Corruption Proofing in Africa

This book outlines evidence-based and data-driven strategies for combating grand corruption in Africa.

Although the causes of corruption vary from country to country, this book suggests that corruption in Africa is often a direct consequence of poorly conceived legislation, policies, and institutional loopholes. The authors in this solution-oriented book converge in arguing that effective strategies to combat corruption (corruption proofing) should integrate an independent enforcement system, vigilant civil society, vibrant media, and political leadership. Utilising empirical evidence and a systems thinking approach, the contributors also uncover root causes of corruption and identify high-leverage interventions to prevent abuse of entrusted power for personal gain. The book recommends an integrated proactive strategy that includes top-down, bottom-up, and multi-stakeholder approaches in the implementation of anti-corruption legislation and policies. Bringing together multidisciplinary and transdisciplinary research, the chapters in this volume include case studies from selected countries on the continent, including Cameroon, Kenya, Malawi, Namibia, Uganda, and Zimbabwe.

Providing readers with a range of effective and functional initiatives in combating corruption in Africa, this book will be of interest to students and researchers of corruption, governance, ethics, peace and security, development, and African studies, as well as policymakers, practitioners, development partners, among other stakeholders.

Dan Kuwali is Professor of International Law at the University of Pretoria, South Africa, Affiliated Professor at the Raoul Wallenberg of Human Rights and Humanitarian Law, Lund University, Sweden, and Commandant of the National Defence College in Malawi.

Routledge Corruption and Anti-Corruption Studies

The series features innovative and original research on the subject of corruption from scholars around the world. As well as documenting and analysing corruption, the series aims to discuss anti-corruption initiatives and endeavours, in an attempt to demonstrate ways forward for countries and institutions where the problem is widespread. The series particularly promotes comparative and interdisciplinary research targeted at a global readership.

In terms of theory and method, rather than basing itself on any one orthodoxy, the series draws broadly on the tool kit of the social sciences in general, emphasizing comparison, the analysis of the structure and processes, and the application of qualitative and quantitative methods.

The Conundrum of Corruption
Reform for Social Justice
Michael Johnston and Scott A. Fritzen

Comparing Police Corruption
Bulgaria, Germany, Russia and Singapore
Leslie Holmes

The Politics of Anti-Corruption Agencies in Latin America
Edited by Joseph Pozsgai-Alvarez

Curbing Corruption
Practical Strategies for Sustainable Change
Bertram I. Spector

Corruption and Development in Nigeria
Edited by Ọláyínká Àkànle and David O. Nkpe

Corruption Proofing in Africa
A Systems Thinking Approach
Edited by Dan Kuwali

For more information about this series, please visit: www.routledge.com/Routledge-Corruption-and-Anti-Corruption-Studies/book-series/RCACS

Corruption Proofing in Africa

A Systems Thinking Approach

Edited by Dan Kuwali

Routledge
Taylor & Francis Group
LONDON AND NEW YORK

First published 2024
by Routledge
4 Park Square, Milton Park, Abingdon, Oxon OX14 4RN

and by Routledge
605 Third Avenue, New York, NY 10158

Routledge is an imprint of the Taylor & Francis Group, an informa business

British Library Cataloguing-in-Publication Data
A catalogue record for this book is available from the British Library

ISBN: 978-1-032-35385-2 (hbk)
ISBN: 978-1-032-35388-3 (pbk)
ISBN: 978-1-003-32664-9 (ebk)

DOI: 10.4324/9781003326649

Typeset in Times New Roman
by Apex CoVantage, LLC

Contents

Contributors

Avitus A. Agbor, Professor of Public International Law, School of Postgraduate Studies, Faculty of Law, North-West University.

Godard Busingye, Chief of Legal Services in the Uganda Peoples' Defence Forces/Ministry of Defence and Veteran Affairs, Uganda; Professor of Public International Law at Kampala International University, Uganda; and Advocate of Courts of Uganda. He has published in the fields of International Humanitarian Law, Human Rights, Gender and the Law, and Environmental Law.

Chikondi Chidzanja, Doctoral Candidate, Stellenbosch University, holds an MA in International Relations and World Order from the University of Leicester. He teaches Law and History at Kamuzu Academy. He published a bestseller "*Kamuzu Academy; Critical perspectives [from] past, [to] present and future of the Eton of Africa.*"

Johan J. Coetzee, Associate Professor (Public Management and Human Sciences), Namibia University of Science and Technology. His publications include several chapters in books, academic peer review journals, magazines, published conference proceedings, and 184 articles in Namibian newspapers on anti-corruption strategies. Co-author of the first Namibian textbook on Namibian Governance (Juta). Editorial Board Member of the Journal of Public Administration and Development Alternatives.

Chevaure du Pokoy, Lecturer at the Faculty of Law, North-West University (NWU), South Africa. She holds Bachelor of Laws and Master of Laws degrees from NWU (LLB and LLM). Her research interests include Criminal Law, Criminal Procedure, and the Law of Evidence.

Michael J. Fratantuono is Emeritus Professor, Department of International Business and Management, Department of International Studies, Dickinson College. He holds a PhD in Economics. He is the recipient of the US Department of the Army Medal for the Outstanding Civilian Service, the 2005 Dickinson's Distinguished Professor Award, and the 2006 Dickinson's Most Inspirational Professor.

Hajer Gueldich, Professor of International Law at the University of Carthage – Tunisia; General Rapporteur of the African Union Commission on International

Law (AUCIL); Visiting Professor at the Universities of Angers (France), Venetia and Siena (Italy), Saint Joseph (Lebanon), Laval University (Canada), and the Pan-African University (Cameroon).

Sandra Fungai Kabaya, Associate, BeraMasamba Law Firm, Zimbabwe. She holds First-Class Bachelor of Laws (LLB) from Midlands State University (MSU). She received Presidential Award for being the overall best LLB student in 2019 and was also honoured by the Law Society of Zimbabwe on the Merit List. Her notable publications include *Managing Anti-Money Laundering Risk at your firm-the role of an Anti-Money Laundering Compliance Officer* and *A critique of Internet Governance Legal Framework in Zimbabwe.*

Charles Kajoloweka holds a master's degree from the University of Pretoria. He is a frontline human rights activist, Founder and Executive Director of Youth and Society (YAS), and Co-founder of the National Anti-Corruption Alliance (NACA). He is a recipient of the prestigious Young African Leaders Initiative (YALI) – USA and the International Anti-Corruption Academy (IACA) – Austria.

Rosemary Kanoel is Advocate of Courts of Judicature of Uganda and Lecturer, School of Law at Kampala International University, where she specializes in Public Law Courses. She is Legal Consultant at M/s Ntegyereize, Ingura and Musiimenta Advocates. She is the Head of the Department of the Diploma in Law Course and Coordinator of the Master of Laws (LLM) at Kampala International University. She has published in the fields of Environmental, Natural Resource Law, and Human Rights generally.

Happy Kayuni, Professor of Political Science and Executive Dean, School of Law, Economics and Governance, University of Malawi, holds a PhD from the University of the Western Cape. He also holds Master of Public Administration degree (MPA) *with Distinction* from the University of Stellenbosch obtained in 2004. He has co-edited books and authored (or co-authored) over 50 peer-reviewed journal articles and book chapters as well as over a hundred research/consultancy reports and conference papers.

Dan Kuwali, Extraordinary Professor of International Law, University of Pretoria; Affiliated Professor, Lund University; Professor of International Law and Strategic Studies, University of Pretoria; Malawi University of Science and Technology; and Commandant of the National Defence College in Malawi.

Thokozire Kuwali, Group Head of Internal Audit at Nico Holdings PLC. She holds Master's in Banking and Finance from Moi University (Kenya) and Bachelor of Accountancy Degree (BAcc) from the University of Malawi. She is Certified Internal Auditor (CIA), Certified Financial Services Auditor (CFSA), Certification in Risk Management Assurance (CRMA), and Fellow of the Association of Chartered Certified Accountants (FCCA); Treasurer of the African Federation of Internal Auditors (AFIIA); Past President of the Institute IIAM (Institute of Internal Auditors in Malawi); and Adjunct Lecturer t Malawi University of Business and Applied Science.

William Kwabiah is Chief Instructor for Joint Studies, Ghana Armed Forces Command and Staff College, and Distinguished Graduate of the US Army War College. He holds a PhD in Business Administration from Walden University in Minnesota.

George Chikondi Lwanda, 2018 Asia Global Fellow, Senior Strategist, and Head of the United Nations Resident Coordinator's office in The Gambia.

Prince Bright Majiga, Officer Commanding – Academic Affairs Department at the MDF Peace Support Operations Training Center. He is also Researcher at the Centre for Strategic Studies, Malawi University of Science and Technology. Captain Majiga has published three chapters in *The Palgrave Handbook of Sustainable Peace and Security in Africa.*

Jonathan Makuwira, Professor of Development Studies and the Deputy Vice Chancellor of Malawi University of Science and Technology (MUST); Research Associate in the Department of Development Studies at Nelson Mandela University (NMU), South Africa; and Visiting Fellow at Airlangga University, Indonesia. He is the author of over 50 journal articles and 30 book chapters. He is the author and co-editor of the following books: *The Routledge Handbook of Global Development* (2022, Routledge); *Rethinking Multilateralism in Foreign Aid: Beyond the Neoliberal Hegemony* (2020, Routledge); and an author of: *Non-Governmental Development Organisations and the Poverty Reduction Agenda: The Moral Crusaders* (2014, Routledge).

Chikondi Mandala, Doctoral Candidate, University of Kent.

Rorisang Matlala, Lecturer, College of Law, University of Kwa-Zulu Natal, Durban.

Salome Chapeyama Mdala, Legal and Compliance Manager, Reunion Insurance Company, Fulbright Scholar with LLM Insurance Law degree from the University of Connecticut, United States. She holds a Master of Laws degree in International Trade, Investment, and Business Law (Cum Laude) from the University of the Western Cape, South Africa, and a master's degree in Anti-Corruption Compliance and Collective Action from the International Anti-Corruption Academy, Vienna, Austria (Cum Laude). She is an adjunct lecturer in International Trade Law, Law of Business Organization and Legal Research Methods in Malawi.

Gilbert Mittawa, Chief of Legal Services, Malawi Defence Force (MDF). He earned a master's degree in public policy from the University of Oxford, a Master of Laws degree with Distinction from the University of Dundee, and Master of Arts in Strategic Studies from the University of Rwanda. He teaches several military and academic courses at the MDF Command and Staff College. He is the current vice president and former legal advisor for the Super League of Malawi.

Kezzie Mkandawire, Senior Lecturer, Department of Accountancy, Malawi University of Business and Applied Sciences, specializing in Governance, Risk and

Strategy. He is a professionally trained and qualified accountant and holder of an MBA.

Maureen Mwalabu is an anti-corruption and anti-money laundering compliance specialist with over 20 years of combined experience in corruption prevention, anti-money laundering and combating the financing of terrorism compliance, having worked with both the Anti-Corruption Bureau (ACB) and the Financial Intelligence Authority (FIA) in Malawi. She is a Certified Anti-Money Laundering Specialist (CAMS) and has a postgraduate certificate in Effective Asset forfeiture from the University of Cape Town. She holds a master's degree in Anti-Corruption Studies from the International Anti-Corruption Academy in Austria, a master's degree in Governance and Public Policy from the University of Queensland in Australia, and a bachelor's degree in Social Sciences from the University of Malawi.

Refilwe Tsatsimpe, Lecturer at North West University. She holds an LLB and an LLM from North West University, and her research interests include Environmental Law, Constitutional law, Family, and Customary law.

Hadijah Yahyah, Doctoral Candidate at the University of Nairobi. She specializes in Environmental and Natural Resources Law and Governance, Rule of Law, Sustainability, Gender Mainstreaming, as well as Local Community Awareness and Empowerment. She earned a Bachelor of Laws degree (LL.B.) from Makerere University and a Master of Laws degree (LL.M.) (Natural Resources) from Kampala International University.

Foreword

Today, corruption is a cancer on society's socio-economic and political fabric, which is condemned even by its "Chief High Priests" and its ardent practitioners. Corruption is a vice that is frowned upon by all in whose vein there is a scintilla of morality, yet paradoxically and ironically, it thrives both overtly and surreptitiously. It cannot be gainsaid that immense intellectual energy has been expended in a bid to understand the anatomy and psychology of corruption. Indeed, many an antidote has been applied to cure the vice. Still, to the chagrin of anti-corruption crusaders, almost every new antidote, its potency notwithstanding, sees the wound of corruption becoming more pernicious.

Dan Kuwali's *Commend and Condemn: Corruption Proofing in Africa* is a collection of well-researched chapters that address the subject of corruption from different perspectives; politics, anthropology, law, and policy. The contributors to this timely book have demonstrated unquestionable knowledge and dexterity in handling corruption issues. Assertions, whenever made, are anchored on firm evidence, making this collection of articles a useful treasury of refreshing ideas on how the vice of corruption is to be understood and tackled on the African continent.

This edited volume promises to use both multidisciplinary and interdisciplinary research methodologies to disentangle the "Gordian Knot" that corruption is, and it fulfils that promise. It is not lost on me, and should not be lost on the reader, that the specific focus is on the state of corruption in Africa, which at the continental level, anchors the combat against corruption on the African Union (AU) Convention on Preventing and Combating Corruption adopted on the 1st day of July 2003 and effective from the 5th day of August 2006. The AU Convention's pioneering prescriptions are also echoed in the United Nations (UN) Convention Against Corruption, which was adopted on the 9th day of December 2003 and came into effect on the 14th day of December 2005. I dare say that the *piece de resistance* of the African Anticorruption Convention gave prevention of corruption pride of place without taking away its *raison d'être* of combating the vice.

The role of leadership in the fight against corruption has received gratifying treatment in the book. Many commentators have repeatedly said that Africa continues to fight against corruption, yet the monster grows bigger and deadlier. In the fight against corruption, there are pessimists who believe that asking the corrupt to leave their ways is like asking vampires to be blood donors. However, the beauty of this volume is that the contributors have not allowed optimism to be sacrificed at the altar of pessimism, notwithstanding that politicians remain infamous for paying lip service to the fight against corruption. The contributors to the volume, who are scholars of note and practitioners with proven experience, have not only exposed the loopholes in the fight against corruption but also how to close those gaps.

All in all, this book is a smorgasbord of beautifully written pieces on an important and evergreen subject. I do not doubt that it is an important arrow in the anti-corruption quiver, and keen readers will discover as much.

Prof PLO Lumumba, LL.D., D. Litt (hc), D.Sc (hc)
FCPS (K), FKIM, FAAS (Hons)
Nairobi

Part I

Quid Pro Quo? – Understanding Corruption in Africa

1 Introduction

*Dan Kuwali**

The purpose of this edited volume was to use empirical evidence to explain common causes of corruption in Africa and analyse cases of some of the effective strategies that have been employed for corruption proofing to prevent, detect, and detect crime on the continent. The main objective of the book was to provide research-based strategies as well as easily accessible academic resources and policy guidelines on combating corruption in Africa. All the chapters in the book provide in erudite detail concrete solution-orientated recommendations anchored in contemporary theory, lessons learned, and best practices to guide the African Union (AU), governments, and policymakers on theoretically and practically proven steps to effectively combat corruption on the continent to achieve sustainable development in line with Goal 16 of the United Nations (UN) Sustainable Development Goals (SDGs) and the AU Agenda 2063, generally.

The contributors to this volume seek to outline an integrated proactive prevention strategy for combating bureaucratic and political corruption in Africa.[1] This approach involves a multi-stakeholder approach in the implementation of selected anti-corruption legislation and policies where leaders set the tone from the top to arrest the insatiable appetite of unscrupulous bureaucrats for public resources; where law enforcement institutions operate independently to deter self-dealing bureaucrats and political elites from embezzling public resources; and where citizens are key players and not spectators in demanding justice and deter potential perpetrators from plundering public resources.[2]

Anchored in systems thinking theory, the hypothesis of this solution-oriented book is that an effective strategy to combat corruption should integrate an independent enforcement system, vigilant civil society, vibrant media, and political leadership to deter abuse of entrusted power for personal gain. As the Corruption Perceptions Index (CPI) has progressively shown, the ineffectiveness of prosecutorial-anchored approaches explains why corruption is still rampant despite the vice being criminalised in nearly every country on the continent.[3] Corruption contributes to Africa being the poorest and least peaceful region of the world.[4] Yet gift-giving and manifestation of appreciation are part of African culture.[5]

Although the African Union (AU) designated 2018 as the year for "winning the fight against corruption" and considering that corruption is a criminal offence in nearly every country on the continent, Africa is still widely considered as the

DOI: 10.4324/9781003326649-2

world's most corrupt continent. Of the ten countries considered most corrupt in the world, six are in sub-Saharan Africa. The continent ranks lowest amongst global regions in the CPI. Countries in Africa average 32 of 100 in their CPI scores. About one billion people (90 per cent) of the continent's 1.2 billion population live under very or extremely corrupt governments, a rate that exceeds most of the rest of the world. Over US$50 billion worth of stolen assets flow out of Africa every year.[6] Hence, ending corruption is a top priority for peace, security, and development in Africa.[7]

Including the private sector, corruption is commonplace in the public sector involving all the three branches of government (the judiciary, the executive, and the legislature). Corruption involves different types of malpractices, namely graft, cheating, grand, and petty corruption.[8] Existing anti-corruption approaches have only targeted the African political elite as perpetrators, eluding foreign collaborators and beneficiaries who have been excluded from the loop. Hence, the need for a different and systems approach is espoused in this volume to complement the reactive prosecutorial strategy often employed by African countries. In agreement with the renowned African anticorruption guru, John Mukum Mbaku, Paul Collier also notes that corruption was "made" in Africa and that it can equally be "unmade" on the continent once the opportunities for rent-seeking behaviour are reduced, and better scrutiny of government behaviour is established.[9] This transformation may help to spur economic development on the continent.[10]

While some argue that corruption greases the gears of commerce and economic development, others contend that corruption acts as the sand that grinds and slows down these same gears.[11] Research has shown that, overall, corruption creates more inefficiency than it corrects as it fuels inequalities and undermines access to public service and scares off investors, and discourages further development.[12] Although causes of corruption unfold differently in different countries, the political economy and moral and anthropological perspectives in most African countries reveal that corruption is a direct consequence of poorly conceived legislation, policies, and institutional loopholes that have promoted rent-seeking and other forms of opportunism.[13] Against this backdrop, this book unites scholars and practitioners to diagnose the structural causes of, and devise evidence-based solutions to, corruption focusing on African states.

While there cannot be a one-size-fits-all approach to fighting corruption, it is generally accepted that strategic leadership setting the tone from the top is key to ending the insatiable appetite of unscrupulous public officials for selfish use of public resources.[14] The discussion takes the African Union (AU) Convention on Preventing Corruption and the United Nations (UN) Convention against Corruption as yardsticks for fighting the vice and investigates approaches in selected countries to discern best practices. The contributors converge to recommend an integrated proactive strategy that includes top-down, bottom-up, and multi-stakeholder approaches in the implementation of anti-corruption legislation and policies to protect public resources from unscrupulous private sector actors, bureaucrats, and politically exposed individuals (PEI). Most authors in this volume lament that a proactive prevention strategy is more worthwhile than prosecution, which is complex, costly, time-consuming, indefinite, and reactive after public funds have already been purloined.

All the chapters in this edited volume are research-based and solution-oriented. To remain within the bounds of the theme of the book, the discussion focuses on addressing the question of how to combat corruption in Africa. The hypothesis is that while prosecution is imperative in fighting corruption, it is complex, costly, time-consuming, and indefinite. Therefore, contributors to this edited volume converge on the thesis that proactive prevention strategies are more effective in deterring corruption.

The contributors to the book are highly respected multidisciplinary academics, policymakers, and practitioners with recognised contributions to the anticorruption space in development studies, law, and political economy. The mix of scholars and practitioners contributing to this volume is the reason the book is one that straddles the academic and policy environments; second, the book brings together both multidisciplinary and transdisciplinary research, policy analysis, and strategic thought. Considering that there cannot be a silver bullet for ending corruption in the heterogeneous systems of African bureaucratic, social, and political culture, systems thinking aids in analysing interrelationships in the common causes of corruption and perceiving patterns to discern best practices and holistic solutions to combat corruption.[15]

The book uses both multidisciplinary and interdisciplinary research methodologies to solve the complex question of how to combat corruption in Africa by providing different perspectives on the subject and developing a common approach and generally accepted recommendations. The multidisciplinary approach in this book draws on knowledge from disciplines, such as law, development studies, development economics, ethics, strategic studies, human rights, and democratisation as well as peace and security in Africa. Although each African country faces unique challenges and may require specific strategies, the multidisciplinary approach helps provide recommendations that are universally applicable. The interdisciplinary approach is employed in this book to analyse, synthesise, and harmonise the links between and among the different disciplines into coordinated and coherent recommendations.[16]

To bring coherence and logical analysis to the book for perspectives from different academic disciplines, the contributors use systems thinking. Systems thinking is an approach to problem-solving, by viewing "problems" as parts of an overall system.[17] Systems thinking is a cognitive framework that helps to explain complex phenomena (or outcomes) by considering the contributory components and the interactions between them.[18] A systems thinking approach is different from traditional approaches because causes of corruption defy simple explanations and usually result from numerous factors and processes.[19]

Systems thinking is employed because it is a methodology that causes of corruption defy simple explanation and usually result from numerous factors and processes.[20] Thus, systems thinking helps explain the complexity of the causes of corruption and the complicated patterns of bureaucratic and political corruption.[21] Systems thinking abhors reacting to a specific part of a problem, outcomes, or events and potentially contributing to the further development of unintended consequences.[22] By using systems thinking, authors are able to uncover the root causes of corruption and identify high-leverage interventions to end corruption on the continent.[23] The result is a comprehensive book that provides readers with a range of effective and functional multi-stakeholder initiatives in combating corruption in Africa.[24]

Notes

* Extraordinary Professor of International Law, University of Pretoria.

1 Elinor Ostrom, Roy Gardner, and James Walker, "Rules, Games, and Common-Pool Resources" www.press.umich.edu/titleDetailDesc.do?id=9739 The University of Michigan Press, 1994 (1994) 37.

2 Dan Kuwali, "Combating Corruption in Africa" Chapter 33 in Dan Kuwali, Palgrave Handbook on Sustainable Peace in Africa, 2021.

3 Transparency International, "Corruption Perceptions Index 2020," available at:<2020 - CPI - Transparency.org > (21 August 2021)

4 Charles M. Fombad and Nico Steytler (Eds), *Corruption and Constitutionalism in Africa* (Oxford University Press, 2020).

5 Philip Nel, "Corruption," Tony Binns, Kenneth Lynch and Etienne Nel, *The Routledge Handbook of African Development* (London: Routledge, 2020), 649–650.

6 Organisation for Economic Co-operation and Development (OECD), "Implementing the OECD Principles for Integrity in Public Procurement," available at:<www.oecd-ilibrary.org/governance/implementing-the-oecd-principles-for-integrity-in-public-procurement_9789264201385-en>. (accessed 1 January 2021).

7 The AU Convention on Preventing and Combating Corruption (AUCPCC) was adopted in Maputo, Mozambique on 11 July 2003 and came into force in 2006. The AU has established an Advisory Board on Corruption, which is an organ tasked to advise on, and address the problem of, corruption on the continent. As can be noted, the Board is limited to an advisory role although it is also mandated to rally for the ratification and implementation by member states, the AUCPCC. To date, the Convention has been ratified by 44 of the 55 AU Member States, which explains the slow pace in the determination to fight the vice on the continent. African Union, AU Convention on Preventing and Combating Corruption, available at:<https://au.in/sites/default/files/treaties/36382-treats-0028-african-union-convention-on-preventing-and-combating-corruption-e.pdf> (accessed 20 February 2021).

8 Nel, "Corruption," 652.

9 See Paul Collier, "How to reduce corruption," *African Development Review*, 12, no. 2 (2000): 191–2005. See also Nel, "Corruption", 659.

10 Jimanze Ego-Alowes, *Corruption in Africa: Resolution through New Diagnosis* (Safari Books, 2017).

11 Nel, "Corruption," 649–650.

12 Nel, "Corruption," 649–650.

13 John Mukum Mbaku, *Corruption in Africa: Causes Consequences, and Cleanups* (Rowman & Littlefield Publishing Group Inc, 2010, p. x). John Mukum Mbaku, *Bureaucratic and Political Corruption in Africa: The Public Choice Perspective* (Krieger, 2000). See also Nel, "Corruption," 659. Sarah Muir and Akhil Gupta, "Rethinking the Anthropology of Corruption: An Introduction to Supplement 18," *Current Anthropology*, 59, no. 18 (April 2018): s1–s15, https://doi.org/10.1086/696161. JP Olivier de Sardan, "A Moral Economy of Corruption in Africa?," *Journal of Modern African Studies*, 37 no. 1 (March, 1999): 25–52, https://doi.org/10.1017/S0022278X99002992.

14 See generally, Prof PLO Lumumba, available at:<www.plofoundation.org>.

15 Peter M. Senge, *The Fifth Discipline: The Art and Practice of the learning Organization* (New York: Doubleday/Currency1990), 68.
16 Stephen Menken and Machiel Keesten, Lucas Rutting, Ger Post, and Mieke Roo, *An Introduction to Interdisciplinary Research: Theory and Practice* (Amsterdam: Amsterdam University Press, 2016).
17 Steven Metz, "Systems Thinking," *The Science Teacher*, 79, no. 7 (October 2012): 6–6, www.jstor.org/stable/i40141445. See Willie J. Flucker, *Army Senior Leader Diversity: A Systems Analysis*, Strategic Research Project (Carlisle, PA: United States Army War College, 2015), 2.
18 Steve Metz, "Systems Thinking," *The Science Teacher*, 79, no. 7 (November 2012): 6.
19 David Peter Stroh, *Systems Thinking for Social Change: A Practical Guide to Solving Complex Problems, Avoiding Unintended Consequences, and Achieving Lasting Results* (White River Junctions, VT: Chelsea Green Publishing, 2015), 1–6.
20 David Peter Stroh, *Systems Thinking for Social Change: A Practical Guide to Solving Complex Problems, Avoiding Unintended Consequences, and Achieving Lasting Results* (White River Junctions, VT: Chelsea Green Publishing, 2015), 1–6.
21 Stroh, *Systems Thinking for Social Change*, 1–6.
22 Metz, "Systems Thinking," 6. See also Flucker, *Army Senior Leader Diversity*, 2.
23 Senge, *The Fifth Discipline*, 68.
24 Ostrom, The Institutional Analysis and Development Framework and the Commons, 807.

2 Gift or Graft? – The Legal and Political Economy of Corruption in Africa

*Dan Kuwali**

Introduction

Corruption is so pervasive in Africa and is a direct consequence of poorly conceived legislation, policies, and institutional arrangements that have promoted rent-seeking and other forms of opportunism. Corruption thrives where individuals are unaccountable and non-transparent in decision-making. Corruption benefits a small number of well-connected people. Corruption occurs in all spheres of life and in all countries, big and small, developing and developed. However, it is in the developing world that the impact of corruption is most destructive.[1] Corruption is generally a problem that represents a breakdown in the integrity of a system, such as a person or an institution. Corruption in effect entails a waste of resources that are not being used for their intended purpose (maladministration and mismanagement are inherent features).

After this introduction, the discussion explores the definition of corruption to outline a common understanding of the crime before zooming in on the question of grand corruption. Then, the chapter analyses the political economy of corruption in Africa before turning its attention to establishing why grand corruption is commonplace on the continent. To recommend effective strategies to combat corruption on the continent, the discussion navigates the factors that facilitate graft using systems thinking. Finally, the discussion assesses the challenges and opportunities of anti-corruption politics and provides recommendations to curb crime on the continent.

Defining Corruption

Although corruption has been precisely defined in law and has set standards for its measurement, challenges remain in understanding it and charging offenders for committing the crime. The challenges are commonplace in post-colonial Africa for understanding this elusive notion conceived in Western traditions of political philosophy where it is generally viewed as the deterioration of institutions, culture of integrity, and professionalism.[2] From an anthropological perspective, understanding what constitutes corruption is particularly pertinent in Africa where gift-giving and the manifestation of appreciation are part of the culture in most

DOI: 10.4324/9781003326649-3

communities.[3] The challenge of defining corrupt practices and the need for a common understanding have been aptly captured thus as follows:

> Differentiating between the 'appropriation of public goods for personal gain' and 'privatization', for example, or between 'governmental distortion of the market' and 'regulation', or, indeed, between a 'bribe' and a 'gift', is always a performative judgment that invites disagreement across the entangled fields of legality and legitimacy. In other words, which transactions can be categorized as corrupt can never be a definitional question; it is always necessarily perspectival, evaluative, and performative.[4]

Definitional precision is crucial to understand corruption and to devise effective strategies to combat the vice. According to Transparency International (TI), "[e]xposing corruption and holding the corrupt to account can only happen if we understand the way corruption works and the systems that enable it."[5]

By and large, corruption manifests itself in the logic of quid pro quo exchanges.[6] Often, corruption is loosely defined as "the abuse of public office for private gain."[7] However, this definition of corruption does not acknowledge the interdependent and interrelated role players in other sectors, such as the private sector and civil society, meaning corruption is not being acknowledged as systemic – a concept that conveys the interdependence of deviant behaviours in public and/or private sector institutions.

The United Nations (UN) Convention Against Corruption (UNCAC) does not provide a definition of corruption.[8] The lack of a universally accepted definition in the UNCAC is a fundamental flaw as the vice is not a domestic matter but a transnational phenomenon that affects all societies and economies globally.[9] However, Chapter III of the UNCAC outlines acts that States are obliged to criminalise. These offences include bribery of national public officials, bribery of foreign public officials and officials of public international organisations, embezzlement, misappropriation, or other diversion of property by public officials, trading in influence, abuse of functions, illicit enrichment, bribery in the private sector, embezzlement of property in the private sector, laundering of proceeds of crime, concealment, and obstruction of justice.[10]

Article 8 of the United Nations Convention against Transnational Organized Crime (UNCTOC) provides a better understanding of corruption as:

> promise, offering or giving to a public official, directly or indirectly, of an undue advantage, for the official himself or herself or another person or entity, in order that the official act or refrain from acting in the exercise of his or her official duties", or the "solicitation or acceptance by a public official, directly or indirectly, of an undue advantage, for the official himself or herself or another person or entity, in order that the official act or refrain from acting in the exercise of his or her official duties.[11]

On the continent, Article 1 of the African Union (AU) Union Convention on Preventing and Combating Corruption (AUCPCC) defines corruption as "acts and practices including related offences proscribed in this Convention."[12] To this end, Article 4 of the AUCPCC provides a comprehensive catalogue of acts of corruption and related offences as follows:

[. . .]

(a) the solicitation or acceptance, directly or indirectly, by a public official or any other person, of any goods of monetary value, or other benefit, such as a gift, favour, promise or advantage for himself or herself or for another person or entity, in exchange for any act or omission in the performance of his or her public functions;
(b) the offering or granting, directly or indirectly, to a public official or any other person, of any goods of monetary value, or other benefit, such as a gift, favour, promise or advantage for himself or herself or for another person or entity, in exchange for any act or omission in the performance of his or her public functions;
(c) any act or omission in the discharge of his or her duties by a public official or any other person for the purpose of illicitly obtaining benefits for himself or herself or for a third party;
(d) the diversion by a public official or any other person, for purposes unrelated to those for which they were intended, for his or her own benefit or that of a third party, of any property belonging to the State or its agencies, to an independent agency, or to an individual, that such official has received by virtue of his or her position;
(e) the offering or giving, promising, solicitation or acceptance, directly or indirectly, of any undue advantage to or by any person who directs or works for, in any capacity, a private sector entity, for, himself or herself or for anyone else, for him or her to act, or refrain from acting, in breach of his or her duties;
(f) the offering, giving, solicitation or acceptance directly or indirectly, or promising of any undue advantage to or by any person who asserts or confirms that he or she is able to exert any improper influence over the decision making of any person performing functions in the public or private sector in consideration thereof, whether the undue advantage is for himself or herself or for anyone else, as well as the request, receipt or the acceptance of the offer or the promise of such an advantage, in consideration of that influence, whether or not the influence is exerted or whether or not the supposed influence leads to the intended result;
(g) illicit enrichment;
(h) the use or concealment of proceeds derived from any of the acts referred to in this Article; and
(i) participation as a principal, co-principal, agent, instigator, accomplice or accessory after the fact, or on any other manner in the commission or attempted commission of, in any collaboration or conspiracy to commit, any of the acts referred to in this article.

As both the UNCAC and AUCPCC require States to enact legislation criminalising specific corrupt acts, this means that countries have the obligation to define corruption at the national level. For example, Article 2 of the Nigerian Corrupt Practices and Other Related Offences Act terms corruption as "bribery, fraud, and other related offences."[13] Gratification by an official, corrupt offer to the public officers, corrupt demand by persons, counselling offences relating to corruption, fraudulent acquisition of property, fraudulent receipt of property, deliberate frustration of investigation on by the commission, making a false statement or return, gratification by and through agents, bribery of public officer, offences of using offices and position for gratification, bribery in relation to auctions, bribery for assisting, in regard to contracts, dealing with, using, holding, receiving or concealing gratification, making of a statement which is false or intended to mislead, among others.[14]

A unique and progressive normative framework presented by the Nigerian Corrupt Practices and Other Related Offences Act is the definition of gratification. The Act defines gratification as:

(a) Money, donation, giving, loan, fee, reward, valuable security, property of any description whether movable or immovable or any other similar advantage, given or promised to any person with intent to influence such a person in the performance or non-performance of his dues;
(b) Any office, dignity, employment, contract of empowerment or service, and any agreement to give employment or render services in any capacity;
(c) Any payment, release, discharge or liquidation of any loan, obligation or other liability, whether in whole or in part;
(d) Any valuable consideration of any kind, any discount, commission, rebate, bonus deduction, or percentage;
(e) Any forbearance to demand any money or money's worth or valuable thing;
(f) Any other service or favour of any description, such as protection from any penalty or disability incurred or apprehended or from any ac on or proceedings of a disciplinary, civil or criminal nature, whether or not already instituted, and including the exercise or the proceedings of a disciplinary, civil or criminal nature, whether or not already instituted, and including the exercise or the forbearance from the exercise of any rights or any official power or duty; and
(g) Any offer, undertaking or promise, whether conditional or unconditional, of any gratification within the meaning of any of the preceding paragraphs (a) to (f).[15]

In the same vein, Transparency International (TI) provides a more succinct and widely accepted definition for corruption as a common standard. TI defines corruption as "the abuse of entrusted power for private gain."[16] Regardless of laborious efforts to iteratively define corruption, it has been observed that owing to its complexity and various stakeholders' perceptions about the vice, corruption cannot be limited to a single meaning. However, the common understanding is that corruption entails the abuse of public resources for private gain. The definition of corruption conjures clandestine, illicit, and cryptic transactions outside officially recognised channel relations for personal benefit.

From a public choice theory, corruption can be viewed as attempts by individuals or groups to subvert existing rules and generate extralegal income and wealth for themselves.[17] It includes bribery, extortion, abuse of discretion, abuse of office, conflict of interest, and state capture, among others. Corruption should be distinguished from fraud, which can loosely be seen as wrongful or criminal deception intended to result in financial or personal gain.[18]

The World Bank distinguishes between "isolated" and "systemic" corruption.[19] At first reading the 2007 definition seems to be outdated, because isolated (or accidental) corruption rare and consist of a few acts. The World Bank's expanded definition[20] replaced "public office" with "trusted office." The implication is that private 'office' is included in the expanded definition, which means that there is a growing understanding that corruption is not just a problem occurring in public institutions, but also a problem in the private sector, often acting in conjunction with the public sector.

Corruption is often classified into two categories: grand (political) corruption, which is usually perpetrated by political elites and high-level public officials such as state capture in South Africa. Another category is petty or small-scale corruption such as the type usually practised by some errant traffic police officers on the roads of Kenya, Malawi, Nigeria, and other countries.[21] Petty corruption is straightforward and usually easy to detect and punish.[22] This chapter together with the rest of the chapters in this book will focus on grand corruption focusing on Africa.

Grand Corruption in Africa: Challenges of Measurement and Detection

TI defines "grand corruption" as "the abuse of high-level power that benefits the few at the expense of the many and causes serious and widespread harm to individuals and society."[23] Grand corruption is further seen through the lenses of political corruption, which is typically orchestrated by political elites such as state capture that took place in South Africa, and bureaucratic corruption or administrative corruption, which is typically committed by influential employees in the public sector (public officials), along with their private enablers and beneficiaries.[24]

Grand corruption is defined as "the abuse of high-level power that benefits the few at the expense of the many and causes serious and widespread harm to individuals and society."[25] Examples of grand corruption include state capture, embezzlement, trading in influence, and bribe payments. Grand corruption can be a one-off transaction or systematic pattern often with significant and harmful repercussions to societies, including damage to the rule of law, economic development, and social harmony.

Political or grand corruption is further seen through the lenses of extractive political corruption and power-preserving political corruption. The former is when a politician uses corrupt means to extract wealth for their benefit, their families, friends, and business associates (e.g., embezzlement, bribery, and fraud), whereas the latter takes place when the corruptly gained resources are utilised to strengthen the position of the politician and political party in question. This is one of the ways in which political party funding is achieved.[26]

Understanding different kinds of corruption is important as such a thought process is important in developing actionable and effective responses. For example, TI's Corruption Perceptions Index (CPI) developed cannot effectively measure power-preserving corruption as its nature may not be detected by such a methodology. Additionally, the fact that developed countries show lower levels of perceived corruption than developing countries may mask the involvement of beneficiary countries that provide a safe haven to the illicit financial flows from Africa. Grand corruption is difficult to detect because of the illicit practices of powerful kleptocrats who beat the system with impunity by operating under the anti-corruption radar.[27]

The variables employed in measuring corruption using CPI do not cover grand corruption and compliance with public procurement legislation, among other such factors. As its name suggests, CPI does not reflect the experience of corruption but rather perception, which pervades the public as grand corruption is covert and complex. In this case, train-minded reliance on the CPI only to measure corruption confines policymakers to focus on petty rather than grand corruption, and to see corruption as an African problem only, yet this is a global vice that traverses geographic boundaries, sociocultural contexts, and institutional structures and such perception ignores the role played by the global North in facilitating the vice.[28]

While administrative corruption can be curbed by law enforcement means such as legislation, prosecution, and punishments, political corruption is difficult to detect and complex to combat since its powerful perpetrators can indulge in state capture and undermine anti-corruption efforts.[29] Most strategies to fight corruption hinge on criminal prosecution although this has generally proved ineffective, as cases in most African countries, particularly Nigeria and South Africa have shown.[30] In any event, prosecution usually happens after public resources have already been purloined making asset seizure and recovery largely an academic exercise.

Although the fight against grand corruption is elusive, politically exposed persons (PEP) who are motivated by greed and power are the most likely to commit this form of corruption, hence making it relatively easy for non-state actors to detect red flags. The red flags or risk indicators for grand corruption include unexplained wealth, bid fixing or non-competitive contract steering, and registration of successful suppliers in tax havens suggesting concealment of vested interests. Red flags can also be seen where PEP-connected bank accounts are registered in tax havens, receive a greater percentage of wire transfers from tax havens, have frequent traffic of account activity, and have substantially higher account balances, among other risk factors.[31]

Granted, PEP-connected accounts are not evidence of grand corruption *per se*, but PEPs have a high propensity to grand corruption such that suspicious transactions may point to illegality. Other red flags are prevalent and evident in defence spending and other high stakes procurement of medical supplies, power-generating equipment, agricultural inputs, construction projects, and other high-value procurements, which usually use the single-sourcing method of procurement.

Political Economy of Grand Corruption in Africa

Africa is the poorest region of the world and the only one with poor prospects for the future.[32] Corruption is extraordinarily prevalent on the continent. Corruption is attributed to be one of the most significant contributions of this under-development and impoverishment in many African states, as it fuels inequalities, undermines access to public service and scares off investors, and discourages further development.[33] Political economy analysts have noted that the failure of postcolonial state and market institutions to eradicate mass poverty and to secure access to necessities on the continent has driven some disfranchised Africans to engage in under-the-table activities that fall under the category of petty corruption.[34] The repetition of such survival practices has morphed into a culture of corruption.[35]

Although the AU designated 2018 as the year for "winning the fight against corruption," and considering that corruption is a punishable offence in nearly every country on the continent, the vice remains alive and well, with the continent still widely considered as the world's most corrupt.

Of the ten countries considered the most corrupt globally, six are in sub-Saharan Africa. The continent ranks lowest amongst global regions in the CPI. Countries in Africa average 32 out of 100 in their CPI scores. About one billion people (90%) of the continent's 1.2 billion population live under very or extremely corrupt governments, a rate that exceeds most of the rest of the world. Over US$50 billion worth of stolen assets flows out of Africa every year.[36]

Ending corruption is also considered a top priority for peace, security, and development on the continent. The AU Convention on Preventing and Combating Corruption (AUCPCC) was adopted in Maputo, Mozambique, on 11 July 2003 and came into force in 2006.[37] The AU has established an Advisory Board on Corruption, which is an organ tasked to advise on and address the problem of corruption on the continent. The Board is also mandated to rally for the ratification and implementation by member states of the AU Convention on Preventing and Combating Corruption. To date, the Convention has been ratified by 44 out of the 55 AU Member States, which explains the slow pace of fighting the vice on the continent.[38] Despite the fact that over two-thirds of African states have ratified the AUCPCC, the fight against corruption is going at a snail's pace, and in other states, is facing serious strategic reversals. The stagnation in the fight against the vice suggests that the problem in combating corruption lies elsewhere, particularly in circles of political power, and goes beyond ratification of treaties.

Granted, from an economics point of view, optimists have argued that corruption might further the social good, perhaps by greasing the wheels of rigid bureaucratic machines.[39] The extent to which corruption may do so remains understudied. However, it is widely accepted that corruption is an insidious plague, which is corrosive to the national psyche as it destroys social cohesion and trust, undermines talent and efficiency, rewards the undeserving, and lowers performance standards.[40]

In addition to diverting scarce resources, corruption is regarded as unjust, leads to the squandering of public resources, raises the cost of doing business, distorts everything from law-making and economic decision-making to infrastructure engineering in ways that can cripple development for future generations, and tarnishes the image of a nation for investment, thus making it one of the principal impediments to achieving the United Nations Sustainable Development Goals (SDGs) and African Union Vision 2063.[41]

The former UN Secretary-General, Ghana's Kofi Annan, poignantly pointed out that the evil phenomenon of corruption "is found in all countries – big and small, rich and poor – but it is the developing world that its effects are most destructive."[42] The cancerous growth of corruption destroys the economic growth of a country and deprives the public of resources as it is only the corrupt few who benefit. As duly noted by Annan, the poor are particularly disadvantaged when resources are wasted. It is, therefore, not surprising that corruption has been the flashpoint for political protests on the continent, including the Arab Spring in North Africa and the Middle East.

The AUCPCC was adopted against the background of these negative effects of corruption and impunity on the political, economic, social, and cultural stability of African states and its devastating effects on the economic and social development of African states.[43] For Africa, fighting corruption is not merely a legal or moral obligation, and it is also an economic and social justice imperative just as it is a matter of life and death in certain instances. Unless African countries find ways to effectively deal with grand corruption, then the position that the vice will remain a constraint to economic, social, political, peace, security, and development on the continent will remain highly incontestable.

Factors Promoting Grand Corruption in Africa

Factors that promote political corruption revolve around greed and opportunity.[44] Greed is an inherent ingredient of human nature, and despite its disruptive and corrosive effect on society, it has been around from time immemorial. Invariably, the weak in character are easily corruptible. High inequality levels in Africa have led to a situation whereby policies undermine growth; substantial resources are concentrated in the hands of the elite who in turn ensure that formulated policies are protected and frozen into perpetuity, thereby exacerbating grand corruption.[45]

Grand corruption is facilitated by several factors. These range from the absence of institutional ethical codes of conduct; lack of effective supervision and oversight mechanisms; outdated policies, procedures, and regulations; (deliberate) bureaucratic delays and red-tape in the provision of services and delivery of goods; discretionary powers minus accountability; monopoly in the provision of services which leads to unabated overpricing as a result of lack of competition; an unhealthy competition or peer pressure which leads to individuals living beyond their means; an organisational culture that tolerates corruption; to a lack of effective punitive sanctions and penalties for offenders.[46]

The proliferation of alternative currencies may make it easier to transfer and retain funds anonymously and, therefore, more difficult for anti-corruption agencies to trace and seize dirty money. Fast-paced innovations in Internet gaming and software make it easier for criminals to launder funds across jurisdictions without any footprints.[47] Lack of transparency and secrecy also leave room for corruption in the defence and security sector.[48] Most of these factors that promote graft are systematic and at times deliberately managed by politicians and bureaucrats to benefit elites.

Political or grand corruption is a direct consequence of poorly conceived legislation, policies, and institutional arrangements that have promoted rent-seeking and other forms of opportunism.[49] If left unabated, powerful individuals or political elites will continue to divert public resources for private gain or capture sectors or markets in ways that stifle access and opportunity for others, drive up costs, and drive down the quality and safety of infrastructure and public services, so long as existing oversight and accountability mechanisms fail to serve as a deterrent.

The motive for grand corruption is the accumulation of wealth and power by means that benefit a few individuals at the expense of integrity-based structures that benefit everyone. Therefore, strategies to deter corruption should aim at commending integrity and condemning illegality, naming and shaming kleptocrats, encouraging and protecting whistleblowers, and disincentivising corruption by depriving perpetrators of the proceeds of crime while incentivising repurposing/redirecting of wrongfully diverted assets to the public and a country's economy.

A Systems Approach to Combat Corruption in Africa

The fifth preambular paragraph of the UNCAC acknowledges that prevention and combating corruption require a comprehensive and multidisciplinary approach. Chapter II of the UNCAC outlines measures that States are required to take to combat corruption.[50] These include the adoption of preventive anticorruption policies and practices, the establishment of preventive anti-corruption bodies, the establishment of comprehensive recruitment and promotion processes for the public sector, and adoption of codes of conduct for public officials. Establishment of public procurement and public finance management mechanisms, public reporting of, or whistleblowing on, corruption, maintenance of independent judiciaries, enhancement of effective accounting and auditing standards in the private sector, increasing societal participation, and establishment of money-laundering prevention measures.[51]

Likewise, Article 5 of the AUCPCC charges State Parties to undertake legislative and other measures to combat corruption. Such measures include enacting anti-corruption legislation, establishing national anticorruption authorities of agencies, adopting effective public finance management practices, enacting whistleblower protection law, and adopting anti-corruption education and sensitisation programmes. As can be noted by these two international frameworks, combating corruption cannot be achieved using linear solutions but should be addressed using a systemic approach.[52] Legalistic anticorruption strategies alone can have the effect of distracting people from forms of corruption that might be popularly illegitimate but are nonetheless legal.[53]

Considering that corruption centres on human behaviour, anthropological approaches may be well situated to meet the methodological challenges in studying corruption.[54] In some cases, corruption and anti-corruption may mitigate or exacerbate social inequalities. For example, corruption can be, and has often been, the prerogative of the political elite, where it serves as a gatekeeping mechanism that ensures the ongoing power and distinction of that privileged class. Taking an example of the illegal obtaining of passports in Malawi by foreigners or rampant cases of bribery in Ghana, there are also situations where corruption may function as the last resort of the marginalised to circumvent anti-egalitarian barriers to access social services.[55] Thus, anthropological approaches may help identify effective non-legalistic anti-corruption strategies that escape the logic of audit culture, by employing interpersonal or informal mechanisms to discourage illegitimate behaviour.[56]

As anti-corruption strategies may lead to unforeseeable and unintended consequences, systems thinking helps understand the complex structural causes of corruption and address those challenges more holistically.[57] In this case, the complex challenges in combating corruption on the continent are viewed through the systems lenses of two collective action problems. First is the tragedy of commons where everyone is keen on plundering public funds, which can be addressed by deterrent strategies. Second is the success to the successful, which is the archetype that plays out where disadvantages grow against the marginalised and advantages accrue to the privileged. Success to the successful represents two reinforcing structures that may be in a delicate balance though as soon as one gains a small advantage the resource allocation favours the more successful, and the result is then skewed quickly in the direction of the more successful. In other words, opportunity breeds success, success breeds opportunity, and the opposite is true.[58] This tendency exists in most societies in Africa.

For example, where a tribe that occupies influential positions in society may employ people from their tribe and thus concentrate wealth, that scenario may further lead to more land, higher-quality education, better health care, and access to more influential people. While certain dynamics help the privileged get more privileged, others work directly or indirectly against the disadvantaged, especially minorities.[59]

As Michael J. Fratantuono discusses in Chapter 5, a systems approach aims to change the "culture of corruption" by changing the environment that contributes to corruption such as eliminating factors that promote corruption, developing moral and transformational leaders and role models, and developing innovative, transparent, and accountable institutions.[60] In this case, non-corrupt behaviour is the norm, and public and private sector institutions act with integrity. Both formal (legalised and institutionalised) and informal systems (the social structure that governs how people work together in practice) are strong enough to return the system to a "non-corrupt equilibrium."[61]

The West's approach to combating corruption in Africa has usually been condemnatory in tone rather than laudatory, especially for those countries such as

Botswana and Rwanda, where corruption has generally not been rampant.[62] Moreover, the stolen assets from Africa tend to be stashed or invested in developed States to the benefit of those economies. Such artificial economic successes create political blind spots in receiving States in the Global North, reducing the political will to combat corruption effectively and holistically.[63] However, the tenth preambular paragraph of the UNCAC posits that the prevention and eradication of corruption are the responsibility of all States. Consequently, the West's approach to look the other way when proceeds of corruption in Africa benefit it runs counter to the UNCAC, slow-rolls the fight against grand corruption, and needs to be revisited.

This complicity of the West in facilitating corruption on the continent means that Africa should devise home-grown anticorruption strategies. The fact that corruption is usually perpetrated by political elites entails that anticorruption strategies should be conceived from the grassroots level where most of the victims are. The general principles for fighting corruption include proper management of public resources, fairness, responsibility, responsibility, and equality before the law and the need to safeguard integrity and to foster a culture of rejection of corruption.[64] To fight corruption, these principles should be inculcated in society taking a bottom-up approach. As Thokozire Kuwali advocates in Chapter 18, setting the tone at the top may contribute to achieving a non-corrupt equilibrium where the community abhors and reports the crime.[65]

All in all, prevention and combating corruption in Africa requires a multi-stakeholder approach in the implementation of anti-corruption legislation and policies where leaders set the tone from the top to arrest the apparently insatiable appetite of unscrupulous bureaucrats for public resources, where law enforcement institutions operate independently to deter self-dealing bureaucrats and political elites from embezzling public resources, and where citizens are key players and not spectators in demanding justice and deter potential perpetrators from plundering public resources. Thus, an effective strategy to combat corruption should integrate an independent enforcement system, vigilant civil society, and vibrant media, and political leadership to deter abuse of entrusted power for personal gain.

Corruption, in short, avoids and damages integrity-based structures that benefit everyone. This suggests that efforts to combat corruption in Africa should focus on disincentivising corruption by depriving the perpetrators of the proceeds of crime and incentivising whistleblowing. Such an approach not only would focus more directly on dissuading the primary motivations for corruption and correcting the economic distortions it causes but might motivate the general public to abhor corruption and close the loopholes for political elites to divert private resources for personal gain.[66]

Conclusion

Transparency International provides a commonly understood definition of corruption as the abuse of entrusted power for private gain. At its core, it implies clandestine, illicit, cryptic transactions outside officially recognised channels for private gain.[67] Despite most states on the continent ratifying several international agreements, corruption is a pervasive global phenomenon that undermines stability and security in societies and compromises the institutions and values of ethics, democracy, and justice. The spectre of corruption jeopardises the achievement of sustainable development and respect for the rule of law. Corruption is a threat to the legitimate political-economic order and markets.[68]

The need for a systems approach cannot be emphasised. Criminal prosecution is only one of the available tools in the fight against corruption.[69] While there cannot be a one-size-fits-all approach to combating corruption, the purpose of corruption prevention should be to minimise, as much as possible, its crippling effect on the economy, human rights, national security, social welfare, and sustainable development.[18] Corruption prevention requires a robust system to detect and eliminate the causes and conditions of corruption through the development and implementation of appropriate measures for deterrence.

Since corruption is motivated by greed and power, the efforts to combat corruption in Africa should focus on disincentivising corruption by depriving the perpetrators of the proceeds of crime and incentivising whistleblowing. Such an approach not only would focus more directly on dissuading the primary motivations for corruption and correcting the economic distortions it causes but might motivate the general public to abhor corruption and close the loopholes for political elites to divert private resources for personal gain.[70]

Prevention and combating corruption in Africa requires a multi-stakeholder approach in the implementation of anti-corruption legislation and policies including integrating an independent enforcement system, watchful civil society, vibrant media, to promote integrity, accountability, transparency, and proper management of public resources as well as to arrest impunity for corrupt practices. The fight against corruption is the responsibility of everyone through active participation in the implementation of anti-corruption legislation and strategies by demanding justice. While law enforcement is a vital component of any effective anti-corruption effort, it may be short-term hence the need for proactive prevention strategies to commend merit and condemn mediocrity. This transformation may help to spur economic development on the continent, which is the poorest and least peaceful continent in the world.

Notes

* Extraordinary Professor of International Law, University of Pretoria.

1 Johan J. Coetzee, The Role of the Private Sector in Fighting Corruption, *Briefing Paper, Institute of Public Policy Research*, 2018, 5.

2 Sarah Muir and Akhil Gupta, "Rethinking the Anthropology of Corruption," *Current Anthropology*, vol 59 Supplement 18 (April 2018), 5–6.

3 Muir and Gupta, "Rethinking the Anthropology of Corruption," 6. See also Philip Nel, "Corruption", Tony Binns, Kenneth Lynch, and Etienne Nel (eds), *The Routledge Handbook of African Development* (London, 2020), 649–650.

4 Muir and Gupta, "Rethinking the Anthropology of Corruption," s5.

5 Transparency International, "What Is Corruption?", available at: <www.transparency.org.en.what is corruption> (accessed 26 June 2023).

6 Muir and Gupta, "Rethinking the Anthropology of Corruption," 9.

7 World Bank, *Helping Countries Combat Corruption: The Role of the World Bank. Poverty Reduction and Economic Management*, New York, September, 1997, 9–10.
8 United Nations (UN), "The United Nations Convention against Corruption (UNCAC)," Office on Drugs and Crime" (New York, 2004), Articles 15 to 25.
9 UN, "The United Nations Convention against Corruption."
10 United Nations (UN), "The United Nations Convention against Corruption (UNCAC)," Office on Drugs and Crime" (New York, 2004), Articles 15 to 25.
11 Article 8(1)(a)-(b) of the UNCTOC.
12 African Union, AU Convention on Preventing and Combating Corruption, available at: https://au.in/sites/default/files/treaties/36382-treats-0028-african-union-convention-on-preventing-and-combating-corruption-e.pdf (accessed 20 February 2023). The AU Convention on Preventing and Combating Corruption (AUCPCC) was adopted in Maputo, Mozambique on 11 July 2003 and came into force in 2006.
13 The Independent Corrupt Practices Commission, "Corrupt Practices and Other Related Offences Act, 2000," available at: www. icpc.gov.ng CORRUPT-PRACTICES-ACT-2010.pdf (accessed 26 June 2023).
14 See sections 8 to 26, Corrupt Practices and Other Related Offences Act.
15 See section 2 Corrupt Practices and Other Related Offences Act.
16 Transparency International, "What Is Corruption?"
17 John Mukum Mbaku, *Corruption in Africa: Causes, Consequences and Cleanups* (Lexington Books, 2010), 4.
18 Financial Conduct Authority, "Bribery and Corruption," available at: <www.fca.org.uk/firms/financial-crime/bribery-corruption> (accessed 26 June 2023).
19 World Bank, *Helping*, 9–10.
20 World Bank, *Helping*, 434.
21 Inge Amundsen (ed.), *Political Corruption in Africa: Extraction and Power Preservation* (Cheltenham: Edward Elgar Publishing, 2019).
22 World Bank, *Helping*, 9–10.
23 Transparency International, "Grand Corruption," available at: <www.rtransparency.org/en/grand corruption_our_priorities> (accessed 26 June 2023).
24 Neil Arun, "State capture: Zuma, the Guptas, and the sale of South Africa," *BBC News*, 15 July 2019, available at: <www.bbc.com/news/world-africa-48980964> (accessed 22 May 2023).
25 Transparency International, "Grand Corruption," available at: <www.transparencyinternational/en/our-priorities/grand-corruption> (accessed 1 March 2023).
26 Dan Kuwali, " 'Bloody Bucks: Preventing War Profiteering,' in Juan-Pablo Bohosi and Jerney Letnar Černič (eds), *Making Sovereign Financing and Human Rights Work* (Oxford: Hart Publishing, 2014), 271–288.
27 Amundsen (ed.), *Political Corruption in Africa*. See also Pornanong Budsaratragoon and Boonlert Jitmaneeroj, "A Critique on the Corruption Perceptions Index: An Interdisciplinary approach," *Socio-Economic Planning Sciences*, vol 70 (June 2020), available at: https://doi.org/10.1016/j.seps.2019.100768 (Accessed 22 May 2023).
28 Uzochukwu Mike, "Corruption in Africa: Overview, Causes, Effects, and Solutions," 15 April 2020, available at: <https://discover.hubpages.com/politics/Corruption_ in_Africa_Causes_Solutions> (accessed 20 June 2023).
29 Amundsen, *Political corruption in Africa.*
30 See, for example, Human Rights Watch, "Nigeria: Corruption Fuelling Police Abuses," 17 August 2010, available at: <www.hrw.org/news/2010/08/17/nigeria-corruption-fueling-police-abuses> (accessed 11 May 2023).
31 Sabine E. Nölke, "Toward a More Effective Implementation of Anti-Corruption Measures: Suggestions for the Strengthening of Existing Frameworks and Institutions," Discussion Paper, Canadian Task Force Against Global Corruption, March 2023, 5.
32 James A. Robinson, "Why is Africa Poor?" 8 April 2013, available at: <havard.edu/files/jrobinson/files/maddison_lecture.pdf> (accessed 25 June 2023).

33 Mbaku, *Corruption in Africa*, x.
34 Hart 1973
35 Muir and Gupta, "Rethinking the Anthropology of Corruption," 6.
36 Organisation for Economic Co-operation and Development (OECD), 'Implementing the OECD Principles for Integrity in Public Procurement', available at: <www.oecd-ilibrary.org/governance/implementing-the-oecd-principles-for-integrity-in-public-procurement_9789264201385-en> (accessed 1 January 2023).
37 African Union, "AU Convention on Preventing and Combating Corruption," available at: https://au.in/sites/default/files/treaties/36382-treats-0028-african-union-convention-on-preventing-and-combating-corruption-e.pdf (accessed 20 February 2023).
38 African Union, "AU Convention on Preventing and Combating Corruption."
39 Muir and Gupta, "Rethinking the Anthropology of Corruption," 5–6.
40 Anver Versi, "Let's Exorcise Corruption Once and For All," *African Business*, April 2010, 11.
41 Dan Kuwali, "Governance or Government Reform? – Transforming Governmentality in Malawi," *Malawi Law Journal*, vol 5, no. 2 (2011), 139–147.
42 See Kofi A. Annan, "Foreword," in United Nations Office on Drugs and Crime, *United Nations Convention against Corruption* (New York: United Nations, 2004), iii.
43 African Union, AUCPCC, preambular para. 6.
44 African Union, AUCPCC, preambular para. 8.
45 United Nations Development Programme (UNDP) (Zambia) and the United Nations Economic Commission for Africa (UNECA) (Southern Africa Office), "Economic Growth and Inequality in Southern Africa: Issues and Policy Options", Concept Note, Livingstone, Zambia, 19–20 June 2014, 3.
46 Ministry of Defence, "Strategic Trends Programme: Global Strategic Trends-Out to 2045," Fifth Edition, United Kingdom, 2014, xxii.
47 Ministry of Defence, "Strategic Trends Programme: Global Strategic Trends-Out to 2045," Fifth Edition, United Kingdom, 2014, xxii.
48 Karolina MacLachlan, "Corruption and conflict: Hand in Glove," available at: <Corruption and conflict: hand in glove (nato.int)> (accessed 29 January 2023).
49 Mbaku, *Corruption in Africa,* 4.
50 United Nations, "The United Nations Convention against Corruption (UNCAC), Articles 5 to 14.
51 UNCAC, Articles 5 to 14.
52 See generally Johan J. Coetzee, "Systemic Corruption and Corrective Change Management Strategies: A Study of The Co-Producers of Systemic Corruption and Its Negative Impact on Socio-Economic Development," Dissertation presented for the Degree of Doctor of Business Management and Administration at Stellenbosch University.
53 Muir and Gupta, "Rethinking the Anthropology of Corruption," 6.
54 Muir and Gupta, "Rethinking the Anthropology of Corruption," 6.
55 Augustine Amenyah, "Corruption in Ghana: Causes and Suggestions FOR A Corrupt-Free Society," available at: <corruptionwatchghana.org/2021/06/14/Corruption_in_Ghana_Causes_and_Suggestions_for_A_Corrupt-Free_Society/> (accessed 20 June 2023).
56 Muir and Gupta, "Rethinking the Anthropology of Corruption," 8.
57 See George J. Woods, *Organizing Your Thoughts about Organizations* (Carlisle: United States Army War College, May 2021), 5, 11. See Elinor Ostrom, "The Institutional Analysis and Development Framework and the Commons," *Cornell Law Review*, 95, no. 4 (2010), 807–816, 807, https://scholarship.law.cornell.edu/clr/vol95/iss4/15 (Accessed 14 January 2023).
58 Stroh, *Systems Thinking*, 60–61.
59 Stroh, *Systems Thinking*, 60–61.
60 Coetzee, "Systemic Corruption and Corrective Change Management Strategies."
61 Muir and Gupta, "Rethinking the Anthropology of Corruption," 12.

62 Transparency International, "Corruption Perception Index," available at: <transparency.org/en/cpi/2022> (accessed 26 June 2023).
63 Nölke, "Toward a More Effective Implementation of Anti-Corruption Measures," 5.
64 See the eleventh preambular paragraph of the UNCAC. See also Muir and Gupta, "Rethinking the Anthropology of Corruption," 9.
65 Muir and Gupta, "Rethinking the Anthropology of Corruption," 12.
66 Nölke, "Toward a More Effective Implementation of Anti-Corruption Measures," 16.
67 Muir and Gupta, "Rethinking the Anthropology of Corruption," 1.
68 Muir and Gupta, "Rethinking the Anthropology of Corruption," 5.
69 Nölke, "Toward a More Effective Implementation of Anti-Corruption Measures," 16.
70 Nölke, "Toward a More Effective Implementation of Anti-Corruption Measures," 16.

3 Greed and Grand Corruption Nexus

Lessons From Cameroon

*Avitus A. Agbor**

Introduction

In Cameroon, details of financial racketeering and irreparable moral turpitude perpetrated by leaders of state-owned entities (SOEs) disseminated to the public domain have shocked and puzzled the public following the judgements delivered by the Special Criminal Court (SCC): a judicial institution established by Presidential Decree with special jurisdiction.[1] The judgements handed in the multi-billion Francs CFA (*Coopération Financière en Afrique Centrale*) cases involving Yves-Michel Fotso[2] and Jean-Marie Atangana Mebara in April and June 2016, respectively, disclosed not only the colossal sums of public funds embezzled when they were in public offices, but also the manner in which they perpetrated such fraudulent schemes.[3] A year earlier, the case of Polycarp Abah Abah, former Minister of Economy and Finances, occupied the tongues and lips of Cameroonians as they got to learn of the numerous public properties and funds siphoned by a man who was once central in the Ministry of Economy and Finance[4] and had risen to a crime-made billionaire. Numerous other cases bore significant resemblance with the foregoing three. As perused in the judgements, hundreds of individuals, hailing from the *corps politic*, private sector and public service, were, in one way or the other, involved in orchestrating a profuse bleeding of the national economy by draining, through fraudulent and dishonest means, public funds entrusted under their stewardship.[5] Simply put, an unprecedented racketeering had found a safe haven in Cameroon which, to some extent, would account for the country's ranking by Transparency International as the most corrupt country in the world in two successive years, 1998 and 1999.

More than 98 per cent of the individuals who have been docked at the SCC come from affluent backgrounds and had built their careers in public service. They were all reckoned as successful businessmen across the national territory and were already consigned to enviable economic and social classes. Therefore, lack of money could not explain why they were involved in such financial crimes. The amounts stolen can hardly be deemed acceptable if such gestures were ever rationalized: the figures transcend the borders of what can be considered as acceptable, occasional, and trivial looting. By the former works earlier in their lives, it can be fair to say they had emerged as the economic actors and political elite of

DOI: 10.4324/9781003326649-4

Cameroon – forming the bases upon which their leadership appointments were factored. In view of their accomplishments and statuses, and bearing in mind the income inequality, poverty gap and ramifications of corruption, one can ask: what really could have propelled them to craft and orchestrate the worst financial racketeering ever known to the people and Government of Cameroon?

The notion of greed touches on various (and complex) angles such as religion, psychology, economics, morality, income disparity, wealth inequality, resource distribution, and social justice.[6] For some scholars, greed has been the propellant of both human progress and economic growth as the desire to have more would mean creating and making use of more opportunities, investing in the economy, etc. As was seen during the global economic crises in the first decade of the 21st century, greed can lead to economic crises. In this paper, the focus is not on the broader economic and financial crises that shocked the world. Focus here is on the unfettered desire to have more, and how that drives the commission of theft of public funds.

This paper does not advocate for the criminalization of greed. Neither does it seek to interrogate its occurrence nor stigmatize those who exude it. Rather, it furthers the discussion of a contentious and thorny topic, acknowledging the vast literature thereon, and builds from different perspectives through which the challenge of greed has been approached: religious, psychological, and economic.[7] It is argued that in view of the absence of what has been termed a 'greed line' similar to the broad consensus on the 'poverty line', it becomes difficult to determine with exactitude at what point an individual's quest for wealth delves into, or becomes greed just like one would say that an individual slipped into poverty if that individual's income threshold falls below the poverty line. Arguably, grand corruption involves huge sums of monies stolen from the state that can be probably due to one contributor: greed.

Like every human trait, greed has been a trait for as long as mankind has existed (Seuntjens, Zeelenberg, Van de Ven, et al., 2015, p. 30)[8] condemned by key religions in the world[9] debated by capitalists who argue that it is the propellant for individual initiative and drives creativity, hard work, ambition, and success. A definition of what greed is debunks that same argument. On the one hand, while there should be no limit to what one can acquire lawfully, on the other hand, when entrusted with public funds, no individual must enrich himself by misappropriating or stealing what belongs to the public. That is dishonest, unethical, unlawful, and criminal. It is thus discussed and argued in this paper that when such theft occurs, most often, it can be driven by an untameable and insatiable desire for more, that can be effected through unlawful means. It is argued in this paper that the craving for an insatiable wealth is propelled by greed, and in the context of misappropriation of public funds by the political elite and other senior government officials, greed can be one of the main contributors to such behaviour.

This paper commences by presenting a concise definition of and discussion on greed. It identifies a few individuals, drawn from different societies, who, at any given point in time, would qualify as one of the African gods of greed, or the perpetration of the self at the detriment of others. It then unpacks the differing perspectives on greed. The last part focuses on the relationship between greed and corruption and argues that the theft of state resources can most probably be explained by the existence of gargantuan greed.

Delineating the Notion of Greed

Greed as a human addiction may reflect an individual's upbringing, differing perspectives and indicates why it is difficult to formulate a substantive definition.[10] To better understand how greed acts as a driver of theft of state resources by senior state officials, it is crucial to understand the notion of greed itself: what it means, and the greed syndrome. That would assist in establishing a link between greed as a driving factor and the commission of grand theft or corruption by senior public officials.

Defining the Notion of Greed

To formulate and postulate an all-inclusive definition of greed has been a challenge. There is no consensus on what greed is. It is challenging for scholars to establish at what point a healthy appetite or a natural passion for something gives rise to greed. To arrive at a working definition, it is important to consider some voices echoed by scholars on what greed is. Inspired by the writing of Saint Augustine,[11] and cognizant of the risk of 'oversimplifying' what greed is, Cooey propounds a working definition and explanation of greed as the gratification of one's desires, beyond one's own needs, at the expense of meeting one's needs or the needs of a common good that includes the good of all planetary life.[12]

Excess and hoarding particularly characterize this gratification of desire. When my desire is governed by and limited to my own self-interests or those of my group, narrowly defined, I am greedy. When I place the gratification of my desires, what Augustine and other theologians referred to as 'appetites', first, I reduce other people and other forms of life exclusively to means to accomplish my ends.[13]

Posner defines greed as a '[craving] almost exclusively about making money'.[14] Borrowing from the works of Cooey and Posner, Meadowcroft provides a three-dimensional delineation of what greed is (or could be):

> First, greed may describe a desire for material wealth or consumption beyond one's needs; greed may be the desire to satisfy wants as well as needs or to gratuitously consume things that are not needed. Second, greed may describe consumption that denies others the opportunity to similarly consume. . .. Third, greed may describe an all-encompassing and exclusive desire to accumulate material wealth.

This definition is substantial, because it can be perceived as a deserved attempt to be comprehensive in nature for the purpose of this paper.

Greed is an 'insatiable hunger for getting more than we need, has various connotations in western history and civilization'.[15] The notion of greed has undergone significant conceptual metamorphosis, changing over time within political, economic, cultural, economic, and moral contexts. Even though different English lexicons offer various definitions, they share some commonalities as they agree that it is an intense and selfish desire for something, often, money and power. Greed is the peak of a high, excessive (and unnecessary) level of self-interests or interest for the self to the point that there is little or no concern for others. German philosopher and sociologist, Simmel, notes in *The Philosophy of Money* that 'there's no period of time in which individuals have not been greedy for money'.[16] Newhauser has demonstrated that greed for money and avarice are two phenomena that arose long before the development of the modern economy.[17] Ballot sees it as 'an excessive desire, to get more . . . a primarily materialistic type of desire'.[18] Looking at these three definitions, one finds some common threads with reference to the need to pursue, acquire, or own something, more than what a person already possesses. There is the inclusion of a selfish desire, marked by concern what such an individual pays to himself. Considered by some as an extreme form of self-interest, greed varies from individual to individual.[19]

Considering all definitions consulted, it can be said that no all-inclusive definition of greed exists. However, it is possible to synthesize that greed is an excessive desire for self-interest. Although greed contributes to economic growth in a self-contained environment, it tends to be detrimental to most societies, because excessive accumulation of material wealth and consumption impacts negatively on society, including the environment.

Religious and Scholarly Views on Greed

As old as mankind itself, the issue of greed has featured in discussions as far back as the acquisition of wealth and power has existed.[20] Therefore, greed as a character trait and human behaviour are not new. As such, scholars of different ages have written about greed.[21] Scholars in the humanities and social sciences exude some consensus on the fact that greed is as old as mankind itself,[22] residing amongst us from time immemorial. It has thus been the focus of research by numerous scholars.[23] Research conducted by those scholars attempted to understand the notion of greed.

In capitalist economic systems where the acquisition and retention of wealth and power can drive individual aspirations, there is the tendency of some people to embark on an endless pursuit of wealth and power irrespective of how they are perceived or what impact/costs are involved. To such individuals, it is mainly what they want, and never how they accumulate wealth, in such pursuit, and how it may affect others. In the context of capitalist economics, it has been argued that greed is both good and bad, a virtue and a vice.[24] To Thucydides, greed is not absolutely evil as it motivates progress.[25] To Plato, greed is the cause of social unrest and instability, and wars, civil conflicts, and immorality are, to an extent, attributable to greed.[26] Aristotle, on his part, argued that greed is actually 'confusion' between what we actually need and what we ideally want.[27] To Humes, greed is labelled the double-edged sword as it motivates individuals to perform better and also brings destructive consequences to society.[28] In contemporary societies as in older times, greed has been a driving contributor behind the acquisition of wealth and power, which orchestrates a perception as being productive and beneficial while on the other hand, it has been harmful to relationships.

Diagnosing the Mind of a Greedy Individual

Across the globe, irrespective of race, nationality, gender, or religious beliefs, there are individuals who see life without money and other material things as incomplete and boring, and ultimately, those same individuals, at the point of death, realize that money without life is pointless. Numerous individuals would fit into a case study of greed and its manifestation at the workplace. Unfortunately, this paper cannot capture all such grandiose incidents or manifestations of greed. In discussing the greed syndrome, this paper identifies some of the habits and traits of greedy individuals who offer a 'cocktail' of personality types. It should be acknowledged that greed is a human tendency which can be likened to any human addiction such as drugs, sex, alcohol, gambling, or food. However, greed exceeds addiction: while it may be normal for a couple to create a safe space for addiction to food, sex, or alcohol, without compromising any other person or their resources – greed, in the context of corruption, makes individuals focus mainly on themselves at the expense of others. Greed assaults the social conventions of a society. It weakens the value system.

A greedy individual, worried about the availability of resources in times of crisis, and how survival can be sustained, thinks he or she should amass more than enough for himself or herself to survive. The greedy individual always feels insecure and thinks he has not acquired enough to be settled or contented. To gain comfort, pleasure, and security, such individuals develop an acquisition mentality which subsequently grows into an acquisition game. To such people, the acquisition of wealth is considered a way of overcoming feelings of inadequacy and insecurity and securing the future which they see as uncertain. Unfortunately, such unrelenting and unfettered acquisition of wealth meets no end: they never feel satisfied or think they have had enough. As such, the acquisition of wealth becomes a never ending and end in itself.

Greed is not about, or driven by, a desire to meet one's basic needs in life. Rather, it is a desire to have more than what is needed. According to Konrad Raiser, greed is the 'desire to have more than one's legitimate share of goods', adding that from a New Testament perspective, 'falls under strong condemnation'.

The greedy politician, like any greedy individual, places no limit on his or her desires: desires can change the moment that an opportunity to fuel them occurs. The greedy politician thinks and desires beyond what he or she needs. He tends to crave for almost everything even if not needed and does not measure his acquisitions from a comparative viewpoint like looking at the have-nots. His cravings are endless.

Every individual has the right, and without any limitations, to acquire whatever he or she wants in life: it can be amassing a fleet of aircraft, and/or purchasing real estate in every corner of the world. Or changing luxurious and ostentatious cars every so often. It is legally permissible to do all that, provided the means to do that are legitimate, or do not involve any illegal, improper or immoral act towards achieving those ends at the expense of those deprived.

Global economic structures have developed and defined what is meant by the poverty line.[29] Yet, they fail to define at what point one crosses the 'enough line' and slips into the 'excess area'. This puts most people in complex positions, often involving a battle between leading a principled life that gives them identity or abandoning their values. It involves finding a balance between wealth and poverty; benevolence and malevolence; accumulating so much versus sharing with the have-nots. The fiercest and thorniest of these battles is fuelling the drive to acquire wealth through illegitimate, illegal, and immoral means, of which corruption fits in squarely. The theft of public resources as a means of acquiring wealth deprives rightful owners and stakeholders of their legitimate share.

The narrative on greed can be challenging to present since many people have diverse and opposing viewpoints on ethics and morality, influenced greatly by their religious convictions and their positions in life. However, it can be made much easier when such a discussion is illustrated with a few examples. At home, a child can feign an illness to evade performing household chores. To others in the house, it is unfair because they have to do extra work while someone pretentiously rests in bed playing online games or chatting to pals. In school, a student can enter the library and mutilate specific pages of a research book because they are very relevant to an assignment. Other students can be bereft of those research materials, which may negatively affect their performance. The Chief Executive Officer (CEO) of a corporation hesitates to negotiate a wage increase in employees because he or she contemplates the size of his or her annual bonus. A senior politician can be offended by the meagreness of one's salary to meet their untamed desires for ostentatious cars and ends up siphoning public funds to cater for those desires. In all the foregoing scenarios, an unfair advantage is obtained through dishonest means.

Greed and Corruption

Even if argued from an economic point of view as a driver of innovation, success, and progress, religious and philosophical approaches have qualified greed as 'the tendency to always want more and never being satisfied with what one currently has'.[30] No one has a problem with an individual who craves for the universe and everything in it. Likewise, no one will make an issue with an individual who works extra hard to satiate his or her cravings. A problem arises when such cravings are catered for through dishonest, immoral, unethical, and illegal means. When an individual resorts to dishonest, fraudulent, immoral, unethical, and illegal means to cater for his or her cravings, then, it is highly probable that greed influenced such an individual. Greed can be the propelling contributor that drives such criminal behaviour.

The Uniqueness of Corruption

On several fronts, the misappropriation of public funds and/or property – a manifestation of corruption – stands out as a unique crime.[31] Firstly, it can include a syndicated participation of a multiplicity of individuals who play different roles in facilitating the theft of state resources. The syndicate can stretch across different administrative units. For example, financial services such as banks, insurance companies, and registration offices – all may at some point in time be involved in initiating and completing a specific transaction. In the Fotso cases, he was able to misappropriate over FCFA 42 billion over a period of time because he involved various agencies at different levels, including the assistance of the Commercial Bank of Cameroon (CBC) through which electronic transfers were made, delayed, and charged at the detriment of Cameroon Airlines (CAMAIR).[32]

The syndicated nature of the misappropriation of public funds is reflected in the manner in which most of the cases were indicted and prosecuted: over 95 per cent of those cases involved multiple accused individuals, and in one case, there were more than 25 persons implicated.[33] Secondly, misappropriation of public property can include transactions involving fraudulent and dishonest theft of property or public resources.[34] These resources were at the disposal of a few individuals. Such resources were not stolen in a day: funds were debited in several transactions, planned, and executed, spreading over months and years.

Another dimension of the misappropriation of public resources is that the perpetrator can make use of them to influence legal processes and legal institutions, including the judiciary and law enforcement. They can slow down or terminate investigations, close them, influence witnesses, or bribe prosecutors and top politicians. With the conspicuous absence of an independent judiciary and other compromised law enforcement institutions and personnel, senior politicians who are involved in the management of SOEs can interfere with appointments and investigative processes to absolve or exonerate themselves. This can explain why in most cases of grand corruption that involve the political elite of any given society, anti-corruption efforts come to naught when they are not complemented by the much-needed political will.[35] Anti-corruption measures can be rendered ineffective if they are not complemented by political will and independence to operate and survive.

Thirdly, there is a breach of trust: individuals appointed to lead SOEs and departments are afforded the trust to manage the resources therein. If they steal those resources, it constitutes a serious breach of public trust. Lastly, looking at the ramifications of grand corruption involving the theft of public assets, no one may struggle to argue that such individuals stagnate the development of that country. They deprive the country of the resources needed for socio-economic development; puncture the democratic culture and evolution; assault the rule of law; widen the gap between the rich and the poor; and orchestrate socio-economic injustices and income disparity in the country.[36] They are the architects of illicit financial flows and agents of financial draining through which assets leave the country and continent for other countries.[37]

The extensive, elaborate, and credible literature on the effects of corruption produced and generated by reputable scholars and institutions globally have detailed the negative impact of corruption from both a micro and macro scale in a variety of contexts, that is to say, democracies and democratization;[38] the rule of law;[39] socio-economic development;[40] human capital;[41] and capital flight.[42] Figures of funds siphoned by political leaders in Africa are staggering and give a glimpse of the devastation that is dealt to the economies wherefrom those funds are stolen.[43] But the theft of funds does not constitute the only form of grand corruption: mismanagement of funds entrusted in the custodianship of a senior public official can, in magnitude, also constitute grand corruption.

The Masked Pursuit of Self-interest When in Public Office

When faced with the funds stolen by public officials, one can say that a substantial number of individuals who occupy public offices embody greed and excesses which can be typical of any African politician. Today, Cameroonian politicians are measured by the amount of wealth amassed, the fortunes obtained, and the funds stolen. Cameroonians drifted from a value-driven system where the focus was on lives transformed, structures implemented, and change initiated to an offensive display of wealth that defined class that became a parameter of hollow success.

History has always recorded a few individuals who are never satisfied, who crave for more, even at the expense of others who do get almost nothing to sustain themselves. When a society develops a culture that places a high value on materialism, and rewards success based on material acquisition, it indirectly encourages and rewards greed. The tendency nowadays is to worship those who erect mansions; ride in expensive cars; take vacations overseas; possess private jets; own yachts; and wear designer clothes. As stated by one scholar, 'greed is the price we pay for an economic system based on the pursuit of self-interest'.[44]

Corporate Entities and Self-seeking Individuals – How Greed Drives Human Actions

Cases I of corporate fraud such as the Bernie Madoff scandal and Enron provide us with indications of the greed of some top corporate executives. Greed causes people to focus mainly on themselves. At the point where the quest for more propels hard work, drives motivation and creativity, and brings expansion and profit, undoubtedly and unhesitatingly, we applaud individuals like Oprah Winfrey, Aliko Dangote, and Elon Musk and several others are the few who may reside in the pages of history as icons of hard work, creativity, and success. The drive of the accumulation of their wealth can explain why some economists have theorized on the positive and negative aspects of greed, explained and understood as a desire or craving for more if the assiduity and creativity of such a person remain unlimited.

The desire to acquire more and more at the detriment of others can trigger unethical, immoral, and illegal behaviour like deception, fraud, and corruption. The perpetrator of grand corruption should be seen as an abject failure by specific individuals to uphold public trust and affirm their integrity; a depiction of a political system that rewards looting through systemic cracks and the sheer unwillingness to prevent recurrence by closing those gaps.

Greed stems from human desires, which, by their nature, are unlimited. Individuals always want more and more of something of value. Resources, whether material or immaterial, are limited. There is thus a conflict between the utilization of limited resources to meet unlimited human desires. A meagre salary must cater for monthly rents, school fees, groceries, and other social demands like acquiring and running a car, dining out, attending events, and the required clothing for such events. Within societies, individuals compete (even unknowingly) to change their economic class and social strata – which are often defined by indicators such as the neighbourhood where one lives, the car a person drives, the schools their kids attend, the investments made, and the ability to fund overseas vacations, to mention a few. In addition, and unfortunately, these constitute some of the parameters by which a person's success is assessed. Such indicators can put individuals in different struggles: the struggle between effective management of a meagre salary and the provision of basic needs; the battle between utilization of a small and unchanging salary to catch up with increasing and costly wants; the struggle to meet those indicators and change both their economic class and social structure. Caught in such a predicament, individuals face two choices: maintain the *status quo* and become laughable, or, engage in a deceptive or fraudulent financial scheme and be 'seen' in the community.

Against the background of individual struggles as depicted in the previous paragraph, to be 'seen' in the community, individuals, at the helm of leadership, or entrusted with public resources, do not struggle to become self-seeking. Placed in a position of resource management, they can see it as the perfect opportunity to cater for their life-long struggles: acquiring that dream car, purchasing that piece of land in that upscale market neighbourhood, commencing that big business, enrolling their kids in that prestigious school, and taking that overseas holiday trip. The fulfilment of the foregoing knows no limit except these three factors: they can do that only during their tenure; up to the extent that resources are available; or stop when the law is enforced. But their tenure, as seen in some cases of political leaders, does not end quickly. They may be there for life, for example, Robert Mugabe, a former president of Zimbabwe and Daniel Arab Moi, a former president of Kenya. Some are rotated in different portfolios. The resources are not exhausted quickly; they are constantly renewed, and excuses may be advanced for their depletion.

The law, unfortunately, does not necessarily strike quickly. There can be plenty of time and opportunity for an individual who heads an SOE to nurture a plan to misappropriate public funds and do so over an extended period of time. The theft of such resources, one would image, should halt at the point where such an individual crosses the 'poverty line', or has acquired sufficient resources to ensure he or she does not fall below the poverty line. Unfortunately, when driven by greed, such individuals foment plans on how to make the theft of public resources a hobby: they are fascinated by what they do and what they earn. Even if one were to alter his or her social class or economic status within a short period of time, there are limits which, when crossed, become indecent and unacceptable.

There is no eloquent explanation as to why an individual would misappropriate public funds up to FCFA 6 billion in a country where millions are starving to death and struggle to access socio-economic services. Alternatively, can one think of the employee whose net monthly salary is FCFA 35000 (USD 54) and there is an individual who, in a period of less than ten years, stole over FCFA 42 billion from the national air carrier. It might be difficult to comprehend the impact of such thefts on the poorest of the poor. However, if an analysis is provided from the perspective of individual salaries and livelihoods, then, it becomes much easier to fathom. For example, in Cameroon where the income disparity is already too wide, consider the following: the average salary of a civil servant is in the range of about FCFA 150,000 (USD 230) per month.

Consider the case of an individual who steals over FCFA 42 billion. This means a civil servant's annual salary of FCFA 1,800,000 (USD 2,760) multiplied by 30 years amounts to FCFA 54,000,000 (USD 82,300). It means stealing FCFA 42 billion public assets is equivalent to depriving about 778 civil servants of salaries for a period of 30 years. In other words, 778 employees will, for a period of 30 years, go without a house to live in, food to eat, clothes to wear, and unable to send their children to school and cater for themselves when they are sick. It also means that 778 employees, and their dependants, would reside in poverty until a fluke strikes. On the other hand, there is one individual who has changed his or her economic status, social ranking, has acquired a fleet of cars, purchased landed properties, and escorted his family overseas for vacation.

One may be tempted to think that only those who emerge out of poverty and find themselves in senior positions of leadership would take the trajectory of amassing wealth by engaging in unethical, dishonest, and criminality, for example stealing public resources. Lessons learnt from the Cameroonian experience indicate otherwise. A look at the profiles of those who were indicted, prosecuted, and convicted by the Special Criminal Court indicates that over 98 per cent of them were already enjoying absolute affluence. To corroborate this, two of the convicts who embezzled billions of FCFA are worth considering: Polycarpe Abah Abah and Yves-Michel Fotso. They both constitute egregious examples for some reasons. First, they both embezzled funds that rang up to billions of FCFA. Second, they had established themselves in public service and the private sector and resided as successful directors in public service and business. Third, they were far above the poverty line and had no suspicion of insufficiency or want in their lives. Fourth, looking at the itemized list of properties acquired by both, one would ask the question: what really did they want and/or at what point would their desires be fulfilled? The former, Polycarpe Abah Abah, is a Cameroonian politician who occupied several key administrative positions in the Government of Cameroon.

Having earned a university education in some of the most prestigious institutions in the world and attended the National School of Administration and Magistracy (well-known by its French acronym *ENAM – Ecole Nationale de l'Administration et Magistrature*) where he obtained a Diploma in Financial Management. He quickly occupied pertinent administrative positions in the Government. At first, he accepted an appointment at the oil unit in the Tax Department, having been mandated to set up oil taxation in Cameroon. He later became the Deputy Director of Tax Legislation in 1983, as well as a member of the National Public Procurement Commission where he worked for several years. He grew to the rank of Expert of the Customs and Economic Union of Central Africa and Deputy Director in charge of Investigations and Tax Control in Cameroon. In 1988, he left the Tax Department. From 1988 to 1991, Polycarpe Abah Abah was appointed as Attaché to the General Secretariat at the Presidency.

Core to his portfolio was monitoring the activities of the Ministry of Economy and Finance and relations with international development partners such as the World Bank and IMF under the structural adjustment programme concluded by the Government of Cameroon. Abah Abah was later deployed to the Prime Minister's Office where he served as Charge de Mission from 1991 to 1998 and continued to perform similar services in his previous portfolio. He was then appointed President of the National Commission for Tax Reforms in Cameroon. He became the National Director of Taxes in 1998, a post he occupied until 2004. Under his leadership, there was a significant increase in tax revenue: in less than six years, the amount rose from FCFA 250,000,000,000 in 1998 to exceed FCFA 750,000,000,000 in 2004. Abah Abah served as Minister of Economy and Finances from 2004 to 2008 and earned the 2006 Knight of the Order of Valour and Best African Finance Minister – a title conferred by the General Assembly of the Breton Woods Institutions in Singapore.

Against such an exceptional public service record, the details of his surreptitious transactions only became public knowledge following his arrest, detention, and conviction by the SCC. Convicted of misappropriation of public funds and perpetrated in complicity with others, Abah Abah was sentenced to a 25-year term in prison. The sum of public funds misappropriated by him was FCFA 1,256,000,000. In complicity with Manga Pascal, the sum of FCFA 6,511,307,783 had been stolen from the State. In terms of the term of imprisonment, the SCC ordered the confiscation of over 50 items which were obtained using the stolen funds.

Yves Michel Fotso was educated in the United States of America. Son of a Cameroonian multi-billionaire, Fotso Victor, he (Yves Michel) left the private sector where he headed most of the business entities under the Fotso Group and joined the now-defunct Cameroon Airlines (CAMAIR) as General Manager per appointment by a presidential decree. An already established billionaire running one of the most successful business groups in the country, one would place him in the category of the business gurus in Cameroon with indisputable self-sufficiency. Fotso's management of CAMAIR, unfortunately, as would be seen years later, was not for the advancement or growth of the national airline company.

Neither for its employees. It was using CAMAIR for his self-interest and goals: to amass wealth by fraudulent and dishonest means. Fotso's racketeering involved a network of financial enterprises, for example the Commercial Bank of Cameroon (CBC), owned by the Fotso Group of which he was one of the directors including multiple other companies in the aviation and insurance sectors that became complicit in what he did. He used CBC to conduct transactions with CAMAIR for which he caused delays, imposed charges, and initiated and concluded international transactions in foreign currencies, resulting in huge debits to CAMAIR's accounts. Fotso, unlike Abah Abah, mastered the business of bank-to-bank transactions and knew how and when to initiate transactions that would go through the

CBC, generating huge charges at the expense of CAMAIR. In the short span of time that he managed CAMAIR, Fotso had siphoned over FCFA 42 billion.

Gleaning from the foregoing cases, one gets puzzled by the nature and extent of such thefts. These two individuals pursued a path to self-aggrandizement, to settle their insatiable desires by stealing from the public in complete disregard of the adverse ramifications of their actions. Their gargantuan greed probably propelled their desire to steal that could probably only be stopped by law enforcement when they were ejected from their portfolios. Admired by the public for their successes, only after disclosure of the details did the public get to know what had transpired during their leadership. Abah Abah acquired several properties for himself, his children, and relatives, probably to resolve the insecurity that looms over the acquisition of land in Cameroon. Fotso deposited funds in his account in a bid to sustain his status as a billionaire, not through arduous work, but crime. In these two examples, and several others that have not been discussed, greed was most probably the driving contributor.

The graphic illustrations of the two gentlemen can take an emotive turn when one considers the myriad of ramifications that such actions bring to the broader community. However, the impact on the public seems not to be of relevance. The individual who stole FCFA 42 billion did not stop because he felt he had amassed enough wealth for himself, his family, and generations that would succeed him. He stopped because he could either be removed from the office and therefore had no access to the resources, or the law could bring him into the dragnet. That explains the tricky and complicated part about greed: it grows into an insatiable desire, without any known reasonable explanation except maybe because the individual want to enjoy having so much for himself. The desire for unlimited accumulation of wealth, even when at the public expense, becomes a propellant for deceitful, fraudulent, and criminal conduct.

The capitalist market system, proven beyond doubt as the most successful economic system despite its flaws and braced by many Africans, has been packaged and presented to the deprived, manipulated, and ignorant people taught to believe that market prices and only market prices govern. Such skewed branding can devalue and discount the importance and contribution of some external interventions, such as government regulation and/or civil society.

The SCC judgements unravel the worst individuals in Cameroon who, entrusted with public resources, were driven by an insatiable desire to amass wealth for themselves while profusely bleeding the state entities under their stewardship. The theft of hundreds of millions of FCFA by individuals who, hitherto, were already affluent, can be understood as driven by the endless quest for material possessions and money, no matter at what cost, even when their liberties were imperilled by their own gestures. In those judgements handed to them, one sees an unmasked and unambiguous display and manifestation of a passion for instant and selfish gratification of accumulated of wealth, including the adoration of money obtained through dishonest, fraudulent, and deceitful means and tactics. The sagas point to financial misfeasance that has plagued SOEs and governmental departments. They do constitute some of the rapacious examples of political and corporate turpitude and decadence.

Conclusion

Scanty research on greed as a driver of grand theft of state resources makes it challenging to appraise and apprise the complexity of such human tendency. Greed deprives societies from extoling the need for specific values expected of those who intend to manage public office. Probably engrossed (even if unintended or ignorantly) in the character of people from infancy through childhood to adolescence, a public discussion on the limits to one's desire when entrusted with public resources should be distinguished from a personal drive to motivation, innovation, growth, and expansion. Without the ability to draw a line and find a balance, it can be counterproductive: seeking and rewarding individualism and hard work while ensuring that no one is enriched from unethical, illegal, or immoral actions such as stealing from the public. At a time when people seemingly want to amass wealth at any cost, contentious debates on the challenging issue of greed and excess may not be resolved soon. With several individuals brought into the SCC's spotlight, and the amounts publicly divulged, a debate on how greed and craving for excess drove the commission of financial crimes. Such debate should touch on both positive and adverse economic effects and evoke profound philosophical and religious considerations. Above all, the debate should speak to a general national culture of whether to entrench deeply an ethos of public service that uplifts everyone or a selected few at the expense of others.

Notes

* Professor of Public International Law, School of Postgraduate Studies, Faculty of Law, North-West University.

1 The Special Criminal Court (SCC) was established by *Law No. 2011/028 of 14 December 2011*. Its mandate was stipulated in Section 2.

2 *Affaire Ministere Public Et La Liquidation Camair C/Fotso Yves Michel*, Arret N° 018/Crim/Tcs of 25 April 2016 and *Affaire Ministere Public Et Etat Du Cameroun (La Liquidation Camair) C/Fotso Yves Michel*, Arret N° 011/Crim/Tcs of 29 April 2016.

3 *Affaire Ministère Public Et Etat Du Cameroun C/Atangana Mebara Jean Marie Et Mendouga Jérôme*, Arret N° 019/Crim/Tcs of 22 June 2016.

4 *Ministère Public Et Etat Du Cameroun (Ministère Des Finances) C/Abah Abah Polycarpe; Edou Joseph; Evina Nyangono Sylvie Chantal Épse Avocey; Meke Raphaël; Mewoulou Oyono Épse Mballa Hélène; Eloumba Thérèse; Tenlep Joseph; Etogo Mbezele Luc Evariste; Manga Pascal*, Arret N° 001/Crim/Tcs/15 of 13 January 2015.

5 The purport of Section 184 of the Penal Code is to prohibit and penalise such conduct with severe penalties that are meted out with a deterrent and punitive intent and effect.

6 Haynes, K. T., Josefy, M., & Hitt, M. A. (2015). Tipping point: Managers' self-interest, greed, and altruism. *Journal of Leadership & Organizational Studies*, *22*(3), 265–279. See also Sievers, B. (2012). Towards a socioanalysis of capitalist greed. *Critique*, *40*(1), 15–39.

7 Seuntjens, T. G., Zeelenberg, M., Van de Ven, N., & Breugelmans, S. M. (2015). Dispositional greed. *Journal of Personality and Social Psychology*, *108*(6), 917–933.

8 Ibid.

9 Oka, R., & Kuijt, I. (2014). Greed is bad, neutral, and good: A historical perspective on excessive accumulation and consumption. *Economic Anthropology*, *1*(1), 30–48.

10 Seuntjens, T. G., Zeelenberg, M., Breugelmans, S. M., & Van de Ven, N. (2015). Defining greed. *British Journal of Psychology*, *106*(3), 505–525.

11 Augustine, Saint (2001). *The Confessions*, ed. & trans. Philip Burton. New York: A. A. Knopf.
12 Cooey, 'Christian Perspectives on Overcoming Greed in a Consumeristic Society: Buying Fear as Collusion with Greed versus an Economy of Grace'.
13 Cooey, 'Christian Perspectives on Overcoming Greed in a Consumeristic Society.'
14 Posner, E. A. 'The Jurisprudence of Greed', *University of Pennsylvania Law Review*, 151(3), 2003, 1097.
15 Tickle, P. A. (2006). *Greed. The Seven Deadly Sins*. Oxford University Press.
16 Simmel, G. (1900/2004). The Philosophy of Money, 3rd enlarged edn, ed. D. Frisby, trans. T. Bottomore and D. Frisby from a first draft by Kaethe Mengelberg. Routledge, p. 237, http://copperismoney.com/Files/philosophy_of_money.pdf (accessed 9 August 2010).
17 17 Newhauser, R. G. (2007). *The Early History of Greed: The Sin of Avarice in Early Medieval Thought and Literature* (Cambridge: Cambridge University Press, 2001). See also R. G. Newhauser (ed.), *The Seven Deadly Sins: From Communities to Individuals*. Boston, MA: Brill CF. R. G. Newhauser, 'The Seven Deadly Sins as Cultural Constructions in the Middle Ages', 2004. NEH Summer Seminar 2004 outline, www.trinity.edu/rnewhaus/outline.html (accessed 3 October 2010) in which he focuses his research on the deadly sins in the Middle Ages.
18 Balot, R. K. (2001). *Greed and Injustice in Classical Athens*. Princeton University Press.
19 Haynes, K. T., Josefy, M., & Hitt, M. A. (2015). Tipping point: Managers' self-interest, greed, and altruism. *Journal of Leadership & Organizational Studies, 22*(3), 265–279.
20 Seuntjens, T. G., Zeelenberg, M., Van de Ven, N., & Breugelmans, S. M. (2015). Dispositional greed. *Journal of Personality and Social Psychology, 108*(6), 917–933.
21 Balot, R. K. (2001). *Greed and Injustice in Classical Athens*. Princeton University Press. Goldberg, M. H. (1994). *The Complete Book of Greed: The Strange and Amazing History of Human Excess*. William Morrow & Company. Robertson, A. F. (2013). *Greed: Gut Feelings, Growth, and History*. John Wiley & Sons. Wang, L., & Murnighan, J. K. (2011). On greed. *Academy of Management Annals, 5*(1), 279–316.
22 Seuntjens, T. G., Zeelenberg, M., Van de Ven, N., & Breugelmans, S. M. (2015). Dispositional greed. *Journal of Personality and Social Psychology, 108*(6), 917–933.
23 Goldberg, M. H. (1994). *The Complete Book of Greed: The Strange and Amazing History of Human Excess*. William Morrow & Company. Robertson, A. F. (2013). *Greed: Gut Feelings, Growth, and History*. John Wiley & Sons.
24 Sutherland, S. (2015). *Greed: From Gordon Gekko to David Hume*. Haus Publishing.
25 Zagorin, P. (2005). *Thucydides: An Introduction for the Common Reader*. Princeton University Press.
26 Balot, R. K. (2001). *Greed and Injustice in Classical Athens*. Princeton University Press.
27 Wang, L., & Murnighan, J. K. (2011). On greed. *Academy of Management Annals, 5*(1), 279–316.
28 Seuntjens, T. G., Zeelenberg, M., Van de Ven, N., & Breugelmans, S. M. (2015). Dispositional greed. *Journal of Personality and Social Psychology, 108*(6), 917–933.
29 Goedhart, T., Halberstadt, V., Kapteyn, A., & Van Praag, B. (1977). The poverty line: concept and measurement. *Journal of Human Resources, 12*(4), 503–520. See also Gillie, A. (1996). The origin of the poverty line. *Economic History Review, 49*(4), 715–730.
30 Terri, p. 917: the "tendency to always want more and never being satisfied with what one currently has."
31 Even though Section 2 of *Law No 2011/028 of 14 December 2011* talks of "misappropriation of public funds". *Law No 2012/011 of 16 July 2012* amending Section 2 of *Law No 2011/028 of 14 December 2011*.

32 *Affaire Ministere Public Et La Liquidation Camair C/Fotso Yves Michel*, Arret No. 018/Crim/Tcs of 25 April 2016 and *Ministere Public Et Etat Du Cameroun (La Liquidation Camair) C/Fotso Yves Michel*, Arret No 011/Crim/Tcs of 29 April 2016.
33 *Ministère Public Et Etat Du Cameroun (Ministère Des Enseignements Secondaires) C/ Eyenga Abena Marie Catherine; Olinga Meke René; Ngahzi Gaspard; Nkoe Ndzeng Yannick Et Ekouma Clément Elie*, Arret N° 008/Crim/Tcs/16 of 1 April 2016.
34 See the definition of the offence of misappropriation of public property/funds in Section 184(1) of the Penal Code.
35 Agbor, A. (2019). Cameroon and the corruption conundrum: Highlighting the need for political will in combatting corruption in Cameroon. *African Journal of International and Comparative Law*, *27*(1), 50–75. Ankamah, S. A., & Khoda, S. (2018). Political will and government anti-corruption efforts: What does the evidence say? *Public Administration and Development*, *38*(1), 3–14.
36 Flores Marquez, H., Valderrama Santibañez, A. L., Angeles Castro, G., & Neme Castillo, O. (2021). Corruption, economic growth, and income inequality in Africa. *Economics of Governance*, *3*(3), 183–209. Torgler, B., & Piatti, M. (2013).
37 Integrity, G. F. (2008). *Illicit Financial Flows from Developing Countries: 2002–2006*. Thiao, A. (2021). The effect of illicit financial flows on government revenues in the West African Economic and Monetary Union countries. *Cogent Social Sciences*, *7*(1), 1–24.
38 De la Croix, D., & Delavallade, C. (2011). Democracy, rule of law, corruption incentives, and growth. *Journal of Public Economic Theory*, *13*(2), 155–187. Rubasundram, G. A., & Rasiah, R. (2019). Corruption and good governance. *Journal of Southeast Asian Economies*, *36*(1), 57–70.
39 De la Croix, D., & Delavallade, C. (2011). Democracy, rule of law, corruption incentives, and growth. *Journal of Public Economic Theory*, *13*(2), 155–187. Elbasani, A., & Šabić, S. Š. (2018). Rule of law, corruption and democratic accountability in the course of EU enlargement. *Journal of European Public Policy*, *25*(9), 1317–1335.
40 Omodero, C. O. (2019). Effect of corruption on foreign direct investment inflows in Nigeria. *Studia Universitatis Economics Series*, *29*(2), 54–66.
41 Omodero, C. O. (2019). Effect of corruption on foreign direct investment inflows in Nigeria. *Studia Universitatis Economics Series*, *29*(2), 54–66.
42 Ionescu, L. (2014). The adverse effects of corruption on growth and development. *Economics, Management, and Financial Markets*, *9*(4), 125–130.
43 Rubasundram, G. A. & Rasiah, R. (2019). Corruption and good governance. *Journal of Southeast Asian Economies*, *36*(1), 57–70.
44 Manfred F R Kets de Vries, The GREED Syndrome, p. 7.

4 The Politics and Anthropology of Combating Corruption in Africa

*Happy Kayuni**

Concept of Corruption

Corruption is a universal theme that describes both public and private organizations and businesses. The World Bank definition, on the other hand, imposes uniformity in defining corruption by referring to it specifically as – the abuse of public power for private gain.[1] Many illicit, unlawful, and immoral behaviours fall under this canopy, including, but not limited to, bribery, extortion, embezzlement, inflated payrolls where designated payees do not receive funds (also known as 'ghost salaries'), over-invoicing, theft of foreign aid, turning a blind eye to smuggling, the buying and selling of legislative votes, nepotistic hiring practices, and selling of government licenses and land concessions, to name a few.[2] These autographs can be divided into petty and grand corruption. The former may be exercised by a select few people on lower ranks, such as police officials and customs agents. At the same time, the latter may be institutionalized as well-run kleptocracies intended to enrich a small elite at the expense of the whole populace.

Corruption is generally understood as an evil canker that erodes amenities from the poor masses to the few political and economic elites.[3] Some academics have, however, used the mutability of knowledge to refute the overhyped cancerous effects of corruption. According to them, a society's level of corruption is determined by the quality of its legal and institutional framework, as well as by how well its government functions and its political system. They claim, for instance, that corruption is essential in making up for bureaucracy, the paralysis of institutions, and the way it 'greases the wheels' of an economy. However, it is assumed that this is only true in nations with stringent laws, ineffective government agencies, and weak governance systems.[4] Indeed, the assertion undermines the long-term damages caused by corruption on national output, income and social inequality, the state of institutions, and the quality of governance. Many studies indicate that corruption highly inhibits the conventional roles and responsibilities of the state: resource allocation, political and economic stabilization, and ensuring even distribution of income and wealth. Many researchers argue that corruption distorts government distributional function by compromising budgetary revenues and expenditures which in turn negatively affects economic growth, employment, income inequality, and living standards.[5]

DOI: 10.4324/9781003326649-5

Status of Corruption in Africa

The extension of the concept, from individuals to institutions and from public to private sector, justifies why corruption has been theatrically assumed and empirically found endemic in countries with weak institutions. Weak institutions, especially those dealing with power and control, provide room for patron–client relationships – dubbed as neopatrimonialism. Scholars have primarily argued that neopatrimonialism is a ubiquitous moniker for Africa's governments. The assertion entails that Africa's politics permeates corruption, clientelism, and rent-seeking behaviours by those in power, which limits the analytical ingredients of economic policy and performance.[6] While corruption is a global crisis, it is still most severe in Africa. The 2021 Corruption Perceptions Index (CPI), according to Transparency International, shows that efforts to reduce corruption over the past 10 years have been largely unsuccessful, with no improvement seen in more than 80% of Sub-Saharan African countries.[7]

In most, if not all, African states, corruption is a crime that carries a sentence. The majority of African constitutions and other anticorruption measures vehemently condemn corruption. African leaders and their people are deeply disturbed by the pervasive corruption, to the point where hardly a day goes by without hearing someone in the street or a public enterprise denounce the cancerous effects of corruption. Nevertheless, the grandiloquence in the waves and progress to weeding out corruption in Africa remain infinitesimally small.[8] Somalia sits on the end of the continuum, followed by Nigeria, and South Africa, among other countries with high-profile corruption scandals. In terms of systemic or structural approach, Somalia's corruption in public procurement ranks as the highest risk for enterprises in Africa, where procurement bids are far from transparency and oversight. This phenomenon is followed by the misappropriation of public funds by those in power.[9] Recently, Malawi witnessed the misappropriation of MK270 million for COVID-19 response.[10]

Regarding the interactional paradigm, high-profile corruption scandals in Africa are primarily visible among political elites. Mobutu Sese Seko, for example, accumulated a staggering wealth of up to United States (US)$5 billion, equivalent to his country's (Democratic Republic of the Congo) external debt. The colossal sum made him richer than well-known business tycoons who owned big corporations.[11] The anatomy of grand gold fraud perpetrated by Kenya's Daniel Arap Moi led to the loss of vast sums of money. The fraud originated from Goldenberg International, which falsified export revenues of precious minerals in return for subsidies as a reward for generating forex.[12] Sani Abacha of Nigeria is popularly known for dying before enjoying his looted billions. Nigeria recovered a significant portion of Abacha's loot through his son, who openly declared the US$700 million he received from his father.[13] Recently, the US government entered into a pact to repatriate over 23 million US dollars stolen by Abacha.[14] Malawi's Newton Kambala, Ken Kandodo,[15] South Africa's Jacob Zuma, and the Gupta family constitute government officials implicated in eye-catching corruption scandals.[16]

The 2021 Transparency International's Corruption Perceptions Index indicates that Sub-Saharan Africa is the most highly corrupt region in the world.[17] In 2021, the region scored 33 out of 100 and Africa as a whole scored 33.5 out of 100, which is 10 percentiles shy of the global average Corruption Perceptions Index of 43. The score shows no significant improvement as the gains realized by few countries are offset by the large static countries and the continent's peripatetic performance that sees Seychelles with a stunning score of 70 percentiles, and other four countries, Cabo Verde (58), Botswana (58), Mauritius (54), and Rwanda (53) out of 54 countries assessed by Transparency International (TI) scored above 50 in the 2021 CPI. According to TI, countries with various forms of political turbulences earned the least scores. It is not unfathomable to see Africa's Libya (17), Equatorial Guinea (17), Somalia (13), South Sudan (11), and Democratic Republic of Congo (19). While 46 countries scored below 30 globally, 24 of those are from Africa. Warf (2017) in his geographical study of African corruption concluded that 1 billion (about 90 per cent) of 1.2 billion people in Africa live under very or extremely corrupt political regimes.[18]

Anthropological Conceptualization

An anthropological perspective to understand corruption is critical. In one or two ways, the World Bank's definition of corruption is lacking in detail or is incomplete. For instance, the definition limits corruption to immoral individuals holding public office and personal power acclimatization. However, stories of corruption go beyond specific people to formal and informal systems that support dishonest, unreliable, and egotistical people. The latter is more important if one is to fully comprehend the anthropological nature of corruption. Muir and Gupta point out that this simplistic definition has several implications; for instance, the emphasis on the distinction between private and public is problematic because 'corruption blurs boundaries'.[19]

The definition also fails to distinguish between a gift and a bribe effectively in a cultural context. Identifying transactions that can be categorised as corrupt can hardly be a definitional question as it is invariably 'perspectival, evaluative, and performative,' and raises a complex challenge.[20] However, Muir and Gupta see this lack of precision in the definition as an advantage.[21] This lack of precision helps the concept of corruption to receive universal acceptance. This is the case because it 'traverses geographic boundaries, sociocultural contexts, and institutional structures' so that it is now 'nearly impossible to argue convincingly in favor of corruption'.[22] An anthropological approach allows scholars to discuss the idea of corruption from a local perspective but with a global outlook.[23]

American Anthropology Association define Anthropology as

> the study of humans, past and present.[24] To understand the full sweep and complexity of cultures across all of human history, anthropology draws and builds upon knowledge from the social and biological sciences as well as the humanities and physical sciences. A central concern of anthropologists is the application of knowledge to the solution of human problems.[25]

Muir and Gupta explain that most anthropologists have ended up studying corruption 'by accident rather than by design'.[26] This implies that for a long time, corruption has not been on top of the agenda for anthropological analysis.

Muir and Gupta argue that to pursue questions related to corruption as well as anti-corruption strategies, it is expected that we also examine the 'socially situated judgments about fairness and justice' and political dynamics of power within a polity.[27] Specifically, anti-corruption initiatives almost always, 'challenges the political and bureaucratic apparatus . . . accusations of corruption can function as powerful but unpredictable political weapons'. According to Torsello and Venard, anthropology provides indispensable perspectives in the field of corruption studies.[28] Some of the new perspectives include, but not limited to, 'the definition of the concept, the morality of corruption, the processual approach, the methods of inquiry, and the holistic perspective'.

Political and Anthropological Dimensions of Corruption

The world has grown simultaneously complex and more uncomplicated due to intertwined cultures and increased economic integration. Despite the 'corruption boom' and though overwhelming on the global scene, neither the United States government nor the International Monetary Fund (IMF) considers corporate crimes and corruption flourishing in the private sector.[29] With increased corruption narratives, it is crucial to understand that corruption discourses and practices breed varying actors besides the state. For example, tendencies of client–bureaucracy interaction have created notions of the haves and have-nots, exposition of the powerless, those made silent, and impotence due to the inability to be involved in the complex exchange system. Therefore, the debate on what corruption is, its breeding ground, and its aftermath is far from over.

Corruption must be defined from the narratives of those who believe it has occurred and those who talk from evidence. According to Eriksen, to have a clear-cut understanding of corruption discourses and practices in a seemingly problematic, mystifying, and complex world will require a paradigm of social life that does not buy preconceived propositions about people's daily life, which is alert of the commonalities and variegations, while facing social life from a global and a local perspective.[30] Thus, anthropology is the only academic discipline that satisfies these preconditions due to its broad perspective of social life that accommodates circumstances in a snapshot fashion without stereotyping while observing structures, patterns, and commonalities. Most importantly, anthropology addresses complex questions with easy-to-understand solutions yet critical of a phenomenon.

Indeed, anthropology's intellectual and theoretical explorations will be decisive in various ways of life beyond the public sector. For example, there is a need to locally study and provide comparisons of corruption allegations involving the Botswana Football Association (BFA), retail and I.T. telecommunication line services in Mauritania, an overwhelming concentration of lending to insiders in Burundi – where top bank managers and their workers have access to bank loans at below market rates, among other cases.[31] Specifically, Ndikumana argued for the need for more attention on private-sector corruption due to its disquieting consequences on society and humanity, along with the traditionally commonly narrated public-sector phenomenon.[32]

Anthropologists see corruption as a social process, in contrast to the conventional view of corruption held by other social science disciplines like economics and political science. The perspective aids researchers in employing an anthropological methodology to avoid the concept's synchronized social phenomenon and thus open up a diachronic perspective. As a result, this processual perspective would enable a dynamic analysis of corruption in terms of the conditions and results of its perpetuation. The meanings and interpretations of social facts as perceived by local observers must therefore be taken into consideration.

The Concept of Guanxi in the African Context

Social facts have it that common to conditions perpetuating corruption is the guanxi concept, which originated in the 1994 Chinese era. Guanxi refers to people's tenacity to have personal social connections (networks) based on trust and strong ties with someone or others and mostly catapults moral obligations and trading favours. Since its inception, researchers have commonly used the concept to understand corruption.[33] Since social ties are inevitable, guanxi has its moral dimensions but mainly results in ethically misgiving behaviours to outright corruption. The argument is that it may give some people or business entities advantages. However, the social cost is more remarkable as it may be detrimental to others or firms in a society.[34] For example, in his analysis, Yin observed that guanxi is a moral norm and desirable social behaviour within the Chinese culture in the sense that it provides the standards and rules on the establishment, continuance, and use of relationships and connections, both among businesses and in the government.[35]

Ado examined the use of guanxi among African returns in Ethiopia, Kenya, and Tanzania from China.[36] He observed that the concept is gradually being internalized in Africa, evidenced by establishing the new cultural capital and a diachronic Sino-African entrepreneurial culture. Thus, it is unfathomable that as opposed to the donor orthodox, which stipulates that aid and foreign direct investment (FDI) flows to African countries with strong institutions, notwithstanding China invests in countries with superfluous business challenges, higher global country risk, or weak institutions. Udo attributes China's strategy as an outcome of the guanxi networking systems (opportunities) rather than the risks which help Chinese enterprises gain contracts from African governments.[37] Internally, evidence shows that the exchange of jobs and other favours is based mainly on African social networks. Though this betting game is believed to have been brought to Africa by the Chinese Cantonese, it is increasingly played by natives and has become an essential entrepreneurial language in Africa.[38]

African Political System of Neopatrimonialism

A close analysis of the Chinese guanxi concept brings its African equivalent concept that is seen as a 'common denominator' for various tendencies typical of the features of African politics, namely despotism, clannish behaviour (tribalism), regionalism, patronage, cronyism, prebendalism, corruption, predation, regionalism, factionalism, among others. Mkandawire called these features an African political system of neopatrimonialism.[39] Mkandawire further contends that these terminologies are typical in African literature, known for its rigorous metaphors, and it is distinguished by its unrestrained use of stories, derogatory terminology, and vivid vignettes of the all-too-common incidents of flagrant abuse of state resources and power. The domination of neopatrimonialism in Africa has been outlined in presidentialism, clientelism, and the use of state resources.[40] Similarly, Soest observed that this kind of informal politics of the African leaders encroaches on the administration of taxation and leads to decreased government spending on essential goods and services.[41] Therefore, we argue that embedding neopatrimonialism leads to increasing extractive institutions as opposed to inclusive institutions since the flow of resources will be based on lineages and social networks.

Central to the perpetuation of corruption in Africa is presidentialism – a political, economic system in which overarching political powers lie with the president, who is elected by the majority vote and is autonomous of the legislature.[42] Because of this, African state leaders frequently exercise extreme power and shoulder enormous responsibilities. For instance, the executive exercises broad political authority in 43 of the 48 Sub-Saharan nations, with the exception of the monarchical Eswatini and four parliamentary governments (Botswana, Mauritius, Lesotho, and South Africa). Therefore, it is not improbable that in the majority of African nations, the president has oversight of and control over ministries, departments, and other state agencies. Hastings Kamuzu Banda, the former head of state of Malawi, represents the extreme moniker of presidentialism, as he openly stated to be the owner of all business activities: education, agriculture, transport, and whatnot, to mention but a few.[43]

Consequently, people in Africa perceive their leaders as fathers of the nation. In turn, to maintain acclimatization and political hegemony, most African leaders claim to be endowed with occult or spiritual powers.[44] This ability to create an intimidating presence has often led to the African founders of independence plundering state resources and making the culture persistent in subsequent political parties.

From an ethnographical perspective and its processual view of corruption, it is argued that developmental aid perpetuates a breeding ground for corrupt activities.[45] Further, Torsello and Venard noted that public officials had been triggered to bow to corruption for developmental policies and the use of aid to succeed. This assertion is consistent with Udo's argument in analysing the Chinese aid to Africa.[46] Indeed, many scholars have been perplexed by the steep flow of aid into more corrupt African states and less aid to angelic states.[47] Asongu and Jellal explored the intertwined relationship between aid and corruption in Africa.[48] The study observed that foreign aid, piped through government consumption expenditure, perpetuates corruptible practices as opposed to foreign aid conditioned on private investments.

Tseretse Khama laid the groundwork for Botswana, giving the continent an African base from which to compare and draw the roots of corruption. Botswana is regarded as the shining example of cleanliness on the continent when it comes to the cancerous corruption in Africa. For example, the country scored 55 out of 100 in the 2021 Corruption Perceptions Index, running concurrently with countries such as Saint Lucia, Dominica, Fiji, and Georgia and ahead of countries such as China, Slovakia, Jordan, Cyprus, Malta, and Mauritius. However, what makes Botswana's corruption levels persistently low, going against the unfortunate trend of Sub-Saharan Africa? Ganahl attributes low corruption in Botswana to the meritocracy and efficiency of Khama's leadership, especially how the state has maintained the parastatal sector, which is desirably small and subject to turgid budget constrictions.[49] Indeed, the trait is rare for African countries as the grandiloquence leakage of public resources is higher among countries with large parastatals than other government agencies.

The African 'Two Publics' Concept and Corruption

Ekeh in his classic 'two publics' thesis tries to explain why nepotism, corruption, and other social vices persist in an African context.[50] The first argument is that the public and private realm, as understood in Western society, operates under the same moral expectations; in other words, what is deemed wrong in the public realm is also regarded so in the private realm. Contrary to Western societies, Ekeh argues that African societies have two public realms which do not share a common moral base and this ultimately explains and characterizes some of the problems in African politics. These two publics are the *primordial public realm* and the *civic public realm*. According to Ekeh, the primordial public realm is characterized by traditional attachments and affinities, which influence how an individual behaves in the public realm. In this case, the primordial public is moral and has a common moral base as the private realm. The civic public realm is associated with the colonial period structures of governance and is amoral and does not have the same moral requirements that guide private behaviour. Africans find themselves operating in both realms but they tend to be more committed to the primordial publics and demonstrate less commitment to the civic public realm. In this case, he states that:

> Most educated Africans are citizens of two publics in the same society. On the one hand, they belong to a civic public from which they gain materially but to which they give only grudgingly. On the other hand they belong to a primordial public from which they derive little or no material benefits but to which they are expected to give generously and do give materially. Their relationship to the primordial public is moral, while that to the civic public is amoral.[51]

Ekeh further argues that voluntary associations are created especially in urban centres by educated African elite and assume a civic public appearance but have an underlying primordial public identity. The African elite create and support primordial voluntary associations as a way of securing their status in the civic public realm. Ekeh concludes that these two realms are rivals and the 'civic public is starved of badly needed morality'.[52] In this case, the lack of morality in the civic public is partly the source of most of the problems in African politics, such as corruption and tribalism. The elite are responsible for inventing some of the ethnic practices and traditions. They may also be responsible for setting the political or cultural agenda of a movement.

Based on Ekeh's thesis, several issues can be deduced in relation to this paper. Firstly, the African elite are behind the creation and sustenance of primordial voluntary associations (or ethnic movements). These ethnic organizations (primordial voluntary organizations) guide their motives and decisions in the political realm. In other words, political participation is defined and interpreted through the ethnic perspective, thus politicization of cultural nationalism. Secondly, and more importantly, since Africans are operating in both realms simultaneously, it is difficult in practice to create proper boundaries between these two realms of culture and politics. Thirdly, the membership to these two publics is the main source and possibly also lies the solution to problems of corruption and other social vices.

Rigg's Prismatic Model (Agraria–Industria) of the African Bureaucratic Structure

The bureaucracy in developing countries such as Africa is not completely divorced from what is happening in the wider community. In other words, it 'is just one of the many sub-systems in a society and as a subsystem it is in constant interaction with other subsystems, that is, political, cultural and economic'.[53] Consequently, for scholars to understand how the bureaucracy functions, they need to first of all analyse it in the context of other societal subsystems which constantly interact with it.

Riggs argued that all communities or societies move from a 'fused' mode to a 'diffracted' condition.[54] The diffracted condition is the ideal condition and it implies a high degree of functional specialization. In administrative terms, this means a change from a situation in which a few structures perform a variety of functions, as in very underdeveloped conditions, to one in which many specific structures perform specific functions, as in highly developed societies like the industrial countries of the West. A prismatic situation is a condition whereby the public sector or society is neither fused nor diffracted. In other words, it is a transitional state.[55] In the 'prismatic' condition, 'societies suffer from a mismatch between political and bureaucratic growth.

Due to bureaucratic hegemony the bureaucrats often encroach upon the jurisdiction of the politician and try deliberately to affect the political process and vice versa.'[56] Ikeanyibe points out that although Riggs model has been criticized over the years 'yet aspects of his theory remain relevant towards explaining persistent poor administrative behaviour in most African countries'.[57]

Building on Riggs model, Dzimbiri, argues that the public administration system in Africa 'needs to be understood as a mixture of the traditional indigenous and western structures and values which continue to co-exist side by side' and the problem is that most African countries do not know 'which administrative culture to adopt'.[58] In other words, there is a western and African culture that influences how the bureaucratic system needs to work. These cultures in most cases clash. This is aptly argued by Dzimbiri when he says:

> Thus, the wider culture has a significant impact on the extent to which citizens obey and follow national constitutions, laws, rules and procedures created for the effective functioning of nations and institutions. . . . For example, while the literature talks of merit, competence, official verifiable qualifications for deciding recruitment or promotion of officers in organisations or public service in general, managers as well as trainers are aware that such objectivity or meritocracy is overtaken by extended family considerations, nepotism, bribery and favouritism which are in line with some African cultures . . . . Thus, while anti-corruption reform measures are imported from the West, as long as the mindset or value infrastructure pattern of beliefs, values, traditions, practices remain supportive of corruption, these initiatives aimed at arresting corruption may even exacerbate it.[59]

Ikeanyibe refers to this transitional state as a hybridization of the African bureaucracy.[60] This hybridization has 'led to various challenges of African public administration such as nepotism, ethnic rivalry, and the unquenchable desire to loot public funds for selfish or group interests'; hence, the idea of the 'public' in public administration is neither appreciated nor felt.[61]

Combating Corruption through Ubuntu Philosophy

Although African culture has been blamed for among other things influencing corruption, Samita and Oindo argue that scholars should focus on the same culture for positive results in the fight against corruption.[62] They argue specifically that while 'there are elements in African culture that can be effectively used to curb corruption', 'the legal and institutional anti-corruption measures, as well as scholarly empirical studies, have hardly delved into how African culture can be utilized in the fight against corruption within the continent'.[63] Samita and Oindo start off by explaining Gyekye's conceptualization of 'ethno-cultural' and 'multi-cultural' communities.[64]

Ethno-cultural defines a community of people 'who are bound by some intrinsic ties within a spatial-temporal context', and they normally identify themselves to a common set of traditions, history, ancestry, language, etc. On the other hand, a multicultural community refers to a situation 'when various ethno-cultural communities merge' or when different ethnic groups collaborate without losing their identities.[65] These two perspectives of communities have a significant impact on the issue of anti-corruption initiatives. Public officers who subscribe to ethno-cultural communities tend to demonstrate loyalty towards their ethnic group and not the whole community in general but the opposite is true for those who subscribe to multi-cultural communities. Social values are also not the same in these two types of communities as Samita and Oindo aptly point out:

> Social values which are manifested in ethno-cultural communities, are absent in a multicultural community. It is within such setting that corruption and its links to culture is conceptualized. For example, an individual who has been accused of corruption will not see himself/herself as the accused, but will see his/her community as the accused. That is, the individual displays allegiance to the ethno-cultural community than to the multi-cultural community.[66]

Consequently, Samita and Oindo suggest that in order to combat corruption in Africa, there is a need for African communities to transition from 'ethno-cultural' to 'multi-cultural' communities.[67] They further recommend that this process of transition requires (re)application of an appropriate pre-existing mental model which ubuntu.

Ubuntu is a concept focusing on African humanism, and it has been defined differently by numerous scholars and 'it remains a highly contested phrase, world-view, value system, and problematised notion within Africa'.[68] The concept is generally understood in the South African Xhosa proverb, 'abantu ngabantu ngabanye abantu', which means 'people are people through other people'.[69] Although it might be difficult to fully interpret its meaning in a non-African context, the bottom line is that the concept implies 'communal connectivity' and 'togetherness'.

In other words, some of the values associated with ubuntu are 'participation, communitarianism, humility, love for humanity' 'sharing one's possessions with the needy, being moved by compassion, and always acting in loving kindness'.[70] The general consensus is that Africans in the pre-colonial period learned to live through communal activities, mutual care and support, as well as a shared spirit, primarily drawn from anthropological and ethnographic studies. They began to pool their resources as a community as a result of this way of life. Personal interests were put below the needs of the community. It is argued that these Ubuntu values have been lost over time. However, inculcating these values is said to be a solution to most of the problems that Africa is facing including the problem of corruption.[71] As Mironga points out, ubuntu as an ideology has the potential to be an effective anti-corruption initiative.[72]

> If Africa is to be free of corruption, the Ubuntu ideology must be included into governance. African civic and political leaders, as well as all citizens, should embrace the Ubuntu philosophy, which prioritizes love, sharing, compassion, caring, unity, solidarity, and acceptance before material and personal gain.[73]

Conclusion

The challenge with fighting corruption is deeper than what most policymakers think. Most African societies must undergo a significant cultural transformation in order for the political institutions and public services to 'create a good fit'; otherwise, some of the reforms will resemble 'a leopard wearing a goat's skin'. The gap between lawmaking and its actual application, and between rhetoric and practice, will only get wider.[74] This transformation can be implemented at various levels, but according to Ikeanyibe, the majority of the effort "should be directed towards effective citizenship policies and education aimed at consciously instilling the benefits of larger states to smaller ones in citizens and groups'.[75] Genuine political dialogue should also take place to improve assimilation and common identity. Most scholars agree that, while culture can be blamed for many of the problems encountered in the fight against corruption, the ubuntu concept is better suited to address them.

Notes

* Executive Dean, School of Law, Governance, and Economics, University of Malawi.

1 World Bank, *Helping Countries Combat Corruption*: *The Role of the World Bank* (Washington: World Bank, 1997), 8–9.

2 Barney Warf, "Geographies of African Corruption," *PSU Research Review* 1, no. 1 (2017): 20–38, https://doi.org/10.1108/PRR-12-2016-0012

3 World Bank, "Helping Countries," 8–9

4 Marie Chene and Robin Hodess, "The impact of corruption on growth and inequality". *Transparency International, 2014,* www.transparency.org/files/content/corruptionqas/Impact_of_corruption_on_growth_and_inequality_2014.pdf

5 Sanjeev Gupta, Hamid Davoodi, and Rosa Alonso-Terme. "Does corruption affect income inequality and poverty?." *Economics of Governance* 3, no. 1 (2002): 23–45.

6 Prince Pius Imiera, "The corruption race in Africa: Nigeria versus South Africa, who cleans the mess first?." *De Jure Law Journal* 53, no. 1 (2020): 70–89. Warf, "Geographies of African Corruption," 20–38. Thandika Mkandawire, "Neopatrimonialism and the political economy of economic performance in Africa: Critical reflections." *World Politics* 67, no. 3 (2015): 563–612.

7 Transparency International, "2021 Corruption Perception Index", 2022, www.transparency.org/en/cpi/2021?gclid=CjwKCAjwzY2bBhB6EiwAPpUpZqfsLc2KVy_fuyH77nLhdcm6FKkAswz7uGDhpZjhefgs3Lm9PJb7_hoCbggQAvD_BwE

8 Ndiva Kofele-Kale, "Change or the illusion of change: the war against official corruption in Africa." *The George Washington International Law Review* 38 (2006): 697.

9 Muhammad Habibur Rahman et al. "Can extreme rainfall trigger democratic change? The role of flood-induced corruption." *Public Choice* 171, no. 3 (2017): 331–358.

10 Symon F. Nayupe et al. "Covid-19 and fund mismanagement in Malawi: A major challenge to its effective pandemic containment." *Health Science Reports* 5, no. 3 (2022).

11 Warf, "Geographies of African corruption," 20–38. John-Thor Dahlburge, J. "Nation suffered as a dictator rained riches," *Los Angeles Times*, May 17, 1997, www.latimes.com/archives/la-xpm-1997-05-17-mn-59626-story.html

12 Roman Singogo and Grynberg Mr Fwasa. "An Anatomy of Grand Fraud: The Goldenberg Scandal and the IMF/World Bank." *Public Policy and Administration Research* 10, no. 2 (2020): 17–32, https://core.ac.uk/download/pdf/304991797.pdf Jeevan Vasager, "Charges in Kenya Corruption Scandal," *The Guardian*, March 16, 2006, www.theguardian.com/world/2006/mar/16/kenya.jeevanvasagar

13 David Pallister and Peter Capella, "British banks set to freeze dictator's millions", *The Guardian*, July 8, 2000, www.theguardian.com/uk/2000/jul/08/davidpallister Laura Paola Villa Garcia, "Political Corruption in Nigeria: Sani Abacha," STREINER Anti-corruption bureau STREINER Anticorruption bureau, August 30, 2019, https://streiner.mx/en/case_study/political-corruption-in-nigeria-sani-abacha/

14 Department of Justice, "United States Enters into Agreement with Nigeria to Repatriate Over $23 Million in Assets Stolen by Former Nigerian Dictator General Sani Abacha" August 23, 2022, www.justice.gov/opa/pr/united-states-enters-agreement-nigeria-repatriate-over-23-million-assets-stolen-former

15 Moses Michael Phiri, "Malawian president dissolves Cabinet over corruption scandal," Anadolu Agency, January 25, 2022, www.aa.com.tr/en/africa/malawian-president-dissolves-cabinet-over-corruption-scandal/2484786.
16 Transparency International, "2018 Corruption Perception Index, 2018 https://view.officeapps.live.com/op/view.aspx?src=https%3A%2F%2Fimages.transparencycdn.org%2Fimages%2FCPI2018_Full-Results_1801.xlsx&wdOrigin=BROWSELINK
17 Transparency International, "2021 Corruption Perception Index."
18 Warf, "Geographies of African corruption," 20–38.
19 Sarah Muir and Akhil Gupta. "Rethinking the anthropology of corruption: An introduction to supplement." *Current Anthropology* 59, no.S18 (2018): 4–6.
20 Sarah Muir and Akhil Gupta. "Rethinking the anthropology of corruption", 5
21 Sarah Muir and Akhil Gupta. "Rethinking the anthropology of corruption."
22 Sarah Muir and Akhil Gupta. "Rethinking the anthropology of corruption," 5.
23 Sarah Muir and Akhil Gupta. "Rethinking the anthropology of corruption," 5–6.
24 American Anthropology Association (AAA), "What is Anthropology?", March 23, 2015, www.aaanet.org/about/whatisanthropology.cfm
25 AAA "What is Anthropology?"
26 Muir and Akhil Gupta. "Rethinking the anthropology of corruption," 5.
27 Muir and Akhil Gupta. "Rethinking the anthropology of corruption," 8.
28 Torsello, Davide, and Bertrand Venard. "The anthropology of corruption." *Journal of Management Inquiry* 25, no.1 (2016): 34.
29 Dieter Haller and Cris Shore, eds. *Corruption: Anthropological Perspectives*. London: Pluto, 2005.
30 Stein Eriksen, Sundstøl. "State crisis and the problem of Statehood" (2004): 183–196.
31 Godfrey Mowaneng, "Botswana embroiled in alleged COSAFA bribery allegations," *Sunday Standard*, August 6, 2021, www.sundaystandard.info/botswana-embroiled-in-alleged-cosafa-bribery-allegations Manuela Francisco, and Nicola Pontara. "Does corruption impact on firms' ability to conduct business in Mauritania? evidence from investment climate survey data." *Evidence from Investment Climate Survey Data (December 1, 2007). World Bank Policy Research Working Paper* 4439 (2007). Janvier D. Nkurunziza Léonce Ndikumana, and Prime Nyamoya. "The financial sector in Burundi." *African Successes, Volume III* (2012): 103, http://Www.Nber.Org/Papers/W18289
32 Léonce Ndikumana. *The Private Sector as Culprit and Victim of Corruption in Africa*. (Amherst, MA: PERI, 2013).
33 Xiangru Yin. "An Analysis of Corruption in China: The Guanxi Network Of Chinese High Level Officials And Governors" (Masters diss., Clark University, 2017). https://commons.clarku.edu/idce_masters_papers/140/ Jacob Harding. "Corruption or guanxi: differentiating between the legitimate, unethical, and corrupt activities of Chinese government officials." *UCLA Pacific Basin Law Journal* 31 (2013): 127. Ying Fan, "Ganxi's consequences: Personal gains at social cost." *Journal of Business Ethics* 38, no.4 (2002): 371–380.
34 Ying Fan, "Ganxi's consequences"
35 Yin, "An Analysis of Corruption in China."
36 Abdoulkadre Ado. "Internationalization of Guanxi from China to Africa." *International Journal of Emerging Markets* (2022). DOI: 10.1108/IJOEM-01-2021-0025
37 Ado, "Internationalization of Guanxi"
38 Ying-Ying Tiffany Liu. "Exploring guanxi in a cross-cultural context: The case of Cantonese-Speaking Chinese in Johannesburg." *Journal of Chinese Overseas* 13, no. 2 (2017): 263–286. Ufrieda Ho, *Paper Sons and Daughters: Growing Up Chinese in South Africa* (Ohio University Press, 2012).
39 Mkandawire, "Neopatrimonialism and the political economy."
40 Joseph Patrick Ganahl. *Corruption, good governance, and the African state: A critical analysis of the political-economic foundations of corruption in sub-Saharan Africa.*

Vol. 2. Universitätsverlag Potsdam, 2014. Michael Bratton and Nicholas Van de Walle. *Democratic Experiments in Africa: Regime Transitions in Comparative Perspective* (Cambridge University Press, 1997).

41 Christian Von Soest. "Persistent systemic corruption: why democratisation and economic liberalisation have failed to undo an old evil." *Zeitschrift für vergleichende Politikwissenschaft* 7, no. 1 (2013): 57 87.

42 Robert Elgie. "Presidentialism, parliamentarism and semi-presidentialism: Bringing parties back in." *Government and Opposition* 46, no. 3 (2011): 392–409. Scott Mainwaring and Matthew S. Shugart. "Juan Linz, Presidentialism, and Democracy: A Critical Appraisal Scott." *Comparative Politics* 29, no. 4 (1997): 449–471.

43 Ganahl. "Corruption, good governance" Henry Ng'oma Chingaipe. *Business and the state in Malawi: the politics of institutional formation, maintenance and change*. Diss. University of York, 2010.

44 Hermen Kroesbergen, "African leadership and the kind of reality of the spirit world." *HTS Teologiese Studies/Theological Studies* 76, no. 2 (2020).

45 Davide Torsello and Bertrand Venard. "The anthropology of corruption." *Journal of Management Inquiry* 25, no.1 (2016): 34–54.

46 Albian Krasniqi and Venera Demukaj. "Does aid fuel corruption? New evidence from a cross-country analysis." *Development Studies Research* 8, no. 1 (2021): 122–134.

47 Krasniqi and Venera Demukaj. "Does aid fuel corruption?" David De la Croix and Clara Delavallade. "Why corrupt governments may receive more foreign aid." *Oxford Economic Papers* 66, no. 1 (2014): 51–66. Alberto Alesina and Beatrice Weder. "Do corrupt governments receive less foreign aid?." *American Economic Review* 92, no. 4 (2002): 1126–1137.

48 Simplice Asongu and Mohamed Jellal. "On the channels of foreign aid to corruption." *Economics Bulletin* 33, no. 3 (2013): 2191–2201.

49 Ganahl, "Corruption, good governance"

50 Peter Ekeh, "Colonialism and the two publics in Africa: A theoretical statement." *Comparative Studies in Society and History* 17, no. 1 (1975): 91–112.

51 Ekeh, "Colonialism and the two publics," 108.

52 Ekeh, "Colonialism and the two publics," 111.

53 Rumki Basu, "Revisiting Fred W. Riggs' Model in the Context of 'Prismatic' Societies Today." *Indian Journal of Public Administration* 67, no. 1 (2021): 87

54 Fred W. Riggs, "The prismatic model: Conceptualizing transitional societies." *Comparative Public Administration* (Emerald Group Publishing Limited, 2006).

55 Okechukwu M. Ikeanyibe, "Bureaucratization and administrative development in Africa: A reading of Riggs' theory of prismatic society." *Public Administration and Development* 37, no. 5 (2017): 307–318.

56 Basu, "Revisiting Fred W. Riggs'," 88.

57 Ikeanyibe, "Bureaucratization and administrative development," 307.

58 Lewsi B. Dzimbiri. "Cultural change, the hybrid administrative system and public sector reforms in Africa: The case of anti-corruption measures in Malawi." *African Anthropologist* 16.1&2 (2009): 61

59 Dzimbiri, "Cultural change," 61

60 Ikeanyibe, "Bureaucratization and administrative development."

61 Ikeanyibe, "Bureaucratization and administrative development," 315.

62 Zacharia Samita and Joseph Ouma Oindo. "Culture, Corruption and Commerce: African Culture vis-a-vis Corruption and Sustainable Development in Africa." *AKU: An African Journal of Contemporary Research* 3, no. 2 (2022): 3–12.

63 Samita and Oindo. "Culture, Corruption and Commerce," 3.

64 Kwame Gyekye, *Political Corruption: A Philosophical Analysis of a Moral Problem* (Sankofa Publishing Company, 1997). Samita and Oindo. "Culture, Corruption and Commerce."

65 Samita and Oindo. "Culture, Corruption and Commerce," 3
66 Samita and Oindo. "Culture, Corruption and Commerce," 5.
67 Samita and Oindo. "Culture, Corruption and Commerce."
68 Benson Onyekachukwu Anofuechi, "A critical assessment of ubuntu as a source for moral formation in contemporary Africa" (PhD diss., University of the Western Cape, Cape Town, 2022). 1
69 Anofuechi, "A critical assessment of ubuntu," 1.
70 Godsend Chimbi, and Loyiso Jita. "Reforming the school curriculum for Ubuntu (humanness): A critical discourse analysis." *International Journal of Research in Business and Social Science (2147–4478)* 11, no. 5 (2022): 439. Anofuechi, "A critical assessment of ubuntu," 10
71 Richard Tambulasi and Happy Kayuni. "Can African feet divorce western shoes? The case of 'ubuntu' and democratic good governance in Malawi." *Nordic Journal of African Studies* 14, no. 2 (2005): 15–15. Anofuechi, "A critical assessment of ubuntu." Anesu Mironga, "Corruption and its negative governance output in Africa: An analysis of the drivers of corruption." *Journal of Humanities and Social Science (IOSR-JHSS)* 27, no. 5 (2022): 12–21. Samita and Oindo. "Culture, Corruption and Commerce."
72 Mironga, "Corruption and its negative governance," 19.
73 Mironga, "Corruption and its negative governance," 19.
74 Dzimbiri, "Cultural change," 63
75 Ikeanyibe, "Bureaucratization and administrative development," 316.

5 Systems Thinking in Fighting Corruption

*Michael J. Fratantuono**

Introduction

Since the cessation of European colonialism and imperialism in the 1960s, the countries of Sub-Saharan Africa have been plagued by corruption that has in turn slowed socioeconomic and political development.[1] Indeed, according to standard measures, many of the countries have the world's highest levels of corruption,[2] lowest levels of per capita income,[3] and greatest degrees of income inequality.[4] Collectively, those factors have eroded the government, market, and social foundations of the nation state.[5] Over the past six decades, experts and scholars have engaged in analyses of conditions and made recommendations for change, but progress has been slow in coming.

The contributors to this volume revisit the twin challenges of pervasive corruption and nagging underdevelopment. They do take a new approach, however, in that each contributor explicitly works from a framework that utilizes system concepts. Given their efforts, this chapter has two interrelated purposes. The first is to provide readers who are not familiar with systems concepts an introduction to ideas. The second is to help facilitate conversations about the respective contributions to this volume.

To achieve these purposes, the chapter introduces basic system models that are informed, at a very general level, by the evolving literature about corruption and underdevelopment in Sub-Saharan African countries. The models, schematic in nature, have been created by the author and are intended to serve as a starting point for conversation. They illustrate the structure of corrupt systems, their implications for outcomes in the short and long term, and interventions to promote system transformation. The imagery included in the models is open to criticism, modification, and extrapolation; nonetheless, that too would be beneficial to all parties as they seek to find common ground in efforts to address the serious challenges to well-being confronting millions of Africans. In the final section, the discussion poses questions to promote conversation.

Themes from the Literature

This discussion does not provide a comprehensive review of the literature regarding corruption in Africa. Most contributors to this volume have ably done that.

DOI: 10.4324/9781003326649-6

Instead, this discussion selects a limited number of contributions that inform the system models introduced in subsequent sections.

The volume by Hope Sr. and Chikulo[6] includes papers written in the 1990s that provide both analytical frameworks and case studies. Collectively, insights from the papers are rich variations on a few themes that contribute to four topics: (1) definitions of corruption; (2) causes of corruption; (3) outcomes of corruption; and (4) alternative pathways towards reducing corruption.

Corruption is a concept with many meanings. Corruption can be taken as breaking an ethical or moral code;[7] actions by public officials to secure economic rents;[8] "the abuse of trust in the pursuit of public gain,"[9] bribery, embezzlement, and theft on a grand scale.[10] Corruption arises from political, economic, and social factors.[11] These include the total exercise of power by elites, the expansion of the state sector, poor economic performance, inadequate rule of law, a lack of high-quality leadership, and personalism in social norms;[12] "poorly developed laws and institutions, and distorted incentive structures";[13] a set of personal factors including financial problems and organizational cultures that encourage self-serving behaviour, malice, rivalries, ego, or peer pressures;[14] modernization that challenges existing values.[15]

Corruption can cause inadequate political and administrative development, poor economic performance, including inefficiency and waste, and larger-than-necessary government budget deficits,[16] as well as capital flight from a country and reduced inflows of foreign investment.[17] It can lead civil servants who are unable to make a living wage to turn to corruption.[18] Furthermore, it can have "psychological" or "philosophical effects" such as a pervasive sense of "cynicism and nihilism" that in turn nurtures more corruption.[19]

Pathways forward include promoting an independent media, removing barriers to economic processes, a reformed judiciary, and a strengthened civil society.[20] Efforts to promote transparency and accountability by public officials would be necessary, as would efforts to alter inadequate interconnections with intergovernmental organizations (IGOs).[21] A public choice perspective would concentrate on altering institutions, which are the societal rules that shape human interactions and incentives for human behaviour.[22] In agreement with Thokozire Kuwali in Chapter 18, other arguments call for the presence of effective leadership, which "may be more crucial than social system and structure."[23] Papers from that era also noted actions by Intergovernmental Organizations.

By the late 1990s, both the International Monetary Fund (IMF) and the World Bank had started to address corruption in African countries. Motivated primarily by concerns for the management of public resources and well-managed macroeconomic policies, the IMF approach entailed discussion with national leaders about ways to counter corrupt activities surrounding programmes it supported. The World Bank took a somewhat broader and deeper approach that included consideration of corruption when making loan decisions; preventing corruption in bank-related projects; helping countries combat corruption; and leveraging its own special skill sets, supporting international efforts to combat corruption.[24]

At the turn of the century, the African Union (AU), via the AU Convention on Preventing and Combating Corruption (AU CPCC)[25], presented a comprehensive statement that incorporated most of the ideas that had been articulated by experts in the 1990s. In doing so, the Convention implicitly called for system transformation. Article 2 identifies new goals: reducing and controlling corruption, promoting transparency in public affairs, and enhancing citizens' rights. Article 3 lists five principles that may be regarded as new norms and values. Other Articles identify various forms of corruption; their relevance to stakeholder groups such as public officials, the court system, and the private sector; and go so far as to call for the empowerment of institutions such as the media and civil society to combat corruption.

More recently published works tend to broaden the scope or nature of analysis and use new research methodologies to promote insights about individual countries. Agang, Pillay, and Jones present a collection of multifaceted, well-researched papers that are all based on ethical, spiritual, or religious foundations.[26] While some studies utilize sophisticated qualitative techniques to capture developments such as rising citizen activism,[27] others use quantitative methods to highlight correlations such as that between ethical and effective leadership.[28] Such scholarship examines the degree to which corruption undermines human rights; the link between corruption, globalization, and terrorism; the necessity to empower youth; etc.

Munyai develops a socio-legal framework in his thorough analysis.[29] He describes corruption as a "cumulative and expansionist process that is hardly reversible, and also spreads from top to bottom."[30] As a central component of his work, he emphasizes that without domestic political will, a country will be unable to counter corruption.[31] Political will calls for political leadership, active engagement by citizens and the private sector, and even by the international community.

Researchers have also considered the attributes of external stakeholders, and their relationships with one or more countries. For example, Jatto evaluates the positive aspects of the AU CPCC, as well as two inherent limitations that contribute to deteriorating relationships within and among countries: that is, the absence of mechanisms, respectively, designed to compensate the victims of corruption and to resolve disputes.[32] Michael evaluates the relevance, fit, and specificity of development programs initiated and implemented in Africa by intergovernmental organizations.[33] The results suggest that in addition to the wellbeing of a country's citizens, the programmes are at least in part motivated by the self-serving political and social priorities of the IGOs.

Dunderdale endorses the United States (US) Foreign Corruption Act as a vehicle that prevents US companies from engaging in illicit activities when doing business in Africa.[34] Nonetheless, Brazys and Kotsadam find that corruption in destination countries is reduced to a lesser extent by direct foreign investment made by companies based in low-corruption countries than investments made by companies based in high-corruption countries.[35] While companies in the former group tend to avoid such investments, initiatives by those in the latter group have wealth effects that over time enable both private sector and public sector stakeholders in the destination countries to rise above the need to engage in corruption. Mbaku argues that African countries must first reform domestic political and judicial systems before they can benefit from the strictures of international law.[36]

Ayodeji takes things a step further and advocates an international anti-corruption court to hold accountable agents residing or operating anywhere in the world for their illicit activities.[37]

Additional Considerations

The above literature and the models introduced in subsequent sections suggest three considerations that lie beyond the immediate scope of this paper but are worthy of conversation among contributors to this volume and readers.

First, corruption pervades many states in Sub-Saharan Africa; corruption undermines the multi-dimensional process of development within countries; and efforts by both internal and external stakeholders have been undertaken and will be required in future to forge further fundamental alterations to circumstances. Although the models in the following sections of this chapter emphasize a single country perspective, they nonetheless provide avenues for an extension to include other system structures and dynamics that exist in parallel with those of the individual state and are interconnected in some fashion.

Second, in keeping with opinions over time and geographical boundaries, people will support leaders who are honest, forward-looking, inspiring, and competent,[38] and who act according to clearly held personal values, well-developed capabilities, and clear aspirations.[39] In a context of pervasive corruption, newly emerging leaders will require courage of conviction that may come from either secular or religious paradigms.

Third, collaboration across sectors – state, market, and civil society stakeholders – is an extraordinarily challenging organizational structure that calls for the creation of new subsystems and systems.[40] While such collaboration would overcome siloed approaches to forging change, weaker forms of interconnection may be a necessary compromise, especially in the early going.

System Concepts Applicable to Combating Corruption

The works by Meadows and Stroh each provide an excellent introduction to system concepts. In a fundamental way, they are in concert, in the sense that they share similar understandings but use different points of emphasis when engaged in analysis.[41] With practice, analysts can use those concepts to tackle increasingly difficult problems. This discussion utilizes insights from each expert.

Components of a System

Meadows says that a system has three components: *elements*, *interconnections*, and a *purpose*. In a human system, elements are stakeholders: people and organizations. Interconnections are relationships that hold the elements together, such as cultural or ideologically based values; organizational and institutional norms, rules, and laws; and communication channels. The purpose provides the rationale for the entire system.

Feedback loops provide the foundation of system analysis. They are a source of information crucial to system performance and serve as a control mechanism for the system. Feedback loops are of two types. "Balancing feedback loops are *goal seeking* or *stability seeking*. Each tries to keep a stock at a given value or within a range of values. A balancing feedback loop opposes whatever direction of change is imposed on the system."[42] A reinforcing feedback loop is "amplifying," "self-multiplying," "snowballing" . . . "a vicious or virtuous circle that can cause healthy growth or runaway destruction"[43] While a positive reinforcing feedback loop "generates more input to a stock the more that is already there," a negative reinforcing loop generates "less input to a stock the less that is already there."[44]

Figure 5.1 provides an example that is based on imagery favoured by Meadows. It includes system boundaries, stocks, flows, flow valves, and feedback loops. Each flow valve is labelled with a verb to denote an activity or process. Each stock is labelled with a noun, each can be either tangible or intangible in nature, and each has a measurable magnitude that can rise or fall over time in response to inflows and outflows. Loops are labelled with nouns suggesting there are forces at play beyond the boundaries of analysis.

The circular nodes represent boundaries. The first stock is law-abiding members of the population. Some will choose to engage in corruption. As they do so, they flow into the stock of opportunists and out of the stock of the law-abiding. Although there will always be corruption in any country, the balancing feedback loop suggests that the presence of law enforcement will influence the degree to which the valve is opened and thus the rate at which people will choose to engage in corruption.

Moving along, opportunists will avoid laws – the implications of their actions flow into the stock of human insecurity. Once again, the rate is implied by the degree to which the valve may be opened. As a final action, depending on their awareness of circumstances and capabilities, intergovernmental organizations (IGOs) may step in and give assistance. The second balancing feedback loop indicates that assistance will help nudge the level of insecurity back towards its original level.

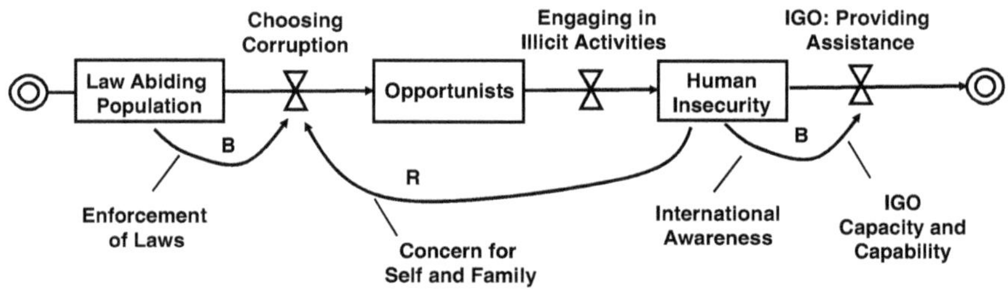

Figure 5.1 Example of Imagery Employed by Meadows

Finally, and quite importantly, there is one positive reinforcing loop. As human insecurity grows in magnitude, people who previously were inclined to be law-abiding are now concerned for their well-being and that of their families, and thus have a stronger incentive to become opportunists.

For his part, Stroh is certainly aware of the imagery used by Meadows. When investigating complex systems, however, he prefers an alternative, as represented in Figure 5.2.

His model consists of only nouns and feedback loops. Unless otherwise stated, a rise in one noun leads to the same change in the direction of a subsequent noun in the feedback loop flow. In this illustration, via reinforcing loop R1, opportunists drawn from the general population engage in illicit activity that leads to rising human insecurity that in turn leads to increased corruption. Balancing loop B1 represents the awareness-informed intervention by IGOs, which helps control – but does not reverse – the rate of growth in human insecurity caused by corruption. Balancing loop B2 represents the prospect that high levels of law enforcement may slow the numbers opting for corruption.

The imagery provided by Meadows can soon become cluttered when dealing with multi-faceted interrelationships. Therefore, this paper gravitates to the approach used by Stroh. The trade-off is that his imagery is more abstract and can at times be hard to navigate. Stroh is mindful of that possibility and encourages all to develop models of appropriate complexity for handling their respective problems. Following his advice, this discussion presents illustrations of subsystems and introduces hybrid forms of imagery that build on, but customize, that of Stroh.

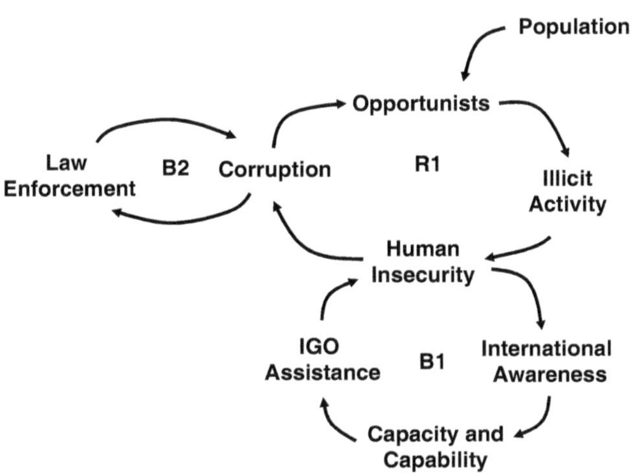

Figure 5.2 Example of Imagery Employed by Stroh

Attributes of a System

Meadows indicates that well-performing systems have three important attributes: *resilience, self-organization,* and *hierarchy*. Resilience is the ability to bounce or spring back into shape or position after being pressed or stretched. The opposite of resilience is brittleness or rigidity Resilience arises from the rich structure of many feedback loops that can work in different ways to restore a system even after a large perturbation.[45] Self-organization is the capacity of a system to make its own structure more complex. Self-organization produces heterogeneity and unpredictability. It is likely to come up with whole new structures and whole new ways of doing things. It requires freedom and experimentation and a certain amount of disorder.[46] Hierarchy is the arrangement of systems and subsystems that tends to arise when self-organizing systems engage in the process of creating new structures and increasing complexity.[47]

System Archetypes, Leverage Points, and Systemic Theories of Change

When dealing with human systems, experienced analysts such as Meadows and Stroh recognize regularly occurring patterns of troublesome or sub-optimal behaviour. These respective patterns are regarded as system *archetypes*. Well-known archetypes carry names such as "Escalation" or "Tragedy of the Commons." As one would expect, each archetype incorporates different sets of components and attributes.

When an archetype exists, Meadows identifies 12 Leverage Points (LPs) for altering system structure and performance and ranks them from least to most influential.[48] This discussion groups Meadows' 12 leverage points into two clusters: those intended to *modify* the existing system (points 12 through 6) and those intended to *transform* the existing system (points 5 through 1).

System modification includes alteration to the magnitude of the stocks, the volume of the flows, the influence of the feedback loops, or the basic configuration of the stock-flow structure. *System Transformation* entails more fundamental changes. This discussion suggests that alteration to a corrupt system calls for transformation and thus employment of one or more of the following five points.

5. Change the Rules: Rules define the scope and boundaries of the system – including the system membership – and the existing incentives, punishments, and constraints.
4. Permit or Enable Self-Organization: The ability to self-organize – the capacity to experiment and innovate in order to add, change, or evolve system structures – is the key to system resilience.
3. Change the Goal: Reimagine or redefine the purpose of the system.
2. Change the Paradigm: A paradigm is the source of a system, "the shared idea in the minds of society, the great big unstated assumptions . . . or deepest set of beliefs about how the world works."[49]

1. Transcend Paradigms: adopt the mindset that no single paradigm is "true" and that each represents a limited understanding of reality. When one does so, then he or she can recognize that an individual is free to choose a paradigm to achieve a purpose.

In cases where systems must be altered, Stroh describes two systemic theories of change. One, Goal Achievement, calls for efforts to bridge a gap between the actual state and the desired state of system performance and is relevant when "people cannot easily identify successes to build on, or if the prospects for creating a positively reinforcing dynamic are tenuous."[50] If so, then the first steps must be based on introducing *balancing feedback loops* to forge incremental change. The other, Success Amplification, is relevant when there are some initial factors that contribute to success, but there are limits to further success confronting the system. To say this another way, a reinforcing loop does exist, but balancing feedback loops impedes further progress. In these circumstances, additional *reinforcing feedback loops* must be introduced to overcome the influence of the balancing loops.

System Archetype: Success to the Successful

As observed by Meadows, "Success to the Successful" is an archetype present in countries at all stages of development. Using accumulated wealth, privilege, special access, or inside information to create more wealth, privilege, and access of information are examples of the archetype called "success to the successful." This system trap is found whenever winners of a competition receive, as part of the reward, the means to compete even more effectively in the future. That's a reinforcing feedback loop, which rapidly divides a system into winners who go on winning and losers who go on losing.[51]

This chapter regards it as the archetype best suited for understanding the structures and consequences of human systems characterized by corruption and underdevelopment, as is the situation for many countries in Africa. Figure 5.3 elaborates on Stroh's illustration of the archetype.[52]

The schema consists of two sets of reinforcing loops, R1-P and R2-N. The first, R1-P, is a *positive* reinforcing loop, a *virtuous cycle* that enriches and empowers a set of elites, a minority of a country's population, the beneficiaries of the corruption that permeates the system. The second, R2-N, is a *negative* reinforcing loop, a *vicious cycle* that disenfranchises and impoverishes the majority of the general citizenry, the victims of corruption. Taken together, the result of the two cycles is an "inequality gap": the difference between the actual inequality and acceptable inequality between the two groups. The notion of acceptable inequality speaks to the reality that inequality cannot be eliminated in any society, but that it must be reduced to a target level that satisfies some articulated sense of morality-informed social responsibility.

Ideally – and perhaps naively speaking – an existing inequality gap could be addressed in the short term by the introduction or strengthening of policies such

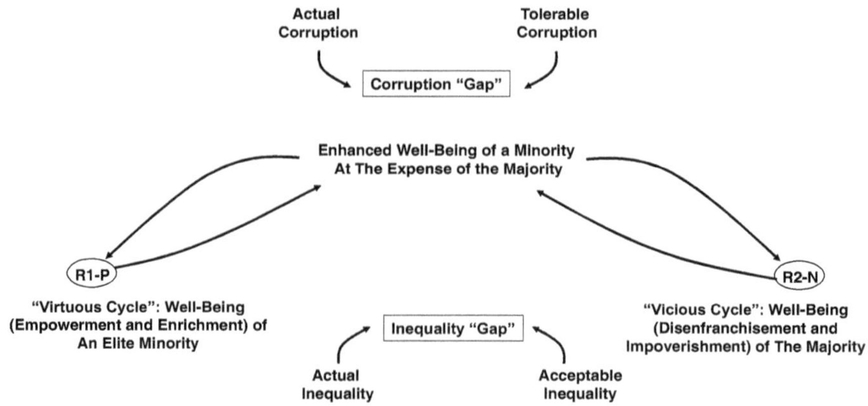

Figure 5.3 The System Trap "Success to the Successful" Complicated by the Presence of Corruption

as progressive taxation and redistribution of income; or thinking about the longer-term horizon, by investment in public goods such as early childhood education. Nonetheless, the challenges of formulating and implementing policies or programmes in developing countries – or in mid-tier developing or even developed countries for that matter – should not be discounted.

When corruption is a catalyst for the system trap, challenges become even more difficult. There is also a "corruption gap," the difference between actual and tolerable levels of corruption. Although the notion of tolerable corruption may sound off-putting, some degree of corruption exists in all societies, in part because the cost of reducing corruption to zero is prohibitive.

Hierarchical Structure in a Corrupt Nation-State

Figure 5.4 takes the first step in further developing Figure 5.3. It is a stylized representation of the hierarchy among three sets of stakeholders often associated with human systems characterized by extensive or systemic corruption. The image includes two balancing loops. In the upper loop labelled B1, the head of state, who may be an autocrat or charismatic individual, provides endorsement, authority, and/or privilege to sectoral power brokers, who may be politicians, military officers, judges, businesspeople, or such other politically exposed persons as discussed by Agbor and his colleagues in Chapter 15. To close the loop, brokers provide pledges, financial payments, and so forth to the head of state. In loop B2, the brokers provide patronage and/or appointments to well-positioned opportunists, who may be bureaucrats, or such kind of administrators. The opportunists serve with compliance or make payments to the brokers.

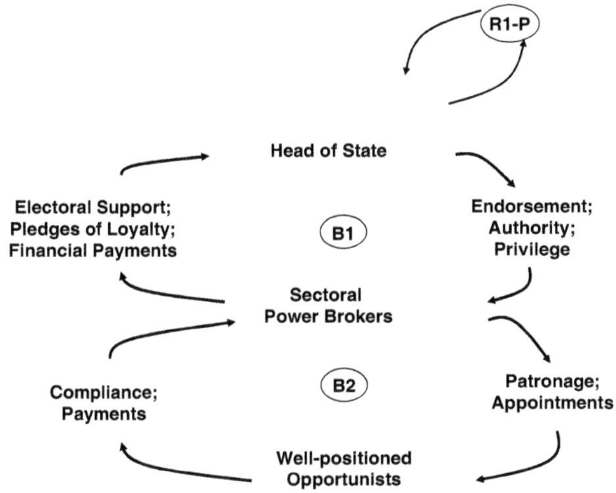

Figure 5.4 Elements and Interconnections at the Apex of the Corrupt System Hierarchy

Inadequacies in the Provision of Public, Economic, and Social Value

Meadows also explains that since systems can be embedded in other systems, which are embedded in yet other systems, then for human systems, there can be purposes embedded inside other purposes. Figure 5.5A, 5B, and 5C (page after next) illustrate subsystems that respectively illustrate shortcomings in the provision of public value, economic value, and social value. They each include balancing loops B1 and B2, from Figure 5.4, but move one step lower in the system structure.

In Figure 5.5a, loop B3 represents the provision of public goods and services by officials. Citizens pay fees and bribes to secure goods that would be provided at no charge in a non-corrupt system. Loop B4 suggests that while the government may identify economic segments that should receive high priority, inept managers of state-owned enterprises are not up to the task. Emerging shortages would enable officials to skim money from sales to those who need supply, including owners of private sector firms.

In Figure 5.5b, loop B5 indicates that power brokers and opportunists award private contracts to crony capitalists for public infrastructure projects. The result is shoddy construction, the ability of those capitalists to capture economic rents, and payments of bribes and kickbacks to brokers and opportunists. Loop B6 indicates that brokers and opportunists require licenses or place burdensome restrictions on for-profit private sector firms. The result is a lack of transparency and poorly functioning markets; higher costs and lower profits; and the need to pay bribes or fees to escape some of the impediments.

Loop B7 of Figure 5.5C indicates that efforts of non-governmental organizations to provide services to citizens are impeded by inadequate public goods and infrastructure. Organizations must solicit support from brokers and opportunists. Loop B8 indicates that the financial assistance provided by IGOs is poorly channelled to appropriate ends and siphoned by brokers and opportunists.

Figures 5.4 and 5A through 5C depict interconnections among stakeholders with balancing loops B1 through B8 that do serve as preconditions for the virtuous and vicious cycles, respectively, designated as reinforcing feedback loops R1-P and R2-N and thus the well-being gap depicted in Figure 5.3. This chapter has opted

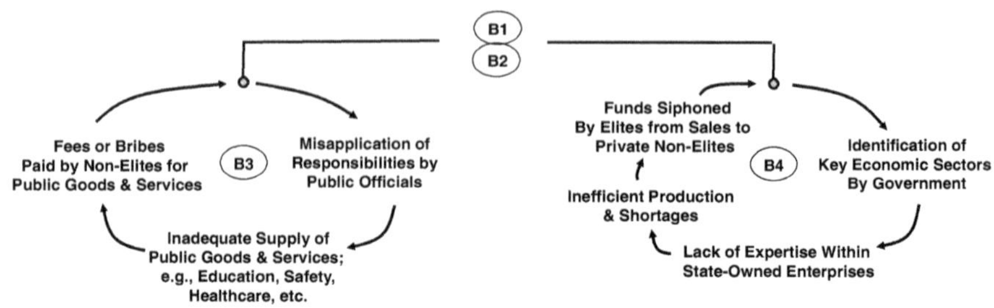

Figure 5.5A Inadequacies in the Provision of Public Value

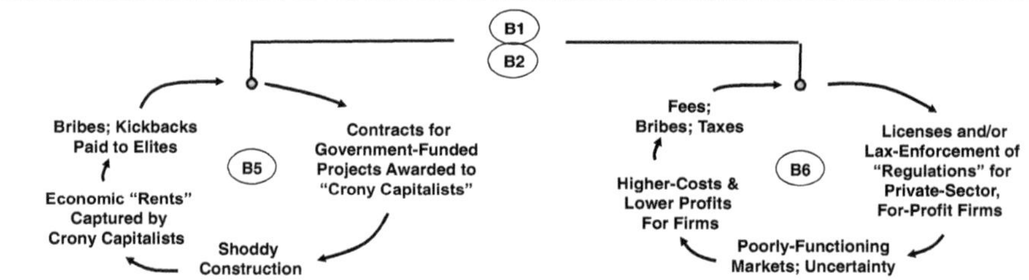

Figure 5.5B Inadequacies in Provision of Economic Value

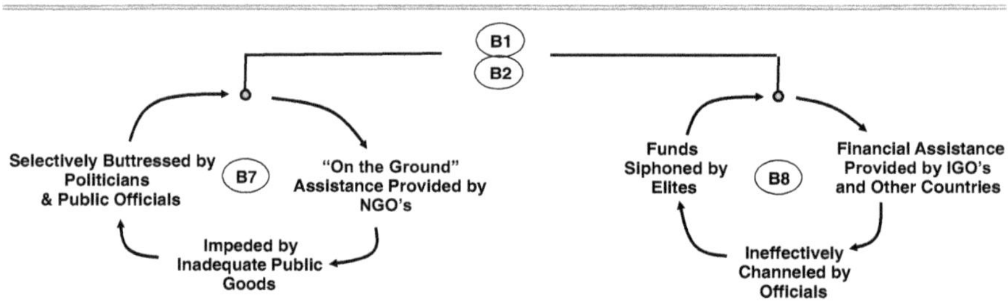

Figure 5.5C Inadequacies in the Provision of Social Value

for that initial balancing loop imagery – which conveys a sense of stability among the subsystems – for a few reasons.

First is a set of observations by Meadows. Complex systems can evolve from simple systems only if there are stable intermediate forms. The resulting complex form will naturally be hierarchic. Among all possible complex forms, hierarchies are the only ones that have had time to evolve.[53] The next two reasons are provided by Coolidge and Rose-Ackerman. Due to their own insecurity about the future of a corrupt system, corrupt leaders assign a higher discount rate to future monetary flows than do average citizens, and therefore favour existing structures and policies that will yield higher short-term economic rents. Furthermore, to the extent possible, in order to limit the degree to which rents must be shared, kleptocrats prefer to prevent rapid growth in subsystem size.[54]

Reinforcing Loops and the Well-Being Gap

Figure 5.6 takes further steps to elaborate on the relationship between the corruption gap and the well-being gap and introduces reinforcing loops. First, the upper segment includes the presence of loops B1-B8 and suggests they individually and collectively have some impact on the lower segment, which comprises six *negative* reinforcing loops, R3-N to R8-N. Second, each of those six loops is pertinent to tangible or intangible stocks that are declining in magnitude. As they do so, the foundation of the nation state is becoming weaker. Third, in a general sense, the labels of each loop tend to speak for themselves Due to length constraints, this paper does not attempt to elaborate the elements in each loop, a topic for useful conversation in general and for respective countries. Fourth, the hexagon in the

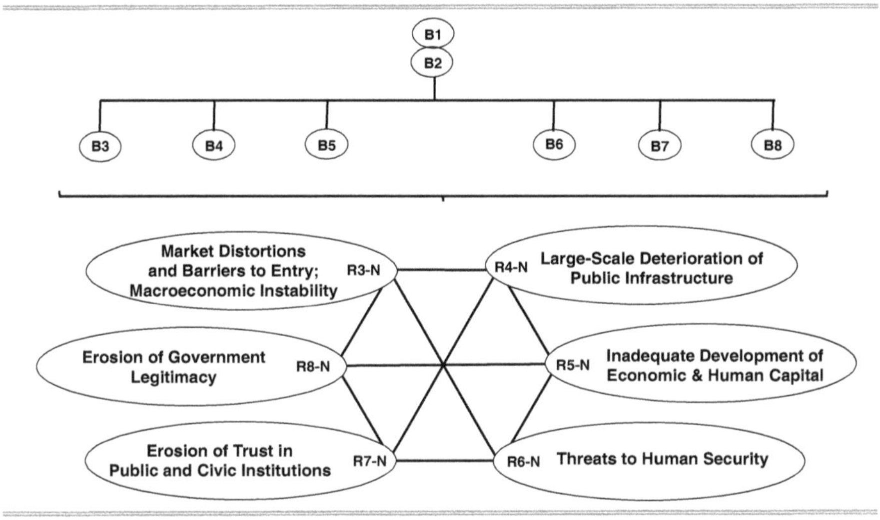

Figure 5.6 The Impact of Corruption on the Foundation of the Nation-State

lower segment indicates that alterations in any one of the reinforcing loops R3-N to R8-N will influence one or more of the other reinforcing loops.

Addressing the Corruption and Well-Being Gap

Through the lenses of systems thinking, the corruption and well-being gaps can be closed as outlined later.

Focusing on Subsystems

In her explanation of hierarchy, Meadows shares insights that prompt strategic thinking about the transformation of corrupt systems. In hierarchical systems relationships *within* each subsystem are denser and stronger than relationships *between* subsystems. When hierarchies break down, they usually split along their subsystem boundaries. However, one should not lose sight of the important relationships that bind each subsystem to the others and to the higher levels of the hierarchy or one will be in for surprises.[55]

Since loops B3 through B8 of Figure 5.5A, 5B and 5C pertain to subsystems that provide support to loops B1 and B2, the apex of the system hierarchy, her comment implies that the best way forward is to focus on actions that will alter individual subsystems and create fissures in the larger system structure.

Systemic Theory: Goal Achievement

At the outset of a system alteration process, there may be a paucity of successes upon which to build. If so, then Stroh recommends goal achievement efforts dedicated to closing existing gaps by introducing balancing loops that will yield incremental change.

Figure 5.7 incorporates the eight balancing loops and associated subsystems included in Figure 5.5A, 5B, and 5C, as well as four new balancing loops: B9, B10, B11, and B12. Each of the four loops is intended to weaken in some way or other one or more of the existing loops B1 through B8. (The notion of weakening is suggested by the introduction of the dashed outlines for the original eight loops.) Weakening those balancing loops will begin to close the corruption gap.

Collectively speaking, alterations intended to introduce or strengthen loops B9 through B12 call for utilizing combinations of leverage points LP5 (rules), LP4 (self-organization), LP3 (goals), and LP2 (paradigms).

Amplifying Success

Ultimately, the hope is that closing the corruption gap via a goal achievement approach will also weaken the influence of reinforcing loops R3-N through R8-N, thereby providing the very first steps towards closing the well-being gap. Ideally, if after some time delay, the influence of negative loops R3 through R8 can be neutralized, and if even one of those loops can be transformed into a positive

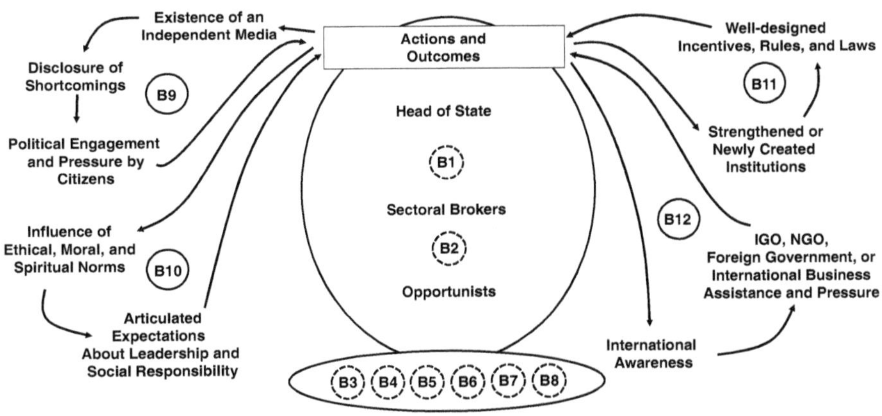

Figure 5.7 Closing the Corruption Gap

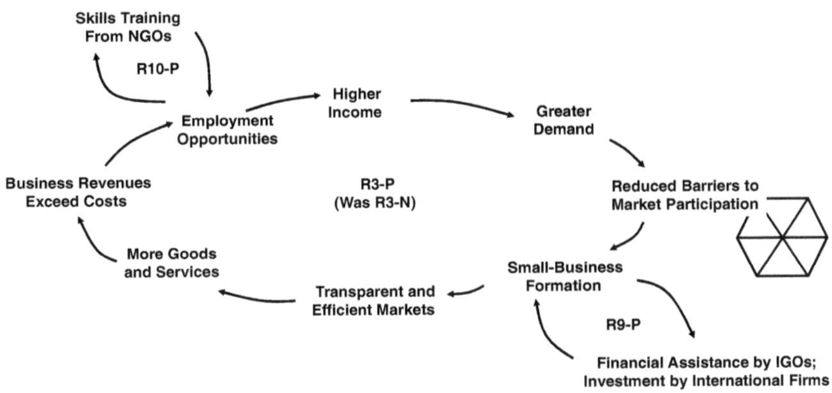

Figure 5.8 Introducing New Positive Reinforcing Feedback Loops

reinforcing loop of minimal or modest influence, then the stage will be set for the possibility of success amplification.

To provide a hypothetical example, Figure 5.8 concentrates upon and enlarges what had been Loop R3-N of Figure 5.6 and designates it as a positive reinforcing loop, relabelled R3-P, thereby indicating initial success. Therein, barriers to entry into sectors have been reduced, small businesses are launched, market distortions have been removed, firms' revenues exceed costs, and formal employment opportunities rise as does the demand for goods and services. To help amplify success, financing is provided to start-up businesses by IGOs and is stimulated by foreign direct investment (Loop R9-P), and skills training is provided by NGOs (R10-P).

Once again speaking in a hopeful fashion, the continued success in R3-P will begin to provide avenues for helping to initiate and then amplify success in arenas represented by what would now be designated as R4-P to R8-P. To illustrate, rising profits by firms will enable them to invest in new plants and equipment, thereby helping to grow economic capital, an element relevant to R5-P.

Intertemporal Considerations

When the Success to the Successful trap exists, Meadows describes the benefit of preemptive system alteration as well as the risk of not addressing conditions before things spin out of control. Reinforcing feedback loops are sources of growth, explosion, erosion, and collapse in systems. A system with an unchecked reinforcing loop ultimately will destroy itself.[56] The trap can be kept under control by putting into place feedback loops that keep any competitor from taking over entirely. Traditional societies instinctively design into their systems some way of equalizing advantages, so the game stays fair.[57] As time passes equalizing mechanisms may derive from simple morality, or they may come from the practical understanding that losers, if they are unable to get out of the game of success to the successful, and if they have no hope of winning, could get frustrated enough to destroy the playing field.[58]

Figure 5.9 suggests possible dynamics over time in the well-being of the elites and the majority, and thus of the well-being gap.

At the outset of the scenario, there is a gap between the well-being of elites and the large majority, as there would be in any society.

In Phase 1, new elites willing to pursue their self-interest at the expense of the general public gain a foothold at the top of the hierarchy and begin to use their influence: the virtuous cycle is initiated, and the well-being gap begins to widen.

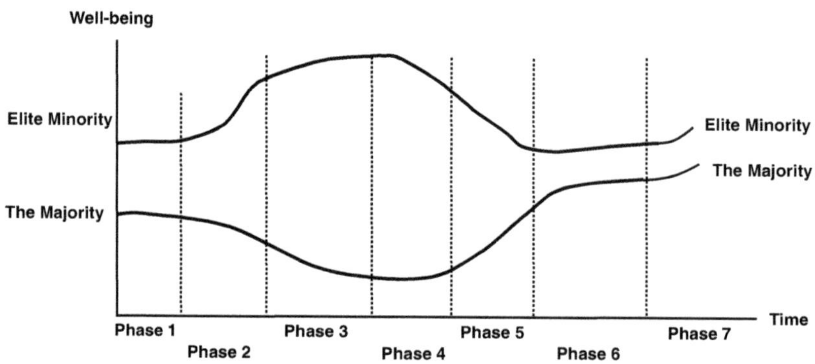

Figure 5.9 The Well-Being Gap Over Time

During Phase 2, the actions of the elite promote the onset of the vicious cycle, the well-being of the majority further declines, and the gap widens at a non-linear rate.

During Phase 3, the well-being of the majority continues to decline; however, the gains to the elite begin to level off, as the impact of reinforcing loops begins to exhaust system capacities and undermines the foundations of the nation state.

In Phase 4, the pillars of the nation state continue to weaken. Steps are taken to address the corruption gap.

It is not until Phase 5, which may lie some years after efforts to address corruption are initiated, that the corruption gap is adequately closed, and the well-being gap becomes stable.

In Phase 6, early indicators of success for the majority in one or two arenas arise, conscious efforts at success amplification are pursued, success begins to spill into other arenas, and success amplification is pursued in those new arenas as well. The well-being of the majority begins to rise at a non-linear rate.

Phase 7 represents the desired situation when the well-being of all segments of society begins to rise at a controlled rate, a proper set of balancing and reinforcing feedback loops are in place, the system is resilient, and socio-economic development occurs under a legitimate and competent government.

How to Combat Corruption in Africa: Questions for Consideration

Following best practices for facilitating conversation, this discussion poses questions intended to promote focused dialogue about concepts and constructive criticism about the models introduced in this paper.[59] Some questions will resonate with those studying a particular country, some with those taking an overview of conditions across countries.

1. What is the source of power of the head of state? How might one characterize the interconnections among the head of state and the other stakeholders at the top of the system hierarchy?
2. In the shorter term, and with respect to the provision of public, economic, or social value – see **Figure 5.5** – which inadequacies are most notable? In terms of outcomes, which are most problematic?
3. Both a corruption gap and a well-being gap exist in a corruption-based success to the successful archetype. Does addressing one of the gaps have higher priority than addressing the other, or is it advisable to address both gaps simultaneously?
4. Thinking of the negative reinforcing loops that undermine the foundations of the nation-state – see **Figure 5.6** – do one or two have greatest impact? Do they unfold in sequential fashion, or do they tend to have simultaneous, synergistic impact?
5. Are any interventions for goal achievement – see **Figure 5.7** – currently at work within or among African countries?
6. Is there any evidence of initial success – see **Figure 5.8** – in the economic, political, or civil aspects of the nation state? If so, has success been amplified in any way?

7. In terms of system dynamics – see **Figure 5.9** – where might countries be located in terms of respective phases associated with closing the corruption and well-being gaps?

Conclusion

Despite countervailing efforts, corrupt human systems have continued to plague African countries for the better part of six decades. External downward pressure for change has been placed on corrupt systems by IGOs, as has external lateral pressure by the African Union, international firms, NGOs, and other stakeholders. Most importantly, there has been internal upward pressure by members of civil society. Nonetheless, due to a combination of effective self-organization and hierarchy, the corrupt systems have exhibited resilience.

The implication is that those hoping to forge system transformation must develop a holistic understanding of system elements and interconnections and attempt to weaken the existing hierarchy by introducing fissures among subsystems. Essentially, that will call for the creation of parallel systems dedicated to articulating new rules, establishing new capacities for self-organization, identifying new goals, and perhaps articulating new paradigms. The challenges are formidable. System transformation will require sustained effort over time.

Notes

* Professor of Economics, International Studies Department, Dickinson College, Pennsylvania.

1 Kostas Rontos and Ioannis Vavouras, "Socioeconomic and Political Development: Their Measurement and Connections," *Global Journal of Human Social Science* 13, no. 5 (Version 1.0, 2013).

2 Transparency International. 2021 Corruption Perceptions Index. www.transparency.org

3 GNI per capita, Atlas method (current US$) | Data (worldbank.org)

4 Gini index | Data (worldbank.org)

5 George B. N. Ayittey, "Combating Corruption in Africa: Analysis and Context," in *Corruption and Development in Africa: Lessons from Country Case-Studies,* eds. Kempe Ronald Hope, Sr., and Bornwell C. Chikulo (New York: St. Martin's Press, 2000), 116.

6 Kempe Ronald Hope, Sr. and Bornwell C. Chikulo, editors, *Corruption and Development in Africa: Lessons from Country Case-Studies* (New York, NY: St. Martin's Press, 2000), 104–118.

7 Hope Sr. "Corruption and Development in Africa," in *Corruption and Development in Africa: Lessons from Country Case-Studies*, eds. Kempe Ronald Hope, Sr., and Bornwell C. Chikulo (New York: St. Martin's Press, 2000), 18.

8 Jacqueline Coolidge and Susan Rose-Ackerman, "Kleptocracy and Reform in African Regimes: Theory and Examples," in *Corruption and Development in Africa: Lessons from Country Case-Studies*, eds. Kempe Ronald Hope, Sr., and Bornwell C. Chikulo (New York: St. Martin's Press, 2000), 58.

9 Bertha Z. Osei-Hwedie and Kwaku Osei-Hwedie. "The Political, Economic, and Cultural Bases of Corruption in Africa," in *Corruption and Development in Africa: Lessons from Country Case-Studies*, eds. Kempe Ronald Hope, Sr., and Bornwell C. Chikulo (New York: St. Martin's Press, 2000), 42.

10 Ayittey, "Combating Corruption", 104.

11 Osei-Hwedie and Osei-Hwedie, "Bases of Corruption," 40.
12 Kempe Ronald Hope, Sr. "Corruption and Development in Africa," in *Corruption and Development in Africa: Lessons from Country Case-Studies*, eds. Kempe Ronald Hope, Sr., and Bornwell C. Chikulo (New York: St. Martin's Press, 2000).
13 John Mukum Mbaku. "Controlling Corruption in Africa: A Public Choice Perspective," in *Corruption and Development in Africa: Lessons from Country Case-Studies,* eds. Kempe Ronald Hope, Sr., and Bornwell C. Chikulo (New York: St. Martin's Press, 2000), 120.
14 Osei-Hwedie and Osie Hwedie, "Bases of Corruption," 43.
15 Osei-Hwedie and Osie Hwedie, "Bases of Corruption," 44.
16 Ayittey, "Combating Corruption," 116.
17 Gervase S. Maipose. "Aid Abuse and Mismanagement in Africa: Problems of Accountability, Transparency, and Ethical Leadership," in *Corruption and Development in Africa: Lessons from Country Case-Studies*, eds. Kempe Ronald Hope, Sr., and Bornwell C. Chikulo (New York: St. Martin's Press, 2000), 97–103, 92.
18 Maipose, *Corruption and Development in Africa*, 93.
19 Osei-Hwedie and Osie Hwedie, "Bases of Corruption," 50.
20 Ayittey. "Combating Corruption," 116
21 Maipose. "Aid Abuse," 95–97; 98–100.
22 Mbaku. "Public Choice," 129–132.
23 Osei-Hwedie and Osei-Hwedie, "Bases of Corruption," 53.
24 Stephen P. Riley. "Western Policies and African Realities: The New Anti-Corruption Agenda," in *Corruption and Development in Africa: Lessons from Country Case-Studies,* eds. Kempe Ronald Hope, Sr., and Bornwell C. Chikulo (New York: St. Martin's Press, 2000), 137–158.
25 African Union Convention on Preventing and Combating Corruption. Date of Adoption: July 1, 2003; Date of last signature, February 10, 2020, Date of entry into force, August 5, 2006. 36382-treaty-0028_-_african_union_convention_on_preventing_and_combating_corruption_e.pdf (au.int)
26 Sunday Bobai Agang, Pregala Pillay, and Chris Jones, eds. *A Multidimensional Perspective on Corruption in Africa: Wealth, Power, Religion and Democracy* (Cambridge: Cambridge Scholars Publishing, 2017).
27 Pregala Pillay and Evangelos Mantzaris. "Citizens' Role in Curbing Corruption in South Africa: Lessons for Africa," in *A Multidimensional Perspective on Corruption in Africa: Wealth, Power, Religion and Democracy*, eds. Sunday Bobai Agang, Pregala Pillay, and Chris Jones (Cambridge: Cambridge Scholars Publishing, 2017).
28 LIdetu Alemu Kefenie, "Towards a Model of Good Leadership: An Empirical Study of Effective Leadership and Ethics in Selected Ethiopian Public Organizations," in *A Multidimensional Perspective on Corruption in Africa: Wealth, Power, Religion and Democracy*, eds. Sunday Bobai Agang, Pregala Pillay, and Chris Jones (Cambridge: Cambridge Scholars Publishing, 2017).
29 Anzanilufuno Munyai, *Overcoming the Corruption Conundrum in Africa: A Socio-Legal Perspective* (Newcastle upon Tyne, UK: Cambridge Scholars Publishing, 2020).
30 Munyai, 14.
31 Munyai, 104.
32 Lucky Bryce Jnr. Jatto, "Africa's Approach to the International War on Corruption: A Critical Appraisal of the African Union Convention on Preventing and Combating Corruption," *Asper Review of International Business and Trade Law*, Vol. 10 (2010).
33 Bryanne Michael, "What Do African Donor-sponsored Anti-corruption Programmes Teach Us about International Development in Africa?" *Social Policy & Administration*, 38, no. 4 (2004).
34 Nellie R. Dunderdale, "The Influence of Corruption on the Developing World: The Foreign Corrupt Practices Act, International Commerce and Africa," *Journal of Law and Commerce*, 33, no. 2 (2015).

35 Samuel Brazys and Andreas Kotsadam, "Sunshine or Curse? Foreign Direct Investment, the OECD Anti-Bribery Convention, and Individual Corruption Experiences in Africa," *International Studies Quarterly*, 64 (2020).
36 John Mukum Mbaku, "International Law and the Fight against Bureaucratic Corruption in Africa," *Arizona Journal of International and Comparative Law,* 33, no. 3 (2016).
37 Gafar Idowu Ayodeji, "Grand Corruption in Sub-Saharan Africa and the Feasibility of Establishing International Anti-Corruption Court," *Acta Universitatis Danubius Administration,* 11, no. 1 (2019).
38 James. M. Kouzes and Barry Z. Posner, *The Leadership Challenge: How to Make Extraordinary Things Happen in Organizations, Sixth Edition* (Hoboken NJ: John Wiley and Sons), 30–31.
39 Michael J. Fratantuono. "The Imperative – and the Challenges – of Introducing a Citizen-Leader Development Program in an Undergraduate Liberal Arts Setting," in *Higher Education – New Approaches to Accreditation, Digitalization, and Globalization in the Age of Covid*, eds. Lee Waller and Sharon Waller (Wales, England: Intech Open, 2021).
40 John M. Bryson, Barbara C. Crosby, and Melissa Middleton Stone, "Designing and Strategically Managing Cross-Sector Collaborations," in *The U.S.-India Relationship: Cross Sector Collaboration to Promote Sustainable Development*, eds. Michel J. Fratantuono, and David M. Sarcone. (Carlisle, PA: Strategic Studies Institute, The United States Army War College, 2014). See also Michael J. Fratantuono, "Collaboration Among Agents of a Human System to Create Distributed Value". *Journal of Creating Value* 6, no. 1 (May 2021).
41 Donella Meadows, *Thinking in Systems: A Primer* (White River Junction, VT: Chelsea Green Publishing, 2008). David Peter Stroh, *Systems Thinking for Social Change* (White River Junction, VT: Chelsea Green Publishing, 2015).
42 Meadows, "A Primer," 28.
43 Meadows, "A Primer," 30–31.
44 Meadows, "A Primer," 31.
45 Meadows, "A Primer," 76.
46 Meadows, "A Primer," 79–80.
47 Meadows, "A Primer," 82–83.
48 Meadows, "A Primer," 145–165.
49 Meadows, "A Primer," 162–163.
50 Meadows, "A Primer," 170.
51 Meadows, "A Primer," 127.
52 Stroh, *Social Change*, Figure 4.7: 60.
53 Meadows, "A Primer," 83.
54 Coolidge and Rose-Ackerman, "Kleptocracy," 60–62.
55 Meadows, "A Primer," 83.
56 Meadows, "A Primer," 155.
57 Meadows, "A Primer," 129.
58 Meadows, "A Primer," 130.
59 C. Roland Christensen, with Abbey Hansen, *Teaching and the Case Method: Text, Cases, and Readings* (Boston: Harvard Business School Publishing, 1987).

6 Beyond Bribes

Legal Framework to Combat Corruption in Africa

*Hajer Gueldich**

Introduction

The socio-political and socio-economic realities of the post-colonial African society have been characterised by paradoxes due to the prevalence of poverty, the absence of essential infrastructure and basic amenities, protracted conflicts, and bad governance despite being gifted with vast mineral deposits and human resources. These are facts evident in Africa's inability to balance against the economic and social severities posed by the coronavirus (COVID-19) outbreak in December 2019. It was evident that most African countries could not feed and provide needed medical assistance for their citizens. In this situation, the African Union (AU) set a goal to raise money to help African countries deal with the effects of the COVID-19 pandemic.[1]

Similarly, the United Nations Conference on Trade and Development (UNCTAD) acknowledged a fall in inclusive growth, which measures growth in poverty and inequality, and the acceleration of poverty by COVID-19 (UNCTAD 2021).[2] The aforementioned conundrums, which are visible across the African continent, are all corollaries of bad governance, which has an excessively corrupt nucleus.[3] As a matter of fact, the issue of bad governance has occupied a robust space in the literature of African politics, but only a few studies have dedicated research to the topic of the causes of corruption and the indelible pattern of corruption in Africa.

The prevalence of corruption as a banal fact of life on the African continent is evident in the Corruption Perceptions Index (CPI), which ranks countries based on their response to issues, such as bribery, state capture, nepotistic appointments, diversion of public funds, and excessive red tape in the public sector. A host of African countries, according to CPI (2021), were ranked as highly corrupt, with Mauritius and Cape Verde ranked as very clean.[4] It is also plausible to note that from 2012 to 2022, Botswana experienced a downward spiral along the CPI curve, with corruption in the country reaching its minimum on the CPI scale. This is a positive change worthy of emulation on the African continent. However, the conundrum exists in the fact that a host of African nations are majorly corrupt and are classified as highly corrupt by the CPI.[5]

The prevalence of corruption on the continent is the single most important reason the African Union Convention on Preventing and Combating Corruption

DOI: 10.4324/9781003326649-7

(AUCPCC) came into existence. This chapter aims to assist policymakers in developing a pan-African anti-corruption framework by providing an objective evaluation of the AUCPCC. Corruption appears to be endemic across the continent, making the AUCPCC appear ineffective. This chapter seeks to critically evaluate this AUCPCC, which is an existing system. Evidently, like any other system, the AUCPCC embodies strengths and weaknesses. However, the bulk of its weaknesses exist in the fact that the AU is not a supranational organisation like the European Union (EU), where a certain portion of member states' sovereignty is submitted to the EU.

The discussion answers several questions. How does the AUCPCC fare in terms of its strengths and weaknesses? Has there been a noticeable decrease in corrupt practices since the AUCPCC was established? Is the AUCPCC regarded as a formidable force by African heads of state? How firmly set in place is the AUCPCC's moral compass? Is there a mechanism in place at the AUCPCC to keep an eye on the behaviour of powerful politicians and bureaucrats? What is the source of the AUCPCC's budget? Can the AUCPCC create an anti-corruption framework that can be used across the continent?

The rest of this chapter is structured as follows: after this introductory section, there is an examination of anti-corruption laws and policies in the AU, and then, there are sections that evaluate the AUCPCC, pointing out its positive and negative aspects before offering recommendations and concluding the discussion.

Conceptualisation of Corruption

This section explores definitions of corruption from different sources to understand what corruption is. To be corrupt is to engage in any number of dishonest social behaviour, such as bribery, embezzlement, abuse of authority, illicit enrichment, kickbacks, and trading influence. In addition, this includes activities such as money laundering, concealment, and obstruction of justice that help corrupt services be carried out.[6]

According to the United Nations (UN), "grand corruption" is corrupt behaviour that affects the highest levels of government and leads to massive abuses of power. Similarly, the World Bank define grand corruption as "state capture," in which powerful politicians and bureaucrats prioritise the financial or political gain of personal corporations over the public good.[7] World Bank and Transparency International (TI) define corruption as the misuse of public office for private gain.

There are many definitions of corruption put forth by different international organisations. All definitions share two components. First, corruption is characterised by an abuse of power in either the public or private sphere. Second, those abusing their power gain an advantage to which they are not legally entitled. Thus, "corruption" is a catch-all term for a wide range of illegal behaviour, including but not limited to bribery, embezzlement, abuse of authority, extortion, illicit enrichment, kickbacks, and trading in influence, as well as money laundering, concealment, and obstruction of justice, which are often used to facilitate the commission of corrupt activities. Bribery and embezzlement are universally recognised as examples of corruption, even though there is no consensus on what exactly corruption entails or how to define it.[8]

The Context of Corruption In Africa

According to the 2018 AU Commission Report, corruption and illicit financial flows cost Africa US$60 billion annually.[9] The great paradox of Africa is that despite its natural resources, it is one of the world's poorest regions. Additionally, corruption is one of the endogenous and systemic factors that has and will continue to impede Africa's progress. A common concern in this book is that corruption erodes public trust in government and the legal system. It permeates every aspect of life and every stratum of society. The participants range from storefront entrepreneurs to top government officials to public sector employees. All of this points to the fact that corruption is a serious issue that needs to be addressed in every possible way.

The 2003 AU Convention on Preventing and Combating Corruption (AUCPCC)[10]

The AUCPCC presents continental consensus on what African states should do in the areas of prevention, criminalisation, international cooperation, and asset recovery. Going beyond other similar conventions, the AUCPCC calls for the eradication of corruption in the private and public sectors. The continental Convention covers a wide range of offences including bribery (domestic or foreign), diversion of property by public officials, trading in influence, illicit enrichment, money laundering, and concealment of property and primarily consists of mandatory provisions. It also obliges the signatories to introduce open and converted investigations against corruption.[11]

A total of 49 countries signed this Convention on 11 July 2003, in Maputo, Mozambique and it went into effect on 5 August 2006.[12] Its stated goal is to encourage countries to work together to create anti-corruption policies and laws, to ensure the efficacy of measures and actions to prevent, detect, punish, and eradicate corruption, and to facilitate and regulate cooperation among state parties.

The AUCPCC is consistent with the anti-corruption laws and policies already in place across the AU. Consequently, the AU now has a system by which to fight corruption across the continent. However, the AUCPCC's effectiveness has been questioned partly because several African states have been labelled "highly corrupt" despite its existence. Within this framework, the purpose of the following section is to provide answers to some of the questions raised in the introduction. The questions explored in this chapter, which aim to determine why the AUCPCC is failing, were developed using system thinking as aptly demonstrated by Michael J. Fratantuono in the preceding chapter.

The Strengths and Weaknesses of the AUCPCC

There is no doubt that the AUCPCC's policy documents present a formidable framework against corruption. In the event of suspicion, the document states that anyone, including public officials, can be questioned, arrested, and tried in court. Furthermore, the convention allows for the extradition of an accused person to a party state upon request.

Most liberal democratic African states, including Nigeria, South Africa, Ivory Coast, Senegal, Kenya, Tanzania, and many others, have also adopted the AUCPCC preventive measures. However, it is puzzling that in the Corruption Perceptions Index (2021), both liberal democratic African states and autocratic states were categorised as highly corrupt. This is a difficult situation that is not the fault of AUCPCC, as the commission can only make suggestions and cannot mandate that states follow them.

The AU's formation has been blamed for this structural issue because its member states are so protective of their autonomy. On this basis, the AU and the AUCPCC are powerless to ensure compliance with anti-corruption laws and policies in its member states. In addition, the AU and its agencies receive most of their funding from member states. Given this, it is obvious that the AUCPCC has limited ability to combat corruption in African nations. If the AU were a supranational organisation like the EU, it could have challenged the abuses of Africa's political and bureaucratic elites in court. Since the AUCPCC lacks the authority to question its sponsors, the fact that it must rely on the African heads of state for the necessary funds for day-to-day activities is a limiting factor. The AUCPCC could be destroyed if its members condemned the corruption of African government officials and politicians.

All the same, the AUCPCC appears to be the best continentally applicable document and mechanism to combat and prevent corruption in Africa. Article 2 lays out the goals, and Article 3 lays out the principles, which require transparency, respect for liberal democratic values, respect for human and people's rights, and a strong rejection of corrupt practices. The scope of application is the focus of Article 4 of the Convention. Definitions of corruption and its consequences are laid out here. Article 1 (a-f) defines corruption in Africa explicitly, with a focus on financial crimes.[13] Section 1(a) forbids public servants and others from accepting anything of value as a bribe for a favour to be done in the course of their official duties.

As mentioned earlier, the AUCPCC is an all-encompassing anti-corruption document that considers the particularities of each member state. However, the AU's technical flaws in its structure have resulted in a slow pace of achievement. This leaves the AU completely at the whim of its individual member states. If a state is unwilling to investigate or prosecute a powerful public official, then the AUCPCC has no recourse but to leave it alone. Given this empirical evidence, it would be fair to characterise the AUCPCC as purely consultative or advisory.

Implementation of the AUCPCC by African State

Forty-eight out of 55 African countries have ratified the AUCPCC, clearly a majority.[14] However, it was pointed out that nobody knows for sure how well the convention is implemented in practice. The CPI (2021) showed a declining trend in the fight against corruption across the 55 African states, so it would be wrong to say that the AUCPCC is effective. The AUCPCC has been widely criticised for being ineffective, and it is safe to assume that its 44 signatory states feel the same way. This conclusion is supported by the fact that between 2003 and 2020, the AU Advisory Board on Corruption (AUABC), which is responsible for monitoring countries' progress in implementing the convention, has only received 13 reports, and these are not made public.

Based on this premise, Transparency International (TI) evaluated the implementation of AUCPCC in ten African countries, including South Africa, Tunisia, Nigeria, Rwanda, and Congo. Based on the results of the evaluation, TI suggested that countries like Morocco and the Democratic Republic of the Congo (DRC) should move quickly to ratify the convention in full. TI recommended that signatory nations complete and submit an updated report to the AUABC.

Another recommendation was that multiple stakeholder groups should also work together. It was suggested that the AU make available to the public all progress reports submitted to the AUABC so that citizens could keep a close eye on their governments. It was also suggested that governments be more open with their operations so that locals and outsiders can view detailed information about government spending and operations.

Finally, it was suggested that all AUCPCC participants invest in sponsoring technical specialist skills and coordination capacity among investigators and prosecutors in an effort to have them intellectually equipped to pursue complex corruption cases, all while respecting the full independence of prosecutorial and judicial bodies to ensure that corruption cases are dealt with impartially.[15]

The TI recommendations are, of course, subject to the approval of the heads of state of the AU's member states. It is true that AUCPCC signatories have an obligation to uphold the convention's stipulations. While it may be tempting to say that the tiny number of progress reports submitted to the AUABC between 2003 and 2020 indicates progress, the sad truth is that it shows just the opposite. The AU also appears to be complicit in this because the public does not have access to the 13 reports at their disposal.

Keeping the reports secret serves no useful purpose. It would, therefore, be reasonable to conclude that the AUCPCC is hampered by the AU's technical deformity in its structure. This structural defect suggests that member states are unusually powerful and wealthy relative to the AU. Inevitably, this has harmed the AU and its institutions over time. Observers should not be surprised if it turns out that AU heads of state whose names appeared in the submitted progress reports decided to keep them secret.

It is widely acknowledged that corruption in Africa is at the heart of the continent's political and economic problems.[16] The 2021 Corruption Perceptions Index (CPI) has shown that anti-corruption efforts in Africa have been fruitless thus far. As of 2021, only two of Africa's 55 countries were deemed "very clean" by the CPI. It stands to reason that corruption is to blame for issues such as high unemployment, lack of infrastructure development, insecurity, food scarcity, and a government that fails to provide for its citizens' basic needs. All in all, the 2021 CPI shows that the AUCPCC has not made significant progress in the fight against corruption in Africa.

Assessment of the AUCPCC in Preventing Grand Corruption

The TI looked into the AUCPCC in 2020, and they found that despite the fact that the AUCPCC has a monitoring and evaluation mechanism, getting signatories to actually implement the convention has been a difficult nut to crack.[17] This is what TI suggested after conducting the study:

> Tunisia should consider expanding the scope of the money laundering offence to include aiding and abetting and the acquisition, possession or use of property with the knowledge that it is the proceeds of corruption.
>
> Morocco should consider criminalising illicit enrichment as a matter of priority and including this as a predicate offence for money laundering.
>
> Côte d'Ivoire, DRC and Morocco should consider clarifying, through legislative amendments, whether money laundering can be prosecuted autonomously from the predicate offence(s).
>
> Ghana, Morocco and South Africa should consider making illicit enrichment an explicit, standalone offence subject to criminal sanctions.
>
> To help avoid legal uncertainty, Côte d'Ivoire, DRC and Tunisia should stipulate the time period during which a person can be held liable for illicit enrichment.
>
> Côte d'Ivoire, DRC, Mozambique, Nigeria, Rwanda and Tunisia should consider including the "lack of a reasonable justification" for the enrichment as part of the offence.
>
> All countries should prioritise the publication of annual, disaggregated data on the number of money laundering and illicit enrichment cases prosecuted and their outcomes. Prosecution and conviction rates should be disaggregated to identify at least: the predicate offences, the nature of the case (for example individual or company, even if anonymised), and information on sanctions imposed and sums recovered.
>
> Given the complexities often involved in investigating money laundering and illicit enrichment offences, all countries should prioritise investment in specialist technical skills and capacity required to pursue such cases.
>
> All countries should also consider reviewing and strengthening coordination mechanisms between investigators and prosecutors, as well with other specialised professions such as financial analysts and tax inspectors, whose expertise can be critical in bringing complex cases to a successful conclusion.
>
> Where possible, enforcement bodies in all countries should focus not only on pursuing the underlying predicate offences, which tend to be easier to prosecute, but also give due attention to the money laundering offence itself.
>
> All countries should ensure full independence of prosecutorial and judicial bodies so that offences can be prosecuted impartially and without favour to powerful, politically connected individuals.

TI (2020) proposed changes to the AUCPCC framework in order to strengthen its ability to combat and prevent corruption across Africa. Quite a few of the suggestions can be implemented in a variety of different African countries. Political and bureaucratic elites, for instance, are frequently well off, but there appears to be a discrepancy between their annual earnings and their tangible and intangible assets. However, the AUCPCC evaluation mechanism is flawed due to the lack of on-the-ground observers to monitor the activities of member states. The AUCPCC depends instead on reports of progress made by signatories. It has been noted that one weakness in the AUCPCC monitoring mechanism is that the agency in the convention allows signatories to compile the progress report on their own. It is highly unethical to ask a criminal or wanted person to evaluate themselves and submit their findings to a group funded by the criminals or gang. In this case, the agency's inherent weakness is due to the sponsors.

Can the AUCPCC Create a Continent-Wide Anti-Corruption Framework?

Given that 48 out of Africa's 55 countries have signed the AUCPCC, it applies across the continent. However, autocratic societies, where civil society is weak, might not be a good fit for the AUCPCC's terms and conditions. The AUCPCC's laws and policies were distilled from those of the countries whose leaders signed them. Many of the member states, however, have been observed weakening their own legal systems. Laws and policies enacted under the AUCPCC can be undermined because many signatories place them below their own priorities. More so, many signatories do not appear to be fully implementing the convention of the agency in question. The body's definition of corruption is narrowly focused on monetary issues, excluding potential contributors like favouritism, rent-seeking, and a lack of transparency and accountability.

The African Union Advisory Board against Corruption (AUABC)

The Board was established on 26 May 2009, in accordance with Article 22 (1) of the Convention of 2003. It is the only African institution specifically tasked by the African Union to combat corruption and its associated ills.[18] The Board's primary responsibility is to encourage African states to take measures to combat corruption and related crimes. The Board must monitor the implementation of these measures and report on the progress of each State Party in adhering to the Convention's requirements on a regular basis to the Executive Council.

The AU Advisory Board on Corruption (AUABC) was established on 26 May 2009, in accordance with Article 22 (1) of the Convention of 2003. It is the only African institution specifically tasked by the African Union to combat corruption and its associated ills. The Board's primary responsibility is to encourage African states to take measures to combat corruption and related crimes. The Board must monitor the implementation of these measures and report on the progress of each State Party in adhering to the Convention's requirements on a regular basis to the Executive Council.

As an independent organ of the African Union (AU), the African Union Advisory Board on Corruption is responsible for urging and supporting the adoption of measures and actions by State Parties to the AU Convention on Preventing and Combating Corruption in order to reduce the prevalence of corrupt practices and criminal behaviour across the continent. For instance, 48 nations had become States Parties to the Convention by ratifying it.[19]

Members of the AUABC

The Board Members of the African Union Advisory Board against Corruption are elected by the African Union Executive Council ministerial meeting during the AU Summit in either January or July. The Council, by delegated authority, automatically and simultaneously appoints the members after the election. The AUABC is composed of 11 members elected by the Executive Council from among a list of experts of the highest integrity, impartiality, and recognised competence in matters relating to preventing and combating corruption and related offences, proposed by the State Parties. Board Members serve for a term of two years renewable only once.[20]

Election of AUABC Members

During the ministerial meeting of the African Union Executive Council held during the AU Summit (typically in either January or July), board members of the African Union Advisory Board on Corruption are elected. When members are elected, the Council automatically and simultaneously appoints them in accordance with its delegated authority. The Executive Council appoints 11 members to the Advisory Board on Corruption from a list of experts of the highest integrity, impartiality, and recognised competence in matters relating to preventing and combating corruption and related offences that are proposed by the State Parties.

Each board member's term is for 2 years, with the option of renewal given only once.

The Board chooses a chairperson, vice chairperson, and rapporteur from among its members to serve as its bureau. Each member of the Bureau serves a two-year term.

The Bureau is responsible for ensuring that the Board's functions under Article 22 (5) of the Convention are carried out through the proper planning and coordination of its activities.

Mandate of the AUABC

The main mandate of the Board is to promote and encourage the adoption of measures and actions by State Parties to prevent, detect, punish, and eradicate corruption and related offences in Africa as well as to follow up on the application of those measures and submit a report to the Executive Council on a regular basis on the progress made by each State Party in complying with the provisions of the Convention.

The Board's primary responsibility is to urge African states to act against corruption and related crimes. The Board must monitor the implementation of these measures and provide the Executive Council with updates on how each State Party is complying with the Convention's requirements on a regular basis.

Summarised SWOT Analysis of the AUABC

Strengths of AUABC include the following:

1. Board Members' Experience and Competence.
2. Regulation and institutionalisation of new practices.
3. Individuals from a wide range of cultural backgrounds make up its membership.
4. Existence of the force of the AU behind the Board.
5. The Convention spans the entire continent.
6. Compliance with Board Independence Requirements.

Weaknesses of AUABC are as follows:

1. A lack of available resources prevents the AU ABC strategic plan from being put into action.
2. The lack of adequate financial means.
3. Insufficient long-term partnerships.
4. The lack of necessary infrastructure, such as adequate office space or transportation options.
5. The Board's mandate has a short lifespan, which results in multiple transitions within a single strategic planning horizon (in this case, three).

Opportunities of AUABC relate to the following:

1. Better understanding of how corruption harms society.
2. Extreme activity in the anti-corruption movement.
3. Alliances and synergies with anti-corruption groups at the local, national, and international levels (including the United Nations).
4. There has been a rise in the international community's focus on Africa's fight against corruption and the continent's urgent need for effective leadership.

Threats to AUABC, among others, include the following:

1. The AUABC lacks a reliable delivery structure that would speed up the implementation of strategic plans.
2. States Parties have not shown sufficient political will to develop a legal framework consistent with the requirements of the Convention.
3. Lack of political will on the part of AU Member States to ratify and implement the Convention (AUABC 2017).

Africa Anti-corruption Techniques

It is obvious that in spite of all this tremendous AU Law and policy in order to combat corruption in Africa, there is still a lot of work to do. Corruption plays a major role in the disruption of constitutional democracies in Africa. Corruption weakens constitutional democracies and undermines the advancement of and respect for the rule of law of any country by, among other things, weakening institutions that are core to the observance of constitutional democracy.

In light of AU Agenda 2063, Aspiration 1 "A prosperous Africa based on inclusive growth and sustainable development" and Aspiration 3 "An Africa of good governance, democracy, respect for human rights, justice and the rule of law," there is a need to look at how constitutional democracy and the rule of law can contribute to a commitment to prevent and eliminate corruption while advancing these aspirations. It takes all the measurements which aims to minimising the size and weight of criminality, by either limiting the conditions which ease the occurrence of criminal activities and controlling the environment or by directly influencing the potential perpetrators of criminal actions and the public. Thus, both preventive and repressive measures are necessary to combat this scourge.

Preventive Measures

Preventive measures against corruption in the public sector begin with the recruitment system. There should be recruitment systems and methods that must be done on the basis of merit, transparency, and equality. Related to the same, all public officials are required to declare their assets when they take up their duties, during and at the end of their mandate. Moreover, it is important to establish codes of conduct. In practice, this should be reflected in the establishment of an internal committee or a body responsible for drawing up a code of conduct and ensuring the application of this code, raising awareness and training public officials in this area of respect for ethics within the public service. Hence, transparency at the level of the administrative is important. One of the more important aspects in the fight against corruption is transparency, which can best be described as follows: to be clear in the process of decision-making and be open to the public in the performance of duties. The complete application of the principle of transparency should have been the best guarantee of public powers to be used to achieve the benefit of the community.

To combat corruption, States must publish information, through periodic reports on the risks of corruption within the public administration. Transparency in the funding of political parties. This rule extends to the prohibition of the use of funds acquired through illegal and corrupt practices to finance political parties, the integration of the principle of transparency in the funding of political parties, adoption of a participatory approach in preventing corruption States will have to set up, make operational, and strengthen the authorities or agencies responsible for combating corruption.

States must adopt legislative and other measures to make operational and strengthen internal systems of accounting, auditing, and monitoring with regard to public revenues, customs and tax revenues, rental expenditure and procedure, procurement and management of public goods and services. The preventive measures against corruption in the private sector consist in requiring State Parties to adopt legislative and other measures to prevent acts of corruption and related offences committed in the private sector and by agents of this sector. This is to prevent companies from paying bribes against the award of contracts.

Repressive Measures

Responsibility means that a person or representative from the government must explain and justify its action in front of citizens. The principle of accountability means that nobody can be excluded from oversight or from reconsidering review. Applying this principle also proves whether other principles such as the rule of law, openness, impartiality, and equality in front of the law are respected.

Accountability is necessary to provide important assumptions about the efficiency and effectiveness of public administration. A well-established system of accountability is the link between the administration and the political system. It is that link which should bind the administrative part of government with the policy and citizens.

It has also been observed that many corruption lawsuits against African states are brought outside African jurisdictions, in particular the International Centre for Settlement of Investment Disputes. It would be appropriate for the AU to be able to assert its own mechanisms in the context of the fight against corruption. This will create a climate in which corruption would be considered high-risk and low-rewarding activity. Also, the cooperation between African states and the other states is necessary. This cooperation can be possible by mutual legal assistance in investigation and extradition.

Citizen Activism

The decisive role of each citizen and civil society by establishing a platform of civil society and a group of investigative journalists dedicated to fighting corruption is very important to tickle the problem of corruption. In fact, political rights are the basis of the control of the state by the citizens. Unfortunately, the low level of civic participation in political processes allows serious systematic corruption. Despite the numerous public campaigns to raise awareness and institutional and legal reforms to improve public administration, research shows that corruption continues to occur on a large scale. One of the main principles for the successful participation of citizens is raising the level of political culture in which the common interests of citizens' rise above the daily political needs and that require solutions to common problems through cooperation.

Conclusion

The struggle against corruption in Africa depends on the economic situation in the African countries, branch of economic structure and foundation of the same political manipulation, social structure, and traditions, and many others having any influence on the occurrence, distribution, and immunity of corruption by legal and political measures. The analysis shows that success in suppression will depend primarily on taking preventive measures and policies, strengthening the awareness of citizens and officials to respect the basic principles of good governance in Africa.

In sum, the AUCPCC is an all-encompassing anti-corruption framework that is hampered by the political superstructure of the AU, as the agency can only proffer recommendations and it functions based on states' consent. Similarly, the AUCPCC does not have the human resources to keep tabs on how signatories are carrying out their commitments. Considering this shortcoming, the agency is overly reliant on the progress reports submitted by them. Many signatories have been hesitant to submit progress reports despite having the authority to do so on their own accord. The AUCPCC needs to figure out how to deal with this dilemma. If the AUCPCC is going to be an effective watchdog over the proper execution of its mission, it needs to be an autonomous organisation.

The reluctance of the AU to make the progress report public and the reluctance of 26 signatories to present a progress report of anti-corruption strides are indicative of this. Since successive governments at the national level have not shown a full commitment to fighting corruption[21], the fight against corruption at the national, regional, and continental levels has an undertone of reluctance. At the regional level, the war against corruption is hampered by the same leaders who are notorious for manipulating policies and laws designed to combat and prevent corruption.

The activities of political elites and bureaucrats can be more effectively monitored by an AUCPCC that is autonomous, self-sufficient and in control of its own resources. Even if the agency is unable to bring corrupt leaders to justice, it will at least be able to act unilaterally and expose the faults of political and bureaucratic elites. The spread of corruption in Africa can be slowed by adopting such a strategy. Corruption persists if the public is kept in the dark about the corrupt actions of their leaders.

Notes

* Professor of International Law at the University of Carthage – Tunisia and Chairperson of the African Union Commission on International Law (AUCIL).

1 African Union Commission. n.d. *About the Fund.* https://au.int/en/aucovid19responsefund

2 UNCATAD. 2021. *Economic Development in Africa Report 2021: Reaping the potential benefits of the African Continental Free Trade Area for inclusive growth.* December 8. https://unctad.org/press-material/facts-and-figures-7 See also *The Impact of the COVID-19 Pandemic on Trade and Development: Lessons Learned*, UNCTAD/OSG/2022/1, https://unctad.org/system/files/official-document/osg 2022d1_en.pdf

3 Transparency International. 2020. *Implementing and Enforcing the African Union Convention on Preventing and Combating Corruption: Comparative Review.* December 04. www.transparency.org/en/publications/aucpcc-comparative-review

4 Transparency international, 2021, www.transparency.org/en/cpi/2021

5 *Idem*, op. cit.

6 International Institute for Democracy and Electoral Assistance (IDEA) *Annual Results Report 2014* Stockholm, 2014), idea.int/sites/default/files/reference-docs/inter national-idea-annula-results-report-2014.

7 United Nations Development Programme (UNDP), "UNDP's Global Anticorruption Initiative Campaign (GAIN) 2014–2017, 2014, www.undp.org/sites/g/files/zskgke326/files/publications/globalanticorruption_final_web2.pdf (accessed 29 September 2019).
8 Institute for Democracy and Electoral Assistance (IDEA), "Combating Corruption Constitutional Frameworks for the Middle East and North Africa," https://constitutionnet.org/vl/item/combating-corruption-constitutional-frameworks-middle-east-and-north-africa (accessed 29 September 2022).
9 Ligane J. Massamba Sène, "Mobilization of Domestic Resources: Fighting against Corruption and Illicit Financial Flows," African Union Commission Department of Economic Affairs, April 2018 https://au.int/sites/default/files/newsevents/workingdocuments/34086-wd-dea_paper_stc_2018_mobilization_of_domestic_resources_fighting_against_corruption_iff_english_0.pdf
10 Sène, "Mobilization of Domestic Resources."
11 Akeem Olajide Bello, "United Nations and African Union Conventions on Corruption and Anti-corruption Legislations in Nigeria: A Comparative Analysis." *African Journal of International & Comparative Law* 22 (2) (2014): 308–333. Peter W. Schroth, "The African Union Convention on Preventing and Combating Corruption." *Journal of African Law* 49 (1) (2005): 24–38.
12 African Union, *African Union Convention on Preventing and Combating Corruption (The Convention),* https://anticorruption.au.int/en#:~:text=The%202018%2D2022%20Strategic%20Plan,the%20Board's%20Short%20Term%20vision (28 September 2022).
13 Access the AUCPCC policy document at https://au.int/sites/default/files/treaties/36382-treaty-0028_-_african_union_convention_on_preventing_and_combating_corruption_e.pdf (September 2022).
14 Transparency International, "Corruption Perceptions Index (CPI)," 2021., www.transparency.org/en/cpi/2021(accessed 28 September 2022).
15 Transparency International, "Corruption Perceptions Index."
16 Transparency International, "Corruption Perceptions Index."
17 Transparency International, "Corruption Perceptions Index."
18 African Union, *African Union Convention on Preventing and Combating Corruption.*
19 African Union, *African Union Convention on Preventing and Combating Corruption.*
20 African Union, *African Union Convention on Preventing and Combating Corruption.*
21 Human Rights Watch, "Corruption on Trial? The Record of Nigeria's Financial and Economic Crimes Commission," August 25, 2011, www.hrw.org/report/2011/08/25/corruption-trial/record-nigerias-economic-and-financial-crimes-commission (29 September 2022).

7 Perfect Storm

Corruption, Peace, Security, and Development in Africa

*Jonathan Makuwira**

Introduction

The linkage between corruption, peace and/or conflict, insecurity and development has, in recent times, captured the attention of scholars in the academy as irrefutable evidence emerges about how complex the issues are, in Africa, as is the case globally "corruption is the global devil that has devoured human intelligibility in its social context."[1] The authenticity of this claim cannot be overemphasised in the current African society. The academy is replete with evidence that Africa is the most corrupt continent in the world, underscoring the stagnation of development progress on a continent endowed with natural resources.[2] Corruption, rather than a mere practice of mismanagement, has become a governance issue with consequences far and beyond. From a development perspective, one has to appreciate that Africa is home to the least developed countries in the world, severely punctuated with pockets of conflicts – an indication of heavy vulnerabilities enmeshed in a tapestry of weak institutions, poor governance, low socio-economic status, the widening gap between the *haves* and the *have nots*, just to mention but a few factors. Over and above all these, it is out of those factors which breed elements of underdevelopment, insecurity, instability, and conflicts.

Not only have these factors brought constraint on the development of peaceful and sustainable societies, but they have further encouraged a downward spiral on peaceful co-existence. Buttressed by the destabilising effects of corruption, we see that where it (corruption) exists, there have been increased criminal networks which have made conflicts continue prevailing. In such environments, hopes of lasting peace and stability can only be fleeting unless solutions are found for the root causes of instability. When corruption becomes entrenched, it undermines the development of state authority and its institutions, thereby leaving a weak state with potentially more space for breeding more insurgents to operate. Leaders also feel the cost of corruption, but they pay in the currency of losing the trust of their citizens.

Thus, the purpose of this chapter is to critically examine the linkage between corruption, insecurity, peace, and development within the African context. It draws lessons from a few African countries and links these to how corruption can be eliminated in order to engender development, peace and security. The chapter is

DOI: 10.4324/9781003326649-8

outlined in three major sections. The first section critically examines in more depth and building on the previous chapter, what corruption is, and is not. This discussion builds into a further analysis of what peace, security, and development are. The second section compasses the link between peace, (human) security, and development. The idea is to show that each of those concepts cannot exist on their own – essentially showing the intricacies and interlinkages. The third section critically analyses how corruption weakens peace, security, and development. This will be discussed within the context of popular theories of corruption and development.

The major thesis of this paper/chapter is that corruption breeds a kind of behaviour that disregards elements of good stewardship. In addition, the fact that corruption undermines public confidence the resultant effect is that there is a tendency to breed mistrust, andaves and/or networks of nepotism and state capture by elites who think they possess a high level of authority beyond state-sanctioned authority.

What Corruption Is and What It Is Not

While the idea may have different definitions, "corruption" is the manifestation of the failure of government and, in many cases, a serious behavioural issue. Scholars such as Hope and Chikulo have called it the "Aids of democracy" from an African perspective.[3] The pervasiveness of this practice is not only puzzling given that the majority of the cases are those whose perpetrators are essentially high-level managers or people not only in positions of power and influence but also those who, on the surface, look to be people of high integrity and respect. Put it another way, corruption is perpetrated by people who are "educated." This not only raises some contradictions on the role and kind of education but also questions the morals and ethics of the nature of education that we go through. In some cases, corruption has been linked to "politicians" – again, highlighting the influence of power and corrupt behaviour among people. This is why in this volume, the theme of "*abuse of power,*" has been consistently used in defining what corruption is.

Furthermore, in making definitions, there is also the issue of "gains" – as individuals or a collective; meaning that corruption is much more than a single act; but rather an act beyond an individual to a network.[4] Such networks thrive on well-planned acts. Corruption does not happen by accident, but it is propagated by a systematic and highly coordinated thinking and action. In many ways, it is also sponsored. The "powerful" – in other words, people with influence, will in many instances, avoid being in front but will instead, send or engage an "infantry" to do the dirty job on their behalf, making the whole act more subtle and complex to the eyes of those who may want to delve deep into exposing such acts.

Macedo and Valaderes (2021) have given their theoretical opinions on how corruption is endemic in the public sector as it is the case in the private; and have concluded that, theoretically, there are three dominant theoretical frameworks – the "Functionalist," "Economic," and "Legal Positivist." In the context of the definition of corruption, a functionalist perspective will often be defined by low political and economic development. Clarity of corruption is seen through the behaviour of public agents who deviate from accepting public norms in preference for private interests. This theoretical perspective is often rife when there is a high level of monopoly and privileges in the public sector.

The Legal Positivist theory, unlike the first two, is premised on the belief that the actions of the state may sometimes be seen to undermine its own legal instruments, thereby seen to delegitimise the effectiveness of the state. In all these theories though, this 'overlap' of private interest to serving the public good is the key frontier in our understanding of how corruption can be tackled. In other words, the rational choices and the seemingly institutionalised economic gains accruing from corruption seem inseparable in our attempt to really get to the bottom of the matter.

When a close analysis of these perspectives is put under sharp microscopic scrutiny, one would be tempted to challenge the linearity of the thinking which may be argued to fit into the cognitive theoretical platform and, perhaps, lack depth in analytical vigour. Here, I struggle with the lack of the confluence between technical, practical, and emancipatory approaches to discerning corruption in its full sense. This is especially the case where the debate on corruption, raises questions about human morality and ethics. Furthermore, it raises the question as to whether or not we can fully understand corruption without applying the social, political, and civic virtues.[5] Because we are predominantly theorising the abstract, the key to understanding corruption is to also ask the question as to why we are unable to control our obsession with personal interests. This point is more crucial considering the contours when I bring the four issues together – corruption, peace, security, and development.

Peace in the Context of Corruption

The purpose of this section is to explore the correlation between corruption and peace/conflict. Does corruption cause conflict? Is the pursuant of anti-corruption effort detrimental to achieving peace? Or better put, "under what conditions can peace be realised in corrupt-ridden environment?" These, and other questions, are not easy to navigate; neither are they easy to get proper answers to. Nevertheless, I have canvassed the definition of corruption and one obvious thing is that corrupt practices do have a negative effect not only on the economy but also on the entire fabric of society. The argument that corruption weakens institutions is a good premise to understand the interface between corruption and conflict.[6] More important is the issue of order.

As we have seen in Malawi lately (see Kateta, 2021), corruption cases have been on the rise yet the country is bleeding economically. Crucially, instead of the government focusing on delivery, the focus is on damage controls under the pretext that all is good. Disorder and the level of corruption cases are evidence of the potential conflict because, the erosion of confidence and trust, has, in one way or the other, created a sense of hopelessness and despair. Corruption has become a class struggle when state apparatus has been captured by a few individuals who render the state ineffective and dysfunctional, using the state. This state of affairs creates inequality, which in the short, medium, and long term produces an asymmetry power system, which, in turn, excludes others.

The marginalisation of certain voices and social stratification can be a fertile recipe for conflict. The more there exists a high level of self-interests, the more the public system gets weaker, resulting in very little or no transparency and accountability. In the words of Koechlin, "a still entrenched understanding is that the more corruption, the more illegitimate the political regime, the more ineffective the public institutions, the greater the propensity of conflict."[7] While the claim may sound rosy, scholars have struggled to prove the correlation between corruption and legitimacy, rendering the corruption-peace and/or conflict, problematic.

While articulating this issue, I am also conscious that we need to be careful not to forget that conflict or peace are social constructs laden with values, practices, and identities. In the context of corruption, it is a dynamic idea. As such, I want to offer caution that if corruption is part of the social struggle, then the state is at the centre of the struggle and cannot be removed from being part of the social and political order. The expectations from the public or if you like, from society, is to state that when corruption (a medium of social struggle) has increased, the resistance that is created as the society seeks to balance the state's social contract, the state loses its legitimacy to a certain extent.

One would argue that as the state seeks to balance power relationships, instability sets in. All this can be construed as "conflict" yet in essence, it is a normative way society expresses itself in demanding accountability and transparency. Equally, the opposite is true – where accountable regime and regimes that deliver on their promise may experience peace by the mere absence of oust conflict yet, structurally, inequality may be high but how citizens express themselves may paint a picture that a corruption-free environment engenders peace. Therefore, when corruption is so deeply rooted in society that it has become institutionalised, it can be perceived as a structural violence-sustaining system in which private interests prevail over the common good.

The premise to analyse the corruption-peace nexus is state fragility. If corruption creates and perpetuates inequality and discontent, the potential for fragility, violent extremism and conflict is high. So, how do we deal with such a potentially explosive situation? The section that follows attempts to respond to this question by looking and critically examining the concept of security which, for the sake of extending the debate will dwell on "human security" as opposed to just "security."

Human Security

The main point to ponder in this section is: does corruption cause insecurity or, is it a threat to security in general, and specifically, in Africa? I have argued that corruption weakens democratic institutions. It is these very institutions which have to operate to engender positive development results. But exactly what is security and what is human security? Why does it matter at all in the context of peace and development?

Human security is a complex concept. Its relevance to peace cannot be overemphasised. I share and appreciate the views of Dowdeswell who aptly argued that

> the battle of peace has to be fought on two fronts.[8] The first is security front where victory spells freedom from fear. The second is the economic and social front where victory means freedom from want. Only victory on both fronts can assure the world of an enduring peace.

While I want to avoid introducing the concept of development at this stage, the sentiments expressed by Dowdeswell above undergird the essence of combating corruption as an enemy number one of human security in whatever form and meaning it ought to be understood.

A closer examination of the literature suggests a big shift in thinking where "human security" has moved from the traditional "national security" through military security intervention to focusing on "global vulnerabilities."[9] This paradigm shift has seen the narrative of "human" security having a combined focus on the human rather than the national. The 1994 *UNDP Human Development Report* was very instrumental in coining the idea. Unsurprisingly, in 2005, the former and late UN Secretary General, Mr Kofi Annan, produced a report "*In Larger Freedom: Towards Development, Security and Human Right for All.*" Not only did the report trigger new reforms within the UN system, but it also ushered in new ways of thinking about the human condition and, this time, using "sustainable ways." It is from this rethinking of the notion of security, human security, and sustainable human security that, today, we talk of "sustainable development goals."

In his article "*The Many – headed Hydra: How Grand Corruption Robs Us of A Sustainable Future,*" Mathews Jenkins argues that "there can be no sustainable development where corruption thrives, yet it is all too easy to find examples of high-level public officials implicated in corrupted schemes resulting in the gross misappropriation of public funds or resources."[10] However, the achievement of this is dependent on our understanding of what human security entails.

The metamorphosis of the notion of human security has been rapid. Since 1994, the concept has had different underpinnings, but overall, human security is about the protection of the vital core of human lives in ways that uphold and enhance human freedoms and fulfilment. These are freedoms at the centre of life. In other words, placing an individual at the centre of analysis – meaning that whatever the case, attention has to be paid to their survival, livelihood, and dignity. It is therefore out of this critical analysis that scholarly work agrees that human security should and must ensure that it integrates three freedoms: freedom from fear; freedom from want; and freedom from indignity. In a nutshell, two fundamental issues emerge out of these principles – that of "protection" and "empowerment." These two are key strategies which can be used to achieve the ends.

Having established that one of the roles of the state is to protect, it follows, therefore, that the key to protecting people is to remove "unfreedoms" – elements that stand in the way of progress. The state, as the public institution, has to shield people from menace. It means a deliberate effort to employ a 'top-down' approach where state structures can intervene in a timely manner where ordinary people encounter threats to their lives like, for example, natural disasters, conflicts, and diseases, just to mention a few. In a way, such protection may not be a sole responsibility of a state but a concerted effort with stakeholders. Similarly, human security is also about "enabling" people to develop their own resilient mechanisms to cope with difficult situations.

Unlike "the protection" strategy where the approach is top-down, the empowerment strategy will have to be a "bottom-up" – by building people's capacities and creating the so-called enabling environment for people to solve their own problems as it is the case that corruption has a domino effect, so too is human insecurity. For example, if corruption is rife in any public or private space, it will rob people of their dignity. A good example is the lack of medicine in the hospitals or, better put, poor health care. A sick nation cannot produce. This will lead to other forms of insecurity-food insecurity, economic insecurity, personal insecurity, community insecurity, and, ultimately, political insecurity. A closer look at these "insecurities", we can argue that corruption attacks "development" in a subtle manner. The section that follows attempts to explain the linkages between corruption and development.

Corruption Against Nature

We have so far firmly established that corruption has an adverse effect on the functionality of public as well as private organisations. Corruption corrodes peace. More importantly, corruption creates a variety of insecurities. However, over the past decade, there has been an increased interest in understanding the link between corruption and nature – where "nature" is used to connate the "environment."[11] Nature sustains humanity and if there is one thing that humans have to take seriously are the effects of corrupting the environment.

As argued by Domas, "society's development is built among other things, on the environment. Indeed, natural resources are production inputs, but simultaneously, they are elements of nature. Furthermore, the environment is at the centre of where we live and thrive. Hence, an imbalance of nature affects development possibilities and societies, not to mention animals, plants and other biotic elements" (link). A Wildlife and Forest Crime Resources Ella-Micallef makes reference to the 2019 World Bank Report which estimates that the true economic impact of illegal logging, fishing, and wildlife trade is estimated to be more than US$1 trillion.

Grand corruption in which laws and regulation are shaped by corrupt actors who benefit from the laws and regulations can have grave consequences for the environment and its protections. For example, the extractive industry, tourism, and the construction of resorts in megacities have direct connections to high-profile public (government) officials who are custodians of policies that are supposed to guide such projects. Not only do those people involved in them pounce on weak environmental regulations, but they also fail to regulate the laws through regulatory enforcement. This is typical where regulations are strong on paper but weak in practice as witnessed when government officials ask for bribes in exchange for approval, for example, of opening up land which is supposed to be under environmental protection.[12]

A 2020 study by Yahaya, Mohd-Jali, and Raji, in eight sub-Saharan countries, explored the effects of corruption on financial development projects and environmental degradation using "fully modified ordinary least square" (FMOLS) and concluded that corruption, along with interaction with financial development, do have a positive and significant influence on environmental degradation.[13] Other studies on carbon emission have also cast a shadow of doubt on environmental sustainability as a result of failure to follow regulations either by choice or through negligence to enforce rules that allow compliance.[14] This has been evident in Zimbabwe, South Africa, Malawi, the Democratic Republic of Congo, and Mozambique where corruption has been reported to be on the increase and worsening – an indication that the decay in moral and ethical conduct is not only an issue of economics but also a direct attack on all efforts geared to enhance environmental sustainability and protecting the biodiversity.[15]

The battle for wildlife has further put the discourse on corruption and nature in sharp focus when headlines like these are in the media: "*British soldier dies in Malawi during ant-poaching operation*"; "*Another day, another dead wildlife ranger. Where is the outrage?*"; "*The price of protecting Rhinos*". As if this is not enough, similar headlines are also common in the extractive industry where illegal mining activities are rife – signalling weaknesses in the industry. In fact, in Malawi, a 2021 study by Haundi, Tsokonombwe, Ghambi, Mkandawire, and Kasambara affirms this occurrence. What is striking is that, despite irrefutable evidence of the positive effects of systematic mining controlled by the government, nothing is being done to safeguard the numerous sites across the country.[16] In their conclusion, Haundi et al. note that the "Lack of clear information on whether a country allows artisanal small-scale mining (ASM) or not, and the underlying conditions regardless of land titles and mining licenses, speak volumes of how the sector is marginalised."[17] Not only has the state lost control before it has fully started but this highlights the fragility of the potential damage to nature and environment due to weak legislative landscape.

Corruption and Development

So far I have argued that nature sustains development efforts. The ecosystem of nature is where development thrives, and hence, any attempts to disturb this ecosystem create disequilibrium which eventually affects other development efforts. But what exactly is development and how does corruption affect development?

Development means different things to people. It is context-specific. I want to start defining development from the conceptualisation of security. Robert Chambers (1997) defines development as "good change." However, what is "good" is relative and problematic.[18] Others have argued that development is about closing the gap on inequality.[19] As we discussed in the previous section, there is an inextricable link between corruption and human security. Likewise, the link between development and human security cannot be overemphasised. Development is about freedoms; it is about social justice and the fulfilment of human dignity. A nation that is poor, hungry, sick, and destitute is in perpetual vulnerability that leads to all sorts of unfreedoms and insecurities.

On 4 December 1996, the United Nations General Assembly Resolution 41/128, and in Article 1, paragraph 1, clearly stipulates that "the right to development is an inalienable human Right by virtue of which every human person and all peoples are entitled to participate in, contribute to, and enjoy economic, social and political development, in which all human rights and fundamental freedoms can be fully realised." A meander through the various provisions in the declaration requires states to take steps towards eliminating obstacles to development resulting from the failure to observe civil and political rights, as well as social and cultural rights (article 6, para 3). Crucial to this article is the "removal of obstacles." In the current debate, corruption is one of the critical obstacles standing in the way of development. This point takes us back to my point where not only is development about protecting the vulnerable but also about empowerment of ordinary people to "holding the giants to account."[20] Furthermore, empowerment, in this context, is also aimed to enhance the active participation of ordinary people – "active" in the sense of saying "no" to top-down and pre-determined decisions that affect their lives. It is only if this is done that corruption will be under constant check.

Case Studies

There is no doubt that the conversation on corruption is always disturbing because of the fact that such a topic hinges on moral and ethical discourses. In this section, I want to highlight a few examples that offer a sense of discomfort among a set of non-state actors in various parts of the world. Of course, the "state" has always been the centre of analysis and, this is where we miss the gist of corruption. In the current case, I highlight a case in Malawi – that of an NGO in the development sector.[21] A critical analysis of the case study which, to me, is a highly reputable International NGO, signals what I have argued as "structural" failures in the NGO sector.[22] Oftentimes, the leadership of the NGO sector in Africa lacks a solid theoretical foundation in development issues in general. This lacuna not only sets a fertile ground for failure but also creates a vacuum for governance issues, one of which is how to strengthen oversight on various aspects of the operations of an organisation. A highlight of Sandbrook's "warning Signals" is a common theme in structural setups in development discourse as outlined in Table 7.1.

A close analysis of Sandbrook's model of "corruption chameleon" has shed more light on a number of salient issues that are common not only in the NGO sector but also in both the public, private, and third-sector organisations. It is also evident that what is emerging is a framework common to the corruption debater where money, opportunistic tendencies, self-interests – in other words, "greed," issues of entitlement, among others, are dominant.[23] Going through the "warning signs," we can discern a correlation between state-controlled entities and the private sector, insofar as corruption is concerned. On the one hand, there is a clear

Table 7.1 Warning Signals in an International NGO in Malawi

No.	*Warning Signs*	*Examples*
1	`Inadequate governance mechanisms and no clear accountability structure.	Facility heads were not involved in the budgeting process, or provided with financial information relating to the performance of their facilities.
2	All powers rests with one or a small member of persons.	Disproportionate power was retained by key National Office no staff, in particular, the Financial Controller (FC) (and a lesser extent, the Country Director).
3	All tasks related to money are centralised to one or a small number of staff members.	Centralised accounting system predominantly controlled by the FC at NO level, with little segregation of power.
4	The Head of Finance has inadequate formal qualifications and lacks experience.	FC held a certificate only, and appeared to lack the skills set required to properly fulfil his duties.
5	The reports are late and unclear	Monthly facility heed reports were extremely superficial, and were only provided when specifically asked for. Deadlines tended to be missed, needing constant reminders from the CD
6	The project budget is . . . . and is difficult to relate planned activities.	While an annual budget was prepared, it was based on an incremental increase, and was not linked to any facility or overall national action plans.

Source: Sandbrook 2012, p. 110

evidence that power and control are at play while, on the other, issues of elitism are equally embedded in a web of relationships.

Furthermore, it also seems clear that corruption, at least in this case, is enhanced in the deliberate distortion of information – again, an issue exceedingly common in many parts of the world which, if not well guarded, makes those in positions of power, more powerful in their attempt to safeguard their positions and malpractices while, on the other, more powerless because of their inability to uphold principles of integrity, accountability, and transparency.[24] While such people are in positions of power, and due to their inability to act accordingly, they become powerless. This is where monitoring and evaluation matters most. At the same time, the model has also revealed the subtleties of power where it is not only about the elite but also how vulnerable institutional systems are, and the need for greater clarity on how rules and regulations can be enforced at all levels of public and private systems.

Another very important point to make regarding the "corruption chameleon" is to understand the changing nature of corruption as a system. Reflecting on this case study brings to the fore an issue, which basically underscores the point that people will always find an escape route when accountability and transparency are implemented at an institutional level where corruption is rampant. This is where human behaviour is at play and is (behaviour) in a state of flux.

Not going too far, over the past few years, Malawi has been under the spotlight of media attention due to common occurrences of corruption cases. Lameck

Masina of Voice of America (VoA) News of 10 August 2021 carried a news article titled "*Malawi's Corruption Monitor Arrests Cabinet Minister, Two others officials over fuel deals*." Similar news by the same source and authors appeared in a newspaper of VoA of 8 August 2022 headed – *Former Anti-Corruption Chief arrested over graft*." These sorts of headlines and, many more, are a daily occurrence in Malawi. While the discourse does not need any amplification in this chapter, the little snapshots are a testimony to the complexity of the matter and affirm what many commentators have made reference to as "Like Chameleon."[25] In essence, meaning that corrupt behaviour changes and/or mutates to ensure the truth is obscured and the status quo is maintained by the few. Perhaps the question we ought to be asking is, where does all this lead to? I will attempt to address this next.

Conclusion

In this chapter, I have attempted to demonstrate the linkages between the concepts of corruption, security, development, and peace. The "trio" of peace, development, and security is perhaps easier to understand as, aptly demonstrated, one cannot exist without the other. However, standing in the way of all these is our enemy number one – corruption. If there is anything, combating corruption is like attempting to relocate a cemetery where the "inmates" do not cooperate. As I have already alluded to earlier, corruption must now be looked at from a different analytical lens. For me, the behavioural analysis approach is more suited to the debate than anything else. It may look like a tall order given the various attempts using well-researched ways.

Anti-corruption attitudes have changed significantly over the past two decades. It is no longer regarded as a subject to be avoided, but rather to bring it to the mainstream debates. I think this is why the topic has attracted the attention of other stakeholders, neither am I suggesting that we have to abandon all efforts. Furthermore, the view of the private sector in the corruption equation is changing as well. Companies are no longer viewed only as facilitators of corruption – they are increasingly recognised as victims and a valuable source of working solutions, and anti-corruption efforts are seen as integral to good corporate governance, unless there is a special medium of communicating messages to curb such behaviours. This takes me to the issue of education. Nothing, in my view, matters unless "education" is considered to be a key driver in fighting corruption. Sadly, though, the contradiction is that perpetrators of corrupt behaviour are people who have gone to school. So, one may argue, how would education work? Anti-corruption education is much more than just having corruption issues promulgated through teachers and books. It will require the high-level effort of transformation of human behaviour while anti-corruption campaigns go on.

Notes

* Deputy Vice Chancellor, Malawi University of Science and Technology

1 Ikupong Cletus, Theories of corruption and their applications in business environment. *Journal of Innovation in Accounting and Information Management*, 2022, 6(2): 42–48,

p. 1; Julien Joly, Addressing the nexus between corruption and conflict through Security sector reform. https://ti-defence.org/security-sector-reform-west-africa-corruption-conflict/, 2021.

2 Barney Warf, Geographies of African corruption. *PSU Research Review*, 2017, 1(1), 20–38.

3 Kempe R. Hope and Bornwell C. Chikulo, *Corruption and development in Africa*. London: Macmillan Press, 2000, p. 17.

4 Emmanuel P. Clocte, *A critical analysis of the relationships between political transformation and corruption*, 2013. Doctoral Thesis. University of Free State. https://scholar.ufs.ac.za:8080/bitstream/handle/11660/927/CloeteEP.pdf?sequence=1&isAllowed=y

5 N. Bignotto, Corrupção e Opinião Pública. In: Leonardo Avritzer, & Fernando Filgueiras. (Orgs.), *Corrupção e sistema político no Brasil*. Belo Horizonte, MG: Editora UFMG, 2011, pp. 15–42.

6 Murat Sofuoglu, *Why war and corruption, conflict are inseparable*, 2021, TRT World; Koechlin Lucy, Conceptualising corruption, conflict, and cities in Africa: Towards a typology of urban political articulation. Basel Papers on Political Transformations #9.https://ethnologie.philhist.unibas.ch/fileadmin/user_upload/ethnologie/Publikationen/Basel_Papers_No_9.pdf, 2015

7 As above.

8 Elizabeth Dowdeswell, Sustainable development, security and the United Nations. *Irish Studies in International Affairs*, 1996, 7, 25–30, 20.

9 Alexander Lautensach & Sabina W. Lautensach (eds.) *Human security in World Affairs: Problems and opportunities*. Prince George, Canada: UNBC and Victoria, Canada: BCcampus, 2nd edition 2020, https://opentextbc.ca/humansecurity/; Garry King & Christopher Murray, Rethinking human security. *Political Science Quarterly*, 2001, 116(4), 585–610.

10 Mathews Jenkins, The many-headed hydra: how grand corruption robs us of a sustainable future, 2019, www.transparency.org/en/blog/the-many-headed-hydra-how-grand-corruption-robs-us-of-a-sustainable-future

11 Kelsey Landau & Joseph Glandory, *Corruption is a Threat to Planet Earth*, 2020; Avik Sinha, Monica Gupta & Mohammad Shahbaz, Tuhin Sengupta Impact of corruption in public sector on environmental quality: implications for sustainability in BRICS and next 11 countries. *Journal of Cleaner Production*, 2019, 232, 1379–1393.

12 Jamie Sommer, Corrupt actions and forests loss: a cross-national analysis. *International Journal of Social Science Studies*, 2018, 6(10), 23–34.

13 Nura S. Yahaya, Mohd Razan Mohd-Jali & Jimoh O. Raji, The role of financial development and corruption in environmental degradation of Sub-Saharan African countries. *Management of Environmental Quality*, 2020, 31(4): 895–913. https://doi.org/10.1108/MEQ-09-2019-0190

14 Reza Akhbari & Mehd Nejati, The effect of corruption on carbon emissions in developed and developing countries: empirical investigation of a claim. *Heliyon*, 2019, 5(9): 1–9, e02516

15 Fortune Ganda, The influence of corruption on environmental sustainability in the developing economies of Southern Africa. *Heliyon*, 2020, 6, e04387 https://doi.org/10.1016/j.heliyon.2020.e04387

16 Tiyamike Haundi, Gift Tsokonombwe, Steven Ghambi, Theresa Mkandawire & Ainsley Kasambara, An investigation of the socio-economic benefits of small-scale gold mining in Malawi. *Mining*, 2021, 1, 19–34. https://doi.org/10.3390/mining1010003

17 Tiyamike Haundi, Gift Tsokonombwe, Steven Ghambi, Theresa Mkandawire & Ansley Kasambara, "An Investigation of the Socio-Economic Benefits of Small-Scale Gold Mining in Malawi," *Mining*, 2021, 1(1): 19–34, 24.

18 Robert Chambers, *Whose reality counts? Putting the first last*. London: Intermediate Technology Publications, 1997.

19 Jonathan Makuwira, *Non-Governmental development organisations and the poverty reduction agenda: The moral crusaders*. London: Routledge, 2014; Jonathan Makuwira, Development? Freedom? whose development and freedom? *Development in Practice*, 2006, 16(2): 193–200. Linje Manyozo, The day development dies. *Development in Practice*, 2010, 20(2): 265–269; Wolfgang Sachs, Introduction. In: Wolfgang Sachs (ed.) *The Development Dictionary: A Guide to Knowledge as Power*. London: Zed Books, 1992, 6–25.

20 Noore Siddiquee & Md Gofran Faroqi, Holding the giants to account? Constraints on NGO accountability in Bangladesh. *Asian Journal of Political Science*, 2009, 17(3), 243–264.

21 Jeremy Sandbrook, The corruption chameleon: A case study of corruption within a Malawian NGO. MPhil Thesis, Massey University, 2012. https://mro.massey.ac.nz/bitstream/handle/10179/4014/01_front.pdf?sequence=2&isAllowed=y

22 Makuwira 2014.

23 M. Gibelman & S. R. Gelman, Very public scandals: An analysis of how and why non-governmental organisations get in trouble. Working paper presented at the International Society for Third Sector Research (ISTR), Fourth International Conference, Dublin, Ireland, 2000.

24 Deborah Ajulu, *Holism in Development: An African Perspective on Empowering communities*. New York: World Vision Publication, 2001.

25 Gerhard Anders, Like chameleons: Civil servants and corruption in Malawi. https://journals.openedition.org/apad/137, 2002

Part II

Do Not Feed Greed: Grand Corruption in Africa

8 What's in It for Me? Fraud and Corruption in Public Procurement

*Johan J. Coetzee**

Introduction

Africa is a continent where the Fourth Industrial Revolution depends on primary resources. For the efficient extraction of primary resources for the benefit of Africans, existing procurement systems are lucrative for exploitation by foreign companies and Africans. It is critical that African countries transform their procurement systems to reap the benefits of this revolution and to fast-track the development of the continent. Procurement is one of the most strategic public functions. It involves the buying and delivering of goods required for public services. If provided in a transparent, indiscriminatory and goal-oriented manner, procurement enables large capital-intensive infrastructure to be realised such as the provision of airports and roads, which are essential for the private sector to conclude transactions and show a profit. Procurement is critical for delivering social services and increasing the comprehensive socio-economic security of citizens.

However, experience has shown that public procurement contracts often do not translate into implementation, are not transparent enough, and do not make provision for failure. With several decision-makers involved in the procurement process, it is not uncommon that no one accepts accountability or liability. Politicians and public office bearers often abuse their powers for personal gain. Checks and balances are often circumvented, and conflict of interest is not disclosed.[1]

This chapter aimed to identify the most common contributors to corruption in procurement and to develop goal-oriented and innovative turnaround strategies for African countries. The research design in this chapter is based on systems-thinking methodologies, specifically the soft systems approach. The meta-assumptions associated with this methodology are based on the following: Within the context of a country as an open system, interactions in procurement and related system(s) follow a network structure of interdependent relations. For example, a change in procurement policy can contribute to several changes in anti-corruption strategies.[2]

Contributors to Corruption in Procurement

Due to the inherent weaknesses of colonialism (such as a complete disregard for human rights and dignity), traditional cultures (associated with autocratic

DOI: 10.4324/9781003326649-10

leadership), and liberation movements (radicalism and terrorism), neither colonial nor traditional regimes nor liberation struggles prepared Africans for sustainable governance. Political elites have centralised power and facilitated a plethora of manifestations of corruption, for example, bid rigging, contract-splitting, and the sale of bidding documents. Kleptocrat-crafted project cost overruns that manifest in sub-standard specifications and contracts are planned to fail.[3] "Tenderpreneurs"[4] facilitate bids with minimum value addition. To understand the ease with which procurement corruption is possible, it is crucial to understand the contributors to corruption.[5]

Access to Scarce Resources and Opportunities

Corruption creates scarcity – scarcity of access to services, scarcity of service providers to provide goods, and scarcity of opportunities to compete in a market by limiting competition for tendering.[6] Scarcity and general feelings of inequality in society affect the nature of competition for access to scarce resources for profiteering, such as tenders, minerals, and business rights. Access to scarce opportunities can become a motivator for gaining political and/or economic power. Benefitting from such opportunities occurs through the abuse of power and 'greasing the wheels' during tendering.

Centralisation of Power

In developing countries, once a party seizes power, it creates monopolies by gaining control of institutions, appointments and tenders. Centralisation of power creates opportunities for ruling parties to control and increase their hold on power and the benefits resulting from such abuse, evidenced in, for example, the allocation of tenders. In such a culture, where institutions and systems of the state are weakened, organised syndicates deliberately infiltrate strategic components, such as procurement, customs and excise, and the police service.

Procurement, being one of the strategic institutions, is important, because the levels of organised crime and public sector corruption are determined by the quality of what can be called "central state institutions."[7] Centralisation of power over decades by African governments has contributed to extremely powerful governments.

Poor Planning, Schedule, and Cost Overruns

The following discussion will deal with the causes of schedule and cost overruns of megaprojects in the energy sector in South Africa, one of the largest economies in Africa. Then, the focus will shift to Namibian projects to highlight some lessons learnt. Namibia is consistently rated annually by Transparency International (TI) on corruption and governance as one of the top six least corrupt countries in Africa. If the current situation in procurement in Namibia is illustrative of some of the better procurement practices in Africa, one may deduce that in most other African countries, procurement practices are much worse.

The focus of this discussion now falls on some South African projects. The first is Medupi–Kusile where two coal-fired power plants are being built in South Africa under the auspices of ESKOM, a public power producer and supplier. The initial planned completion date of these projects was 2014/15 and then moved to 2023.[8] The initial project cost estimate for the project was ZAR81 billion (US$). However, the project cost in March 2021 had risen to ZAR 300 billion: ZAR145 billion for Medupi and ZAR161 billion for Kusile.[9] The difference between the initial project cost of ZAR81 billion and the March 2021 cost equates to a cost overrun of 370 per cent. Because the project has not been completed, this percentage is likely to increase.

Reasons for the schedule and cost overruns include the following: "slow decision making, shortages of skilled labour, inaccurate material estimating, unforeseen ground conditions, poor material planning, changes in scope of work on-site, contractual claims, variation orders and poor site management."[10] The top five challenges include "poor site management, inadequate managerial skills, poor monitoring and control, unstable management structure, and lack of experience together with poor organisation structures." All these findings are management – and organisationally-related. Tshidavhu and Khateli deduced that "there is not enough local management and organisational expertise in South Africa to ensure the proper planning and effective implementation of energy megaprojects."[11] However, neither their literature nor their survey questions included an investigation into possible political influence. Due to cadre deployment by the ruling party, the African National Congress (ANC), several professionals, including engineers, have left ESKOM since 1994. The political contribution factor to cost and schedule overruns could be relevant here because of cadre deployment.[12]

From an analysis of all sources cited in this section, the following key contributors to the cost overruns at Medupi–Kusile emerge: dysfunctional internal and external auditors, inadequate managerial skills, unstable management, lack of experience, design flaws of the boilers, poor site management, high turnover of project and site managers, corruption in contract amendments, years of extensive delays, ESKOM staff resignations due to alleged corruption not being investigated, poor monitoring and control of projects, and finally, the mismanagement of funds. South Africa's neighbour, Namibia, is dealing with related challenges in water and energy projects. The planned cost of the Neckartal dam increased from ZAR/N$ 900 million to ZAR/N$ 3.5 billion. The Walvis Bay Petroleum facility project cost increased from a planned ZAR/N$ 950 million to more than ZAR/N$ 3 billion. The project cost overrun of the Neckartal dam is 389 per cent and the Walvis Bay petroleum facility 316 per cent. Against the backdrop of a Namibian government budget of less than ZAR/N$ 60 billion, these cost overruns do have huge opportunity cost implications.

As in energy and water, road construction in Namibia is also tainted with schedule and cost overruns. Kruger, a Namibian consulting civil engineer who specialises in road construction projects and has executed projects in the Democratic Republic of the Congo (DRC), Angola, Kuwait, and Saudi Arabia, states that in Namibia, schedule and cost overruns since Independence in 1990 have become the norm.[13]

Checks and balances for completing projects on time and within budget have been watered down since 1990. Project Control Engineers (PCE), appointed in charge of large road construction projects, were appointed without adequate expertise, and often without experience in road construction. For example, the Windhoek–Okahandja double-lane highway of 70 kilometres (km) is being built at a cost of N$78 million/km. The going rate for a single-lane road is N$8/km. The amount of traffic on this road does not justify the cost of what can be called a 'dream road'. Currently, all public road construction projects have schedule and cost overruns running into hundreds of percentages.

If one analyses the bidding and tendering processes of road construction projects, the problem starts with specifications written in such broad terms that they are open to manipulation. The weighting attached to technical specifications versus other specifications, for example, financials, is often changed to favour a specific tenderer with connections to a public official in charge of a specific tender. After the technical evaluation and during the bidding process when cost estimation is requested from bidders, information about the cost of a specific tenderer is often leaked to competitors by a public official in a tender office in exchange for undue benefits.

For project funding, external loans are generally secured from the Export-Import (EXIM) Bank of China. Conditions of such loans include the fact that Chinese State-Owned Enterprises (SOEs) must be allowed to tender. Such Chinese SOEs are controlled by a holding company. These companies collude in price fixing. The EXIM Bank does not have strict control measures for releasing funds at different project stages, because the more a borrower is indebted, the more advantageous it is for China. However, the African Development Bank (ADB), which is seldom used for funding Namibian road construction projects, has strict control measures such as processes for verification of project progress before releasing funds as well as for auditing before they release money directly to contractors and not to governments, thereby limiting cost overruns and corruption.

For purposes of this discussion, it is appropriate to focus on Namibian public contracting in general. In terms of procuring and tendering of, among others, radar equipment requiring extreme accuracy in technical specifications, clear and transparent contract specifications must be available to all bidders. These include the evaluation criteria as well as the weightings of such criteria and the ratios attached to such weightings. Kruger indicated that there is often inconsistency in the evaluation of tenders by the Procurement Board, which is the centralised authority for evaluating and approving public tenders of Offices/Ministries/Agencies and SOEs. Any small inconsistency often creates a loophole for manipulation.

In an online survey initiated on behalf of the present author, members of the Construction Industry Federation (CIF)[14] of Namibia were asked the following questions by the Managing Director of the CIF, Bärbel Kirchner: 'Are you aware of any bribery taking place?' and 'Can you give examples of bribery that has taken place?' They responded that tender officials award tenders to companies for a bribe of 2–3% of the contract value. As an example, in 2014, a contractor received a tender for executing work for a Regional Council despite the tender being ZAR/N$

1.2 million more expensive than the closest bid. The owner of the successful company contacted a member of the CIF and asked his company to execute the tender on his behalf for ZAR/N$500,000 more than the amount the unsuccessful company had tendered for. Being N$1.2 million more expensive enabled the successful tenderer to make a profit of ZAR/N$500, 000 for himself, with ZAR/N$200, 000 going to corrupt official(s).

One CIF member commented that he knew of an official in the Ministry of Finance who requests payment to process documents. Without bribes, documents are not processed. Another member's tender was rejected, and the feedback received was that the bid price was too high. A signed copy of the same tender was found, revealing that the tenderer had exceeded the going rate by approximately 65%. Some companies pay municipal officials to execute 'favourable' inspections and 'fast approvals'. One member was approached by officials of the Ministry of Works and Transport to provide them with 'cooldrink money'. In return, they would channel 'work' his way. The member did not comply with the request, and he did not receive any work. It is alleged that officials of the Roads Authority approached consulting engineering companies and offered them assurances that certain contracts would be awarded to them if the companies offered kickbacks.[15]

Consultants informed a CIF member about many projects awarded by decision-makers in government which did not comply with technical tender specifications. Front companies pay bribes to public officials. A Chinese company offered a CIF member money for a prospective tender/project. It was clear to the said member that political connections were influential in awarding this tender and future tenders/projects. Some consulting companies are awarded large contracts without these contracts being advertised or treated as open or public tenders. A CIF member said his company does not perform work for the government. The company had applied some time previously to be approved as a contractor. The company was informed that the application was successful. After approval, they received phone calls at least once a month from public officials who wanted to conclude deals if the company would execute work for the government. The company refused to conclude such deals, informing public officials that they were not interested if no official documents were available when tenders were invited. Another member stated that he thought that companies receiving tenders often offer kickbacks to public officials. For example, the contractor was approached with the bribe: 'To ensure you get a contract, you must give us 5% of the tender value'. This happened a day before the tender was adjudicated by the Tender Board.

Corruption occurs if projects are large and numerous, as revenues for bribes increase in proportion to the total amount of money allocated. If projects are technically complex, corrupt payments are easier to hide in one-of-a-kind projects compared with less technical and standardised projects. Illegal payments 'can increase the cost and lower the quality of public works projects by as much as 30 to 50%'.[16] Corrupt bidders persuade public officials to manage an SOE badly to lower its value, and then when such an SOE is privatised due to mismanagement and causing a drain of scarce public resources, they emerge as the successful bidder. Payoffs are not limited to a few thousand dollars but to billions that in turn impact other processes.[17] Winning public contracts and concessions are generally a sphere that is only accessible to large businesses and high-level public officials. The process of concluding and awarding winning contracts creates numerous opportunities for corruption in dealings with politicians and officials.[18]

Although the references in this section are dated, being illustrative of contributors to corruption, they remain relevant. This section illustrates that the bigger capital-intensive infrastructure projects in the energy and water sectors are, the bigger the bribes (also known as payoffs) tend to be.

Manifestations of Corruption in Procurement

Corruption occurs in several forms, known as 'manifestations'. These manifestations mutate continuously. The author's field of expertise is corruption and anti-corruption strategies, and he has identified more than 40 manifestations of corruption.[19] All manifestations are not related to procurement. This section focuses only on some of the most common forms.

Bribery

Bribery is one of the most common forms of corruption. In a bribe, one party (first party) agrees to pay and/or incentivise another party (second party) to do something so that the first party will benefit. Such an agreement is to the disadvantage of society at large, is generally not in writing, is illegal and cannot be used to force the other party to comply. For example, the second party abuses his or her influence so that the first party is awarded a tender, which does not meet specifications. In general, a bribe is paid in advance by the first party to the second party before the second party acts on the request by the first party. A few examples of bribery will be discussed later.

The following investigations and prosecutions by the United States Government provide an indication of the scale of bribery in Nigerian federal procurement. For example, Halliburton was found to have 'channelled' US$182 million to several former Nigerian presidents and officials through an agent in 1994 bid to build a US$2 billion natural gas plant for the Nigerian Government. Although Halliburton faced stiff penalties in the USA for their role in this scandal in Nigeria, no officials fingered in investigations were investigated. In January 2016, the then-Nigerian President demanded that the files be re-opened.[20]

The Airbel Group paid bribes of US$2.1 million to Nigerian customs officials and other public officials in connection with oil exploration contracts. In 2009, an executive of Willbros International admitted to having paid bribes of more than US$6 million to officials in Nigeria's state-owned petroleum corporation to obtain pipeline construction contracts. In 2010, Panalpina World Transport admitted to having paid bribes worth US$27 million to public officials in seven countries, including Nigeria. As the term 'bribe' is a very general and loosely described term, it can also manifest differently. Some of these manifestations are discussed later.

Price Fixing

Although the following citation is mainly based on US legislation, it illustrates the comprehensiveness of price fixing, bid rigging, and market division that occur outside as well as inside Africa. Price fixing is an agreement amongst competitors 'to raise, fix, or otherwise maintain the price at which their goods or services are sold'. Competitors do not have to charge the same price or 'that every competitor in a given industry join the conspiracy'. Price fixing can take numerous forms because any agreement that "restricts price competition violates the law."[21] Price fixing can include several forms that are not always related to procurement corruption.

Bid Rigging and Market Division

If government purchasers obtain goods or services by soliciting competing bids on behalf of competitors who mutually agree (conspire) on prices to increase bids, this process is known as 'bid rigging'.[22] Competitors agree in advance 'who will submit the winning bid on a contract being let through the competitive bidding process'. Like price fixing, not all bidders have to participate in the conspiracy to agree on who will bid at what price. Bid rigging, also known as 'tender fixing', can manifest in many forms. However, bid rigging usually falls into one of several categories which are beyond the focus of this chapter. All forms of bid rigging have an agreement among some and/or all bidders so that the winning bidder is agreed upon before a bid, thereby limiting or eliminating competition. In the market division, competitors divide markets among themselves. For example, competitors decide themselves who will target and who will withdraw from specific customers or types of customers, products, or territories.

Arms, COVID-19, Emergencies, and Other Exemptions

Corruption increases in proportion to higher military spending because such spending is not subject to parliamentary questioning and scrutiny. Corruption also increases in relation to an increase in the percentage of total government spending and in relation to the percentage of increased military hardware procurement. Military spending is a monopoly of the state, and contracts are often concluded in secrecy and under extensive discretionary power. In most parliaments, including in Africa, parliamentarians may not question procurement-spending on military contracts. Since no accountability is required under such blanket coverage, spending on defence and national intelligence are major areas of corruption. It is general practice in defence not to invite tenders and to make use of a single sourcing method of procurement. Procurement of armaments with the protection offered by the secrecy of defence tenders and its large capital-intensive projects is a favourite area of lucrative benefits for individuals active in organised crime.[23]

Military projects and staged emergencies enable exemptions and massive corruption to occur. During the coronavirus disease 2019 (COVID-19) pandemic and often because of poor planning and even 'planned emergencies', medical supplies, for example oxygen, are often exempted from regulations and bought at short notice, based on quotations, without inviting tenders. COVID-19 vaccines are also often bought on an emergency basis. This means that there is extremely limited transparency in the procurement process. An increasing number of corruption cases in procuring items for COVID-19 projects have been recorded.

In Zimbabwe, the former Minister of Health, Obadiah Moyo, was charged with criminal abuse of office over the alleged awarding of an inflated US$60 million contract for COVID-19 supplies at inflated prices to Drax International LLC, without having followed proper procurement procedures.[24] In Uganda, top public officials were arrested for inflating COVID-19 relief food prices and causing government losses in excess of $528,000.[25] In Malawi, several public servants were arrested following a report that unearthed corrupt practices in public procurement of COVID-19 goods and services. These cases are only a fraction of examples illustrating corruption resulting from the COVID-19 pandemic. Manifestations of corruption overlap and cannot be clearly demarcated. This means that effective turnaround strategies cannot be developed to address only one specific manifestation.

Turnaround Strategies

Corruption is a systemic and complex issue that cannot be addressed by a linear (cause and effect) and/or a one-size-fits-all approach and/or strategy. A combination of a state- and citizen-centric approach that is multifaceted and country-specific is proposed by this author in line with the central theme of this book. Political support is paramount if successful reform over the shortest timeframe is to be attained. However, if such political commitment cannot be secured, then an alternative solution is the creation of citizen awareness and activism secured over a longer time.

Back to Basics

From the discussion of mega-infrastructure projects in the energy, water, and road construction sectors, it can be deduced that the basics of procurement and tendering need to be revisited. Contracts should be written with accurate contract specifications which meet exact project requirements. Public officials who leak cost estimations should be brought to justice for this unethical behaviour. The evaluation of tenders should occur against pre-determined criteria and weightings should be included in tender specifications and applied consistently. Project Contract Engineers of large infrastructure projects should have extensive experience in the type of project(s) they manage. Regular internal and external audits should be executed of project phases and schedules prior to the release of funds attached to each phase. The turnaround strategy discussed later will focus on reducing incentives for corruption and increasing the ratio of cost (risks): benefits of procurement corruption.

Litigation, Prosecution, and Conviction

Construction of the Katze Dam, also known as the Lesotho Highlands Water case, was a first for a developing country to take multi-national companies

(MNCs) to court because of tender corruption and to win the case. The Lesotho official in charge of the bid and tender evaluation process had been bribed by several MNCs to facilitate their tenders 'successfully'. Lahmeyer International was fined the sum of US$1.4 million for having bribed the former head of the Lesotho Highlands Water Project.[26] The Lesotho Highlands Water case is a best-practice example of what can and should be done about the corruption of large capital-intensive projects in which MNCs bribe officials in developing countries and Africa.

Companies convicted of corruption should be banned and dissolved to discourage corruption. The Bribe Code (a Nigerian Bill for the Corporate Communication Act), which focuses on personal liability and dissolving companies of convicted owners, is an excellent example of a name-and-shame strategy that extends beyond blacklisting.[27] The Bribe Code proposes that when a company is convicted of corruption, the penalty will be liquidation. For large companies, the penalty will not be liquidation, however, the employment of board members and senior management will be terminated. The shares of principal shareholders will be expropriated to the Treasury. Thereafter, the Board can be reconstituted, and such a public company can continue to operate. Whistleblowers will be protected and rewarded with a percentage of the shares of the liquidated company. The principles of the Bribe Code can be replicated in other African countries, customised in such a way that fits particular contexts.

Based on a study of best practices in reforming four systemically corrupt countries, it was found that to detect corruption, punish the corrupt, and reward whistleblowers, the probability of detection by law enforcement agencies should increase at the same rate as the punishment of corruption.[28] The risks of detection and punishment for the corrupt should always be greater than the possible benefits from corrupt opportunities. Shifting the focus to the prevention of corruption can reduce the temptation of exploiting corrupt opportunities such as bidding and tendering.

Public Awareness, Education, and Community Oversight

In general, civil society is not very actively involved in challenging systems, which contribute to corruption, if Transparency International indices are consulted for any year. Creating public awareness about the opportunity cost of corruption is a mechanism to make civil society aware and to actively demand accountability from government offices and officials. Awareness about the destructive impact of procurement corruption should be raised so that the public can realise what the cost of corruption is in monetary terms. For example, the number of schools and houses that could have been built using any of the project cost overruns discussed in this chapter should be publicised. Citizens should be incentivised to participate in evaluating tenders and auditing delivered goods.

Redress mechanisms and citizen oversight bodies are much-needed mechanisms to institutionalise citizen oversight. Citizens can oversee the opening of tenders, the allocation of tenders, and the auditing of delivered goods. For example, when educational materials and equipment are delivered, parents can oversee the process and verify that what has been quoted for, tendered, and delivered is indeed delivered within the agreed price, specifications, and quality. Citizen oversight can also be increased through creating electronic procurement systems, as discussed later.

E-governance and E-tendering

E-governance is a trend in decision-making where multiple stakeholders, each having their own accountability, can make decisions in a participatory and transparent manner by using electronic platforms, which provide access to all stakeholders. Such mechanisms can provide unlimited public access to legislation, tenders, contracts, and procedures.[29] If tenders are electronically available, this will increase the probability of detection by competitors in cases where tenders have been written to meet a single supplier's specifications. E-tendering can be used annually to simplify the awarding of tenders compared to the physical submission of tenders. Recurring tenders is one form of corruption in procurement that should be eliminated where possible.

In most African countries where public offices have websites, these are usually poorly managed and are rarely updated. Customers still go to public offices to pay manually for services. Such offices cannot receive or register tenders online. In most African countries, public offices' websites are not interactive. If tenders can be received and recorded online, this can enable a revolutionary increase in transparency, reduce tender corruption, and increase trust in procurement and tendering systems. E-tendering can track the bidding process and ensure procedural transparency. Other strategies could include contingency planning for contract failure and enforcing punitive measures. An integrated digitisation approach for e-procurement (electronic) and e-tendering systems to be functional is discussed later.

Digitalisation and Blockchain

To enable e-tendering, digitalisation of data is a must. After digitalisation, only then can blockchain be developed for a specific database application. Blockchain is a decentralised database that links electronic data ledgers between billions of computers. These ledgers record transactions that can be verified and are tamper-proof. Information that can be verified includes the identification of the sender and transactions and contract specifications.[30]

The adoption rate of blockchain is faster than the uptake of the Internet during the 1990s. Blockchain is an institutional technology that will revolutionise institutional infrastructure. Any inventory system can be integrated with blockchain to create country- and African-wide inventory system(s) of all procurement projects, contracts, and tenders. Blockchain can ensure that procurement transactions are cheaper and faster because verification of data is automated, does not rely on manual verification and minimises verification delays. With blockchain, the identity of people who tender can be verified; supporting documents can be submitted. Examples include date received, cost overruns, and authorised changes after contract agreements. Once procurement information is digital and in the most optimised 'block', it cannot be changed. Such a 'block' then becomes the 'gold standard' of digitised procurement information.

Blockchain will reduce fraud in procurement and financial systems.[31] All information about tenders awarded can be made publicly accessible. Blockchain can increase institutional trust in procurement systems and reduce centralised government control. Blockchain can fast-track Africa's sustainable development.

If the African Union (AU) could have the mandate and accountability for coordinating transnational procurement projects such as electricity generation and water supply, integrated electronic procurement systems can be developed to track the progress of such projects and tenders to prevent and reduce corruption. Companies convicted of corruption, having a poor track record, can be blacklisted by the AU, and all procurement and tender authorities can have access to such information. For blockchain to be institutionalised, it requires digitalisation. Such digitalisation is very limited in especially public systems in Africa. Ethiopia has signed contracts with Cardano, a blockchain platform (operating on the principles of sustainability, interoperability, and scalability) to digitalise the Ethiopian education system.[32]

Turnaround strategies for procurement transformation require digitisation and electronic platforms. Hence, in the above discussion of blockchain, it is clear that this institutional technology has the potential to revolutionise systems of supply chain, inventory, accounting, and tendering and can enable radical improvement in transparency, community oversight, and institutional trust.

Policy Reform

Globally, standard project phases are Exploration (E) coined from mining projects, which includes financial closure; Engineering; Processing (P) and Construction; Commissioning (C) which includes Operations; and Exit (E).[33] The acronym EPCC represents these project phases. The government is involved in all project phases of EPCC. For decades, political interference, bureaucracy, poor contract planning, and management by government have led to delays in and failure of projects in Africa. Several examples have been discussed in this chapter to illustrate the government's monopoly in infrastructure development projects. The dominant role of government in especially large capital-intensive infrastructure projects needs to be reduced and the role of the private sector in the project phases should be increased. Only if equity investors are not interested in funding large capital-intensive projects, the government should be allowed to increase its funding role to less than 50 per cent of total funding. These changed roles can be realised by forming joint ventures between the government and the private sector, bringing in joint management of project phases.

In such joint ventures, a managing agent should be introduced who assumes accountability for exploration, processing, and construction, until operations are executed. The standard project framework should be changed to EPCC-M, M – representing management. The government: private sector funding ratio should be changed. Most funding should be provided by the private sector (equity investors) and the government should be a minority shareholder. If the government becomes a minority shareholder, projects can progress much faster and be less prone to political and technocratic delays. If equity investors are the majority shareholders and a competent and trustworthy managing agent is accountable after financial closure, projects can be completed on time, within budget and meeting pre-agreed contract specifications. Policy reform is a prerequisite for making the government a minority shareholder of projects and institutionalising the project phases of EPCC-M.

Global trends in sustainable governance such as value-added and network governance require that a government should facilitate and not necessarily be responsible for project implementation. In network governance, the community should drive the process of overseeing projects. The dominant role of government which contributes to excessive bureaucracy and delays in project implementation should be reduced to a facilitation role.

Regulation Prior to Divesting State Assets

One way of improving project governance is by means of private sector-driven development projects in which the government is a minority shareholder. Privatisation could be an option if it could reduce monopolistic behaviour, increase competition, and reduce prices. However, if corruption is systemic in a country with a small economy and limited competition, privatisation will probably increase corruption. To reduce the probability of such corruption, an independent regulator should guide and monitor the transition towards a transparent privatisation process. It is critical that an independent regulator and regulatory framework should be in place before tendering for the divesting of state assets begins.[34] A transparent legal and regulatory environment should be created, not only for disseminating information and declaring vested interests in managing conflict of interest but also to create transparent procurement systems. The World Bank Procurement Regulations for Investment Project Financing (IPF) Borrowers could be applied.[35] Innovative and effective procurement systems should be developed by African countries with preferably assistance of the African Union that need to assist, which makes use of the 'track record' of contractors for awarding tenders, because contractors with an above-normal ratio of schedule and cost overruns compared with the industry average, are at higher risk of default. A well-organised bidding process should be created. In such a process, tenders should be advertised locally as well as internationally to increase competition. Public institutions should be encouraged to compete with the private sector for the tendering of services. To bring public services up to standard with private sector services, benchmarking can be applied as the United Kingdom Civil Service has done since 1980.

Standardised Products

One way that is used to inflate prices is to deliberately draft contract specifications for non-standardised products that are unique while standardised products are available. Standardised products meet most suppliers' specifications, are open to rigorous competition, are cheaper, and are supplied with fewer delays.

These products should be purchased because they are generally of superior quality and often come with guarantees and/or warranties, which is not true of non-standardised products.

Transforming Strategic Institutions and 'Hot Spots'

Strategic public institutions need to be transformed as part of a public sector reform and/or transformation programme aimed at reducing corruption. Klitgaard called the process of transforming such strategic leverage points 'picking visible low-hanging fruit'.[36] These are the organisational units or components in public service with the largest potential for change; however, these units/components generally resist transformation. Examples are tax and customs offices; budgeting and accounting offices (inventory); procurement (public works and tendering), and social benefits (pension and motor vehicle accident funds). The purpose is to break the recurring negative loops of self-serving organisational behaviour. Other 'hot-spots' of administrative and regulatory control units, where corruption is most often found, include the following: quotas and licences (e.g. fishing, transport, and mining), permits and regulations (e.g. environmental, occupational health and safety, and labour units). Procurement that includes tendering depends on several support functions. Examples are inventory, accounting, auditing, and financial systems, which are also strategic institutions and 'hot spots' of corruption. It is appropriate to conclude that procurement reform can only be successful if it is part and parcel of a comprehensive public service reform and/or transformation initiative.

Subverting the Subversive

Procurement corruption can be attacked by disseminating information that corrupters and corruptees would prefer to keep hidden. Information about the allocation of tenders where bribery, price fixing, and bid rigging prevail can, for instance, be made public. Price fixing, bid rigging, and market division can be avoided by planting 'informers' with the aim of uncovering the corrupt and spreading disinformation to harm bribers and colluders. Informer and covert agents in 'hot spots', such as revenue and tax component(s), customs and excise, police and procurement should observe and report transgressions. These informers and covert agents should be used to spread 'misinformation', for example about bid rigging, to create fear, and/or to provide suspects with leeway for error to 'hang themselves'.

External Reporting

Internal reporting measures of corruption such as a complaint system that is overseen internally are most often not effective because institutions seldom have the ability and commitment to rectify their own failures. However, external reporting measures can be much more effective, if they are overseen by a body operating independently from the institution being reported on. Examples include reporting to an anti-corruption ombudsman and/or agency that is backed and/or protected by strong political support of their independence and overseen by community oversight mechanisms.

To encourage the reporting of transgressions (e.g. bidding, evaluation, and allocation of tenders) whistleblowers should feel secure that they will not face risks such as intimidation, harassment and losing their income as a direct and/or indirect result of such reporting. A reporting mechanism such as external whistleblowing generally carries with it more risks than incentives, especially if those public office bearers are reported to have abused their power in the awarding of contracts and tenders. In bidding, where mega-construction projects are at stake with billion-dollar incentives, it is highly likely that corrupt practices will occur. Based on best practices of whistleblowing, lucrative financial incentives must incentivise reporters. Such incentives must exceed the risks of reporting.[37]

Implementation Challenges

Considering the range of turnaround strategies discussed, one may deduce that for procurement reform to be long-lasting, it should form part and parcel of a comprehensive public service reform and/or transformation initiative. Merely focusing on procurement is unlikely to be effective. Focusing on only one or two turnaround strategies is also unlikely to be effective because, in a systemically corrupt system, a single anti-corruption strategy can have no sustainable impact on the effectiveness of other strategies and can, therefore, be counterproductive in terms of the desired outcome which is to reduce corruption.

The biggest limitation to the implementation of turnaround strategies in reducing corruption in procurement is political commitment. A further limitation is the lack of digitalisation of procurement and supporting systems. Digitalisation is required for implementing e-governance and e-tendering and is paramount for implementing blockchain as infrastructural and institutional procurement technology.

Conclusion

From the above discussion of procurement corruption, it becomes clear that turnaround strategies are a combination of state and citizen-centric approaches. Since political support for a state-centric approach is unlikely, a two-pronged approach increases the probability of sustainable reform and/or transformation. Those in control of government, politicians, and public officials, are most often those who participate in, and benefit from, corruption, and, therefore, also resist turnaround strategies.

If political commitment is not present to reduce procurement corruption, a citizen-centric approach can create and maintain the momentum for change. Creating citizen awareness about the impact of corruption and quantifying it by means of estimating the opportunity cost of corruption cases can assist in educating the public. Civil society should understand the severity of the impact of corruption. Once they are aware of and knowledgeable about the impact, citizens will most often demand accountability from politicians and public officials and initiate community oversight mechanisms.

Blockchain is the institutional infrastructure and technology that can improve and integrate procurement and tender-related systems and enable e-governance and e-tendering. All procurement supporting systems should be revolutionised by adopting blockchain technology to enhance institutional transparency, community oversight, and verification of information. Of all probable turnaround strategies, blockchain technology will have the biggest impact on preventing and reducing procurement corruption in Africa.

The government's dominant role in large capital-intensive infrastructure projects and in controlling all project phases should be changed. The private sector should be the majority shareholder of projects, and joint ventures should be formed between the private sector and the government. In the current standard project planning approach of EPCC, an additional phase should be included, that of managing agent: EPCC – M. This managing agent should be an independent party and should manage projects from the processing phase until the end of the commissioning phase. To conclude, turnaround strategies as discussed in this chapter will enable sustainable project development and reduce procurement corruption and fast-track projects in Africa.

Notes

* Senior Lecturer in the Faculty of Human Sciences at the Namibia University of Science and Technology.

1 Charles Keyter (ed.), Oliver Anton, Thomas Erika, Schwella Erwin, Coetzee Johan, Lwendo Sitali, Sazita Vincent, & Maritz Yrika, *Namibian Governance. A Public Administration and Management Perspective*, Claremont, Juta, 2018, pp. 92–100.

2 Johan Coetzee, *Systemic corruption and corrective change management strategies: A study of the co-producers of systemic corruption and its negative impact on socio-economic development*, unpublished PhD dissertation, 2012, Stellenbosch, University of Stellenbosch <https://scholar.sun.ac.za/handle/10019.1/71904> (accessed on 15 September 2021) 19.

3 A 'kleptocrat' is an autocratic ruler whose goal is personal wealth accumulation by exercising corruption. Susan Rose-Ackerman, *Corruption and Government Causes, Consequences and Reform,* Cambridge: Cambridge University Press, 1999, 114–115.

4 A 'tenderpreneur' is a person who uses their political connections to secure government contracts for personal advantage, <www.lexico.com › definition › tenderpreneur> (accessed 20 December 2021).

5 Susan Rose-Ackerman, *Corruption and Government Causes, Consequences and Reform,* Cambridge: Cambridge University Press, 1999, 114–115.

6 Coetzee, *Systemic corruption and corrective change management strategies,* 68.

7 Edgardo Buscaglia, Samuel Gonzalez-Ruiz & William Ratliff, "Undermining Foundations of Organized Crime and Public Sector Corruption", *Essays in Public Policy* (2005) 114, 10 <https://papers.ssrn.com/sol3/papers.cfm?abstract_id=930988> (accessed on 25 September 2021).

8 Melani Nathan, Falling short: Medupi and Kusile an ESKOM plan designed to fail – Chris Yelland, <www.biznews.com/thought-leaders/2021/03/17/eskom-medupi-kusile-yelland> (accessed on 17 March 2021).

9 Thanduxolo Jika, & Sabelo Skiti, More woes for Medupi Kusile, *Mail and Guardian,* https://mg.co.za/article/2020-03-19-more-woes-for-medupi-and-kusile/ (accessed on 19 March 2020).

10 Fhumulani Tshidavhu, & Nthatisi Khateli, "An assessment of the causes of schedule and cost overruns in South African megaprojects: A case of the critical energy sector projects of Medupi and Kusile", *Acta Structilia* (June 2020) 26(2), 119–120, <http://journals.ufs.ac.za/index.[hp/as> (accessed on 27 August 2021).
11 Tshidavhu & Khateli, "An assessment of the causes of schedule and cost overruns in South African megaprojects, 119–120.
12 William Gumede, Cadre Deployment: Building or breaking a capable state? Catholic Parliamentary Liaison Office (CPLO) South Africa, Webinar series, 22 September 2021 <https://youtu.be/UCLPaMg5MoA> (accessed on 8 October 2021).
13 Hendrik Kruger, Road construction projects, retired and formerly from Namibia Project Managers & Consultants, (Windhoek), interview, 22 September 2021.
14 Construction Industry Federation of Namibia, *Online survey conducted: The Role of the CIF and the private sector in tackling corruption*, 21–23 August 2017.
15 Johan Coetzee, The Role of the Private Sector in Fighting Corruption, *Briefing Paper, Institute of Public Policy Research*, April 2018, pp. 13–14 <https://ippr.org.na/wp-content/uploads/2018/05/Private Sector Tackling Corruption_WEB.pdf> (accessed on 15 September 2021).
16 Susan Rose-Ackerman, The Political Economy of Corruption – Causes and Consequences, *Public Policy for the Private Sector*, The World Bank, (74), 1996, <www.worldbank.org/viewpoint/HTMLNotes/74/74ackerman.pdf> (accessed on 1 February 2004) 3–4.
17 Rose-Ackermann, The Political Economy of Corruption, 19.
18 Rose-Ackermann, The Political Economy of Corruption, 19.
19 Johan Coetzee, Good governance as a conceptual paradigm of institutional reform and transformation, *3rd SAAPAM Limpopo Chapter Annual Conference, Conference Proceedings, Corruption and Democracy in Africa*, 2014, 119.
20 Sope Williams-Elegbe, "Systemic corruption and public procurement in developing countries: Are there any solutions?", *Journal of Public Procurement*, (2018) 18(2), 135 <www.emeraldinsight.com/1535-0118.htm> (accessed on 15 September 2021).
21 United States Antitrust Division New Case Unit, *Price Fixing, Bid Rigging, and Market Allocation Schemes: What They Are and What to Look For. Antitrust Primer*, 2–5 <www.justice.gov/atr/file/810261/download> (accessed on 26 September 2021).
22 United States Antitrust Division New Case Unit, *Price Fixing, Bid Rigging, and Market Allocation Schemes*, 2–5.
23 Coetzee, *Systemic corruption and corrective change management strategies*, 5.
24 *The Guardian*, Zimbabwe Health Minister facing Coronavirus corruption charged sacked, <www.theguardian.com/global-development/2020/jul/09/zimbabwe-health-minister-facing-coronavirus-corruption-charge-sacked> (accessed on 15 September 2021).
25 Halima Athumani, Top Ugandan officials arrested in Covid -19 purchasing scandal, VOA News <www.voanews.com/science-health/coronavirus-outbreak/top-ugandan-officials-arrested-covid-19-purchasing-scandal> (accessed on 15 September 2021).
26 H. (first name unknown) Dembowski, 2003. Lesotho: Lahmeyer International Fined. *Development and Cooperation*, 30(10), October 2003, 359.
27 Chuma Nwokolo, The Bribe Code Rethinking Corporate Corruption (A Nigerian Bill for the Corporate Communication Act), <https://bribecode.org/a-bill-for-the-corporation-corruption-act/> (accessed on 25 September 2021).
28 Johan Coetzee, "Comparative best practices to manage corruption", *Journal for Studies in Humanities and Social Sciences*, University of Namibia (2016) 5(2), 101–110.
29 Coetzee, *Systemic corruption and corrective change management strategies*, 105.
30 Andrew Fenton, Blockchain is as revolutionary as electricity: Big ideas with Jason Potts Magazine by Cointelegraph, 23 August 2021, <https://cointelegraph.com/magazine/2021/08/23/blockchain-is-as-revoluntionary-as-electricity-big ideas-with-jason-potts> (accessed on 24 August 2021).

31 Simplilearn, How to start a career in blockchain technology? <www.simplilearn.com/how-to-start-a-career-in-blockchain-technology-article> (accessed on 27 August 2021).

32 CoinDesk, Cardano in Africa: Inside IOHK's Ethiopia Blockchain Deal, <www.coindesk.com/markets/2021/04/30/cardano-in-africa-inside-iohks-ethiopia-blockchain-deal/> (accessed on 20 September 2021).

33 Abara Ayuk, Peter Nutt, Taburu Colin Uirab & Edwin Igili-Edwards, A Generic Project Approach. Project Consortium Africana, Nigeria South-South Seminar, Windhoek, 23 April 2019.

34 Coetzee, *Systemic corruption and corrective change management strategies* 2, 3.

35 The World Bank, *World Bank Procurement Guidelines for IPF Borrowers*, available at: <https://thedocs.worldbank.org/en/doc/178331533065871195-0290022020/original/Procurement Regulations.pdf> (accessed on 7 October 2020) Fourth Edition, November 2020, pp. 1–142.

36 Robert Klitgaard, *Addressing Corruption in Haiti*, 2010 <www.cgu.edu/PDFFiles/Presidents%20Office/Addressing%20Systemic%20Corruption%20in%20Haiti%20version%202.pdf> (accessed on 13 June 2010) p. 18.

37 Johan Coetzee, "Speaking truth to power: Whistleblower challenges and options. A Namibian perspective", *Journal of Namibian Studies – History, Politics, Culture*, ISSN print 1863-5954, ISSN online 2197-5523, 27, 2020, 91–107.

9 Corruption in Public Service Delivery

Kezzie Mkandawire and Maureen Mwalabu***

Introduction

Corruption is a universal problem with a significant impact in developing nations since resources meant for socio-economic development are times diverted to the benefit of a few corrupt elites, undermining the developmental goals of these nations.[1] Governments have a duty to provide essential services to their populace but the efficient provision of such services is a challenge in many countries due to corruption among other things.[2] Transparency International (TI) broadly defines public service delivery as the provision of services by governments to their citizens.

Public service delivery also encompasses the provision of a wide range of services such as healthcare, education, water and sanitation, identification documents (such as voter registries and passports), telecommunications, licenses, and many other services that governments undertake for the benefit of citizens. This is done either directly through the public sector via public providers or by nongovernment organisations (NGOs) receiving a subsidy from the government for service provision.[3]

As they accomplish their obligations of delivering public services to their citizens, Governments are, at the same time, complying with the requirements of the Universal Declaration of Human Rights (UDHR), which considers access to public services as a fundamental human right, as stated in Article 21(2) of the UDHR that "[e] has the right of equal access to public service in his country," while Article 25(1) emphasises that "[e]veryone has the right to a standard of living adequate for the health and well-being of himself and of his family, including food, clothing, housing, and medical care and necessary social services," and Article 26(1) states that "[e]veryone has the right to education."

Corruption is a major concern today in the delivery of public services for many countries and donors. Wherever money is involved, some corruption will likely occur. For instance, a survey conducted by the Global Corruption Barometer of Transparency International in 2013 revealed that one in four people paid bribes for getting access to the most basic needs.[4] According to Transparency International, certain forms of corruption in service delivery such as clientelism, patronage, and bribery undermine the human right of equal access to public services and exacerbate fundamental inequalities that violate citizens' access, affecting the most marginalised and underrepresented segments of the population the most.

DOI: 10.4324/9781003326649-11

Moreover, rampant corruption can lead to breakdowns in the service delivery chain, preventing the state from fulfilling its obligations to safeguard its citizens, with catastrophic consequences such as a lack of basic medical supplies. This creates a greater divide and inequality in society as the wealthy can afford private services. There is, therefore, a compelling argument to consider the fight against corruption in service delivery as an integral part of the human rights-based approach (HRBA) to development.[5]

This chapter examines six dimensions of corruption in public service delivery, namely; forms of corruption that subsist in public service delivery, factors that promote corruption in public service delivery, and effects of corruption in public service delivery. In addition, it also recommends strategies for curbing corruption as well as means of monitoring and detecting corruption in public service delivery. Finally, it highlights challenges that are likely to be faced when addressing corruption in public service delivery. Throughout the chapter, discussions are restricted to public service delivery in the education, health and water and sanitation sectors as case studies.

Forms of Corruption That Subsists in the Public Service Delivery

Other Forms of Corruption

Table 9.1 shows various forms of corruption that can manifest in public service delivery.

Forms of Corruption in the Education Sector

According to a 2011 UNDP report on fighting corruption in the education sector, corruption in the education sector takes many forms and may occur at national, sub-national, and institutional levels.[6] The examples of corrupt practices in different areas of educational planning and management in Table 9.2 are not exhaustive, but they nevertheless show the range of risk and locus of corrupt practices that have been identified by observers.

Corruption takes many forms in the education sector and occurs at all stages of the service delivery chain, from school planning and management to student admissions and examinations, to academic research, and to teachers' management and professional conduct. There are areas of concerns at the policy formulation stage, as well as the management of organisational resources and the service delivery phases.[7]

Forms of Corruption in the Health Sector

According to Transparency International (2017), all major forms of corruption are present in the health sector, ranging from petty bribery and nepotism to informal payments and mismanagement of resources, absenteeism, and state capture. In many countries, health services are also affected by various forms of clientelism as

Table 9.1 Various Forms of Corruption

Categories of Corruption	*Description*
Bribery	The act of dishonestly persuading someone to act in one's favour by a payment or other inducement. Inducements can take the form of gifts, loans, fees, rewards or other advantages (taxes, services, donations, etc.). The use of bribes can lead to collusion (e.g. inspectors' under-reporting offences in exchange for bribes) and/or extortion (e.g. bribes extracted against the threat of over-reporting).
Embezzlement	To steal, misdirect or misappropriate funds or assets placed in one's trust or under one's control. From a legal point of view, embezzlement need not necessarily be or involve corruption.
Facilitation Payment	A small payment, also called a "speed" or "grease" payment, made to secure or expedite the performance of a routine or necessary action to which the payer has legal or other entitlement.
Fraud	The act of intentionally and dishonestly deceiving someone in order to gain an unfair or illegal advantage (financial, political or otherwise).
Collusion	An arrangement between two or more parties designed to achieve an improper purpose, including influencing improperly the actions of another party.
Extortion	The act of impairing or harming, or threatening to impair or harm, directly or indirectly, any party or the property of the party to influence improperly the actions of a party.
Patronage, Clientelism and Nepotism	Patronage at its core means the support given by a patron. In government, it refers to the practice of appointing people directly

Source: Johnsøn, 2014; World Bank, 2011a in DFID, 2015, 12)

Table 9.2 Forms of Corruption in the Education Sector

Area	*Corruption Practices*
Finance	• Transgression rules/procedures • Inflation of costs and activities in budget estimates • Embezzlement
Specific allowances (fellowships, subsidies, etc)	• Favouritism • Nepotism • Bribes • By passing criteria • Discrimination (political, social ethnic)
Construction, maintenance and school repairs	• Fraud in public tendering • Collusion among suppliers • Embezzlement • Manipulating data • bypass of school mapping • Ghost deliveries
Distribution of equipment, furniture and material (including transport, boarding, textbooks, canteens and school meals)	• Fraud in public tendering • Collusion among suppliers • Siphoning of school supplies • Purchase of unnecessary equipment • Bypass of allocation criteria • Manipulating data • Ghost deliveries

Area	*Corruption Practices*
Writing and assigning of textbooks	• Fraud in the selection of authors (favouritism, bribes, gifts) • Bypass of copyright law • Students forced to buy material copyrighted by instructors
Teacher appointment, management, payment and training	• Fraud in the appointment, deployment, transfers, promotion of teachers (favouritism, bribes, gifts) • Using teachers to campaign for politicians • Where and what type of school to build • Discrimination (political, social ethnic) • Falsification of credentials/use of fake diplomas • Bypass of criteria • Pay delay, sometimes with unauthorized reductions
Teacher/school staff behaviour (professional misconduct)	• Ghost teachers • Absenteeism • Illegal fees (for school entrance exams, assessment, private tutoring, etc.) • Favouritism, nepotism and acceptance of gifts • Discrimination (political, social and ethnic) • Private tutoring (including use of schools for private purpose) • Sexual harassment or exploitation • Bribes or favours during inspection visits
Information systems	• Manipulating data to misrepresent • Selecting/suppressing information • Irregularity in producing and publishing information • Payment for information that should be provided free
Examinations, diplomas and access to universities	• Selling exam information • Examination fraud (personification, cheating, favouritism, gifts) • Bribes (for high marks, grades, selection to specialized programmes, diplomas and admission to universities • Diploma mills and false credentials • Fraudulent research, plagiarism
Institutional accreditation	• Fraud in the inspection and accreditation process (favouritism, bribes gifts)

Source: Fighting Corruption in the Education Sector

personal relationships between patients, doctors, or even key bureaucrats help people gain access to healthcare programmes take the form of patron–client relationships. Corruption can affect all stages of the health service delivery chain, including policy formulation, management of organisational resources and procurement of medical supplies, as well as bribery and extortion at the point of service delivery. Areas that are particularly vulnerable to corruption include the provision of services by medical personnel, human resources management, drug selection and use, procurement of drugs and medical equipment, distribution and storage of drugs, regulatory systems, budgeting, and pricing.

As part of general healthcare reforms in certain regions, other areas of vulnerability include the construction and equipping of new healthcare centres as public–private partnership projects, with specific corruption risks associated with such partnerships.[8] Often, these centres may become hotbeds of corruption when

Table 9.3 Actors in the Health System and Their Involvement in Corruption

Health care providers	• Absenteeism • Theft of drugs and medical supplies • Informal payments to fast track or receive a service • Fraud – pocketing user fees by a service provider or overcharging of a health insurance agency by a physician, collusion between a hospital administrator and a purchasing agent
Government regulators in the pharmaceutical market	• Drug registration and marketing regulation agencies, poorly funded, understaffed and under capacitated • Weak legislation and regulation environment • Lack of transparency and accountability in the regulation processes may necessitate bribery government officials being bribed to register substandard drugs or government officials may deliberately delay registration processes in order to solicit bribes
Procurement of pharmaceuticals and medical supplies	• Manipulation of specifications in favour of a specific supplier • Suppliers bribing procurement officials to gain advantage in the procurement process • Overpayment of products • Procurement of products without a justification
Distribution and storage of drugs	• Poor storage conditions leading to losses or outright theft • Shipments being stolen along the way in the delivery system • Theft by custodians of the drugs
Health budgets	• Lack of oversight over budget performance • Limited budget management systems making budget monitoring to be a challenge • Missing of critical data thereby rendering financial information to be flawed • Weak budget formulation process providing an opportunity for interested parties to

Source: (Hussman 2020)

considering the types of machinery being purchased and used. In other countries, special healthcare programmes (such as prevention, monitoring, and educational programmes) are not available to all, particularly not low-income and indigenous populations.[9] Table 9.3 shows some actors in the health system and how they are involved in corruption.

Forms of Corruption in the Water and Sanitation Sector

In water and sanitation, as shown in Figure 9.1, corruption risks can be grouped into different stages of the water supply chain, from policy formulation to the management of organisational resources and the point of service delivery.[10] As with other public services, corruption can occur at all stages of the water supply chain, from policy formulation to the management of organisational resources and to the point of service delivery.

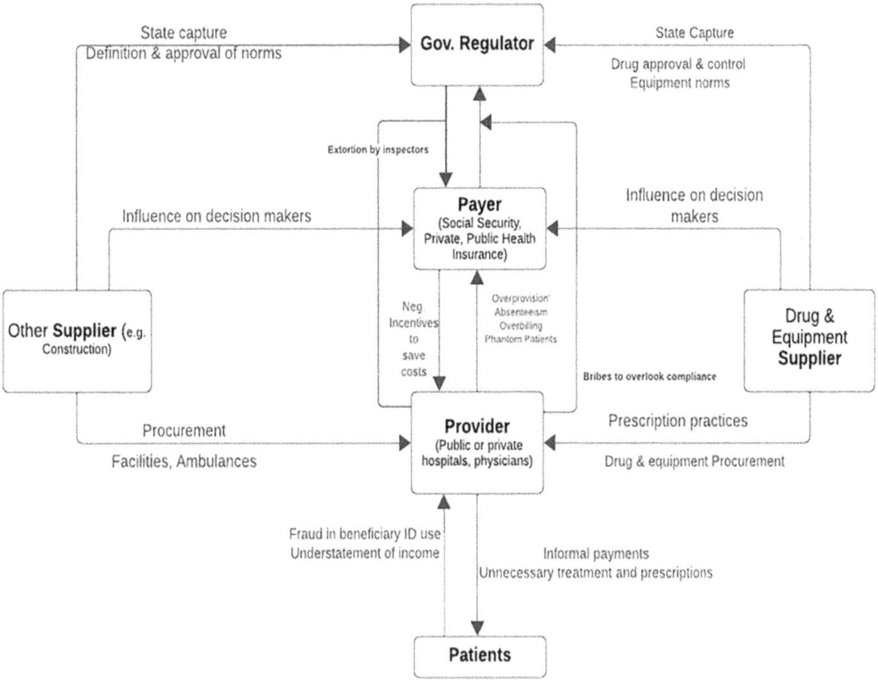

Figure 9.1 Stakeholders in the Health Sector and Corruption Risks

Factors That Promote Corruption in Public Service Delivery

Factors that drive corruption in public service delivery are both intrinsic and extrinsic. This section starts by exploring general factors that promote corruption in public service delivery before providing an overview of factors that provide fertile grounds for corruption to thrive in the education, health and water and sanitation sectors of the public service delivery value chain.

Public Service Delivery Corruption Drivers

Transparency International (2017) singles out the following as some of the general key drivers of corruption in the public service delivery: large-scale investments and significant financial commitments, complex processes and overlapping responsibilities and jurisdictions, scarcity of resources; and composite structures and bureaucracies.[11]

Drivers of Corruption in the Education Sector

In the education sector, the specific corruption drivers include the large sums allocated to the education, monopoly by government in recruitment, redeployment, payroll, and the huge number of human resources employed; and that education is a high-stakes endeavour by governments, parents, and students.[12]

Drivers of Corruption in the Heath Sector

Some of the factors that make the health sector particularly vulnerable to corruption include the vast quantities of resources flowing through health systems, for example, procurement of drugs; the high level of uncertainty of possible patience challenges the predictability of the required supplies and services; asymmetry of information between providers and patients as well as suppliers and providers, especially where physicians prescribe products not based on the patient's need by because of incentives offered by pharmaceutical companies; the complexity and fragmentation of national health systems; and the globalised nature of the supply chain for drugs and medical devices make health systems particularly susceptible to corruption;[13] a large number of actors/stakeholders with limited and/or indirect accountability exist throughout the sector and they interact in complex ways; weak on non-existent rules and regulation, over-regulation, lack of accountability; low salaries; and limited offer of services.[14]

According to the World Bank (2013), a key characteristic that distinguishes education and health services is that these services are determined by provider behaviour; they are discretionary and transaction-intensive, complicating how relationships of accountability for education and health services are structured.

Finally, in the health sector, the distinction between corruption and inefficiency is often difficult to discern due to poor management/administration. Another challenge is that although the issue of accountability is a relatively new area of enquiry in the health sector, desired health gains may be hindered or obstructed completely unless efforts are made to improve accountability and transparency and understand how to prevent corruption within the health system.[15]

Drivers of Corruption in the Water and Sanitation Sector

In water and sanitation, water management typically involves huge infrastructure projects, technical complexity making it difficult for civil society oversight, and incentives for corruption.

Strategies for Curbing Corruption in Public Service Delivery

Service delivery is part of a complex relationship between government, society, and citizens.[16] Complex because it involves various dimensions, it is dynamic, and because the government is itself a complex body.[17] In service delivery, the processes and structures are often complex with overlapping responsibilities and jurisdictions.[18] On the other hand, corruption is multifaceted, characterised by varying economic, political, administrative, social, and cultural factors, and it is a consequence of dynamic relationships between multiple actors.[19]

Therefore, when designing strategies for curbing corruption in public service delivery, it should be borne in mind that the strategies are targeting a complex issue in an intricate setting. This requires a systems-thinking approach, defined as a discipline for seeing wholes, a framework for seeing interrelationships rather than things, and for seeing patterns of change rather than static 'snapshots'.[20] In other words, it is a framework for describing, evaluating, and understanding the elements and relationships that shape the behaviour of a system. Systems thinking focuses on 'qualitative analysis, developing a system map, designing an intervention, and developing an evaluation framework'.[21]

The first step in the systems thinking approach would be to understand public service delivery corruption including the context in which it occurs. This can be done through consultations with all relevant stakeholders and coming up with key issues. The systems map of the complex relationships should be drawn explaining the drivers/enablers and the role of corruption in the system including all the links (refer to Figure 9.2). The third step would be to design the strategies through consultations with various stakeholders including policymakers and users. Finally

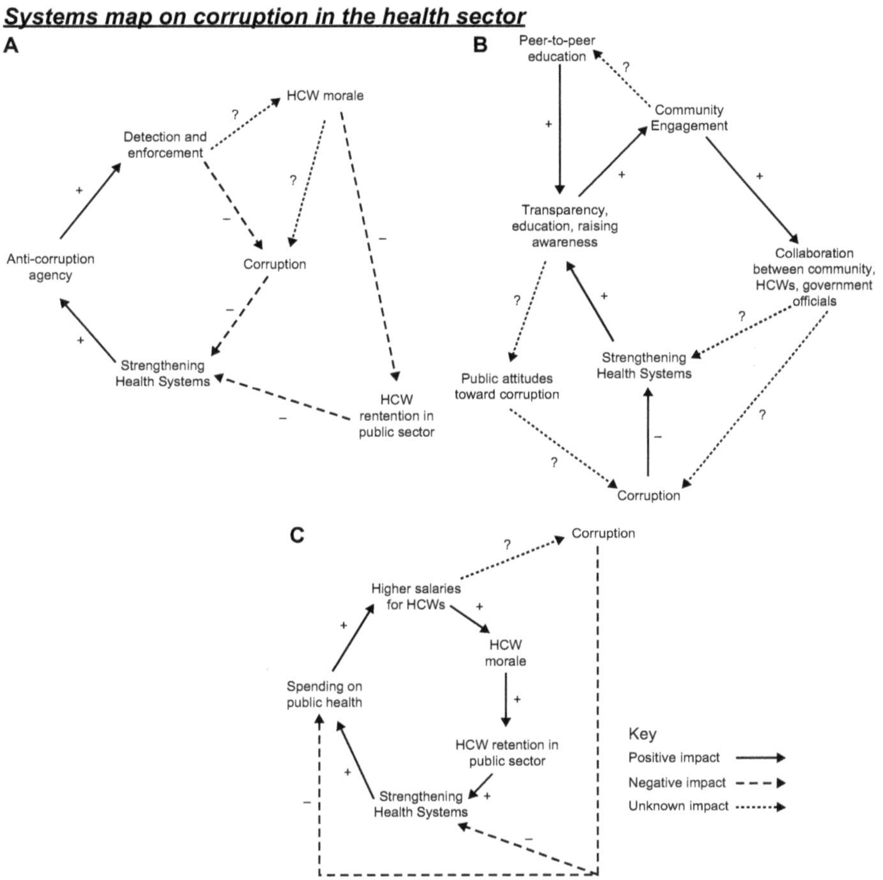

Figure 9.2 A Systems Map on Corruption in the Health Sector

designing an evaluation framework to audit progress in the implementation of the strategies by understanding the types of existing corruption in a sector to devise appropriate and feasible solutions.[22]

All in all, anti-corruption measures are most effective when other contextual factors support them and when they are integrated into a broader package of institutional reforms. Based on the systems-thinking approach, this section, therefore focuses on the key strategies that can be used to address corruption in the public service delivery, but first, it starts by looking at how to assess corruption risks drivers and enablers of corruption.

Preparing for New Measures

To be effective and sustainable, there is a need to consider some basic principles before designing anti-corruption interventions. For instance, sector-specific interventions must be embedded in broader, integrated reform efforts involving large parts of the public sector as well as have adequate data on the corruption problem in the country.[23] In addition, country dynamics and sector contexts must be kept in mind and also that all research, programme design and implementation should take place in close cooperation with government counterparts. Above all, an assessment of the current mindset in the country is critical: to what degree do players in the country respect the rule of law, encourage transparency, act against violations, and exhibit integrity in their own transactions?[24]

Assessing Drivers of Corruption

A first step in curbing corruption is to understand the circumstances that are conducive to corruption. According to Hussman, people are more likely to cross the line between honest and corrupt behaviour when they have an opportunity to misuse their power (in part because the probability of the consequences is low);[25] when they feel pressured or incentivised to do so; and when personal or social beliefs and norms allow them to rationalise corrupt behaviour. As such, before designing corruption mitigating measures, there is a need to assess which of the three risks is prevalent so that interventions can be designed targeting those identified risks in any of the three areas of opportunity to abuse, pressures to abuse and rationalisation or all of them. Hussman also emphasise that corrupt behaviour is more likely in situations where some or all of the following conditions are present:[26]

(a) The agent with entrusted authority has *monopoly powers*. The agent might be the only provider of public services like health services, medical treatment, or medicines and supplies.
(b) Officials have *discretion without adequate control* of their decision-making authority. Such decisions might concern the definition of treatments and drugs to be covered by health insurance, or the prescription of medicines, diagnostic tests, or treatments. Discretion is a complex issue due to the tension between control and medical autonomy.

(c) There is *not enough accountability* for decisions and actions. Accountability comes through the measurement of results and sanctions for non-performance.
(d) *Citizen voice and participation are insufficient* to allow for social control – for example, by generating experience-based data on absenteeism, monitoring drug procurement or hospital construction, or exposing undue influence in regulatory and policy decisions.
(e) *Transparency is lacking*, in the form of active disclosure of and access to information. This affects, for example, the regulation of market access of drugs and medical devices, the prices of medicines, or prescription behaviour.
(f) *Enforcement is weak*. Abuse or corruption is not detected and punished through administrative, fiscal, or penal enforcement or through social sanctions.

Upholding the Rule of Law and Integrity

Enactment of anti-corruption legislation is a necessary condition for tackling corruption as it signifies the government's willingness to address corruption. In addition, the legislation establishes anti-corruption institutions with powers to investigate corrupt practices.[27] Further, the institution of criminal sanctions and disciplinary measures deters corruption. Similarly, the establishment of codes of conduct for personnel contributes to improving professional behaviour and performance of staff. This in turn helps to reduce corrupt practices in institutions.[28]

Public Administration and Systems Reform

Preventing corruption under public administration and systems reform entails improving accounting and information systems, increased use of independent and external bodies, software and information technology, community participation, and policy development amongst others. Other measures include the institution of efficient financial management systems, improving systems using independence and externality, and digitising operations in service delivery and use of software and information technology to reduce corruption.

Transparency and Accountability

Advocacy for including anti-corruption programmes in the education system is in line with Article 13 of the United Nations Convention Against Corruption (UNCAC), which obliges States to include values, integrity, and anti-corruption education in school curricula as a long-term anti-corruption strategy. Other means include the adoption and use of open and transparent procurement processes, instituting participatory monitoring and social accountability, and use of media and information technology to disseminate information; frequent surveys such as public expenditure tracking surveys (PETS), social audits, quantitative service delivery surveys, and other types of diagnostic surveys in order to assess the risky areas and identify points of potential action, raise awareness, and also disseminate quantitative evidence of corruption for purposes of auctioning, and build the capacity of institutions, organisations, and individuals.

Monitoring and Detecting Corruption in Public Service Delivery

This section gives a synopsis of some of the means that can be used to monitor and detect corruption in public service delivery. It is, however, important to note that some of the measures listed under mitigating measures can equally be used to monitor corruption in public services, for example PETS, social audit, and use of independent audit bodies. All these can be used to detect corruption as well.

The use of information communication technologies (ICTs) in general and mobile phones in particular can be instrumental in detecting corruption. In Zimbabwe, for example, a corrupt public official was recorded soliciting a bribe, while in India, the Central Bureau of Investigation launched a campaign urging citizens to report corruption via SMS with the view to building a database of officials to be monitored.[29]

In the health sector, various applications have been developed, using video, audio, touch-screen quizzes, global positioning system (GPS), and short message service (SMS) to collect, store, transmit, and analyse large amounts of health-related data[30] Applied to the anti-corruption agenda, such approaches can be promoted as a citizen-based monitoring tool, including but not exclusively for collecting feedback on the quality and quantity of public service delivery.[31] Specialised audits (e.g. forensic and performance audits) may be more effective in detecting and reducing corruption.[32]

Finally, Supreme Audit Institutions (SAIs) play a unique role in detecting and preventing corruption, when they have the mandate, tools and trust of the government to take on the fight against corruption. SAIs' audit mandate generally is broad enough to cover the entire public sector and flexible enough to examine government activities at any level. SAIs are expected to raise red flags that would deter and detect fraud and corruption and assist law enforcement agencies in bringing perpetrators to justice.[33] Surprise audits that may be conducted for detection, act as a good deterrent. Some SAIs have institutionalised the detection function by setting up a designated unit and developing forensic and investigative audit guidelines and manuals.[34]

Challenges in Addressing Corruption in Public Service Delivery

This final section of the chapter reviews some of the challenges faced when fighting corruption in public service delivery. Fighting corruption is not an easy task as it faces a few challenges. The multi-faceted and complex nature of corruption has shown that technical solutions and compliance measures are rarely sufficient in themselves to root out corruption. In many societies, corrupt behaviour is deeply rooted in the historical origins, social norms, and political culture; it is therefore not unusual to find strong inter-linkages between power, politics, and money. The scope for reformers to make changes is therefore constrained by the limits of their political influence, and any significant impact on corruption usually takes a long time.[35] Another challenge is the high degree of persistence of corrupt tendencies due to decades of prevalence of bribery practices in public sector service delivery, despite reforms and the creation of incentives and sanctions, which are supposed to induce good public governance patterns.[36]

Further, in an environment where corruption is widespread, establishing the integrity of Supreme Audit Institutions (SAIs) can be a challenge as SAIs move closer to the frontline of fighting corruption, the temptations and risks to the auditors will grow.[37] Besides, the continued culture of silence in many countries is a serious challenge undermining the fight against corruption.[38] Overall, the combination of composite structures and bureaucracies as well as a competition for resources make service delivery monitoring processes and accountability mechanisms challenging and costly to create and implement. This lack of adequate oversight can lead to high levels of discretionary power, which can produce arbitrary outcomes as well as significantly raise the risks of corruption in the supply chain. Where this is the case, corruption in service delivery can become a low-risk, high-profit activity.[39]

Conclusion

This chapter has described the forms of corruption that occur in public service delivery, factors that promote corruption as well as effects of corruption in public service delivery, and tools that can be used to curb it mainly approaching it from the systems perspective but bordering on rule of law/integrity, public administration and systems reforms, and transparency and accountability with education, health and water and sanitation sectors as examples. It is, however, critical that the prescribed instruments for mitigating corruption be a blend of the top-down and bottom-up strategies. The top-down strategies are processes or institutions used by government or service providers to make information accessible to citizens such as open data, e-government, e-procurement and the like, while bottom-up instruments are those that empower citizens to make processes more transparent like participatory budgeting, citizen report cards, and citizen inputs through ICT.

In addition, the chapter has also briefly prescribed means of monitoring and detecting corruption the public service delivery and challenges which stakeholders are likely to face in the fight against corruption. Finally, emphasis has been placed on the choice of the anticorruption strategy as being determined by the outcome of the corruption risk assessment, the political context, capacity, cost of implementation, and socioeconomic and other relevant factors. The bottom line is that there is no magic bullet that can solve corruption problems, but progress must be made in reducing resource leakages and wastages and also in controlling criminal and unethical behaviour that comprises the quality of public service delivery.

Notes

* Senior Lecturer, Department of Accountancy, Malawi University of Business and Applied Sciences.

** Anti-corruption and Anti-money Laundering Compliance Specialist.

1 R.K. Manyaka and N.W. Nkuna, "The Phenomenon of Corruption in the South African Public Sector: Challenges and Opportunities", *Mediterranean Journal of Social Sciences*, 2014, 5(27), 1572.

2 Anil B. Deolalikar, Shikha Jha, and Pilipinas F. Quisin, (eds.), *Governance in Developing Asia: Public Service Delivery and Empowerment* (Cheltenham: Asian Development Bank and Edward Elgar Publishing, 2015), 4.
3 Jha Deolalikar and Quisin (eds.), *Governance in Developing Asia*, 3.
4 Anwar Shah (ed), *Public Sector Governance and Accountability Series: Public Services Delivery* (Washington, DC: World Bank, 2005), 98.
5 Transparency International, *Corruption in Service Delivery: Topic Guide*, (2017), 4.
6 United Nations Development Program, *Fighting Corruption in the Education Sector Methods, Tools and Good Practices*, 2011.
7 Transparency International, *Corruption in Service Delivery*, 2017.
8 Transparency International, *Corruption in Service Delivery*, 2017.
9 Transparency International, *Corruption in Service Delivery*, 2017.
10 Transparency International, *Corruption in Service Delivery*, 2017.
11 Rose-Ackerman, and Palifka, *Corruption and Government* (New York: Cambridge University Press, 2016), 12.
12 United Nations Development Program, *Fighting Corruption in the Education Sector*, 2011.
13 Karen Hussman, "*Health Sector Corruption – Practical Recommendations for Donors*," 2020, Anticorruption Resource Centre, U4 Issue 2020:10
14 United Nations Development Program, *Fighting Corruption in the Education Sector*, 2011.
15 United Nations Development Program, *Fighting Corruption in the Education Sector*, 2011.
16 Jean Eigeman, *Service Delivery, a Challenge for Local Governments*, VNG International, 2007, p. 5.
17 Eigeman, *Service Delivery*, 5.
18 Transparency International, *Corruption in Service Delivery, 2017.*
19 Department for International Development, *Why corruption matter*, 14.
20 P. M. Senge, *The fifth discipline: The art and practice of the learning organization* (New York, NY: Doubleday, 2006).
21 Emily H. Glynn, *Corruption in the health sector: A problem in need of a systems-thinking approach*, 2022, 11.
22 World Bank, *Enhancing Government Effectiveness and Transparency*, 2020
23 Monica Kirya, *Education Sector Corruption: How to Assess It and Ways to Address It*, U4 Issue 2019:5
24 Monica Kirya, *Education Sector Corruption*, 5.
25 Hussman, *Health Sector Corruption*, Issue 202:10.
26 Hussman, *Health Sector corruption*, 10.
27 United Nations Development Program, *Fighting Corruption in the Education Sector*, 2011
28 Department for International Development, *Why corruption matters: understanding causes, effects and how to address them*. Evidence paper on corruption, (2015), 7.
29 Marie Chene, *Use of mobile phones to detect and deter corruption,* 12 April 2011 Number: 280, 2.
30 (Mobleactive.org, 2011).
31 Chene, *Use of mobile phones to detect and deter corruption*, 4.
32 Department for International Development, *Why corruption matters: understanding causes, effects and how to address them*. Evidence paper on corruption (2015), p. 63.
33 World Bank, *Enhancing Government Effectiveness and Transparency: The Fight Against Corruption* 2020, Global report, September 2020 Revised on October 3, 2020, 305.
34 World Bank, *Enhancing Government Effectiveness and Transparency*, 305.

35 World Bank, *Enhancing Government Effectiveness and Transparency*, 305.
36 Sadik-Zada, Gatto & Ibrahim (2022): E-government and petty corruption in public sector service delivery, Technology Analysis & Strategic Management, 2022
37 World Bank, *Enhancing Government Effectiveness and Transparency*, 306.
38 Anil B. Deolalikar, Shikha Jha, and Pilipinas F. Quisin, (eds.), *Governance in Developing Asia: Public Service Delivery and Empowerment* (Asian Development Bank and Edward Elgar Publishing, 2015), 130.
39 Transparency International, *Corruption in Service Delivery Topic Guide*, 2017, p. 6.

10 Palm Oiling

Corruption in the Natural Resources Sector

*George Chikondi Lwanda**

Introduction

Corruption at the licensing stage of the oil and natural gas value chain can have long-lasting negative political, economic, and social consequences that hamper sustainable development. It increases transaction costs borne by investors. Besides, corruption deprives countries of critical revenue, making it more challenging to meet their development goals.[1] This chapter will use data from the Natural Resources Governance Institute (NRGI), 2017 and 2021 Resource Governance Index (RGI) to examine the corruption risks in Africa's oil and gas licensing process.

The chapter discusses how corruption happens in the hydrocarbon licensing process before examining the licensing process in the 19 African countries listed in Figure 10.1. It concludes that corruption remains a significant risk in Africa's oil and gas licensing process, despite improvements in licensing enforcement. The discussion ends with recommendations on how African countries can combat corruption in oil and gas licensing.

Importance of the Hydrocarbons Sector and Why It Is Prone to Corruption

Although the oil and gas industry is declining as the world moves away from fossil fuels, it is still essential to Africa's economy.[2] African economic growth depends on the fortunes of the global oil and gas industry. According to Statistica 2020, the hydrocarbons sector accounts for approximately 57 per cent of the continent's export earnings. The sector also finances over half of the national budgets of at least 12 African countries. The oil and gas sector also contributes significantly to the gross domestic product (GDP) of at least 14 African countries.[3] For example, Statistica reports that oil and gas account for over half of Libya's GDP and over a third of the GDP in Gabon, Chad, and Angola, respectively.

Corruption is pervasive in the oil and gas industry.[4,5,6] According to the OECD, the oil and gas sector accounts for one in every five instances of bribery globally.[7,8] The oil and gas industry is prone to corruption for at least two reasons.[9,10,11] The oil and gas sector generates enormous sums of money. These sums are sometimes several times the size of the GDP of an oil-producing country.[12,13] For example, an oil

DOI: 10.4324/9781003326649-12

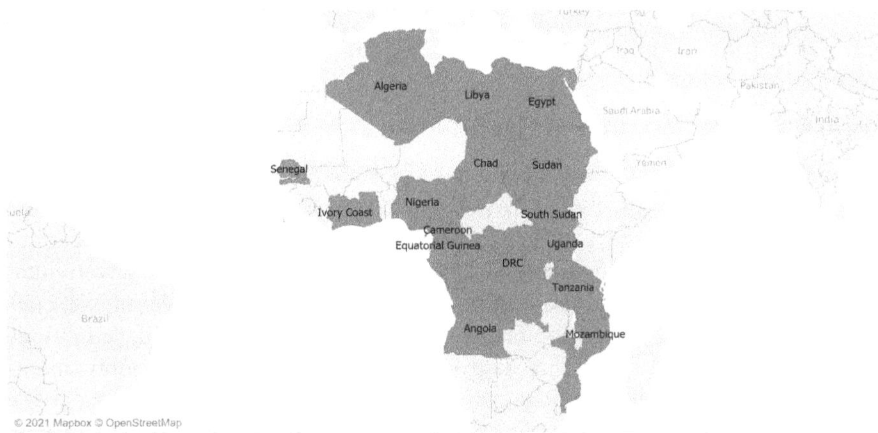

Figure 10.1 The 19 countries examined in the Chapter[14]

company secured US$16 billion in 2020 for a gas project in Mozambique, a country with a GDP of US$14 billion (Reuters staff, 2020; Bloomberg News, 2020). Further to that, the oil sector involves complicated financial transactions, making it easy for malign actors to conceal corrupt activities.[15,16] These two characteristics enable the oil and gas industry to serve as a source of economic and political power for individuals and groups, while also providing enormous profits. As a result, oil companies vying for licences engage in significant lobbying, distorting policymaking, and skewing laws and policies to favour their private interests.[17]

Decoding Corruption

As discussed by Kuwali in Chapter 1, there are several competing definitions of corruption, owing to the evolving and complicated nature of the vice. According to Transparency International and the OECD, corruption is the abuse of public or private office for personal gain.[18,19] This broad definition encompasses various activities, including fraud, political capture and interference, conflicts of interest, bribery and extortion, and misappropriation and illicit enrichment.

Corruption is often defined to include activities such as fraud and embezzlement. As a result, the terms "corruption," "fraud," and "embezzlement" are often used interchangeably.[20] While corrupt behaviour manifests itself in various ways, such as when a public official abuses his or her position for personal gain or when a business violates rules to further its interests, as Kuwali narrated in Chapter 1, it always involves the following three components: (a) professional standards violations resulting in partial decision-making, (b) abuse of traditional or professional authority, and (c) private gain at the expense of society by those involved in corruption.[21] This chapter limits the discussion to the aspect of corruption relating to influence trading. Influence trading is the act of trading one's power or apparent control over a public official's decision-making for an unfair advantage.

Corruption in the Awarding of Hydrocarbon Licenses

Licensing, the first stage of the oil and gas value chain, is prone to influence trading.[22,23] In most countries, the government owns all oil and gas reserves. To that end, only entities that the government issues licences may explore and exploit oil and gas reserves. Consequently, the licensing process is how the government decides who can explore and produce oil and gas. It is also how governments conduct due diligence on licence applicants to avoid issuing licences to unscrupulous businesses. As a result, it is at this stage where companies and people lobby intensively, leading to influence trading.

As an extension, influence trading includes situations of political interference, such as when someone with political influence wields undue influence over public officials' decision-making. One of the most common consequences of influence trading is that it leads to authorities favouring companies in whom politically exposed people have interests. For example, in 1998, the Nigerian government granted a licence to one of the country's most valuable offshore oil blocks to a politically connected company formed just five days before.[24] This example has the three components of corruption referred to earlier. Authorities violated professional standards and abused their offices by giving a company with no operational experience a licence. Granting a licence to an undeserving company resulted in private gain for politicians with shares in the company.

Influence trading thrives when no conflict-of-interest checks exist, and public officials deciding who gets a licence do not need to disclose their interests in the sector. Part of its negative consequences is that influence trading can lead public officials to negotiate unfair contracts for the government. It can also make public officials favour unscrupulous businesses, such as companies attempting to avoid paying taxes and royalties. The 2012 High-Level Panel on Illicit Financial Flows in Africa (HLP) reported two such cases.[25] There was one in which a company negotiated a corporate tax rate of just 1 per cent and the other in which the government set the royalty rates at 20 per cent of the legal rate. Influence trading can allow senior government officials to embezzle or misappropriate funds using multiple shell companies with hidden beneficial owners to conceal their identities. One example is in the Republic of Congo (Brazzaville), where senior public officials embezzled or misappropriated state funds between 2003 and 2005 by concealing their identities through a sophisticated web of offshore shell companies.[26]

Influence trading is not a phenomenon unique to Africa. Three examples show the global scope and impact of influence trading. For example, in 2015, the Venezuelan government awarded a US$4.5 million oil drilling contract to a small trucking firm with political ties.[27] Another case is where an American court convicted a US citizen in 2009 for conspiring to bribe Azerbaijani senior oil and gas officials.[28] In Europe, for instance, Norwegian authorities found in 2004 that Statoil, a Norwegian oil company, paid US$15 million to influence Iranian oil and gas policymakers.[29,30]

The opacity of licensing laws and norms is a prerequisite for influence trading.[31,32,33] Whether opacity is by design or a result of an unfortunate default, it creates both the motivation and the opportunity for personal benefit from corruption. In fact, opacity helps corruption by making it difficult to hold businesses and authorities accountable for their actions, resulting in no consequences for corrupt practices. In contrast, transparency is a prerequisite for reducing corruption.

Unlike opacity, transparency lessens the probability of personal benefit, demotivating and reducing the opportunity for corruption. Corruption-busting transparency requires governments to disclose information about the entire chain of decisions with a complete, complementary set of data in the oil and gas licensing process. To combat influence trading in oil and gas licensing, governments must reveal (a) the licence winners' names, (b) the licensing process rules, and (c) their contracts with the licence winners (NRGI, 2018, OECD, 2016).[34,35]

Hydrocarbon Licensing in Africa: Law and Practice

This section examines corruption risks associated with licensing law and practice in the 19 African countries shown in Figure 10.1. These 19 countries account for 82 per cent of Africa's total oil production and include all of Africa's major oil producers (Nigeria, Angola, Algeria, Egypt, Libya, Congo (Brazzaville), Gabon, South Sudan, Equatorial Guinea, Chad, and Sudan).

The section uses data from the NRGI's Resource Governance Indices for 2017 and 2021. It examines four aspects of licensing law and practice, financial interest disclosure, licensing rules disclosure, licence winner disclosure, and contract disclosure. The analysis of each component starts with why transparency is vital in the fight against corruption. Then comes a look at global law and practice before concluding with an analysis of the law and practice in Africa.

Law and Practice in Financial Interest Disclosure

Financial interest disclosure is a critical component of anti-corruption efforts.[36,37] It is paramount that citizens know whether oil and gas companies use sophisticated corporate structures to evade taxes. Similarly, citizens must know whether officials have interests in the companies they regulate. It requires the government to collect and disclose public officials' asset declarations and the identities of corporations' beneficial owners, those who benefit from a corporation's operations, besides the legal owners.

Public officials' asset declarations are an effective tool for detecting and preventing conflicts of interest and corruption. Public disclosures enable the public to track a public employee's wealth. If an employee makes periodic disclosures, authorities may question the employee about suspicious financial transactions or extravagant spending. Asset disclosure laws are also vital for law enforcement agencies. They allow law enforcement agencies to monitor the consistency of public officials'

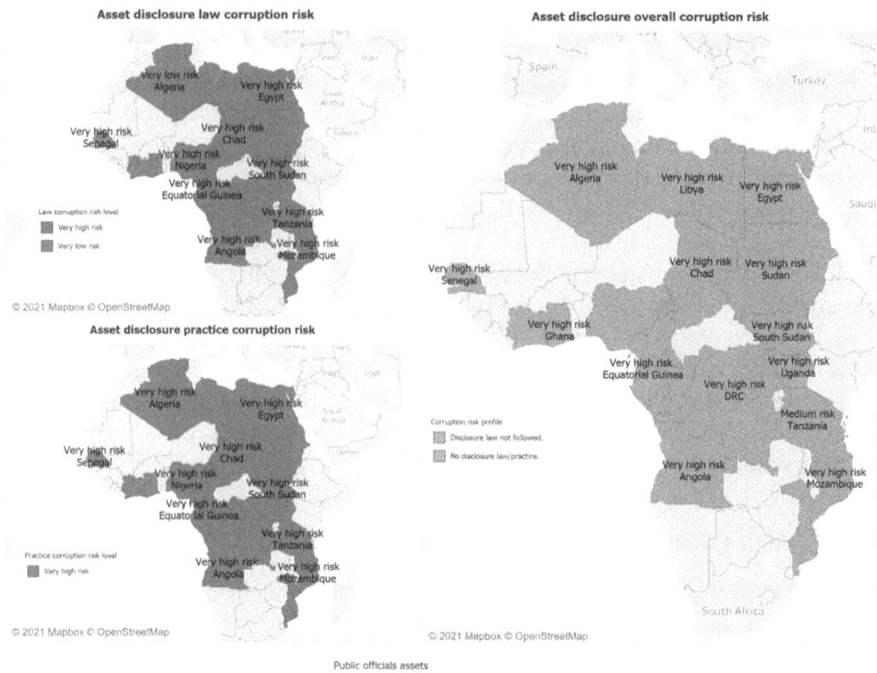

Figure 10.2 Declaration of the Assets of Public Officials' Law and Practice in Africa[41]

income and asset disclosure statements, facilitating the prosecution and conviction of corrupt officials. For example, Indonesian authorities used public officials' disclosure records to detect corrupt payments to the then-head of the Indonesian oil and gas regulator, resulting in that official's conviction.[38,39]

Financial interest opacity is a defining feature of the oil and gas industry globally. According to the 2017 Resource Governance Index (NRGI 2017), seven out of every ten oil-producing countries globally do not disclose public officials' financial holdings. Additionally, only Vietnam and Ukraine have laws that require public officials and corporations to disclose their assets. Africa is no exception; secrecy surrounding the assets of public officials is the continent's biggest facilitator of influence trading. None of the African countries disclose the wealth of public officials (see Figure 10.2). In addition, only Algeria and Uganda have enacted legislation requiring public officials to disclose commercial ties to the sector. The law does not require public officials to declare their assets in the remaining countries (Angola, Cameroon, Chad, Congo, Democratic Republic of the Congo, Egypt, Equatorial Guinea, Gabon, Côte d'Ivoire, Libya, Nigeria, Mozambique, Tanzania, Senegal, South Sudan, and Sudan).

Beneficial ownership disclosure makes it harder to use complex corporate structures or offshore companies to hide corrupt activities.[40] Despite this, only 29 per cent of the world's oil-producing countries have enacted beneficial ownership

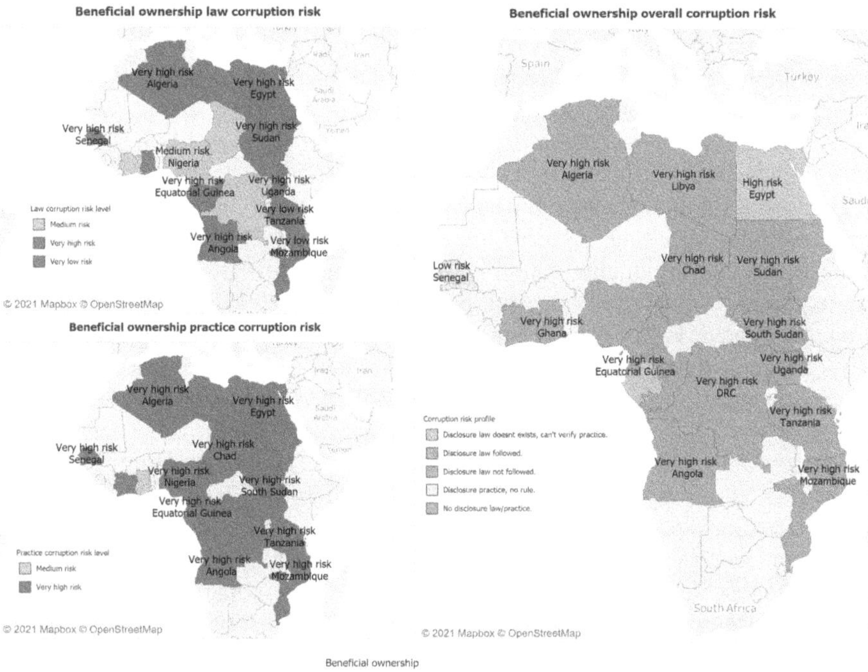

Figure 10.3 Beneficial Ownership Law and Practice in Africa[42]

disclosure legislation or policies. Alarmingly, none of the world's oil and gas producers disclose beneficial ownership information.

The situation is no different in Africa. No African state has disclosed beneficial owners since a high-level panel recommended it in 2012. Most (53 per cent) of the countries have not passed legislation requiring the disclosure of beneficial owners (Algeria, Angola, Congo, Equatorial Guinea, Gabon, Libya, Senegal, Sudan, Uganda, and Tanzania). Of the nine countries with beneficial ownership laws, Cameroon, Chad, DRC, Ghana, Côte d'Ivoire, Mozambique, Nigeria, South Sudan, and Tanzania, only Ghana discloses some beneficial ownership information.[43] Structural weakness in oversight and compliance in Angola shows how corrupt people can take advantage of the lack of beneficial ownership information disclosure. Between 2012 and 2018, politically exposed individuals in Angola took advantage of weak beneficial ownership disclosure requirements to conceal corrupt activities as outlined in Figure 10.3.[44]

Law and Practice in Disclosure of Licensing Process Rules

Public disclosure of rules governing the licensing process is critical to deterring corruption. It helps prevent corruption in two ways. First, it allows anyone interested to check how well the licensing process aligns with a country's development goals, policies, and laws. More people can take part in national development policy decision-making because of this. For example, it allows any person or entity to suggest improvements to the licensing process to better align with national goals or reduce corruption risks. Second, it is easier for any interested stakeholder to discover and investigate cases where companies get licenses when they do not deserve them.

The global oil and gas industry has not fully embraced disclosure of licensing procedure rules, resulting in secrecy in the sector. Only 45 per cent (or 23 of 52) of the world's oil-producing countries have enacted legislation or adopted policies requiring disclosure of licensing process rules. Thirty-seven per cent (or 19) of countries have laws, while 8 per cent (or four countries) have policies. Similarly, only four of the ten oil-producing countries in the world disclose their licensing process rules. Brazil, China, Iran, Norway, the United Kingdom, and Ukraine are global leaders in licensing process rule disclosure. African countries account for slightly more than a quarter (26 per cent) of the 19 global leaders in licensing process rules disclosure (Algeria, Angola, Cameroon, Equatorial Guinea, and Mozambique).

African countries are making strides towards enacting laws to disclose the hydrocarbon licensing process rules. Two-thirds of the countries with licensing process disclosure laws enforce them. They have the lowest risk of corruption during the licensing process (Algeria, Angola, Cameroon, Ghana, Mozambique, and Senegal). However, like the global trend, the African hydrocarbon licensing process remains susceptible to influence trading because of the opacity of the licensing rules (see Figure 10.4). While the number of countries that enforce licensing process disclosure laws is high, it only accounts for 32 per cent of all oil-producing countries. Less than half of the countries (47 per cent) have passed legislation mandating the disclosure of licensing process rules. They are Algeria, Angola, Cameroon, Congo (Brazzaville), Equatorial Guinea, Ghana, Mozambique, Senegal, and Uganda. Uganda and Congo (Brazzaville) are the two countries that do not enforce licensing process disclosure laws.

Law and Practice in the Disclosure of Licence Winners

Disclosing licence winners helps reduce corruption during the licensing process. It enables anyone to know the identity of the licence winners.[45] Knowing the winners' identities allows interested parties to investigate their integrity, reducing the corrupt practice of favouring undeserving applicants. The disclosure of licence winners is the norm in the global oil and gas industry. The majority (65 per cent) of oil-producing countries reveal the identity of licence winners. Global leaders in licence winner disclosure include Brazil, Canada, Ukraine, and Norway. Algeria, Angola, Côte d'Ivoire, Gabon, Ghana, Mozambique, Sudan, and Tunisia are among the African countries that are global leaders in licence winner disclosure.

While the global trend is to reveal licence winners, a culture of not disclosing the identity of the licence winner, despite laws requiring it, still reigns in Africa. It is a practice that exposes the oil and gas licensing process to a greater risk of

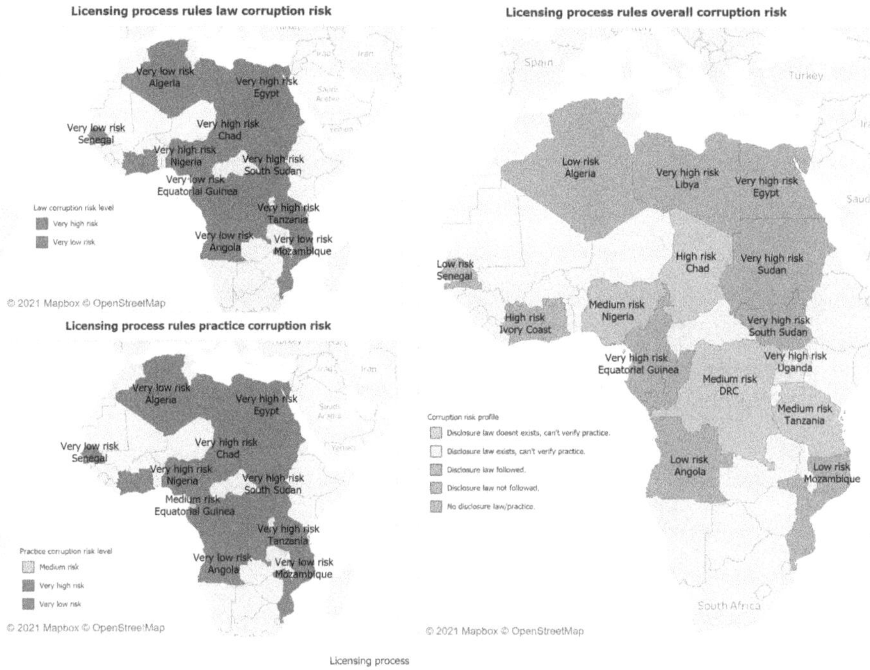

Figure 10.4 Licensing Process Law and Practice in Africa[46]

corruption (see Figure 10.5). Despite most (58 per cent) countries having licence winner disclosure laws (Algeria, Angola, Congo, the Democratic Republic of the Congo (DRC), Egypt, Equatorial Guinea, Côte d'Ivoire, Ghana, Mozambique, Senegal, and South Sudan), only 37 per cent of these countries disclose licence winners (Algeria, Angola, Côte d'Ivoire, Ghana, and Mozambique). Additionally, a quarter of the countries have yet to implement the law, requiring licence holders to reveal their identities (DRC, Egypt, Equatorial Guinea, Senegal, and South Sudan). On the other hand, Sudan and Gabon disclose licence winners, even though there is no law requiring it.

Law and Practice in the Disclosure of Contracts

Contract transparency is essential for fighting corruption in the oil and gas industry.[47] It helps citizens analyse the multi-billion-dollar contracts that governments sign. Such transparency helps citizens understand the obligations placed on businesses and the government, allowing citizens to track compliance. Contract disclosure also strengthens a company's social licence to operate by allowing companies to show how they meet their social and financial obligations.[48,49] Governments benefit from disclosed contracts because all government agencies know the contract

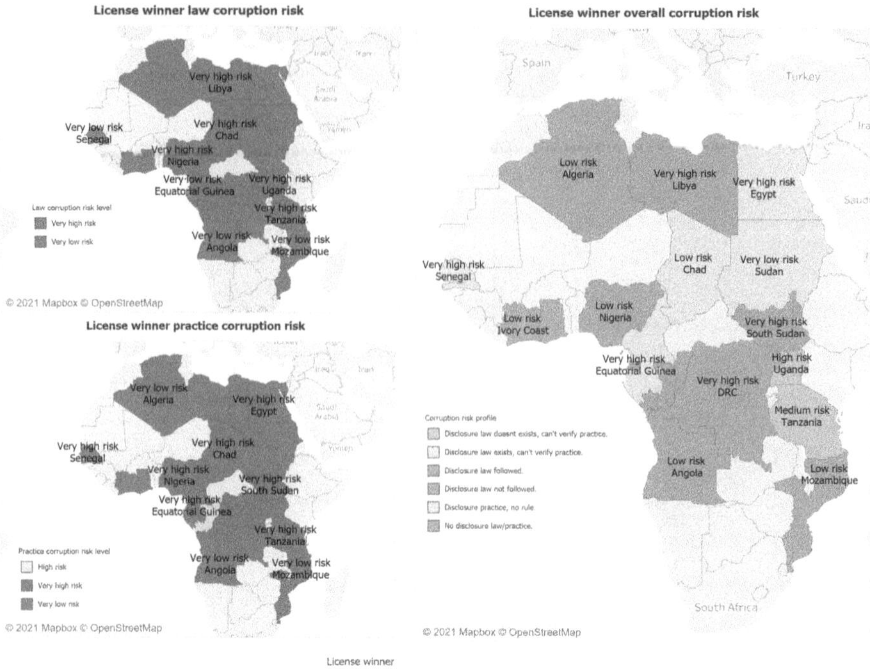

Figure 10.5 License Winner Law and Practice in Africa[50]

terms and can work together to ensure compliance.[51,52] All this builds trust between citizens and governments.

Contract opacity is a global trend in the oil and gas sector. Eight out of ten oil-producing nations globally do not have contract transparency laws. Nine out of ten oil-producing countries globally do not publish oil and gas contracts. Together with Colombia, Ecuador, Mexico, and the United States, Mozambique is the only African oil- and gas-producing country that discloses contracts.

As is the case globally, Africa's hydrocarbon licensing process is susceptible to corruption due to contract opacity (as illustrated in Figure 10.6.) Only Mozambique makes all signed contracts public, out of the 19 countries examined. Congo (Brazzaville), Democratic Republic of Congo (DRC), Equatorial Guinea, Ghana, Cote d'Ivoire, Senegal, South Sudan, and Tanzania do not disclose contracts or licences in violation of their national contract disclosure laws. The remaining countries lack contract disclosure legislation and do not make contracts or licences public (Angola, Algeria, Cameroon, Chad, Equatorial Guinea, Gabon, Libya, Nigeria, and Sudan).

The Corruption Risks in Hydrocarbon Law and Practice in Africa

Table 10.1 compares African hydrocarbon licensing laws and practices to global hydrocarbon licensing laws and practices.

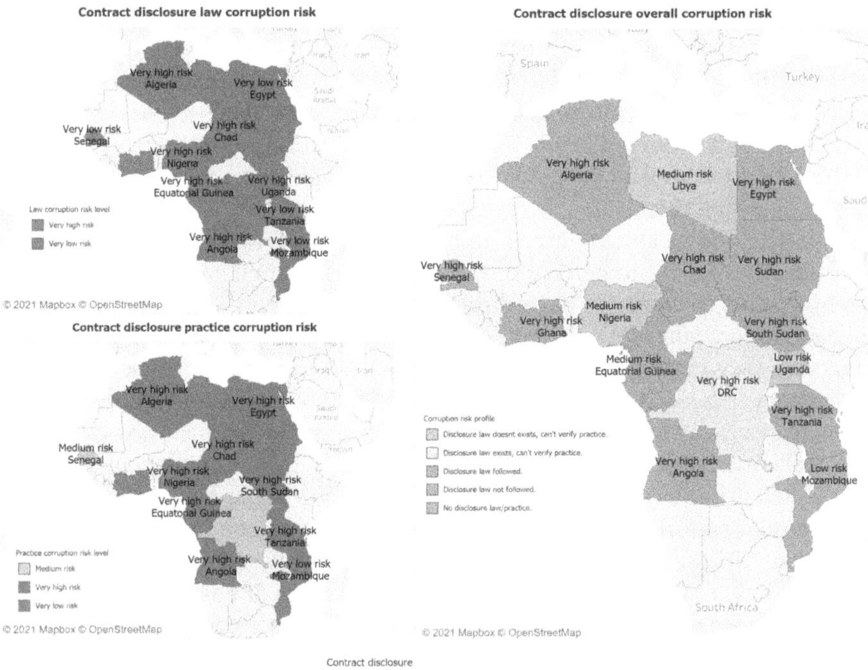

Figure 10.6 Contract Disclosure Law and Practice in Africa[53]

Table 10.1 Comparison of Law and Practice in Africa and the World

Licensing component	*Per cent countries globally with disclosure law*	*Per cent African countries with disclosure law*	*Per cent countries globally disclosing*	*Per cent African countries disclosing*
Disclosure of public officials' assets	29%	16%	13%	0%
Beneficial ownership disclosure	9%	21%	0%	0%
Licensing process disclosure	45%	47%	40%	32%
Licence winner disclosure	43%	58%	65%	37%
Contract disclosure	20%	47%	10%	5%

Source: Author's analysis of the NRGI Resource Governance Index 2017 and 2021

Two things are worth noting from Table 10.1. First, financial interest secrecy, licensing procedure rules opacity, and contract secrecy are all risks in African and global hydrocarbon licensing processes. Second, while African oil producers are pioneers in enacting disclosure laws, they lag behind global practice trends. As a result, while there are 27 per cent more African countries with contract disclosure laws than the global average, 5 per cent more countries worldwide disclose contracts. Similarly, while 15 per cent more African countries have license-winner disclosure laws than the global average, 28 per cent more countries worldwide disclose license winners. And, while 2 per cent more African countries have licensing rules disclosure laws than the global average, 8 per cent more countries worldwide disclose licensing rules.

Table 10.2 shows at least three significant corruption risks among the 19 countries studied. A failure to enforce disclosure laws is the first source of corruption. Only one-third of countries have disclosure laws, and only one-quarter of those with laws enforce them. As a result, African oil-producing countries are less transparent than their global peers. The second source of corruption is a lack of financial transparency. Almost all countries do not require public officials to disclose their commercial interests in the oil and gas sector, while 84 per cent do not require beneficial ownership disclosure. The third source of corruption is contract opacity. As shown in the preceding section, Mozambique is the only country on the continent that publishes oil and gas contracts. On a positive note, Table 10.2 also shows that African countries are increasing transparency of licensing procedure rules and licence winners. Over two-thirds (67 per cent) of countries with licence winner disclosure laws implement them. Similarly, 64 per cent of countries with laws requiring licence winner disclosure do so.

Based on the preceding, corruption risks abound in Africa's hydrocarbon licensing process. From the 19 countries examined, African countries must take three steps to reduce the risk of influence trading in hydrocarbon licensing. First, they must prioritise the disclosure of licence winners and licensing process rules. The two areas have seen the most progress and are thus the most amenable to improvement. Second, African oil-producing countries must prioritise enacting financial disclosure, beneficial ownership, and contract disclosure laws. These are the three areas where disclosure falls short and assistance is most needed. Third, countries must strengthen their national institutions' capacity to enforce contract and beneficial ownership disclosure laws. The area where practice falls far short of the law is contract disclosure.

Table 10.2 Summary of Law and Practice in Oil and Gas Licensing in Africa

Licensing component	*Per cent countries without disclosure laws*	*Per cent, countries that do not disclose*
Public officials' assets	84%	100%
Licensing process	53%	68%
Licence winner	42%	63%
Beneficial ownership	53%	95%
Contract disclosure	53%	95%

Source: Author's analysis of the NRGI Resource Governance Index 2017 and 2021

Preventing Corruption in the Award of Hydrocarbon Licences

African countries can reduce corruption risks associated with hydrocarbon licensing by expanding the Africa Mining Vision (AMV) to include the hydrocarbon sector.

In 2009, the African Union's Heads of State and Government adopted the Africa Mining Vision (AMV) as a key continental framework for promoting good governance in Africa's mining sector. The AMV's ultimate goal is to ensure transparent, fair, and optimal mineral resource exploitation. The Africa Mineral Development Centre is in charge of putting the AMV into action (AMDC). Since the AMV's inception in 2013, at least 14 countries have implemented significant mining legislation reforms with the help of the AMDC. While the AMV is not without flaws, its achievements are undeniable and show the importance of continental efforts to improve natural resource governance.

The AMV has a serious flaw because it continues to draw a distinction between mining and hydrocarbons. The distinction is understandable, given how much more complex the oil and gas industry is than the mining industry. As a result of this distinction, the oil and gas industry has received less reform than the mining industry. For instance, while 14 countries have amended their mining legislation since 2013, only four have amended their hydrocarbon legislation.[54]

Mozambique and Ghana provide the most compelling evidence of the benefits of expanding the AMV to include the oil sector. Both countries used the AMV in the development of their hydrocarbon laws. The results are undeniable. As demonstrated in the chapter, Mozambique and Ghana are leaders in terms of hydrocarbon licensing process rules and disclosure of licence winners. Mozambique is also a trailblazer when it comes to contract transparency. At the same time, Ghana is a trailblazer for beneficial ownership transparency.

Importantly, expanding the AMV to include the oil and gas industries is critical because it will allow African countries to develop a systemic approach to learning from one another. The countries that are leaders in the hydrocarbon licensing components examined in this chapter are summarised in Table 10.3 to demonstrate how each country can learn from one another. For example, Ghana can teach Mozambique about beneficial ownership disclosure, and Mozambique can teach Ghana

Table 10.3 Summary of the Countries Leading in Disclosure

Licensing process rules disclosure	*Licence winner disclosure*	*Beneficial ownership disclosure*	*Contract disclosure*
Angola Cameroon Ghana Senegal	Algeria Angola Ivory Coast Ghana Mozambique Sudan	Ghana	Mozambique

about contract disclosure. Similarly, Algeria can teach Cameroon about licence winner disclosure, and Cameroon can teach Algeria about licensing process rules disclosure.

Notes

* 2018 Asia Global Fellow; Senior Strategist and Head of the United Nations Resident Coordinator's office in The Gambia.

1 OECD 2016. *Corruption in the extractives value chain: Typology of risks, mitigation and incentives*. Paris, France: OECD.

2 COHEN, S. 2021. *The Future of the Fossil Fuel Business* [Online]. Columbia Climate School. Available: https://news.climate.columbia.edu/2021/06/01/the-future-of-the-fossil-fuel-business/ [Accessed 30 September 2021]. COPENHAGEN ECONOMICS 2017. The future of fossil fuels: How to steer fossil fuel use in a transition to a low-carbon energy system. Energy transitions committee, MUFSON.

3 Global Business Reports 2020. Africa oil and gas 2020 [Online]. Available at www.gbreports.com, accessed 15 September 2021.

4 Helena, M., Dolve, M. & Mullard, S. 2019. *Addressing illicit financial flows for anti-corruption at country level: A primer for development practitioners*. Bergen, Norway: CMR Michelsen Institute.

5 Obioma, B. 2012. Corruption reduction in the petroleum sector in Nigeria: Challenges and prospects. *Mediterranean Journal of Social Sciences*, 3.

6 Sayne, A., Gillies, A. & Watkins, A. 2017. *Twelve red flags: Corruption in the award of extractive sector licenses and contracts*. London, United Kingdom: Natural Resources Governance Index.

7 Transparency International. 2013. Corruption in the extractive industries [Online]. Berlin, Germany: Transparency International. Available on: www.transparency.org/en/our-priorities/extractive-industries [Accessed on 16 October 2021].

8 OECD 2016. *Corruption in the extractives value chain: Typology of risks, mitigation, and incentives*. Paris, France: OECD.

9 PL Billon, 2011. Extractive sectors and illicit financial flows: What role for revenue governance initiatives? In: CENTRE, A.-C. R. (ed.). Bergen, Norway: Chr. Michelson Institute.

10 Buenaventura, M. & Biyani, N. 2020. Combating illicit financial flows in extractives sector in Asia: A toolkit on illicit financial flows. Financial transparency coalition.

11 Centre for Natural Resource Governance 2013. Illicit financial flows in Zimbabwe's artisanal mining sector. Harare, Zimbabwe.

12 Ndikumana, L. & Boyce, J. 2011. Capital Flight from Sub-Saharan Africa: Linkages with External Borrowing and Policy Options. *International Review of Applied Economics*, 25, 149–70.

13 Alao, A. 2015. *Natural Resources and Conflict in Africa the Tragedy of Endowment*. Texas: University of Rochester Press.

14 Source: OpenStreetMap.

15 Signé, L., Sow, M., & Madden, P. 2020. *Illicit Financial Flows in Africa: Drivers, Destinations, and Policy Options*. Brookings Institute.

16 Almounsor, A. (ed.) 2005. *A Development Comparative Approach to Capital Flight: The Case of the Middle East and North Africa, 1970–2002*. Cheltenham, United Kingdom: Edward Elgar.

17 Transparency International. 2013. Corruption in the extractive industries [Online]. Berlin, Germany: Transparency International. Available on: www.transparency.org/en/our-priorities/extractive-industries [Accessed on 16 October 2021].

18 Al-Kasim, F., Søreide, T. & Williams, A. 2008. Grand corruption in the regulation of oil. In: CENTRE, A.-C. (ed.) U4 Issue. Bergen, Norway: CHI Michelsen Institute. U4 Anti-Corruption Resource Centre, 2017

19 Eisen, N., Kaufmann, D., Heller, N., Whitt, J. P., Picón, M. G., Bassetti, V. & Hudak, J. 2020. *The TAP-Plus Approach to Anti-Corruption in the Natural Resources Value Chain*. Washington DC, USA: Brookings Institute.
20 U4 Anti-Corruption Resource Centre. 2017. Defining corruption [Online]. Oslo, Norway. Available on: www.u4.no/topics/anti-corruption-basics/basics [Accessed on 16 October 2021].
21 Transparency International. 2013. Corruption in the extractive industries [Online]. Berlin, Germany: Transparency International. Available on: www.transparency.org/en/our-priorities/extractive-industries [Accessed on 16 October 2021].
22 Forstater, M. 2018. *Defining and measuring illicit financial flows*. New York, USA: Council on Foreign Relations.
23 U4 Anti-Corruption Resource Centre 2011. Good practices in mitigating corruption risks in the extractives sector. Oslo, Norway: U4 Anti-Corruption Resource Centre.
24 Sayne, A., Gillies, A. & Watkins, A. 2017. *Twelve red flags: Corruption in the award of extractive sector licenses and contracts*. London, United Kingdom: Natural Resources Governance Index.
25 UNECA 2014. *Illicit financial flows: Report of the high-level panel on illicit financial flows from Africa*. Addis Ababa: UNECA.
26 Sayne, A., Gillies, A. & Watkins, A. 2017. *Twelve red flags: Corruption in the award of extractive sector licenses and contracts*. London, U.K.: Natural Resources Governance Index.
27 Ulmer, A. & Gupta, G. 2016. Special Report: In Venezuela's murky oil industry, the deal that went too far [Online]. New York, USA: Reuters. Available on: www.reuters.com/article/us-venezuela-pdvsa-contract-specialrepor-idUSKCN1061U9 [Accessed on 17 October 2021].
28 U.S. Department of Justice. 2009. Connecticut Investor Found Guilty in Massive Scheme to Bribe Senior Government Officials in the Republic of Azerbaijan [Online]. Washington DC, USA. Available on: www.justice.gov/opa/pr/connecticut-investor-found-guilty-massive-scheme-bribe-senior-government-officials-republic [Accessed on 16 October 2021].
29 Uchitelle, L. 2005. Three Indicted for Bribery in Oil Scheme in Azerbaijan [Online]. New York, USA: New York Times. Available on: www.nytimes.com/2005/10/07/business/three-indicted-for-bribery-in-oil-scheme-in-azerbaijan.html [Accessed on 17 October 2021].
30 BBC News. 2004. Statoil fined over Iranian bribes [Online]. London, U.K.: BBC. Available: http://news.bbc.co.uk/2/hi/business/3849147.stm [Accessed on 17 October 2021].
31 Nrgi 2018. Resource governance index: From legal reform to implementation in Sub-Saharan Africa. London, U.K. Eisen et al., 2020.
32 OECD 2016. *Corruption in the extractives value chain: Typology of risks, mitigation, and incentives*. Paris, France: OECD.
33 Eisen, N., Kaufmann, D., Heller, N., Whitt, J. P., Picón, M. G., Bassetti, V. & Hudak, J. 2020. *The TAP-plus approach to anti-corruption in the natural resources value chain*. Washington, DC: Brookings Institute.
34 Nrgi 2018. *Resource governance index: From legal reform to implementation in Sub-Saharan Africa*. London, U.K.
35 OECD 2016. *Corruption in the extractives value chain: Typology of risks, mitigation, and incentives*. Paris, France: OECD.
36 Rossi, I., Pop, L. & Berger, T. 2017. Getting the full picture public officials: A how-to guide for effective financial disclosure [Online]. Washington DC, USA: World Bank. Available on: https://star.worldbank.org/sites/star/files/getting-the-full-picture-on-public-officials-how-to-guide.pdf [Accessed on 17 October 2021].
37 OECD 2011. *Assets declarations for public officials: A tool to prevent corruption*. Paris, France: OECD.
38 Indonesia Investments. 2014. Corruption in Indonesia: Rudi Rubiandini Guilty of Receiving Bribes [Online]. Jakarta, Indonesia. Available on: www.indonesia-invest

ments.com/news/news-columns/corruption-in-indonesia-rudi-rubiandini-found-guilty-of-receiving-bribes/item1938 [Accessed on 15 October 2021].

39 Sayne, A., Gillies, A. & Watkins, A. 2017. *Twelve red flags: Corruption in the award of extractive sector licenses and contracts*. London, United Kingdom: Natural Resources Governance Index.

40 Westenberg, E. 2018. *Leveraging beneficial ownership information in the extractive sector*. New York, USA: Council for Foreign Relations

41 Source: Author's analysis of the NRGI Resource Governance Index 2017 and 2021

42 Source: Author's analysis of the NRGI Resource Governance Index 2017 and 2021

43 Cameroon, Chad, DRC, Ghana, Côte d'Ivoire, Mozambique, Nigeria, South Sudan, and Tanzania

44 (Bassetti et al., 2020, Control Risks, 2020, Freedberg et al., 2020)

45 (Buenaventura and Biyani, 2020, NRGI, 2017, NRGI, 2018, OECD, 2016, Sayne et al., 2017)

46 Source: Author's analysis of the NRGI Resource Governance Index 2017 and 2021

47 Price Waterhouse Coopers 2019. *From promise to performance: Africa oil and gas review*. Johannesburg, South Africa: Price Waterhouse Coopers.

48 Publish What You Pay. 2021. #DiscloseTheDeal [Online]. London, U.K.: Publish What You Pay. Available on: www.disclosethedeal.org/ [Accessed on 8 October 2021, 2021].

49 Deepak, S. 2020. Why the oil curb is getting worse for Africa [Online]. New York: International Finance. Available: https://internationalfinance.com/why-oil-curb-is-getting-worse-for-africa/ [Accessed 15 October 2021].

50 Source: Author's analysis of the NRGI Resource Governance Index 2017 and 2021

51 EITI. 2015. Contract transparency: Making contracts accessible for citizens [Online]. Oslo, Norway: EITI. Available on: https://eiti.org/contract-transparency [Accessed on 8 October 2021].)

52 Sayne, A., Gillies, A. & Watkins, A. 2017. *Twelve red flags: Corruption in the award of extractive sector licenses and contracts*. London, U.K.: Natural Resources Governance Index.

53 Source: Author's analysis of the NRGI Resource Governance Index 2017 and 2021

54 Angola (2019), Cameroon (2019), Gabon (2018) and Nigeria (2021).

11 Closing the Loop

The Role of External Actors in Corruption

Chikondi Chidzanja and Charles Kajoloweka***

Introduction

Global financial integrity (GFI) estimates that Malawi loses an average of 650 million USD each year to illicit financial flows[1], ultimately distorting government spending, disrupting reforms, impeding service delivery, further marginalising the vulnerable, compromising development support, and undermining democracy. Malawi also risks significant losses in direct foreign investment as high levels of corruption deter foreign direct investment by potential investors. Crucially, corruption poses a significant threat to achieving Malawi's Vision 2063, a long-term development plan which seeks to catapult the country into a middle upper income status by 2063 by investing in physical and human capital. Thus, tackling corruption has become a central governance element for aid to Malawi among development partners (DPs).

On average, foreign donor aid constitutes over 40% of Malawi's annual budget, in addition to direct budgetary and technical support to NGOs, and over US$5.1 trillion in debt. In 2020, for example, the US Government alone contributed US$124.3 million in aid targeting health, education, agriculture, environment, and governance. Malawi ranks 110 on the Transparency International's (TI's) 2021 Corruption Perceptions Index out of 180 countries. With reference to Malawi, the chapter analyses the anti-corruption legal and policy landscape, categories of external actors, the type and effectiveness of support rendered to Malawi, and the influence and dynamics of external actors in the fight against corruption in Malawi. The chapter also highlights possible solutions to strengthen the positive role of external actors in the anti-corruption drive in Malawi.

Legal Framework for Combating Corruption in Malawi

International development partners have been critical in shaping the institutional architecture of Anti-Corruption Bureau of Malawi (ACB). Their role in stamping out corruption and related crimes in Malawi has been significant. This has been motivated by the self-serving need to protect their taxpayer's money, which is given to the country through development aid and the need to promote the growth of democratic governance.

DOI: 10.4324/9781003326649-13

The development partners' role in the anti-corruption crusade in Africa, and in particular, Malawi, should also be understood in the context of the liberalisation of the latter's economy and the new democratic dispensation introduced in the 1990s, as well as the existing national and international anti-corruption frameworks. When Malawi adopted a democratic Constitution in 1995 following the General Elections of 1994, it committed the State to ensure public trust and good governance under section 13 (o). The section further committed the state to "guarantee accountability, transparency, personal integrity and financial probity and which by virtue of their effectiveness and transparency will strengthen confidence in public institutions."[2] In agreement with democratic principles of good governance, the Corrupt Practices Act (CPA) became operational on 15 February 1996, marking a new chapter in Malawi's democratic governance structure. The World Bank called the legislation "a comprehensive and well-designed piece of legislation; it provides a much better basis for the control of corruption than the original anti-bribery provisions in the penal code."[3]

So far, the national legal framework pertinent to corruption comprises the Penal Code (PC 1930), Criminal Procedure and Evidence Code (CPC), Corrupt Practices Act (CPA), Public Finance Management Act (2003 PFMA) Public Procurement and Disposal of Public Assets Act (PPDPA), and the Financial Crimes Act (FCA, which replaced the repealed 2006 Money Laundering, Proceeds of Serious Crime and Terrorist Financing Act (MLA).[4]

Despite some registered initial successes of the legal regime, several gaps and deficiencies were exposed following the high-profile Cashgate scandal.[5] It was observed that the Penal Code provisions were not well-suited to prosecute "modern" crimes of theft of intangible assets, computer-based fraud and associated offences. It was further observed that the introduction of laws such as the 1995 Corrupt Practices Act and the 2006 Money Laundering Act had not been matched by efforts to address inconsistencies, gaps, and ambiguous provisions arising from the heterogeneous assemblage of modern statutes and those mainly reproducing English law of the 1950s and 1960s. The clumsy money laundering law was also new territory for law enforcement officials and untested in court.[6] The response to Cashgate was the active operationalisation of the Money Laundering, Proceeds of Serious Crimes and Terrorist Financing Act.

Alignment with International and Regional Legal Framework

Malawi signed the United Nations Convention against Corruption on 21 September 2004. The instrument of ratification was signed by the President of the Republic on 31 October 2007. Consequently, Malawi deposited its instrument of ratification with the Secretary-General of the United Nations on 4 December 2007.[7] Malawi implements its obligations under the Convention through a variety of laws, principally: the Corrupt Practices Act, the Penal Code, the Criminal Procedure and Evidence Code (CP and EC), the Money Laundering, Proceeds of Serious Crimes and Terrorist Financing Act, the Extradition Act and the Mutual Legal Assistance in Criminal Matters Act (MLACMA).

Malawi is also a member of the Southern African Development Community (SADC), the Eastern and South African Anti-Money Laundering Group (ESAAMLG) and the Asset Recovery Inter-Agency Network of Southern Africa (ARINSA). The ACB is also a member of the SADC Anti-Corruption Committee (SACC) and the African Association of Anti-Corruption Authorities (AAACA). The exchange of personnel for investigative and training purposes, in particular with neighbouring countries, helps to strengthen law enforcement cooperation at the international level.

Categories of External Actors in Fighting Corruption

The major bilateral DPs in Malawi's anti-corruption fight include the European Union, United Kingdom (UK), United States of America (USA), Germany, Irish and Norwegian governments. These external actors can be categorised into two: those that provided financial assistance and those that provided technical assistance. However, in most instances, these categories would overlap as some actors would provide for both. Outstanding among them is the British Department for International Development (DfID), now the Foreign Commonwealth and Development Office (FCDO) has been supporting the ACB since shortly after its inception in 1998 as the traditional donor. In fact, ACB has always had a technical advisor from the DfID. The Royal Norwegian Embassy (RNE) started supporting it in 2001. Before suspending its aid in 2001 prompted by Malawi's "corruption and political intolerance," Denmark was also one of the outstanding supporters of ACB's operations.

Malawi's drive for international convention inclusion has seen it engaging with the multilateral Bretton Woods institutions: the International Monetary Fund (IMF) and the World Bank (WB). These have been influencing policy reforms in Malawi since the early 1990s, in a wider push to apparently improve governance. The IMF through its country reviews engage the Malawi Government on governance issues including corruption. For example, in its 2021 Country Report for Malawi, IMF highlights corruption as one of the major governance deficits.

The Bretton Woods institution called on Malawi to strengthen public sector governance and institutions that "would help safeguard scarce resources, reduce vulnerabilities to corruption, and strengthen policy effectiveness." On a specific note, the IMF also noted the abuse of funds meant for the COVID-19 pandemic in 2020 and urged the government to swiftly act on audit reports of the National Audit Office (NAO), which identified irregularities and mismanagement in the procurement and contract awarded process of COVID-19-related public funds.[8] There is no doubt, therefore, that Bretton Wood institutions are crucial in influencing the government's interventions in the fight against corruption.

DPs coordination in governance-related fields has been effective, and ACB has relied heavily on its support. These donors have fashioned the operational style and approaches of ACB through financial backing and the provision of technical assistance. Funding from various partners has helped to build the capacity of members of staff of the Bureau such as through training of investigators, prosecutors, and other members of staff. Some of the donors provide commodity assistance in the form of equipment and vehicles. Other DPs provide support for the development and later review of the National Anti-Corruption Strategy.

Donor Funding

Fighting corruption is not cheap. This is the case because corruption cases mostly involve political elites with the wherewithal to fight back. For a country like Malawi with a lot of competing budgetary priorities, the allocation of money and other resources to the graft-fighting body has been dodgy. The ACB has always faced acute resource constraints which are compounded by erratic funding by the government. Sometimes months pass without funding, and once the funding is in, most of it goes towards administrative costs such as rent, electricity, water bills, and car servicing.[9]

The result has been that the ACB is incessantly overwhelmed with a backlog of cases that need to be investigated and prosecuted. Lack of budgetary independence has also impacted negatively on its effectiveness. Therefore, to some significant extent, the ACB has relied heavily on DPs for its operational budget since its formation. Before the Cashgate scandal, donors funded the ACB through a funding pool under the arrangement termed common approach to budgetary support (CABS). However, the CABS became defunct due to DPs withdrawing after the Cashgate scandal.[10]

Before the Cashgate scandal, DPs were fully committed to funding the Bureau. For example, in 2007, the RNE and DfID joined into a funding agreement. The programme phase ran until the end of 2011 and had sourced 2.5 million British pounds from DfID and an additional 20 million Norwegian Kroner from RNE (together an equivalent of approximately seven million US dollars). The goal of this phase was "the elimination of corruption in all its forms in order to enhance the socio-economic well-being of all the people of Malawi"[11], the purpose was "to prevent and reduce corrupt practices in Malawi."[12] Both were aligned with the vision of the ACB five-year Strategic Plan 2007–2011. In February 2010, the review team was tasked by DfID/RNE to review the progress of the ACB over the last 1.5 years. The insecure funding called for more donor engagement. DfID Malawi's budget for 2012/13 to 2014/15 was set at 307.5 million British pounds of which 45 per cent among others was to assist the operations of key institutions such as the Anti-Corruption Bureau and the judiciary.[13]

It should be observed that not all DPs suspended their funding to Malawi's graft cause. The Royal RNE and Irish Aid, for instance, did not withdraw their financial support to the ACB. The RNE supported the capacity development of the ACB to investigate financial and computer-related corruption through the establishment of a forensic unit. The operation of the unit required staff training in computer forensics and purchasing equipment, including computer software for analysis. On the other hand, Irish Aid supported investigations of corrupt practices related to the Farm Input Subsidy Programme (FISP).

Furthermore, the DfID also provided funding in support of the process and development of The National Anti-Corruption Strategy II (NACSII).[14] Experts from the Basel Institute of Governance provided technical support to the Drafting and Oversight Committees as well.

Technical Assistance

Since its establishment, the ACB has been criticised for being slow in handling cases. This is true and the criticism is justified, to an extent. However, it should be noted that the bureau lacks technical expertise in both investigations and prosecutions in terms of staff capacity. Consequently, at the height of Cashgate case trials; the DfID supplied two advisors to provide technical support in the prosecutions department of ACB. The technical advisors were seasoned lawyers from the UK tasked to analyse cases and guide investigators and prosecutors on how to handle them to ensure an increased conviction rate in court.

To aid prosecution of Cashgate cases, the United Nations Office on Drugs and Crime (UNODC), in collaboration with the Assets Recovery Interagency Network of Southern Africa (ARINSA), organised training of ACB officers on money laundering and asset tracing, to facilitate the seizure of property tainted by money-laundering crimes. In addition to that initiative, Malawi has benefited a lot from ARINSA's capacity-building efforts. Since ARINSA's inception, a good number of officers from the Financial Intelligence Authority, investigators and prosecutors from the Anti-Corruption Bureau (ACB) and the Malawi Police Service (MPS) as well as prosecutors from the Director of Public Prosecution (DPP's) office have attended different training workshops organised by ARINSA.[15]

In 2016, the DFID, Royal Norwegian Embassy and Irish Aid financially assisted the opening of the Forensic Data Unit (FDU) within the investigations department of the Bureau. The FDU is responsible for running the Forensic Laboratory to collect, secure, and preserve digital data evidence seized from suspects and ensure that it is in a form admissible in the court of Law.[16] So far, the FDU has been assisting the MPS, Director of Public Prosecutions (DPP) and Malawi Revenue Authority (MRA).

In the wake of Cashgate, USAID and DfID partnered to establish "Tackling Serious and Organised Corruption in Malawi" (TSOC) programme. The programme commenced in July 2016 and is expected to end in March 2024. The aim of this bilateral programme is to enhance the technical capacity and coordination of key Malawian law enforcement agencies, including the Anti-Corruption Bureau, Director of Public Prosecutions, Financial Intelligence Unit (FIU), and Drug Theft Implementation Unit.[17]

With a Project budget of GB£8,271,367, TSOC aligned itself with the anti-corruption priorities of the Malawi government with an enhanced focus on asset confiscations in high-visibility/high-impact cases. The objective of the TSOC programme is to increase the likelihood and severity of sanctions for high-level corruption and in doing so deter future crimes. The main component is delivered by the Basel Institute's International Centre for Asset Recovery (ICAR). This component offers technical assistance and responds to strategic needs requested and agreed upon the Anti-Corruption Bureau (ACB), the Financial Intelligence Authority

(FIA) the office of the DPP, and more recently the MPS. ICAR-embedded experts have access to a "Strategic Fund" to support the tactical needs of the beneficiary agencies.[18]

TSOC has also contributed towards supporting the approved Coordination Strategy on Investigation and Prosecution of Financial and Related Crimes (2020). Furthermore, the programme has strengthened Malawi's anti-corruption and asset recovery regime by supporting the establishment of the Asset Forfeiture Unit (AFU), as well as providing proposed amendments to the reviews of the Financial Crimes and Corrupt Practices Acts. However, beyond its establishment, the management of AFU has been chaotic marred by opaqueness in the disposal of seized assets and poor coordination among law enforcement agencies. Notably, some of the assets seized from Cashgate cases in 2014/2015 have significantly depreciated for lying idle for years.

At the writing, there were efforts by the government and DPs particularly TSOC under the International Asset Recovery to strengthen the asset recovery regime including AFU. A new Asset Recovery Strategy should focus on establishing a structure for policy-making and a whole system response, including a multi-agency asset-tracing and recovery scheme, as well as transparency to the public. From a prevention perspective, the programme further enhanced Malawi's ability to curb money laundering in line with the East and Southern Africa Anti-Money Laundering Group (ESAAMLG) recommendations – with, for example, a focus on strengthening oversight of estate agents – and continued to support investigative journalism with an emphasis on corruption through the continuous Journalist Education (CJE) programme.[19]

Effectiveness of Developing Partners in Combating Corruption

International DPs have had a significant influence on the anti-corruption value chain in Malawi, prominently featuring in designing and funding anti-corruption interventions. It is not uncommon that like the Government of Malawi, DPs recognise corruption as one of the major threats to the country's development aspirations. However, they have also had some setbacks.

Assessing the Methods

In 1995, the World Bank supported the government of Malawi in reforming the public financial system. One of the first reforms was to replace the manual financial system with a Public Financial Management System (PFMS). The pilot trial covered several key government ministries. However, due to problems with suppliers, know-how, coordination, and implementation, the pilot trial was abandoned.[20] Another unsuccessful attempt was implemented in 2003. In 2005, however, the Integrated Financial and Management Information System (IFMIS) was successfully operationalised. Notably, the implementation of IFMIS was a precondition for Malawi's qualification for the Highly Indebted Poor Country Initiative debt cancellation.[21]

The new system sought to strengthen financial management and fiscal discipline. However, evidence shows that IFMIS miserably tumbled as it turned out to be at the heart of cashgate cases and the grand plunder of public resources in government. Investigative audits into Cashgate show that IFMIS was extensively manipulated and abused due to weaknesses in system security and auditing.[22] Thus, the reforms were introduced without relevant investment in human capacity development.

The World Bank also carries out country assessments on governance including corruption. For years, Malawi's performance has been rated as extremely poor on the World Bank's Country Policy and Institutional Assessment (CPIA) which assesses the conduciveness of a country's policy and institutional framework to poverty reduction, sustainable growth, and the effective use of development assistance. The CPA rates countries on a scale of 1 to 6, where 1 represents the worst performance while 6 depicts the best performance on a series of indicators. For the period between 2013 and 2017, Malawi's CPIA rating remained between 2.9 and 2.8; while in 2018, the rate dropped to 2.5.

Whereas the CPIA rating improved to 3.2 in 2019, the score on corruption, Transparency, and Accountability in the Public Sector remained low at 2.5, signifying significant failures in tackling corruption. This calls for honest conversations on the effectiveness of the anti-corruption approaches and interventions by DPs, government, and other stakeholders. Sadly, DPs in Malawi are beyond reproach considering the power play, no one including civil society is prepared to challenge the significant failures of the DPs in this anti-corruption value chain. This ugly picture depicts the country's collective failure in uprooting corruption.

External Actors: A Double-Edged Sword?

External actors in the anti-corruption value chain in Malawi have evidently proven to be a double-edged sword. On the one hand, as demonstrated earlier in this chapter, DPs have succeeded in fortifying law enforcement agencies and spurring the government into action during major corruption scandals. On the other hand, their efforts have been disruptive, inhibiting the cohesion and independence of law enforcement agencies, stirring rivalry, undermining local ownership, and interfering with the independence of the agencies. Multinational corporations (MNCs) have also engaged in various bureaucratic and systematic corruption and extractive activities, yet with limited sanctions.

A critical reflection on Cashgate cases and the recent "state capture cases" involving one business tycoon, as well as aid management politics, illuminate the disruptive role external actors have had in Malawi. Crucially, some foreign actors have also been at the heart of systemic and bureaucratic corruption, in a country where the government is the biggest buyer of goods and services. Yet foreign actors induced corruption and other inadequacies have not received adequate attention.

Further, a closer look at the role of DPs in cashgate and the recent corruption cases raises some significant questions about the intrusive nature of their participation with the potential of inhibiting the independence and coordination of law enforcement agencies. In the Cashgate case, some DPs literary sat in the inter-agency coordination task force. Such an approach can be dangerous to the independence of the law enforcement agencies. It creates a perception that law enforcement agencies are controlled, captured and driven by external interests, which has the potential to undermine public trust and local ownership. It also creates unwarranted pressure on law enforcement agencies blurring independent decision-making as each time they have to pay attention to the interests of donors sitting at the table. Similarly, some DPs have attached their own expatriates to law enforcement agencies such as the Anti-Corruption Bureau to provide technical support.

Hence, donors have direct access to all critical information about the country's graft-busting body. This may undermine the independence of the Bureau and national sovereignty. Interestingly, law enforcement agencies have been at the mercy of projects designed by DPs. This has resulted in individual law enforcement agencies aligning with the respective donor agencies more than inter-agency coordination. This has in turn fuelled rivalry, suspicion, and competition among agencies. Crucially, this approach by DPs possibly also explains the lack of commitment by the Government of Malawi to uprooting corruption to the extent that DPs are pushed to take over the government's core anti-corruption obligations including financing and human capacity investment.

DPs have also been selective in their support of law enforcement agencies with the ACB as their favourite, leaving other agencies such as FIA and the Director of Public Prosecutions under-resourced. This has contributed to rivalry, unnecessary, and unhealthy competition among law enforcement agencies. The most recent case of perceived state capture involving one business tycoon and some senior government officials exposed a lack of cohesion between the ACB and other agencies in which ACB is seen not cooperating with other law enforcement agencies, but Britain's National Crimes Agency (NCA).

There are claims that the ACB could not share any credible information with other law enforcement agencies and was neither willing to work with others in the Sattar case. In a leaked audio clip with one social media political operative, the ACB Director is on record that the British Government trusted no one but herself in dealing with the Sattar case and that the success of the entire case solely depended on her personal integrity. This exposes the depth of foreign influence in the lifeblood of the Bureau. It was no surprise to witness another wave of running battles between the ACB and DPP on one hand, and the ACB and Attorney General on the other. While the ACB had the NCA report implicating high-profile public officials, the DPP and Attorney General had no idea about the report, despite their critical role in the prosecution of cases.

While it may be arguable that the Bureau did not trust other law enforcement agencies in handling such high-profile cases which implicated senior government officials and politicians including the country's Vice President Saulos Chilima; it may also be true that the Bureau was on instructions by the British authorities not to share their report with other agencies for reasons best known to them. The lack of cohesion among law enforcement agencies and its cost are huge that no external allies should overlook. The Cashgate cases offer a good example of how crucial interagency coordination is crucial in tackling complex corruption cases.

There are also growing conversations in Malawi about the lack of transparency and accountability in the management of aid by DPs in Malawi. Some quarters including civil society actors have accused DPs in Malawi of clandestinely awarding grants and consultants to their preferred INGOs and consultants. A good amount of aid destined for Malawi actually ends up in the pockets of a few foreign agents disguised as expert researchers and INGOs whose criteria for their selection remain opaque. It is widely believed that most grants and contracts destined for Malawi are clandestinely shared up global north through connivance. It is no secret that most INGOs and consultants from the Global North are given more advantage over locals. This form of corruption is widespread yet not confronted. This has continued to erode the perception of the integrity of donors in Malawi.

While DPs have been on the frontlines calling for transparency and accountability in Malawi, their operations remain heavily shrouded in secrecy. This raises questions about DPs' moral standing, which is supposed to be on a high ground. In fact, some foreign agencies are actively engaged in corrupt practices. Around 2015, the ACB investigated World Vision, an international NGO over allegations of abuse of funds for a community project in a rural district, Nkhata Bay. However, the Bureau could not proceed with the case despite credible evidence after intervention by the Foreign Affairs Ministry citing immunity from prosecution enjoyed by international agencies including IGOs. Such a selective and regressive approach is counterproductive to tackling organised corruption, particularly in a country where IGOs control over 95 per cent of external funding channelled through NGOs.

Way Forward: Strengthen the Positive Role of External Actors

Corruption deterrence is a multi-causal process. This is why the US Ambassador, David Young, called on Malawians to fully embrace the fight against corruption as their own.[23] This should not be interpreted as a sign of donor fatigue but rather a call to the need for more civic engagement by corruption-fighting agencies to promote the involvement of the demand side of accountability. So far, the graft fight by DPs has been dominated by the top-to-bottom supply side of accountability through strengthening the legal and policy governmental checks and balances without fully engaging the demand side through the bottom-to-top approach. To some extent, donors have been blamed for hijacking ACB's agenda as Doig et al (2006) pointed out:

> In the case of the Malawi ACC, a 2003 NORAD/DFID report noted, 'the evolution of donor support has tended to accentuate, rather than abate, ACB's difficulties. Compartmentalised funding by donors division-by-division has, albeit unintentionally, held back the development of internal ownership of corporate strategic management [. . .] Effectively, ACB priorities remain determined by donors through their individual funding choices.[24]

Perhaps investing resources in promoting citizen ownership of the crusade will complement the strides already achieved in the supply side of governance accountability. An examination of the social norms that have entrenched corruption among the local citizenry is important to build ownership. This approach will absolve and inoculate external actors from accusations of intrusion and favouring a particular institution on the supply side of governance accountability. Furthermore, this holistic approach will ensure a levelled play field for all institutions without creating a favourite as with the case with ACB.

Favouring one institution over others creates issues of suspicion and lack of trust. More importantly, favouring one institution is unwise because "for donors to place their anti-corruption expectations in a single agency is a risky strategy that gives them little room for manoeuvre and limits the development of a wider governance organisational framework that may have complementary approaches and structures."[25] Therefore, the holistic approach will create equilibrium as it will balance the efforts on the supply side of improving the capacity and strengthening systems of graft fighting with the efforts on the demand side of non-state stakeholders through the promotion of public participation. Governance is best when the supply-and-demand side of governance is both strong and is used to complement each other imaginatively.[26]

DPs should explore alternative networks in the demand side of governance accountability. The recent explosion of the NCA–ACB relationship in the media is an example of how transparency is the panacea for holding the government to account. Without the alertness of the media and CSOs, and the bravery of investigative journalists like the Platform for Investigative Journalism and whistleblowers, corruption will continue to succeed. Academia is another network that needs to be engaged to promote civic engagement. The academia can champion a national integrity approach through the development of anti-corruption and ethics studies and research for use by policymakers and practitioners.

In 2014, The Basel Institute on Governance together with UNODC initiated an Anti-Corruption Academic Initiative (ACAD) platform with the aim of effective teaching and pedagogy in anti-corruption studies within institutions of higher learning. However, this initiative did not extend to African institutions of higher learning. This initiative can yield positive strides towards combating graft as academicians in Malawi are often also activists and play a first-hand role in modelling public opinion and policy issues. More importantly, academics are uniquely positioned as they typically operate under fewer political constraints and can speak and write more freely about sensitive corruption issues.[27] These are some of the networks that need to be engaged and empowered to promote civic engagement and ownership of the graft fight.

Ultimately, the government has a huge role to play in the graft fight in order to signal and promote ownership. It can be said that since the advent of multiparty democracy, successive administrations have given convincing lip service campaigns against corruption without effecting feasible positive results on the ground. Successive governments are aware that graft fight is a prerequisite to development but their commitment levels have always been mild. Government therefore should take steps to provide adequate financial and technical support towards the graft. Therefore, the issue of DP intervention may be mitigated by increased state support to corruption fighting bodies. This would counter-balance DPs' intrusive practices, while ensuring that the state continues to benefit from other potentially rewarding initiatives by the former.

Conclusion

The ACB has the right institutional form; its functionality is beholden to the interests of the politically powerful and connected – so much so that operational independence, enforcement, and accountability for effective anti-corruption remain challenges.[28] However, despite the challenges, it should be asked whether without financial and technical assistance, graft-fighting institutions would have survived and managed to operate in a hostile political and economic environment and recorded some achievements. Without any iota of doubt, DPs ensured that these institutions acquired a sound pre-requisite graft fighting structure and operating system.

DPs have been critical to the evolving organisation development outlook of ACB and its attendant supporting institutions. They have made critical contributions towards closing the loop and their efforts have seen fortification of the supply side of governance accountability through funding and technical support of graft-fighting institutions legal and policy framework. Indeed, there are gaps in the demand side of governance accountability that need to be strengthened through civic engagement to encourage ownership of the graft fight.

However, the onus is on the DPs to operate without seen to be favouring, intruding, and playing double standards. The credibility of DPs is dependent on their outlook as architects and facilitators of good governance and accountability practices. Their invaluable expertise and experience should be seen to be complimenting other than dictating and prescribing the direction of graft fighting in Malawi. This is how local ownership can be successfully enhanced. DPs can close the loop and turn Malawi into a paragon of integrity if they assume a holistic other than a heuristic approach only to fighting corruption.

Notes

* Doctoral candidate, Stellenbosch University.

** Founder and Executive Director of Youth and Society (YAS); and Co-founder of the National Anti-Corruption Alliance (NACA).

1 Global Financial Integrity, Illicit Financial Flows and Development Indices: 2008–2012 – available at: www.gfintegrity.org/report/illicit-financial-flows-and-development-indices-2008-2012/ (accessed on 20 July 2022)

2 ACB History – available at: https://acbmw.org/acb-history/ (accessed on 09 July 2022).

3 Support to the Government of Malawi's Anti – Corruption Program available at: http://www1.worldbank.org/publicsector/anticorrupt/MalawiGCA.pdf (accessed on 15 August 2022)

4 Gerhard Anders Law Enforcement and High-Level Corruption in Malawi: Learning from Cashgate
5 Cashgate was a financial scandal involving looting, theft and corruption that happened at Capital Hill the seat of the Government of Malawi between 2012 and 2013.
6 Gerhard Anders Law Enforcement and High-Level Corruption in Malawi: Learning from Cashgate
7 Malawi Final Country report available at: www.unodc.org/documents/treaties/UNCAC/CountryVisitFinalReports/2017_03_09_Malawi_Final_Country_Report.pdf (accessed on 24 July 2022)
8 IMF Country Report No. 21/269.
9 Chingayipe, Henry in OSISA report on Effectiveness of Anti-Corruption Agencies in Southern Africa available at: www.corruptionwatch.org.za/wp-content/uploads/2017/08/osisa_acc_text_29mar1130_web2.pdf (accessed on 1 August 2022)
10 Chingayipe, Henry in OSISA report on Effectiveness of Anti-Corruption Agencies in Southern Africa available at: www.corruptionwatch.org.za/wp-content/uploads/2017/08/osisa_acc_text_29mar1130_web2.pdf (accessed on 1 August 2022)
11 Nawaz, F. (2012), 'Overview of corruption and anti-corruption in Malawi' U4 Anti – Corruption Resource Center, No 329 available at:https://knowledgehub.transparency.org/assets/uploads/helpdesk/329_Overview-of_corruption_and_anti-corruption_in_Malawi.pdf (accessed on 05 August 2022)
12 Nawaz, F, (2012), 'Overview of corruption and anti-corruption in Malawi' U4 Anti – Corruption Resource Center, No. 329 available at:https://knowledgehub.transparency.org/assets/uploads/helpdesk/329_Overview-of_corruption_and_anti-corruption_in_Malawi.pdf (accessed on 5 August 2022)
13 DFID's Anti-Corruption Strategy for Malawi available at: https://assets.publishing.service.gov.uk/government/uploads/system/uploads/attachment_data/file/213920/anti-corruption-strategy-mw.pdf (accessed on 13 July 2022)
14 The National Anti-Corruption Strategy II available at: https://acbmw.org/wp-content/uploads/2020/03/NACS-II-1.pdf (accessed on 20 July 2022)
15 Taking the Proceeds from Crime: The Story of ARINSA available at: www.unodc.org/documents/southernafrica/The_story_of_ARINSA.pdf (accessed on 26 July 2022)
16 ACB Investigations Department available at: https://acbmw.org/investigations/ (accessed on 27 July 2022)
17 https://devtracker.fcdo.gov.uk/projects/GB-1-205173/summary (accessed on 20 August 2022)
18 Annual Review Template – April 2022 available at: http://iati.dfid.gov.uk/iati_documents/5631652.odt (accessed on 15 August 2022)
19 Annual review (4) 205173 (Published - December 2021) https://devtracker.fcdo.gov.uk/projects/GB-1-205173/documents (accessed on 10 August 2022)
20 Gerhard Anders, Law Enforcement and High Level Corruption in Malawi: Learning from Cashgate
21 Gerhard Anders, Law Enforcement and High Level Corruption in Malawi: Learning from Cashgate
22 Gerhard Anders, Law Enforcement and High Level Corruption in Malawi: Learning from Cashgate
23 The Sunday Times, *'US urges Malawi to own graft fight'* 05 June 2022
24 Doig, A, 'Hands-On or Hands-Off? Anti-Corruption Agencies in Action, Donor Expectations, and a Good Enough Reality, 170.
25 Doig, A, 'Hands-On or Hands-Off? Anti-Corruption Agencies in Action, Donor Expectations, and a Good Enough Reality.
26 Naazneen Barma Matching governance demand and supply, available at: https://blogs.worldbank.org/eastasiapacific/matching-governance-demand-and-supply (accessed on 18 August 2022).

27 Virna Di Palma The role of academia in anti-corruption Collective Action, available at: https://baselgovernance.org/blog/role-academia-anti-corruption-collective-action (accessed on 18 August 2022)

28 OSISA report on Effectiveness of Anti-Corruption Agencies in Southern Africa, available at: www.corruptionwatch.org.za/wp-content/uploads/2017/08/osisa_acc_text_29mar1130_web2.pdf (accessed on 16 July 2022)

12 Combating Illicit Enrichment in Cameroon's Public and Private Sectors

Avitus A. Agbor and Rorisang Matlala***

Funding for the research of this chapter was obtained from the South Africa National Research Foundation (NRF) and Justice in Practice Project, Law, Justice, and Sustainability Research Unit in the Faculty of Law. Thanks to Professor Mitzi Wiese and Dr Natasha Ravyshe.

Introduction

Typical of most legal systems that seek to tackle the plight of corruption within both public and private sectors are the following: the development and deployment of anti-corruption measures that target both the private and public sectors; the criminalization of illicit enrichment or inexplicable personal wealth; and the utilization of conviction-based confiscation of assets that were obtained from the proceeds of crime or used in the commission of a crime. These strategies are informed by the need to achieve deterrent and punitive effects as they punish the perpetrators while discouraging others from engaging in similar criminal conduct.

International and regional instruments dealing with the broader issue of transnational organized crime and corruption specifically require States Parties thereto to undertake legislative and other measures within their legal systems, that investigate and punish corruption within the private sector, prohibit illicit enrichment and extend the powers of the judiciary and law enforcement by drifting from conviction-based confiscation to non-confiscation-based confiscation: a recent tool whose usage within domestic legal systems has increased dramatically.

In view of the anti-corruption strategies adopted by Cameroon, a few arguments can be made: first, they are narrowed to the public sector, thereby (inadvertently) neglecting the private sector. Secondly, illicit enrichment is yet to be criminalized. That means numerous individuals, in both the public and private sectors, are not interrogated (and subsequently investigated) on the legitimate source(s) of the assets they acquire and amass. Thirdly, the legal system still relies on conviction-based confiscation as evidenced by the numerous confiscation orders imposed by the Special Criminal Court in decided cases.

Informed by international and regional anti-corruption instruments and taking two hypothetical scenarios that highlight the regular interface between the public and private sectors and how that may result in illicit enrichment, this paper argues

DOI: 10.4324/9781003326649-14

that the various anti-corruption mechanisms taken and implemented by Cameroon will be effective in achieving the ultimate goal of eliminating corruption if and only when those measures are extended to the private sector. That would mean that the legal system is reformed, with legislation enacted that does not only criminalize illicit enrichment but also drifts from a conviction-based confiscation model to a non-conviction-based confiscation.

The anti-corruption strategies adopted by Cameroon in combatting corruption, not so much would be achieved if corruption is limited to the public sector only, illicit enrichment is not criminalized, and confiscation is based on conviction. The paper kicks off with the presentation of two hypothetical cases that expose some of the complex clandestine relationships that exist between individuals in the private and public sectors, and how that would result in what can be called a negative misappropriation of public funds (described later); illicit enrichment; and why, in the absence of evidence of misappropriation of public funds, the individuals involved would amass assets that were procured through illegitimate means which they would retain since confiscation requires conviction for a predicate offence.

Implementation of Anti-Corruption Measures in Cameroon

The imposition of forfeiture and confiscation as accessory penalties upon criminal conviction of an individual is a key feature of most legal systems in the world. Where a person is convicted of an offence, it is relatively much easier to impose such accessory penalties such as forfeiture and confiscation of specific items often listed in the judgement itself. This remarkable ease is attributable to the fact that there is a nexus between the offence and the property in question: such a property could have been used in the commission of a crime, or itself is derived from the commission of a crime. Secondly, in such situations, issues relating to the right to property and the right to privacy are not contended.

As seen in the numerous judgements delivered by the Special Criminal Court (SCC) in cases involving public officials who misappropriated public funds,[1] in addition to the imposition of a term of imprisonment, fines, and reparations, specific assets "belonging" to the convicts were confiscated by the State. Polycarpe Abah Abah used his office as a Minister of Finance and networks to misappropriate funds and properties that belonged to the state, details which were made public only after his arrest, prosecution, and conviction. Sentenced to 25 years' imprisonment for the offence of misappropriation of public funds, confiscation of assets he had acquired was part of the judgement.[2] The Abah Abah case like the others tells us about the involvement of individuals in the private sector in the planning, preparation, and commission of corruption within the public sector.

Anti-corruption efforts are often directed at public officials, or corruption that occurs within the public sphere. The design and implementation of anti-corruption efforts hardly consider the instances and incidents of corruption that take place in the private sector. International instruments do not exclude the private sector: in fact, a holistic approach to fighting corruption would require that the private sector is actively involved, and the activities therein investigated. The question is this: in view of the millions of small- to large-scale transactions that occur within the private sector, is it feasible for the state to deploy its finite resources to every transaction? Or it must limit itself to specific ones? If so, how does it identify and investigate?

These are complex questions of law enforcement, and the lawmaker is challenged with developing and adopting legal instruments that must empower law enforcement and judicial authorities to zoom into those areas without encroaching into citizens' private spaces. At least, international instruments are unequivocal in describing the nature of legal obligations that must be fulfilled by states to achieve the ultimate goal of preventing and combating corruption in their respective countries. In addition, those instruments are clear on the following: extend corruption to the private sector instead of limiting it to the public sector; make illicit enrichment a crime; engage civil society in the fight against corruption; give corruption the status of a universal jurisdiction crime; and lastly, utilize confiscation and seizure of assets in cases where the owner is unable to justify the legitimate source(s) of an asset.

Cameroon and the Corruption Conundrum

Cameroon is a perfect example of a country that manifests the multi-faceted dimensions and depths of corruption: good governance has been compromised, democracy, democratization, and democratic institutions polluted and rendered incredible, systemic violations of human rights that are ensued by selective accountability for the cases involving law-enforcement personnel; a widening gap between the rich and the poor; the subjugation of millions to poverty while a selected few are uplifted to wealth through illegal and unethical means. Corruption has triggered inflation, felt mostly in the acquisition of landed property as individuals with stolen funds outmatch their competitors. It has stagnated socio-economic and political development and accounts for the dilapidating and unsightly infrastructure in the country. With a venal criminal justice system, the spike in violent crimes is, to a greater extent, attributable to corruption as the key actors in the criminal justice system, from investigation through trial to conviction and imprisonment, influence both the processes and outcomes with money. Corruption has also compromised the delivery of basic services.

In Cameroon, the corruption problem is unique for a few reasons: first, it is deeply entrenched in the social fabric of Cameroonian society and exists at all levels. Secondly, it has become the logic of negotiations, infiltrating, and residing in all sectors of Cameroonian life, whether public or private. Scandals of huge financial racketeering have been reported in the clergy, financial institutions, such as banks, cooperatives, and micro-financial institutions; law enforcement; the military, educational institutions; alumni associations; professional bodies and schools; the judiciary; and other civil society entities. Thirdly, Cameroon's criminal law contains over 50 different offences related to corruption, in both the public and private sectors. In addition to her criminal law provisions, other legal instruments and institutional mechanisms have been put in place to combat corruption.

Unfortunately, lacking the requisite political will to drive these initiatives, they have appeared to be more cosmetic and eventually ineffective to fulfil the mission for which they were established.

Cameroon's fight against corruption has been limited to and focused on the misappropriation of public funds, especially those cases committed by senior public officials and top politicians. Evidenced by the legal and institutional developments such as the CONAC, Supreme Audit and the SCC, the investigation, arraignment, prosecution, and conviction of individuals who have misappropriated state property have dominated national news in the past decade. In all objectivity, the SCC has succeeded in recovering stolen funds while consigning its convicts to a penal complex for repentance.

The SCC: Confiscation and Forfeitures as Accessory Penalties

Section 18 of the Cameroonian Penal Code stipulates three principal penalties for natural persons: death penalty, imprisonment, and fine.[3] In addition to those principal penalties, there are alternative penalties;[4] accessory penalties;[5] and preventive measures,[6] applicable to natural persons and corporate bodies. Confiscation as an accessory penalty and a preventive measure is further detailed in Section 35 of the Penal Code, captioned as "confiscation of the 'corpus delicti.'"

Within Cameroon's criminal system, confiscation requires three things: first, it can only be prescribed as an accessory penalty or preventive measure upon the conviction of the accused. In other words, if an accused is acquitted of the crimes for which he is charged, confiscation cannot be ordered. Secondly, it must be ordered by the court. Thirdly, the property that is the subject of the confiscation must belong to the offender. Fourthly, such property must have been used as an instrument in the commission of a crime or is derived from the proceeds of the offence. The words "or is the proceeds of the offence" require some clarification: the proceeds must be related to the offence for which the offender has been convicted, and not for any other offence he might have committed. This, therefore, limits the execution of a confiscation order: a specific property that belongs to the convicted person because such property was used in the commission of the crime for which he is convicted or obtained using the proceeds of the crime for which he has been convicted.

The wording of that clause restricts law enforcement and the judiciary to ensure that the confiscation order, contained in the judgement that convicts the offender, is limited to a specific property (rather than a widened scope to all his properties or assets) for the specific reason that such property or asset was used in the commission of the crime for which he was convicted or proceeds derived from the commission of that crime (and not any crime) were used in the acquisition of the property. The characterization used by the lawmaker in detailing confiscation as an accessory penalty and preventive measure makes the argument more persuasive: "confiscation of the 'corpus delicti'": this means that confiscation is limited to a *corpus delicti* which must be tied to the crime for which the accused has been convicted, such *corpus delicti* having been used as an instrument to facilitate the commission of a crime or was obtained with the proceeds from the crime for which the accused was convicted.

Confiscation as an accessory penalty and preventive measure features in two key parts in the Penal Code: first, Chapter One of Book II of the Penal Code (offences against the Security of the State). Offences appearing in Sections 102 to 117 inclusive deal with both internal and external security of the state. In addition to the principal penalties that are attached to the definition of those offences, accessory penalties and features are imposed mandatorily and discretionarily. For those offences, especially those involving the use of weapons in committing specific offences whether against the internal or external security of the state, the Penal Code stipulates that accessory penalties such as confiscation should be ordered. Those accessory penalties, applicable to that genre of offences, include specific confiscation; confiscation of unlawful property; general confiscation; and forfeitures.[7] As explained earlier, such confiscation as an accessory penalty is conviction-based: an accused must have been convicted for the offence before confiscation can be ordered, and such confiscation shall be limited to a specific property, including the weapon, linked to the commission of the offence for which the accused was convicted.

For the offence of misappropriation of public funds, confiscation of the corpus delicti as an accessory penalty has never been more utilized by any judicial institution like the Special Criminal Court. Dealing with a special category of misappropriation of public property or funds, the SCC had under its ambit the different kinds of principal and accessory penalties to impose on convicted individuals. Different considerations would inform such choices, some of which include the following: first, the deterrent effect. The convicted individual should receive a sentence and penalties that would ultimately deter others from engaging in such unlawful conduct. Secondly, the need to repair the harm: repay the funds misappropriated and assets stolen from the State. By directing such assets to their personal use, they deprive the state of its own resources.

Section 184(4) of the Penal Code states that "[c]onfiscation under Section 35 of this Code shall be ordered in every case and the forfeitures described in Section 30 shall be imposed for 5 (five) to 10 (ten) years." If the phrasing of Section 184(4) of the Penal Code is an authority to go by, then, a trial court dealing with the offence of misappropriation of public funds has no option but to order accessory penalties: confiscation and forfeitures. The SCC judgements contained, amongst other things, orders for confiscation of the corpus delicti. The principle underlying this aspect of the judgements is simple: the property did not belong to that individual; therefore, the law must restore the said property to its rightful owner: the State. Even though written with so much precision and clarity, confiscation of property in Cameroonian criminal law is conviction-based: an individual must be convicted before a competent court can make an order for confiscation, which further requires the articulation of specific details such as the property in question, belonging to the convicted person, used as an instrument in the commission of a crime or obtained through the proceeds of a crime.

Corruption in the Private Sector: Some Criminal Provisions

In Cameroon, the legal system punishes corruption in both the public and private sectors. However, public perception and understanding is that corruption is perpetrated by only public officials: a view that is, to some extent, shaped by the publicity given to the investigation and prosecution of corruption within the public sector, committed by senior state officials. Numerous acts of corruption, in both the public and private sectors, are criminalized in Cameroon. The amended Penal Code of 2016[8] contains numerous corruption-related offences that occur in both the public and private sectors. Some of those offences include forgery; misappropriation of public funds; concealment and fabrication of evidence; false oath; false expert report; perjury; abuse of function; fraud at examinations; corruption in administrative competitive examinations; favouritism; forgery of official act; insider trading; passive corruption; active corruption; misappropriation of public funds in election matters; corruption and violence in election matters (such as gifts, favours, or promises of employment or benefits); interest in concern; interference with the financial market; prohibited employment; electoral fraud (use of false identity or concealment of information related to an individual's civil status); interest in grant; and procuring influence.[9]

Despite these legislative provisions, nationwide anti-corruption measures have been narrowed to corruption in the public sector. This is evidenced by the establishment of nationwide state institutions.[10] The profiles of the individuals indicted, investigated, prosecuted, and convicted speak to the specialized focus the state has infused into corruption within the public sector. Thirdly, at the interface between individuals in the private and public sectors, it is difficult to rule out the existence of corruption in the private sector: itself taking the guise of organized or syndicated crime with the resultant effect being illicit enrichment. Despite the incontrovertible evidence that points to the occurrence of corruption in the private sector, and the criminal participation of private sector individuals in the commission of corruption in the public sector, such evidence has been largely ignored: the private sector is hardly the focus of criminal investigation when it comes to corruption.

The investigation and prosecution of corruption in Cameroon has largely been limited to the public sector. Without any evidence to explain why this trend, probably, it is because of a couple of reasons: capacity-related issues within law enforcement to be able to identify and investigate cases of corruption within the private sector. Another reason could be the business culture: keep the deal secret if it is a win-win for everyone. If corruption is perpetuated by senior state officials within the political realm, why then bother about petty corruption committed by the rank and file of society which has become a way of life and a means to an end? As always argued in criminal justice, you are a criminal only when you are caught. Therefore, for as long as you are undetected, you go undeterred. These are the typical mindsets that have provided a fecund territory for the perpetration of corruption in Cameroon, normalizing it within the country's social fabric wherein even law enforcement personnel know that a fight against corruption would ultimately mean that they are deprived of booties to sustain their families.

Rethinking Unexplained Wealth Orders as a Legal Tool

An aspect common to all three international and regional instruments mentioned earlier is the power given to State Parties to adopt legislative and other measures that require individuals to justify the legitimate source(s) of their assets. If illicit enrichment is criminalized and has to be combated and prevented, then, requiring that owners of assets provide justifications on how such assets were obtained. This is one of the most effective tools in combating the crime of illicit enrichment: as explained later, it shifts the burden of proof to the owner of the asset who must explain and justify the sources of the assets in question.

Confiscating the Proceeds of Crime to Deter Corruption

People engage in criminal activities for different reasons: revenge, adventurism, heroism and money. For organized crime, research points to one overriding motive: the making of profit or financial gain as the driver. The profits from criminal activities are used to either live lavishly or fund other crimes. Therefore, an effective dissuasion to organized crime would require depriving the culprits from enjoying the proceeds therefrom, which can only be achieved through confiscation and forfeiture. Confiscating such property fulfils two purposes: it prevents the funding of future crimes and deters criminals from criminals as it reduces their capacity to invest in other criminal activities. This strategy touches individuals in organized crime at the core: their pockets. By striking them where it hurts most, they end up scaling down on their operations since they know that ultimately, whatever property they acquire from such crimes would be confiscated by the State. Confiscation and forfeitures have a devastating effect on the psyche of those who engage in organized crime. Informed and driven by evidence of the successes of UWOs, many states have explored the possibility of adopting them in their legal systems.

UWOs in Combatting Illicit Enrichment

In the fight against corruption, law enforcement personnel and the judiciary have one critical tool at their disposal: unexplained wealth orders. Quite a recent legal development that has been utilized by many countries in the world, this tool targets proceeds obtained from criminal proceedings, having as its primary objective depriving criminals from acquiring or benefiting from the proceeds from lawful activities. From an operational perspective, this tool has two distinct features: first, the state must not prove a criminal charge, unlike the situation where there is confiscation or forfeiture based on conviction. Secondly, the state is not required to prove that the property in question is the proceed of a crime. Traditional criminal law requires the state as an adducer to prove every allegation in a criminal charge. The UWO alters this: it shifts the burden of proof to the owner of the property who is required to provide a legitimate source for the wealth in question.

Confiscation or forfeiture procedures are instituted against such a property rather than against the individual who would not necessarily be subjected to a criminal procedure and have such accessory penalties imposed post-conviction. Due to such features, the tool takes a radical approach in dealing with individuals who might benefit from the proceeds of unlawful activities, shifting the evidentiary burden of proving the legitimacy of the funds to acquire such property to the owner. Appearing as radical, law enforcement agents such as the police and prosecutors and courts have tried to water down its utility, ensuring that it becomes one of the most extreme measures in cases where the seizure of assets proves impracticable and ineffective.

Its drastic manner of operation and the likelihood of encroaching on the right to privacy are some of the key concerns that linger around the adoption of this anti-corruption tool in most legal systems where the debate remains much alive as to whether to maintain and grow the current tools in detecting and combatting corruption as traditional methods or infusing the unexplained wealth orders as an additional and contentious tool in such operations.

Recognizing that legal systems and traditions differ and that states weigh on the multiple options that could be used in combatting corruption in both the public and private sectors, this paper argues that UWO becomes an additional tool that would enable law enforcement personnel to open inquiries in cases of inexplicable personal wealth. It is further argued that in view of the obligations imposed by international instruments dealing with the criminalization of corruption and highlighting the need to combat corruption even within the private sector, UWOs become a critical tool towards those ends as they shift the evidentiary burden to the property or wealth owner to disclose the legitimate source of his or her wealth.

The United Nations Convention against Corruption (UNCAC) and the AU Convention on the Prevention and Punishment of Corruption criminalize illicit enrichment, as well as the proceeds therefrom. These instruments urge States Parties thereto to adopt domestic legislation towards this end as well. Despite this, a practical challenge would be how to initiate investigations of suspected cases since most of them are in the private sector. It, therefore, becomes critically important to initiate a paradigm shift in the legal system: to shirt or reverse the burden of proof from the state as it would be in criminal cases, to the individuals who own the assets, requiring them to justify the lawful source(s) of the assets in question. Legal systems like Australia, Colombia, and Ireland have opted for full UWOs: they do not require proof that the property was connected to a crime. In doing so, they reversed the burden of proof to the owner of the asset(s) in question.

If the investigation and prosecution of corruption must go beyond public officials, then, novel tools should be introduced to the Cameroonian legal system. Firstly, and within the legal system, the criminalization of illicit enrichment with appropriate sanctions. Secondly, empowering the judiciary and law enforcement officials to open investigations into any suspected cases of illicit enrichment. Such broadened powers must, however, be exercised with due regard to human rights, consistency, and uniformity, with approved guidelines on the conduct of such operations. Thirdly, suspected cases of illicit enrichment must detail the assets in question, with questions on their lawful origin posed to their owners, who must be given a reasonable time to respond and if possible, provide documentary evidence.

These approaches and legal tools would, undoubtedly, be useful in tackling the crime of illicit enrichment and taking the focus of anti-corruption measures to the private sector. They will put Cameroon in compliance with her international obligations. They will also prevent participants in organized crime from reaping from the proceeds of a crime and also deny them the assets they need to fund further criminal operations. However, legal challenges would erupt: they may have some implications on criminal procedure and human rights. More than likely, it would be argued that no one should be compelled to disclose his or her personal information, especially with regard to wealth. That touches on the right to privacy, and it brings an individual's personal information to the public arena.

In cases of suspected criminal activity, the traditional burden of proof rests on the state as it is the state that alleges. That burden, fortunately, is shifted to the owner of an asset: explain the legitimate sources of the property. In other words, the property owner asserts that his or her property is lawfully acquired and all that is needed to discharge this burden is to provide the evidence. Furthermore, the criminalization of illicit enrichment and the need to adopt non-conviction-based confiscation are measures prescribed by international instruments, which were adopted with an understanding of the potential human rights implications. From a commonsensical perspective, it can be argued that if the lawful origin of an asset is required for an insurance coverage to be provided, then, states may as well require that the lawfulness of a property be established before it can be afforded legal recognition and protection. Just like a state has the power to ask anyone at any time to identify themselves and the legality of their stay on their territory, it can do the same with assets on its territory.

The divulgence of an individual's pertinent information to the state does not throw that information into the public domain. Neither does it infringe on the individual's privacy: if the state has an obligation to protect the property of those in its jurisdiction, then, the state may have a vested interest in knowing what it is protecting, its source, and who owns it. Cameroon's legal system takes a post-conviction confiscation and forfeiture approach, requiring that only upon and after the conviction of an individual and with the pronunciation of the court can confiscation and forfeiture be executed. What then happens to those individuals who have not been prosecuted? Would that approach be effective in dealing with the offence of illicit enrichment?

The state must develop sound methodologies to deploy effective techniques that do not trigger apprehensiveness in property owners on the one hand while, on the other hand, ensuring that proceeds from criminal activities are not left in the hands of criminals. Departing from the legal requirement of a post-conviction-based confiscation and forfeiture to government confiscation because of the lack of a justification for the possession of the property may, in all fairness, be an effective tool in fighting corruption in the private sector and the crime of illicit enrichment. Instances of arbitrariness inconsistencies and misconduct may be curtailed by introducing safety valves such as adequate training of specialized financial crimes investigators and the adoption of guidelines that serve as the working document in their operations.

Applying Unexplained Wealth Orders (UWOs) in the Private Sector

To combat corruption in the private sector and illicit enrichment specifically, it is suggested that Cameroon should depart from the traditional conviction-based confiscation and forfeiture formula to a confiscation–forfeiture without conviction. Alternatively known as civil forfeiture or non-conviction-based confiscation, the state brings an action against a property itself (*in rem*).[11] Such a procedure requires the state to prove that the property in question is derived from the proceeds of a crime or used in the commission or facilitation of a crime. For such a process, the standard of proof is a preponderance of evidence which is the usual civil burden of proof (as opposed to beyond reasonable doubt in criminal matters). Countries like the United Kingdom, the United States, among others, use this as the standard barometer.[12] Some countries have departed from this standard: for example, South Africa where the requirement is "proof on a balance of probabilities" that the property in question was derived from unlawful activities or used in the commission or facilitation of an offence.[13]

UWOs, in operation, would mean that asset confiscation and forfeiture will not be based on a criminal conviction. In substance, they are markedly different from the conviction-based-confiscation model in three ways: first, they are not related to the existence of a criminal investigation or conviction. Rather, a legal action is brought against a person who owns or possesses an unexplained wealth or property. Secondly, the state is not required to prove a predicate offence. Neither is it relevant for the state to show that the owner has been engaged in criminal behaviour. Thirdly, the state is required to show on a preponderance of evidence (that it is more likely than not) that such a person, the defendant or respondent, owns or possesses unexplained wealth, without specifying the criminal activity in which the person might have been involved in. In effect, the burden of proof is shifted from the state that has identified such a property and seeking answers, to the respondent (the owner) who must explain or justify the manner in which such wealth was acquired. In other words, the respondent must show that the property was acquired through lawful means.

Application of Confiscation and Forfeiture Orders

The Cameroonian legal system must be designed to resolve inefficiencies and structural deficiencies that make it cumbersome and impracticable to identify, investigate, and prosecute corruption in the private sector, especially the crime of illicit enrichment. UWOs should be applied in the following scenarios: illicit enrichment, any corruption crime, organized crime, transnational crime, etc. It should be extended to inheritance property where it is established or suspected that the property in question was derived from any of the foregoing listed crimes.

The courts should be empowered to order confiscation or forfeiture of property in the following instances: when there has been an unjustified increase in personal assets, including moveable and immoveable property, cash, at any time, for which no explanation on the origin of the assets has been given; where the property in question is derived from illegal activities, whether directly or indirectly; where the property was used in the facilitation or commission of a crime; where the property is derived from illegal activities; and where the legal origin of the said property cannot be established by the owner.

Reversal of burden should be permitted by law: it shifts from the state that seeks an answer on the legitimacy of the sources of funds to acquire the property to the owner of the property to explain and establish that the property was acquired lawfully. This creates a dynamic burden of proof, as it requires the person who is better able to prove a fact to be able to prove it. For owners of property, they should be in a better position to prove the lawful origin of their property which in effect undermines the state's attempt to prove otherwise. The law must protect only those who have acquired property through lawful means. Those with a source of income have no challenge in proving the legitimacy of their funds used in acquiring property, but such property must be evaluated vis-à-vis the person's income. In doing this, the law would be able to pick the results of unlawful activities committed in the private sector.

Conclusion

Cameroon has not yet criminalized illicit enrichment and empowers law enforcement personnel to investigate suspected instances of illicit enrichment. In the multi-faceted transactions between individuals in the private and public sectors, numerous individuals have acquired assets which they would struggle to justify in view of their incomes. That means illicit enrichment is heavily present in Cameroon, yet, it has not been criminalized within the legal framework. This also means that those transactions continue, hurting the national economy; enriching a few individuals; and making the anti-corruption efforts more of a waste of time.

To combat and contain organized crime more broadly, and illicit wealth and inexplicable wealth as specific kinds of corruption, it is suggested that Cameroon must adopt legal reforms that grant law enforcement personnel and the judiciary an investigative tool: unexplained wealth orders. With its increased usage in numerous legal systems and documented evidence corroborating its effectiveness, it is recommended that Cameroon should consider taking similar approaches that would help in fighting the crime of illicit enrichment and also put her in compliance with her international law obligations. As a society with strong roots in liberal democratic principles, Cameroon has a challenging scenario when it comes to seizing the proceeds of illegal activity or illicit assets. These liberal democratic principles encompass the right to private property, as well as the assertion that the state can only confiscate property once the owner has been convicted of a particular crime (conviction-based confiscation).

Nonetheless, when the state fails to employ non-conviction-based confiscation in cases involving illicit enrichment or unexplained personal wealth, it neglects its responsibility to restore the legal status quo by depriving offenders of what does not rightfully belong to them (ultimately fulfilling its international law obligations). This failure gives rise to numerous instances of justice being miscarried, as the criminal justice system merely focuses on creating the appearance of curbing crime of illicit enrichment rather than unravelling the problem from its core. Thus, departing from conviction-based confiscation to non-conviction-based confiscation is an approach that would empower law enforcement personnel and the state to not only confiscate proceeds from criminal activities, but it would also deprive criminals from reaping the proceeds of crime and prevent them from (re)investing in future criminal activities. By denying them access to such assets, this strategy would ensure that the legal system uses legal tools to strike at the root and hit criminals where it hurts most: their pockets.

Notes

* Research Professor of Law, Faculty of Law, North-West University.
** Lecturer, College of Law, University of Kwa-Zulu Natal, Durban.

1 See Law No 2011/028 of 14 December 2011 set up the Special Criminal Court (SCC).
2 *Ministère Public et Etat du Cameroun (Ministère des Finances) C/ABAH ABAH Polycarpe; EDOU Joseph; EVINA NYANGONO Sylvie Chantal épse AVOCEY.*
3 Section 18(a) of the Penal Code.
4 Alternative penalties are community service (detailed further under Section 26 of the Penal Code) and reparatory sentence (provided in detail in Section 26–1 of the Penal Code): Section 18–1 of the Penal Code.
5 Accessory penalties for natural persons are forfeiture; publication of the judgment; closure of an establishment and confiscation. See Section 19 of the Penal Code.
6 See Section 20(a) of the Penal Code.
7 Sections 118 to 121 of the Penal Code.
8 Law No. 2016/007 of 12 July 2016 relating to the Penal Code (the Penal Code).
9 Generally see sections 122 to 165 of the Penal Code.
10 In addition to the numerous legislative instruments, there have been institutional mechanisms put in place to combat corruption in the country: for example, the National Anti-Corruption Commission (commonly known by its French acronym *CONAC*), established by Presidential Decree N° 2006/088 of 11 March 2006. See the following: <www.prc.cm/en/the-presidency/49-organisation/attached-services/79-minstry-of-the-supreme-state-audit-mincsp> accessed on 27 June 2023.
11 See Sections 12, 36; Stat. 39, 47 of the Act of 31 July 1789 which is Congress' first enacted statute that authorized civil forfeiture as a sanction for the use of a ship in customs violations.
12 Article 54(1)(c) of the UNCAC recommends the preponderance of evidence as the standard of evidence in such proceedings.
13 This requirement and standard of "proof-balance" of probability is not different from what other jurisdictions use and is the same as the US standard in civil cases: the preponderance of evidence. See South African Prevention of Organized Crime Act of 1998, Chapter 5, Part 1.

13 Blind Spot

Corruption in Sports

Gilbert Mittawa and William Kwabiah***

Introduction

Corruption, in its simplest form, entails abuse of authority for private gain. In the context of sport, corruption is understood as "any illegal, immoral or unethical activity that attempts to deliberately distort the outcome of a sporting contest for the personal material gain of one or more parties involved in that activity."[1] Corruption in sport is multifaceted and complex and includes several qualifications of magnitude, for example, petty and grand corruption and unlimited manifestations, for example, fraud, bribery and doping.

While the phenomenon of corruption in sport is nothing new, the context in which some frauds and acts of corruption occur has changed. The evolution of sport from amateur to professional status, the manipulation of sport as a form of national propaganda, and the increased commercialization of sport have all contributed to increased corruption. While this chapter builds on previous research on sport corruption, the researchers will attempt to analyse the phenomenon from a systems-thinking perspective for the purpose of identifying and closing the blind spots and gaps inherent in the fight against corruption in sport.

This chapter begins with an understanding of the nature and forms of corruption in sport. It then assesses the impact of corruption in sport. Among others, the chapter notes that corruption undermines sport integrity, reduces competition, offers an undue advantage to non-deserving athletes and overall, brings the discipline and institutions of sport into disrepute. The chapter then makes proposals on addressing corruption in sport in Africa. Among others, this chapter advocates for a comprehensive policy approach to address corruption in sport. At the minimum, such an approach must deal with the push-and-pull factors. However, most critical, there should be a blend of coercive and incentives-based approaches to enable transformation. A coordinated and strict sanctions regime should be put in place to deter offenders and would-be offenders. Such coercive interventions should be combined with transformative interventions, such as commending merit and condemning mediocrity.

The Nature and Forms of Corruption in Sports

Sport corruption can be traced as far back as the time of the first Olympic Games. In the first documented case of corruption in sport, the fist fighter Eupolos bribed

DOI: 10.4324/9781003326649-15

three of his competitors at the Olympic Games of 388 BC.[2] However, the phenomenon did not assume a topical global issue until recently due to the increased professionalization and commercialization of sport. Sport management scholars have joined academic conversations about corruption to examine the vice and devise ways of addressing it. An emerging body of literature has focused mainly on examining specific types of corruption (e.g. doping, match fixing, academic fraud, and illegal gambling).[3] While in previous research has provided context for a better understanding of sport corruption, the nature and complexities have not been fully explored.

A single acceptable definition of *corruption in sport* is problematic because the common definitions of corruption tend to be limited by the definer's perspective. For example, the now classic view for political scientists defines corruption as "behaviour which deviates from the formal duties of a public role because of private pecuniary or status gains; or violates rules against the exercise of certain types of private-regarding influence."[4] On the other hand, Adam Masters proposed a new definition of corruption in sport as "any illegal, immoral or unethical activity that attempts to deliberately distort the result of a sporting contest for the personal material gain of one or more parties involved in that activity."[5]

Corruption in sport takes several forms. Maennig divided sport corruption into two categories. The first category is about competition results, whereby the provider and the recipient of bribes can be athletes only, sporting officials and other non-athletes such as referees, or athletes and officials. The second category is about corruption related to sporting bodies and officials regarding host venues for important competitions, allocation of rights, or nomination for positions, and several others. Gorse and Chadwick classified sport corruption into four types: bribe, match-fixing, misuse of inside information for betting purposes, and doping. It was noted that 95.64% of corruption cases in sport was related to doping and many athletes used prohibited drugs to enhance performance in sport games.[6]

Sport corruption has, to a great extent, been influenced by the ever-growing gambling business. During a 2015 convention organized by the International Centre for Sport Security and the United Nations Office on Drugs and Crime (UNODC), experts noted that the real figure for illegal and irregular gambling in the world alone was approximately two trillion to three trillion US dollars per year across all sport. When parties have particular and substantial financial interest in the outcome of sporting fixtures, individuals and institutions have the tendency to manipulate results.[7]

Impact of Corruption in Sports

Meaning affirmed that the extent, level, and intensity of sport corruption have varying impacts on individuals, organizations, and societies at large. Sport is more than an athletic endeavour and reaches beyond the "pitch and track" into the worlds of politics, business, fashion, entertainment, film, and crime. Sport administrators often use sport as a tool to promote a nation's credentials on the international stage.[8] Sport has therefore provided legitimacy to regimes, increased international prestige and national pride, and stimulated economic and commercial success in a host of countries.[9] Sport can therefore be described as playing a collective social, political, and cultural role apart from the associated elements of commercial interests, of which commercial is a recent development. The critical roles of and in sport are however vulnerable to manipulation.

Corruption in sport continues to threaten the fundamental values, ethics, and integrity of the sport industry, including managers, participants, organizations, and governments. The management of unethical behaviour in sport is imperative for addressing corruption, which at the minimum demand a holistic approach focusing on a combination of detection, prevention, and managerial strategies.

The development of sport worldwide has created lucrative business opportunities for athletes, associations, and business corporations. It has created a big market in the form of merchandize, services, and recently betting. "Aware of this global appeal, companies have sought to capitalise and pay millions of dollars to be associated with various sport brands."[10] However, every corporate entity should rely on a sustainable corporate image which is likely to be undermined by cases of corruption. The net effect of corruption in sport is that corporate entities are discouraged from investing in sport and less money is available for sport development.

There is evidence that societal and organizational culture impacts corruption in sport. Despite an ordinary understanding of what constitutes corruption, what may be considered unethical in one culture may be considered as a norm depending on the prevailing culture of a society. The approach to dealing with corruption in sport should therefore be crafted with a particular attention to the traditions prevailing within a society. A study of Taiwanese professional baseball found that match fixing across the cases occurred because of various forms of Wulun cultural social relationships, including obedience to individuals in authority, collective harmony, friendships, and loyalty buttressing the complex nature of corruption.[11]

Corruption in Sports: Mapping the Way Forward

Corruption in sport is undesirable. It distorts sporting outcomes, infringes the rules of the game, dampens sport credibility, and undermines sport integrity. Addressing corruption in sport is not an easy task, but it is hittable. It requires a comprehensive policy direction grounded on strong sanctions, incentives, and a change in mindset.

To proffer effective mechanisms to address corruption in sport, one must understand the fundamental factors that underline sport management and its intricacies. First, organizational leaders should recognize sport corruption as a multidimensional phenomenon that transcends beyond the fields, offices, and sport rooms. The world of sport constitutes a multibillion-dollar industry, employing vast numbers across several interlinked sectors including marketing, tourism, media, sponsorship, health, events management, and clothing, to name a few.[12] Effective mechanisms for addressing sport corruption should impact positively in reducing corruption in several sectors and industries. An anticipated cross-sectoral impact requires a comprehensive approach such as a systems approach to cure the social disease, corruption. A deeper understanding and greater application of systems thinking would facilitate an improved understanding of the multidimensional nature of sport corruption.

There is a need to distinguish sports corruption from other types of corruption. Sport corruption as a societal problem should be distinguished from other types of corruption to make the problem unique and identifiable in a particular way. One unique characteristic of sport is the increased autonomy of International Sport Governing Bodies (ISGB), whose independent status extends to local sport administrators and governing bodies. As much as autonomy is necessary to maintain the sanctity of sport and minimize interference, governments and other stakeholders have a role and accountability in ensuring that such bodies do not violate sport integrity. The need for autonomy and the requirement for oversight generate a gap that must be carefully diagnosed and cured.

To effectively attain the proposition in the preceding paragraph, components of sport corruption should be demarcated into parts to understand how each part contributes to the whole. Such parts include ISGBs, sport administrators, game officials, government officials, possible gaps in the regulations, and how each group's unique roles, and actions impact on the problem of corruption, in other groups. For example, there is a need to interrogate the role of game officials. How do they influence betting? How does it impact on the integrity of the sport?

Fighting corruption in sport requires a complete mindset change. Efforts to curb the vice ought to be grounded in understanding the context and perceptions of several stakeholders. A few examples follow. How do sport administrators view sport corruption? Are the views different from each other? What are the key differences in perceptions towards corruption? These questions should preoccupy the minds of officials investigating corruption in sport, sport officials, and other stakeholders. All stakeholders should be trained to acquire competencies in understanding sport corruption and its negative impact on societies. Such training and competencies should form the basic requirements and qualifications to ensure a mutual understanding of the intricacies of sport corruption and how a new mindset can be changed to reduce sport corruption.

There is also a need to adopt a progressive punishment regime. It cannot be disputed that punishment has a considerable deterring effect, for both offenders and would-be offenders. However, it should also be understood that the increasing profits and power of Multi-National Corporations that can with ease evade tax in tax havens, sponsor sport, and the benefits from sport corruption are so lucrative that MNCs, individuals, and leaders of sport institutions are willing to take the risks inherent in the crime, knowing that the financial gains accruing from such unlawful conduct is adequate to offset punishments and consequences arising therefrom. It is recommended that sanctions and punishments should be broad-based, all-encompassing to include imprisonment, heavy fines, confiscation of properties, and a combination of all the previously mentioned to address the problem. The risks attached to punishments should supersede the benefits of corruption to effectively deter offenders.

Criminal interventions may sometimes be inadequate because corruption is not only a problem of enforcing laws and regulations. It is recommended that such interventions should be complemented by other transformative interventions. Critical is the need to commend and condemn. Organizations and sport officials who have conducted themselves credibly in upholding the values, ethics, and integrity of sport over a period should be listed for national and international awards (incentives). The process for selecting recipients that qualify for awards should be transparent to all nominees and once made should be confidential. Transparency can motivate and encourage sport personalities and officials to aspire to greatness with a legacy of servant leadership. For example, referees and other sport officials who have distinguished themselves should be rewarded financially and acknowledged in an International Hall of Fame even if posthumously. On the contrary, those engaged in corrupt practices must be publicly condemned. Such condemnation should, however, be based on valid and reliable evidence to avoid character assassination. Condemnation should be done after thorough investigations and after the alleged perpetrators have been given their right to be heard.

Committees of inquiry should be constituted to investigate sport corruption and be given specific terms of references consistent with the multifaceted and interdisciplinary nature of sport to limit the ambit of investigations. Sport governing bodies and national leaders should encourage stakeholders in sport to undergo professional training. Sport officials should encompass sport corruption training as part of sport training curricula to facilitate mutual understanding of the problem of corruption. They should also collaborate with Interpol and UNODC in pre-emptive investigations and supervision of sport events. Local and national sport officials should create a forum to enable dialogue and engage continuously with traditional leaders where the cultural and traditional practices support acts of bribery directly and/or indirectly.

Sport governing bodies should adopt a policy of assets declaration by officials. All stakeholders intending to administer sport at a higher level should be made to declare all their assets before taking office. Such officials would be required to declare assets again on expiration of their terms of office. Officials should also agree to comprehensive scrutiny as part of measures to inculcate transparency in sport administration. Individuals, traditional and organizational leaders at all levels, should understand the difference between amateur and professional sport and the role of elected and nominated officials. Sport oversight must be the responsibility of government, non-governmental and civil society oversight bodies with basic relevant training in the administration and management of sport. Government should not be the regulator and policymaker of sport, only the facilitator of policy and on equal footing with non-governmental and civil society oversight bodies. Oversight cannot be limited to one role player in society or leader. The aspiration is that increased transparency will reduce corruption and restore integrity in sport.

Conclusion

Dealing with corruption in sport can be compared to trying to push a horse through a needle's eye. It is a cumbersome enterprise that requires a holistic approach premised on penalties, incentives and transformation. At the minimum, policies tackling corruption in sport should aim at rooting out the key drivers of the vice. The development of sport policy should be a multi-stakeholder engagement process involving sport officials, government officials, and public representations to ensure that policies are widely representative of the several industries that interface with sport corruption.

Sport governing bodies should encourage responsible engagement of national governments in the administration of sport to ensure that sport officials are accountable to the people. The need for autonomy of sport administrators should be rigorously monitored by national and international oversight institutions to reduce blind spots and gaps that officials leverage to commit corrupt acts.

Regulations must be enhanced to introduce stiff and enforced punishments for people convicted of corruption in sport. Such stiff punishments can serve as a deterrent to both offenders and would-be offenders. However, these punishments should be complemented by deliberate efforts to commend merit (incentives) and condemn mediocrity and indifference to sport corruption.

Notes

* Chief of Legal Services, Malawi Defence Force.
** Chief Instructor for Joint Forces, Ghana Armed Forces Command and Staff College.

1 S Gorse and S Chadwick Conceptualising corruption in sport: Implications for sponsorship programmes" ', *European Business Review* (July/August 2010).
2 Wolfgang, Maennig, Corruption in International Sport and Sport Management: Forms, Tendencies, Extent, and Countermeasures, *European Sport Management Quarterly*, 5:2, pp. 187–225.
3 Lisa A. Kihl, James Skinner, Terry Engelberg, Corruption in Sport: Understanding the Complexity of Corruption, *European Sport Management Quarterly*, 17:1 (2017): pp. 1–5.
4 Adam, Masters, Corruption in Sport: From the Playing Field to the Field of Policy, *Policy and Society*, 34:2 (2015): pp. 111–123.
5 Ibid.
6 S. Gorse, S. Chadwick, "Conceptualising corruption in sport: Implications for sponsorship programmes" ', *European Business Review*, July/August 2010.
7 Lea Cleret, Mike McNamee, Stuart Page, Sports Integrity Needs Sports Ethics (Sports Philosophers and Sports Ethicists Too), *Sport, Ethics and Philosophy*, 9:1 (2015): pp. 1–5.
8 G. Brooks, A. Aleem, M. Button, Introduction: *Fraud, Corruption and Sport. In: Fraud, Corruption and Sport*. Palgrave Macmillan, London (2013).
9 Jan Haut, Jonathan Grix, Paul Michael Brannagan, Ivo van Hilvoorde, International Prestige through 'Sporting Success': An Evaluation of the Evidence, *European Journal for Sport and Society*, 14:4 (2017): pp. 311–326.
10 S. Gorse, S. Chadwick, "Conceptualising corruption in sport: Implications for sponsorship programmes" ', *European Business Review*, July/August 2010.
11 Lisa A. Kihl, James Skinner, Terry Engelberg, Corruption in Sport: Understanding the Complexity of Corruption, *European Sport Management Quarterly*, 17:1 (2017): pp. 1–5.
12 United Nations Office on Drugs and Crime, *Preventing Corruption in Sports, and Manipulations of Competitions*, (2021), available at: < www.unodc.org/documents/Safeguardingsport > (accessed on 10 June 2022).

Part III

Bark or Bite? – Emerging Strategies in Preventing Corruption

14 Duty to Report

Prevention of Money Laundering

*Salome Chapeyama Mdala**

Introduction

Today, corruption is no longer a hidden agenda as it has become a vital topic for discussion in Africa and beyond. This chapter discusses the anti-money laundering (AML) reporting obligation for lawyers as a tool to fight corruption in Africa. Considering that lawyers may be used as channels for laundering proceeds of corruption, lawyers' AML reporting obligations can increase the detection of money laundering and deter corruption.[1] However, the AML reporting obligation can potentially conflict with the fundamental principles of the legal profession, such as independence, confidentiality and lawyer–client privilege.[2]

With a focus on African countries, this chapter discusses how to strike a balance between the lawyers' AML reporting obligation and lawyer–client privilege. The chapter is structured as follows: first, a discussion of corruption in the context of Africa; second, the principal–agent theory; third, the interaction between corruption and money laundering; fourth, the obligation of lawyers to report money laundering; fifth, AML traffic lights for lawyers; and finally, conclusion and recommendations. The discussion focuses on the Financial Action Task Force (FATF) standards of AML as about 16 African countries are members of the Eastern and Southern Africa Anti-Money Laundering Group (ESAAMLG) and subscribe to the FATF standards to combat money laundering and the financing of terrorism.[3]

Corruption in the African Context

What comes first between poverty and corruption in African countries is a chicken and egg situation. Poverty can fuel corruption, whereas poverty perpetuates corruption; it is a vicious cycle with a cause becoming a result and the result later reinforcing the cause.[4] Grand corruption depletes government resources, resulting in low pay for public servants and scarce resources in public institutions.[5] As such, people see the need to pay or demand bribes to get or give a service that ordinarily does not require reciprocity.[6] The scarcity of resources affects public utilities, resulting in poor road infrastructure, a lack of drugs in hospitals, and poor educational institutions.[7] If corruption was eliminated and resources were allocated

DOI: 10.4324/9781003326649-17

adequately, public institutions would be well-funded, thereby reducing poverty and ultimately reducing corruption in African countries.

The broader definition of corruption by Transparency International (TI) is the abuse of entrusted power for private gain. A narrower definition by the World Bank is the abuse of public office for private gain.[8] Corruption manifests in many forms, including bribery, embezzlement, abuse of office, gifts and hospitality, extortion of any advantage, money laundering, and nepotism.[9] Corruption has a widespread prevalence on the continent, with similar features of slang or euphemism for bribery and corruption in several African countries. Even though one may not understand the textbook definition of corruption, people seem to recognise corruption when they see it. From the responses, the features of bribery denote a sense of begging or giving an advantage in exchange for a favour. The street words are usually used in the context of ordinary begging but are perceived as corruption when the person asking is in a position of power, such as in public service. Corruption is also understood in street language as not only bribery but also, as embezzlement or abuse of office by people in the position of power, in either private or public.[10]

Corruption in Africa usually involves a person in power (referred to as a "big man/big boss") abusing their power by asking for an incentive (such as a cold drink, tea, lunch, or breakfast) for their benefit. In other scenarios, the "big man/big boss" would abuse their power, status, or office to coerce someone to accept a bribe. For example, in Uganda, some common coercive phrases in the native language include *Toli muna'uganda* (are you not Ugandan?) or *Yogera Oluganda* (Speak Luganda). Corruption is distinguished from the usual friendly chat because it usually involves an act that is illegal, unprocedural, or unethical.

Some street words support the notion that bribery is something secretive or inconspicuous. For example, the common English expression of "brown envelope" and the Nigerian "Ghana must go" bag. This euphonism for corruption in Africa also serves to dilute the seriousness of the crime of corruption and reduces it to a social norm. This may explain why there is a striking similarity in the African countries in using food items such as tea or cold drinks as euphonism for a bribe. The understanding of corruption in most countries supports the textbook definition who corruption as the abuse of entrusted power or public office for private gain.

Corruption as the Principal–Agent Problem

Initiatives to combat corruption often fail when they are based on the wrong theory of why corruption happens.[11] This chapter defines corruption as the abuse of public office for private gain. The principal–agent theory explains why corruption occurs in the public service. Corruption is a principal–agent problem that results from information asymmetry between the principal and the agent.[12] For example, the government ministries as the "principal" assign duties to the public officials, "agents," who are authorised to act on behalf of the principal, expecting that the agents will adhere to the law. Another principal–agent scenario is where public officials are elected into office as agents by the citizens as the principal. The principal–agent theory explains that corruption occurs whenever agents are more knowledgeable about their work than the principal, making it easy to engage in corruption.

Fighting corruption using anti-money laundering is an idea based on the theory that corruption is a principal–agent problem. Measures based on the principal–agent theory focus on deterring agents from participating in corrupt behaviour by increasing accountability. The following formula by Robert Klitgaard serves as an illustration of the principal–agent theory: Corruption = Monopoly + Discretion – Accountability.[13]

The equation illustrates how reducing monopoly and discretion while promoting accountability are necessary for fighting corruption. Since corruption results from rational individuals making decisions that are influenced by projected costs and rewards, the theory holds that enhancing accountability reduces corruption, almost based on the Faustian Bargain. Arguably, public officials make a cost-benefit analysis weighing the chance of being caught, the potential penalties, and the value of not being caught before participating in corruption.

As per the Klitgaard formula, anti-corruption measures would work effectively if liability exposure and the likelihood of detection were high compared to the gains of corruption.[14] Thus, the higher the risk of getting caught and punished, the less likely an individual will exploit opportunities for corruption. Money laundering is vital to corrupt officials who wish to reduce accountability by disguising the money they get from corrupt activities. While criminals involved in other types of crimes like drug trafficking may depend on remaining anonymous with their large sums of money, public officials begin to attract attention when they are associated with significant sums of money from unknown sources.[15] The desire to legitimise the proceeds of corruption funds explains why money laundering has become an inevitable part of corruption.

The Interplay Between Money Laundering and Corruption

Money laundering schemes and corruption might be metaphorically viewed as two sides of the same coin. Money laundering is the act of concealing illicit gains generated from criminal activity.[16] However, corruption is the criminal activity that creates illicit gains. According to Mugarura, "corruption and money laundering are inextricably linked such that where one exists, the other one will be lurking in the background."[17] The three stages of money laundering are as follows: (1) the introduction of illegally obtained funds into a financial system; (2) the layering stage, in which the launderer engages in a series of transactions designed to conceal the origin of the funds; and (3) the integration stage, in which the launderer seeks to repossess the funds through what appears to be a legitimate transaction.[18]

Following through the process, corrupt individuals engage in money laundering to legitimise the proceeds of corruption. Conversely, corruption perpetuates money laundering processes by using bribery to undermine the detection of money laundering. As a result of the use of money laundering to legitimise corruption proceeds, anti-money laundering measures can be helpful in anti-corruption initiatives. Ivanov suggests cooperation between anti-money laundering compliance programmes and anti-corruption compliance as they aim to prevent two closely connected types of crime.[19]

Money laundering is a huge conduit for corrupt officials in disguising their ownership of corrupt proceeds through corporate vehicles and trust companies and the use of gatekeepers like lawyers.[20] Corrupt officials would opt to use lawyers in their transactions so as to disassociate themselves from the unexplained wealth that can trigger inquiries. This may be done, for example, by instructing lawyers to incorporate a company or a trust and transfer the corrupt proceeds to the legal entity. Further, corrupt officials may use intermediaries such as family members or close associates to distance themselves from corrupt criminal activities. If these schemes are successful, corruption is more likely to go unpunished, especially where the proceeds of such crimes are laundered and not linked to the underlying corrupt activity.[21]

Having access to substantial public finances and the expertise and power to control budgets, public corporations, and contracts, public officials have a strong predisposition to engage in corruption.[22] However, the most obvious cost of corrupt activities to officials is the risk of arrest, prosecution, and punishment.[23] Therefore, if corrupt officials cannot utilise their illegal proceeds and instrumentalities, it removes the incentive for corruption and deters their corrupt activities. Arguably, when lawyers adhere to their AML reporting obligations, it increases accountability and makes corruption risky for such corrupt officials.

Lawyers' Anti-Money Laundering Reporting Obligation

A key component of detecting money laundering is reporting suspicious transactions.[24] Two arguments are made in favour of, and against, requiring lawyers to report money laundering suspicious transactions. According to the first school of thought, lawyers act as a channel for money laundering, and as such, they should disclose suspicious transactions.[25] The opposing viewpoint acknowledges that lawyers should not be authorised to assist their clients in criminal activity, but this view stresses that the duty of confidentiality is a fundamental principle and distinguishing characteristic of the legal profession. The employment of AML to combat corruption does not preclude lawyers from defending clients in court, including those accused of money laundering. However, the AML reporting obligations prevent lawyers from participating in money laundering activities. Nonetheless, the debate on whether AML measures apply to lawyers has centred on the potential conflict with the general professional ethics of lawyers.

According to some scholars, requiring lawyers to report suspicious transactions would be unfair to the legal profession and go against the core values of independence.[26] Others, such as Weinstein, contend that prosecuting lawyers who accept tainted representation fees is incompatible with the adversarial judicial system.[27] He argues that the government's desire to deter money laundering is not interfered with by legal representation because lawyers serve the public by representing and advising those accused of crimes. Weinstein contends that making lawyers susceptible to criminal prosecution if they receive representation fees from corruption gains interferes with their client's constitutional right to access to legal representation.

The "lawyer-client privilege" is another distinctive aspect of the legal profession that may conflict with the AML reporting requirement. According to Itsikowitz, the lawyer–client privilege complicates efforts to include lawyers in the fight against money laundering.[28] The complication comes in because information obtained by the lawyer when giving legal advice or legal representation is privileged and protected from disclosure. Arguably, money laundering laws requiring lawyers to disclose suspicious transactions would potentially conflict with this core value of the profession. Itzkowitz further argues that lawyers have professional integrity and that acting with integrity includes keeping confidential information secret.

Further, some law societies have challenged anti-money laundering laws that require lawyers to report suspicious transactions, arguing that such reporting would be unlawful. The Nigerian Bar Association successfully challenged the AML obligations on lawyers in the Federal High Court.[29] According to the judgement of the court, Nigerian lawyers were exempted from the AML obligations. Zimbabwe's Bank Use Promotion and Suppression of Money Laundering Act was subject to a constitutional challenge by the Law Society of Zimbabwe in January 2005.[30] On 18 January 2005, the Society petitioned the Supreme Court to declare some provisions of the Act unconstitutional.[31]

Through a memorandum of understanding, the parties to the case – the law society, the Reserve Bank, the Attorney General, and the Ministry of Finance in Zimbabwe – decided to create a framework for identifying money laundering without breaching human rights and the core values of the legal profession. Likewise in South Africa, the Law Society sought legal advice over the legality of the Financial Intelligence Centre Act 38 of 2001 (FICA) since the anti-money laundering law threatened the independence of the legal profession.[32] The position of the Financial Intelligence Centre (FIC) was that not all confidential information is privileged information entitled to protection. Like Zimbabwe's Memoranda of Understanding (MoUs), provincial law societies in South Africa entered into MoUs with the FIC pledging their commitment to combating money laundering and the financing of terrorism.[33]

In contrast to the views against AML reporting obligations, lawyers participating in corruption and money-laundering schemes undermine the credibility of the legal profession.[34] Lawyers actively participating in money laundering should not be shielded by lawyer–client privilege. As Weinstein argues, lawyers are not a "special class of citizens"; the law should hold them accountable when involved in money laundering schemes.[35] For example, when a client instructs a lawyer to transact in a money laundering or corruption scheme and the lawyer proceeds to transact, the transaction is illegal and not protected by lawyer–client privilege. Thus, mandatory reporting of suspicious transactions does not affect a lawyer's core values and duties when giving legal advice or representation. Arguably, with a proper understanding of the ambit of lawyers' AML reporting obligations, the AML requirement does not conflict with lawyer–client privilege or lawyers' professional ethics. Therefore, lawyers can play a role in the fight against money laundering and corruption without infringing on lawyers' professional ethics.

Anti-Money Laundering Traffic Lights for Lawyers

A lawyer is effectively obligated to keep his client's economic interests and personal affairs private after a lawyer–client relationship has been established.[36] The duty of confidentiality is so essential to the legal profession to the extent that law societies usually have codified ethical guidelines that specify that lawyers owe their clients a duty of secrecy, which includes the responsibility not to divulge any sensitive information.[37] A lawyer is, however, obligated to disclose information as required by law, and this exception is sometimes explicitly stated in a lawyer's code of ethics.[38] Lawyers can be required, for example, by AML laws to report their clients' suspicious money laundering transactions.[39] This chapter proposes an AML guideline for lawyers given the competing ethical duties to keep confidential client information on the one hand, and the AML duty to report suspicious transactions, on the other hand. The AML guidelines are illustrated by the traffic light colours of green, amber, and red. The discussion uses the phrases "green information" to describe privileged information, "amber information" to describe information that can be privileged or not privileged depending on the circumstances, and "red information" to describe reportable non-privileged information.[40] These AML guidelines would serve to help lawyers abide by their AML reporting obligations while upholding their professional ethics.

Green Information

A lawyer is not required to report green information because such information is protected by lawyer–client privilege. The freedom of confidential communication between lawyers and clients is essential to the smooth operation of the legal system.[41] The notion that clients should consult with their lawyers without worrying about a breach of confidentiality is at the root of the legal system.[42] In constitutional rights discourse, everyone has the right to privacy and legal representation.[43] To ensure that people's rights are effectively protected, lawyers must uphold the values of independence, confidentiality, adherence to ethical standards, and moral integrity, and eliminate conflicts of interest. A breach of the duty of confidentiality is professional malpractice, and a lawyer who breaches such duty can be held accountable by their professional body or the courts.[44] The lawyer–client privilege protects the lawyer's duty of confidentiality by giving communication between lawyers and their clients a privileged status.

According to FATF Recommendation 23, lawyers conducting financial transactions as listed in Recommendation 22 are required to report suspicious transactions.[45] The financial transactions include buying and selling real estate; managing clients' money; and incorporation and management of legal persons. According to the interpretive note to Recommendation 23, lawyers are immune from reporting suspicious transactions provided they get the information under professional confidentiality or legal professional privilege. The FATF has left each nation to ascertain what information is covered by legal professional privilege or professional confidentiality. The FATF guidelines state that the following constitutes privileged information: information acquired while assessing the client's legal position; or while representing a client in matters of judicial, administrative, arbitration, or mediation procedures. In short, information shared with a lawyer that can help them advise or defend a client in court or other legal procedures concerning a legal offence is considered privileged information.

In some cases, there may be disagreement about what exactly constitutes "advice." Would the lawyer–client privilege apply, for instance, if a client asked for suggestions on how to conceal and launder his illicit gains without being discovered? To comply with AML requirements, it is crucial to restrict the scope of advice because some advice encourages crime, and this is not the legal advice the law purports to protect. Courts have helped define what legal advice means in some jurisdictions. Legal advice is defined by the court of appeals in the case of *Three Rivers District Council and Others* v. *Bank of England* as interactions between a lawyer and a client with the primary goal of giving or receiving advice on legal rights and liabilities.[46] The court went on to clarify that advice on presentational matters is not protected unless it is offered in connection with guidance on legal rights and liabilities.[47]

Defining legal advice to exclude any advice that perpetuates criminality would be an exception to the general rule of lawyer–client privilege. In any case, the lawyer–client privilege is not absolute such that communication is not privileged if a client asks a lawyer for help in committing a crime, engaging in fraud, or covering up such crimes.[48] In the case of *Law Society of Zimbabwe* v. *Minister of Transport and Communications and Others*, the court acknowledged that the lawyer–client privilege is not absolute and that there are some exceptions to the rule. The court pointed out that the duty to uphold lawyer–client does not apply to communications that are criminal in themselves or intended to obtain legal advice to facilitate crime. Similarly, in Malawi, the lawyers' Code of Ethics provides that lawyers may not counsel or aid a client in committing a crime or engaging in fraud.[49]

Therefore, lawyers are not required to report "green information," which is information acquired in a lawyer–client relationship and shared with the lawyer while giving legal advice or legal representation. Although a lawyer is excluded from the requirement to report information gained when rendering legal advice, this does not imply that all communication presented as advice is protected. The court's definition of "legal advice" can be as narrow as advice on one's legal rights and liabilities; this definition may exclude casual conversations with a lawyer. Furthermore, the lawyer–client privilege does not protect communication concerning advice that encourages the commission of a crime. To minimise confusion, countries seeking to comply with AML requirements while upholding legal professional ethics would do well to develop AML guidelines for lawyers that assist in providing explanations such as the meaning of lawyer–client privilege and the scope of legal advice.

Amber Information

A lawyer is not required to report "amber information" in two situations: (1) where the lawyer is merely giving advice and not doing the actual transactions and (2) where the lawyer is doing transactions that fall outside the AML reporting obligation. These two situations are amber because they describe information that is nearly reportable or non-reportable depending on the circumstances. The first amber information relating to mere advice will be referred to as "First amber information," and the second amber information, which is outside the scope of the AML reporting obligation, will be referred to as "Second amber information."

First Amber Information

Information obtained in the process of giving mere advice that does not qualify as protected legal advice is still not reportable because the lawyer is not preparing or carrying out transactions. According to AML legislation that mirrors FATF Recommendation 22, the law requires legal practitioners to report suspicious transactions *when they prepare for or carry out transactions* for their clients in the specified activities.[50] The activities include buying and selling real estate, managing clients' money, and creating legal persons. The phrase *when they prepare for or carry out transactions mean*s that the AML obligation does apply where the lawyer is giving mere advice, even if that advice is not privileged.[51] For example, if a client asks a lawyer for advice on how to launder money through buying and selling real estate, the transaction of real estate is reportable. However, if a lawyer advises without preparing or carrying out the actual transaction, he would not be required to report. However, it would turn into "red information" and be reportable if the lawyer proceeds to do the transaction for the client.

The first amber information is not a reportable transaction since a lawyer is only required to report when they actively prepare for or carry out transactions. The phrase prepares for or carries out a transaction is defined in some AML guidelines for lawyers. For instance, the Mauritian AML guidelines for lawyers specify that planning or carrying out transactions may involve creating legal documents in the context of forming a business.[52] In addition, preparing for or carrying out transactions includes drafting incorporation paperwork, arranging for a financial transaction to be completed on behalf of a client, and producing an act of sale of a company or piece of real estate. These guidelines show that lawyers' giving advice that does not result in preparing for or carrying out the transaction does not trigger the reporting obligation.

The exclusion of the first amber as a reportable transaction does not mean that other ethical and legal obligations do not apply. For example, some codes of ethics or laws may provide that a lawyer must disclose confidential information when necessary to prevent a crime or when required by law.[53] Thus, a lawyer can still report the first Amber information to relevant authorities to prevent a crime, although this is outside the scope of the AML reporting obligation. However, the FATF Interpretive Note to Recommendation 23 permits lawyers to dissuade their clients from participating in criminal activity, and FATF does not regard this as a tipping-off.[54] In sum, there is no mandatory reporting requirement for the first Amber information which relates to advice without proceeding with doing the actual transaction. However, a lawyer is allowed to prevent a client from engaging in a crime by letting them know that the transaction they intend to do would be a crime.

Second Amber Information

The second amber information relates to information acquired by the lawyer while preparing for or carrying out transactions that are outside the scope of the AML reporting obligation. According to FATF Recommendation 22 "designated non-financial companies and professions" that are subject to AML reporting obligations include the following:

> Lawyers, notaries, other independent legal professionals and accountants – when they prepare for or carry out transactions for their client concerning the following activities: buying and selling of real estate; managing client money, securities or other assets; management of bank, savings or securities accounts; the organisation of contributions for the creation, operation or management of companies; creation, operation or management of legal persons or arrangements, and buying and selling of business entities.[55]

The activities listed under Recommendation 22 are transactions where a client can likely attempt to use a lawyer as a channel for money laundering. The exhaustive list under Recommendation 22 entails that lawyers do not have to report suspicious transactions discovered while preparing for or carrying out transactions not listed under Recommendation 22. For example, when a lawyer is registering real estate, transferring real estate, or other non-listed financial transactions the reporting obligation is not triggered because the activities although they may be channels for money laundering fall outside the AML reporting obligation. AML laws can broaden the scope of AML reporting obligations by having a long list of activities, such as all the activities listed in Recommendation 22 and more financial transactions.

Another option to broaden the scope of AML reporting obligations would be to require lawyers to report suspicious transactions when preparing for or carrying out the listed transactions or any other financial activity that would allow clients to engage in potential money laundering or terrorist financing transactions. However, a catch-all phrase may raise some implementation challenges. Perhaps the exhaustive list under FATF Recommendation 22 was a way to maintain the lawyer–client privilege by refraining from meddling in too much of the lawyers' business. In any case, even with an exhaustive list that defines the scope of AML reporting obligations, lawyers are still subject to ethical standards that would hold them accountable if they actively participated in money laundering activities. A national set of AML reporting guidelines would help lawyers meet their AML reporting obligations while upholding their professional ethics.

Red Information

The "red information" on the AML traffic lights for lawyers entails that the information is red; the lawyer should report it. The red information is non-privileged; the transactions fall within the scope of an AML reporting obligation, and suspicion arose while the lawyer was preparing for or carrying out the client's transaction. According to the Interpretive Note to FATF Recommendation 23, AML laws may allow lawyers to report suspicious transactions to their relevant self-regulatory organisations provided they collaborate with the Financial Intelligence Units (FIU). For example, the Memorandum of Understandings discussed earlier between the Law Society of Zimbabwe and the FIU, as well as the provincial law societies in South Africa and the FIU, could be examples of such cooperation to report.

The collaboration between the Law Societies and the FIU might be helpful when a lawyer is unsure whether the information acquired is privileged. In such circumstances, the lawyer would report the matter to the Law Society rather than the FIU. The Law Society can subsequently forward the suspicious transaction report to the FIU if the information is non-privileged. Moreover, not all privileged information is subject to protection by law. Codes of Conduct or statutes can allow lawyers to report or disclose information to prevent a crime.[56] The essence of the specific provision in statutes or codes of conduct allowing lawyers to report, in some circumstances, enables lawyers to disclose information without committing professional malpractice resulting from the violation of the secrecy obligation.

Conclusion

This chapter has highlighted that anti-corruption measures would work effectively if liability exposure and the likelihood of detection were high compared to the profits of corruption. The higher the risk of getting caught and punished, the less likely public officials will exploit opportunities for corruption. Since money laundering plays a crucial role for corrupt officials in laundering their corrupt proceeds, increasing the detection of money laundering can decrease corruption. The logic is that if corrupt officials cannot use their illegal gains, it removes the incentive for corruption and deters criminal activity. Arguably, when lawyers adhere to their AML reporting obligations, it increases accountability and makes corruption risky.

The paper also found that if there are no proper guidelines to guide lawyers on their reporting obligation, the AML reporting obligation on lawyers can potentially conflict with the duty of confidentiality. The duty of confidentiality is so essential to the legal profession that divulging a client's confidential information is professional malpractice. In addition, the operation of the legal system relies on lawyer–client confidentiality so that clients can freely consult with their lawyers. On the other hand, the AML requirements on lawyers are essential because lawyers' participation in corruption and money-laundering schemes undermines the credibility of the legal profession. Lawyers actively participating in money laundering should not be shielded by lawyer–client privilege. Consequently, with a proper understanding of the ambit of lawyers' AML reporting obligations, the AML requirement does not conflict with the duty of confidentiality or lawyer–client privilege. Therefore, lawyers can play a role in the fight against money laundering and corruption without infringing on lawyers' professional ethics.

The discussion proposed solutions to the conflict between AML reporting requirements and the lawyer–client privilege by first, developing AML guidelines for lawyers that explain the scope of AML reporting obligations, second, defining privileged information, and third, providing scenarios that guide lawyers in their reporting obligations. The AML traffic lights for lawyers can guide lawyers in determining whether or not to report suspicious transactions. The study found that lawyers should not report green information because it is privileged information. Lawyers should not report amber information because the transaction falls outside the scope of the reporting obligation. Further, lawyers should report the red information as it is non-privileged information acquired while a lawyer prepares for or carries out the activities listed in the specific AML regulations. The proposed AML traffic lights for lawyers would help lawyers abide by their AML reporting obligations while upholding their professional ethics. In sum, lawyers' AML reporting obligation may reduce corruption by enhancing detection, cutting channels for money laundering, and preventing lawyers from taking part in illicit activities.

To enhance AML compliance, law firms can reduce the risks of corruption in their firms by establishing strong anti-corruption and anti-money laundering compliance programmes. National law societies and their members can create a Collective Action Initiative in the form of Integrity Pacts, in which participants pledge to work together to fight corruption. For example, the collective action initiative called *Kuleta Haki* in the Criminal Justice System of the Democratic Republic of the Congo. National law societies should strengthen their oversight and monitoring of AML compliance mechanisms and include supervision and monitoring of AML compliance. The FIU, the law societies, and the Attorney General's office should collaborate in developing country-specific guidelines for the AML reporting requirements for lawyers.

Notes

* Legal and Compliance Manager, Reunion Insurance Company Limited and Adjunct Lecturer in International Trade law, Law of Business Organisation and Legal Research Methods in Malawi.

1 FATF, "The use of FATF recommendations to combat corruption," (2013), Accessed on July 21, 2022. Available at: www.fatf-gafi.org/media/fatf/documents/recommendations/BPP-Use-of-FATF-Recs-Corruption.pdf. (Accessed 15 July 2022).

2 FATF, "Guidance for a risk-based approach: Legal professionals," (2013), www.fatf-gafi.org/media/fatf/Risk-Based-Approach-Legal-Professionals.pdf. (Accessed 21 July 2022).

3 FATF, "Eastern and Southern Africa Anti-Money Laundering Group (ESAAMLG)," www.fatf-gafi.org/pages/easternandsouthernafricaanti-moneylaunderinggroupesaamlg.html. (Accessed 15 July 2022).

4 Transparency International (TI), "Poverty and Corruption in Africa Community Voices break the cycle." www.transparency.org/files/content/activity/2012_PCA_brochure_EN.pdf. (Accessed 15 July 2022)

5 Marie Chêne, "Low salaries, the culture of per diems and corruption," (2009), www.u4.no/publications/low-salaries-the-culture-of-per-diems-and-corruption. (Accessed 15 July 2022).

6 Richard Rose, "Reducing bribery for public services delivered to citizens," (2015), (Accessed 15 July 2022) www.u4.no/publications/reducing-bribery-for-public-services-delivered-to-citizens. (Accessed 15 July 2022).
7 TI, "Poverty and Corruption in Africa Community Voices break the cycle."
8 World Bank, "Helping countries combat corruption: The role of the World Bank," (2012), http://www1.worldbank.org/publicsector/anticorrupt/corruptn/corrptn.pdf. (Accessed 15 July 2022).
9 UNCAC, "United Nations Convention Against Corruption," (2003), www.unodc.org/documents/brussels/UN_Convention_Against_Corruption.pdf. (Accessed 15 July 2022).
10 Malawi uses the phrase "*ku pakula*," meaning serving, to describe a situation where someone is embezzling funds from their institution.
11 Elizabeth Dávid-Barrett, "Business unusual: collective action against bribery in international business," *Crime Law Soc Change,* Vol. 71 (2019): 151–170.
12 Heather Marquette and Caryn Peiffer. "Theoretical (Mis)understanding? Applying Principal-Agent and Collective Action Theories to the Problem of Corruption in Systemically Corrupt Countries." *Routledge Companion to Ethics and Public Service Organizations* (2015).
13 Robert Klitgaard, "Public-private collaboration and corruption," in *Collective action: innovative strategies to prevent corruption,* ed. Mark Pieth, (Zurich: Dike, 2012).
14 Daniel Treisman, "The causes of corruption: a cross-national study," *Journal of Public Economics* Vol. 76 (2000): 399–457.
15 FATF and OECD, "Laundering the proceeds of corruption," (2011), www.fatfgafi.org/media/fatf/documents/reports/Laundering%20the%20Proceeds%20of%20C orruption.pdf. (Accessed 15 July 2022)
16 FATF, "The use of FATF recommendations to combat corruption," Available at: www.fatf-gafi.org/media/fatf/documents/recommendations/BPP-Use-of-FATF-Recs-Corruption.pdf (Accessed 15 July 2022)
17 Norman Mugarura "Uncoupling the relationship between corruption and money laundering crimes," *Journal of Financial Regulation and Compliance*, Vol. 24(1), (2016): 74–89.
18 FATF and OECD, "Laundering the proceeds of corruption."
19 Eduard Ivanov, "AML/CFT and Anti-Corruption Compliance Regulation: Two Parallel Roads?" (2018), Accessed July 15, 2022, www.iaca.int/media/attachments/2018/07/24/research_paper_02_eduard_ivanov_final.pdf.
20 FATF, "Specific risk factors in laundering the proceeds of corruption: Assistance to reporting institutions," (2012) Accessed July 15, 2022, www.fatf-<gafi.org/media/fatf/documents/reports/Specific%20Risk%20Factors%20in%20the%20Laundering%20of%20Proceeds%20of%20Corruption.pdf.
21 FATF, 2013, "The use of FATF recommendations to combat corruption," Accessed July 15, 2022, www.fatf-gafi.org/media/fatf/documents/recommendations/BPP-Use-of-FATF-Recs-Corruption.pdf.
22 FATF and OECD, "Laundering the proceeds of corruption."
23 Daniel Treisman, "The causes of corruption: a cross-national study," *Journal of Public Economics* Vol. 76 (2000): 399–457.
24 Sonja Cindori, "Money laundering: correlation between risk assessment and suspicious transactions." *Financial Theory and Practice*, Vol. 37(2) (2013): 181–206.
25 Laurel Terry and José Carlos Llerena Robles, "The relevance of FATF's recommendations and fourth round of mutual evaluations to the legal profession," *Fordham International Law Journal*, Vol. 42(2) (2018): 627.
26 John Kelley, "International anti-money laundering and professional ethics," *The International Lawyer*, Vol. 40 (2006): 433–443.
27 Adam Weinstein, "Prosecuting attorneys for money laundering: A new and questionable weapon in the war on crime," *Law and Contemporary Problems*, Vol. 51 (1988): 369–386.

28 Angela Itsikowitz, "Legal professional privilege/Intermediary confidentiality: The challenge for anti-money laundering measures," in *Money Laundering Experiences*, ed Charles Goredema (Pretoria: Institute for Security Studies), 73.
29 Registered Trustees of Nigerian Bar Association & Attorney General of the Federation v. Central Bank of Nigeria, Suit No: FHC/BS/173/2014).
30 *Zimbabwe Independent*, "State in climbdown over money laundering," [www.theindependent.co.zw/2005/09/30/state-in-climbdown-over-money-laundering/. (Accessed 15 July 2022)
31 *Zimbabwe Independent*, "State in climbdown over money laundering."
32 Angela Itsikowitz, "Legal professional privilege/Intermediary confidentiality: The challenge for anti-money laundering measures," in *Money Laundering Experiences*, ed Charles Goredema (Pretoria: Institute for Security Studies), 73.
33 FIC, "Law Societies join the financial intelligence fold," www.lssa.org.za/wp-content/uploads/2020/01/FIC-LSSA-media-statement-25-July-2013.pdf. (Accessed 15 July 2022)
34 Transparency International, "What is Corruption?" www.transparency.org/en/what-is-corruption (Accessed 15 July 2022).
35 Adam Weinstein, "Prosecuting attorneys for money laundering: A new and questionable weapon in the war on crime," *Law and Contemporary Problems*, Vol. 51 (1988): 369–386.
36 Susan Martyn et al. *The Law Governing Lawyers National Rules, Standards, Statutes, and State Lawyer Codes* (Aspen Publishers: Boston, 2011).
37 Brunilda Bara et al. "Lawyer-client relationship and the latest legislative changes on the obligation to report money laundering (Albania)," (2019), https://doi.org/10.4000/revdh.6549 (Accessed 15 July 2022)
38 See Malawi's Lawyers' Code of Ethics, Chapter 8 rule 8(i) that a lawyer must disclose confidential information when required by law.
39 FATF, "Guidance for a risk-based approach: Legal professionals," (2019), www.fatf-gafi.org/media/fatf/Risk-Based-Approach-Legal-Professionals.pdf (Accessed 15 July 2022)
40 Salome Chapeyama, "To Tell or Not to Tell: Lawyer's Reporting Obligation as a Tool to Combat Corruption Vis-à-vis Lawyer-Client Privilege," (Masters diss. International Anti-Corruption Academy, 2021) www.iaca.int/media/attachments/2022/05/16/proofread-chapeyama-salome-imacc-thesis-2021_covers.pdf. (Accessed 15 July 2022)
41 Angela Itsikowitz, "Legal professional privilege/Intermediary confidentiality: The challenge for anti-money laundering measures," in *Money Laundering Experiences*, ed Charles Goredema (Pretoria: Institute for Security Studies), 73.
42 Susan Martyn et al., *The Law Governing Lawyers National Rules, Standards, Statutes, and State Lawyer Codes* (Boston: Aspen Publishers, 2011).
43 Lee Goldman, "The Constitutional Right to privacy," *Denver Law Review*, Vol. 84:2 (2006) Article 7.
44 *NBS Bank Limited v. Mbendera Nkhono and Associates and Shabir Latif* (Practicing under the style of Sacraine, Gow and Company. Commercial Cause Number 281 of 2017. Lilongwe Registry. Accessed July 15, 2022, https://media.malawilii.org/files/judgments/mwcommc/2020/7/2020-mwcommc-7.pdf.
45 FATF, "The FATF Recommendations," www.fatf-gafi.org/publications/fatfrecommendations/documents/fatf-recommendations.html. (Accessed 15 July 2022)
46 [200] UKHL 16).
47 Three Rivers District Council and Others v. Bank of England, [200] UKHL 16).
48 *Law Society of Zimbabwe v. Minister of Transport and Communications and Others*, [2004] ZWSC 127. https://globalfreedomofexpression.columbia.edu/wp-content/uploads/2017/08/Law-Society-of-Zimbabwe-v-Minister-of-Transport-and-Communications-and-Another.pdf. (Accessed 15 July 2022)
49 Chapter 11 rule 11.
50 FATF, "The FATF Recommendations."

51 Paul Allan Schott, "Reference Guide to Anti-Money Laundering and Combating the Financing of Terrorism," (2006), https://documents1.worldbank.org/curated/ar/558401468134391014/pdf/350520Referenc1Money01OFFICIAL0USE1.pdf. (Accessed 15 July 2022)

52 Mauritius AG and FIA, "Guidelines on the Measures for the Prevention of Money Laundering and Countering the Financing of Terrorism for Law Firms/Foreign Law Firms/Joint Law Venture/Foreign Lawyers and Individual Law Practitioners (Barristers/Attorneys And Notaries," (2020), https://attorneygeneral.govmu.org/Documents/Law%20Firms/AMLCFTdocuments/LEGALPROFESSIONALSGUIDELINESNOV20.pdf. (Accessed 15 July 2022)

53 Malawi Law Society Code of Ethics, Chapter 11.

54 FATF, "The FATF Recommendations."

55 FATF, "The FATF Recommendations."

56 See Chapter 11 rule 11 Malawi Law Society Code of Ethics.

15 Political Elites and Corruption

The Cases of Cameroon and South Africa

Avitus A. Agbor, Refilwe Tsatsimpe**, and Chevaure du Pokoy****

Introduction

Transparency International's assessment of the most and least corrupt countries in the world places most African countries on the lowest rung: meaning that they are the most corrupt countries.[1] Even though corruption is a global pandemic with effects on every nation,[2] for Africa, the situation is worse. With inherent dysfunctional, weak, and misguided structures and systems, corruption has a huge negative toll on tax revenues;[3] investments;[4] inflation;[5] triggers inequality;[6] assaults the rule of law;[7] delegitimises the government, governmental institutions and processes;[8] makes access to social services and institutions cumbersome;[9] affects service delivery;[10] contributes to illegally acquired (and inexplicable personal) wealth;[11] widens the gap between the rich and the poor; and retards socio-economic and political development.[12] Without a doubt, corruption is one of the biggest enemies to Africans.

From a sociological perspective, corruption takes many different forms,[13] has been given various names within a country's nomenclature,[14] and is so imbued in the social fabric of African societies to the point that it is now a logic of negotiation to get something done, a bribe must be given, or a promise made. As such, those unable or unwilling to make such promises, or pay a bribe, are not assisted, or are largely ignored.

What is more disturbing is the fact that the political elite are so involved in the perpetration of grand corruption, especially the theft or misappropriation of public funds. Senior political elites have been involved in numerous scandals that upon revelation have outraged the public. The perpetration of illicit financial flows (IFFs) in Africa, resulting in over US$800 billion channelled from Africa to different non-African countries through surreptitious transactions is, to a greater extent, attributable to the political elite who are actively involved in such malpractice.[15] The involvement of the political elite in corrupt activities means that they debilitate the legal system: laws, law enforcement personnel, and judicial institutions. They also deprive the legal system of the political will needed to combat corruption.

In sub-Saharan Africa, legal developments in combatting corruption perpetrated by senior state officials have gained momentum and national attention, exuding some degree of political will from the political elites in Cameroon and South

DOI: 10.4324/9781003326649-18

Africa. In the former, the establishment of a Special Criminal Court (SCC) in 2011 to deal with a specific kind of misappropriation has, at the time of publication, brought over 200 individuals to the dock.[16] The accused and convicted individuals include a former Premier; former Ministers; former directors of state-owned enterprises; the rank and file of public service, various professional corps, and the broader civil society. Data of the amounts misappropriated are in billions, exposing the fact that there are systemic cracks exploited by those individuals. In South Africa, the establishment of the Zondo Commission to deal with the issue of state capture committed during the Zuma administration was indicative of a political will to confront and defeat a malaise that was drowning the South African economy and widening the gap between the rich and the poor.

In the investigations that ensued, it came to public knowledge how the political elite were intricately involved in the commission of embezzlement of public funds, and how syndicates were established in various governmental departments to facilitate the commission of those crimes. The legal developments which have so far exposed the political elite deserve some applause yet remain complicated for comprehension given the selectivity that has been infused therein. By taking an evidence-based comparative approach, this paper looks at the involvement of the political elite in grand corruption in Cameroon and South Africa. In doing this, the paper makes some arguments: firstly, the involvement of the political elite in the perpetration of grand corruption means that the battle against corruption may be eternal or even futile. Secondly, with the numerous scandals that have assaulted the images of the countries involved, the political elite must take a greater responsibility for the ugly state of affairs, especially the stagnating socio-economic and political development in those two countries. Thirdly, until the political elite is guided by public service values, and avoids self-seeking opportunities, politics rather than law shall remain as opportunities for self-advancement through theft of state resources at the expense of the state.

The chapter starts off by exploring the notion of political elites as used broadly in the social sciences to a much-narrowed sense guided by a vertical subordination of power model. Later, the model is applied to the Cameroonian and South African constitutional frameworks to identify individuals who are appointed by the President to the cabinet. We argue that such appointments are political because of the processes (defined in a political document like the Constitution); the mandate to be fulfilled (their portfolios are determined by the President but often largely in fulfilment of a defined policy); and such appointees usually come from a political base (such as a political party or from a political body).

We then discuss corruption scandals in South Africa, with a specific focus on three individuals who are the core of the political elite. We investigate the SCC details to identify which political elites were involved in the theft of state funds and articulate the amounts involved, the way they stole the funds and with whom they conspired to commit such crimes. Lastly, we conclude, arguing that if the political elites are involved in grand corruption, the hope of ending corruption or bringing it to a manageable level, must be dashed, unless the enforcement of anti-corruption laws is not limited to the small fishes: the big fishes should and must be brought to the legal dragnet.

The Notion of Political Elites

In politics and political science, the question of who governs the people is key and complex because power is never distributed evenly; the exploration (including exploitation) and management of resources may not be done in an open and accountable manner; and the ultimate questions of who gets what, when, how and why, may, often, result in the alienation of some segments of the population. The way the foregoing aspects are dealt with, in any given country, may foster stability and national cohesion and development, or cause segmentation, alienation, instability, and even intra-state (armed) conflicts. Numerous African countries constitute eloquent testimony to the above.

As such, it is a power play, and irrespective of whether a political system is democratic or autocratic; parliamentary or presidential, there will always be specific individuals who oversee institutions that make key decisions in a system. Those individuals wield a considerable amount of influence over such institutions, play a key role in processes, and across the nation, do exercise some disproportionate power. Together, they may constitute a class that is seen as "untouchable" – often perceived as the preferred, or whose voices must be considered. A social class is created, and the members of that social class are privileged to the point of being placed higher than others. In short, members of such a social class are seen as superior. However, the notion of the rule of law means that no one is above the law, all are equal before the law and when a crime is committed, the perpetrator should be prosecuted for violating the laws of that country. Adherence to the rule of law contributes to a government's legitimacy, stability, continuity, and legacy.

Over time, the notion of the political elite has evolved including the definition and understanding of that concept given the dynamic character of politics and political institutions and processes themselves. The constitution of what fits into the description of a political elite depends on many factors, some of which include the type of political regime (presidential or parliamentary); provisions on processes to fill positions in organs of state; or even the residual power possessed to appoint to specific senior level positions.[17]

Political elite is quite a complex (and fluid) concept just like political violence and terrorism. However, it is relatively much easier to define political violence since it is a specific kind of social violence that is perpetrated with a defined (political) motive, committed with an intention that has a political character, and often, committed by or against political actors, or individuals with a political ideology or grouping. However, if one were to apply such parameters, then, one would likely miss the point: the notion of political elite is quite complex and often frustrating given the fluidity it contains because such a social grouping is reflective of processes (being elected into a political body such as parliament); institutions (voted into an office such as presidency); appointments of a political character such as a cabinet minister and senior public office; positions in politically established institutions such as heads of chairs of commissions with a specific mandate (like Truth and Reconciliation Commission and state capture); heads of institutions requiring validations by political bodies like Chapter Nine institutions in South Africa.[18]

The Notion of Political Elite – Definitional Complexities

In the past decades, political participation, ways of doing and influencing politics and political structures within countries have undergone enormous changes. Also notable is the dynamism and challenges experienced in formulating a watertight definition of what is political elite. At every level of political administration in any country, political elites do exist – local (city mayors and councillors); provincial or state (legislators and governors); and national (state legislative bodies, cabinet officials and state entities). The vertical and horizontal dimensions of political structures and processes, without doubt, constitute the first major challenge in formulating a watertight definition. But belonging to the political structures should not be the defining criterion of political elitism: numerous business individuals, not attached to any structure may well be within such a small social and political group given the considerable wealth and power they possess and exercise.

At the often and complex interplay between law and politics lies the issue of formulating and postulating a definition of concepts agreeable to both the political scientist and lawyer. The literature on politics, human rights, freedom, terrorism, leadership, political violence, and corruption are indicative of some of the instances in which consensus on meaning has been hard to achieve. The notion of "political elites" is another dimension of complexity at the intersection between law and political sciences. Developing a definition that touches on the various aspects of political elites and political elitism, without doubt, is also challenging.

The challenge can be explained by some factors. First, political elites constitute a unique and special social class: a bunch of political figures who wield valuable and disproportionate political power within a given society. The attitude has been to consider political elites based on the power they possess. On one hand, if that approach is to be taken, then, military generals, superintendents of police and prisons, should be locked in that compartment while low-ranking uniformed officers should not be.[19] Using "power" as the main criterion for the determination of who is a political elite comes with the high risk of sinking numerous influential financial gurus who, by their choice or based on rules, engage surreptitiously in political activities. On the other hand, a military general possesses powers over the military but would likely not qualify as a political elite given the nature of the mandate such an authority has to fulfil in society.

Secondly, from the domain of political sciences, plenty of flexibility has been infused into the categorisation process: it has been applied to military officers;[20] business executives;[21] professional scholars with doctorates in law, politics, economics, and political sciences.[22] Also included are mixed groups of government and military personnel who have been hired from specialised executive training programs[23] and elected politicians.[24]

To formulate a definition requires that we reflect, examine the voices of scholars, and articulate what constitutes the political elite. This paper shall not attempt to discredit or puncture the works of scholars (whether legal or political sciences) on the issue of political elitism. Since it is narrowed to the perpetration of a specific kind of corruption by this political group, the focus shall be on the core common elements – senior membership in a top government administration. Considering what we seek to do and achieve, we must start by asking a question: who counts as a political elite? For political scientists, the notion is vast as it touches on politicians, political actors, think tank members, academics and local administrators, presidents, lawmakers, prime ministers, senior cabinet members, chairs of commissions, heads of state-run institutions, appointees by presidents, etc. The examples exude distinct variations in the use of the term which bring forth serious practical implications for delimiting the notion's usage.

Literature on the subject suggests that there is still no consensus on who counts as a political elite.[25] The recent work by Kertzer and Renshon (2022) on who counts as a political elite is critical in both philosophical and practical approaches to the issue.[26] Taking stock of the existing literature prior to theirs, they do acknowledge the existence of definitional disagreements, which would have serious and deep implications in whatever one does.

Kertzer and Renshon propose three approaches in the conceptualisation of political elites: first, the occupational approach which sees political elites as "actors whose institutional roles afford them higher levels of influence over public policy."[27] Fitting into this compartment are presidents, premiers, ministers, directors-general, lawmakers, civil servants, diplomats, bureaucrats, and military officers. In line with this categorisation is Lasswell's definition of elites as "the holders of high positions in a given society"[28] and political elites as "the power holders of a body politic."[29]

This approach considers the (political) character and roles incumbent on the offices they occupy. The compositional model considers specific social and economic traits that they do exude such as wealth, education, and age. The cognitive model, according to Kertzer and Reshton, emphasises "elites" possession of a distinctive constellation of cognitive traits, sometimes conceptualised as a domain-specific expertise or experience.[30] But they further caution on the dangers of reliance on those conceptual methodologies. First, they argue that they are "conceptually intertwined."[31] Secondly, and from a practical point of view, they both consider those approaches as inter-related. Lastly, in spite of the divergent approaches in the definition of what is the political elite, two factors are reflected therein which they sum as variation in the reasons why scholars study elites in the first place as well as practical constraints.[32]

Delimiting the Notion of Political Elites: Vertical Subordination of Political Power

In view of the foregoing analysis, it is important to delimit the notion of political elites. As power structures exist at local, provincial, and national levels, it will be a Herculean task to attempt to bring onto the radar every individual who would be seen as a political elite. Rather, a sensible (and practical) approach is to look at the power structure in place and focus on the vertical (rather than horizontal) distribution and delegation of political authority. In other words, a vertical subordination model zooms in on specific elites to whom power is delegated by a superior authority. To do that, it is important to consider the constitutionality of a vertical allocation and delegation of political authority entrenched in the supreme laws of the various countries.

The South African Constitution contains provisions relating to the President and National Executive. Chapter 5 of the Constitution outlines the powers and functions of the President, cabinet, accountability, and executive decisions. On the powers and functions of the President, most of them are of a political character (and implication). For example, the "making any appointments that the Constitution or legislation requires the President to make, other than as head of the national executive"; "appointing commissions of inquiry"; and "appointing ambassadors, plenipotentiaries, and diplomatic and consular representatives."[33]

The South African Constitution stipulates further that the executive authority of the Republic is vested in the President: such authority, exercised by the President and other members of the Cabinet, can be done through any or all of the following ways stated in the Constitution.[34] In addition to the functions and powers as the Head of the Executive of the Republic, the President heads the cabinet as one of its members and appoints the Deputy President, Ministers, and Deputy Ministers to specific portfolios.

Even though there are some slight differences, the President of the Republic of Cameroon possesses similar powers and performs functions like those of the South African President. Operating a presidential system, the premier, ministers-of-state, ministers, and other senior members of government are appointed by the President, drawn from the broader Cameroonian society, with no restriction to membership in Parliament.

Evidently, from the above, narrowing down the concept of political elite is much easier and practical. Since Presidents are elected through institutionalised political processes, wielding considerable political power, they are required to define the policy of the state. To that end, presidents are required to compose a cabinet that must perform specific political functions and do serve at the president's pleasure, it is logical to argue that such appointees to the cabinet and other senior governmental positions are political. For this paper, our usage of the phrase "political elites" shall be limited to the individuals who have been appointed by the President to serve in cabinet-level positions as well as other top-ranking positions such as directorates of state-owned enterprises.

Political Elites and Grand Corruption

Common to both Cameroon and South Africa are the following: penal provisions relating to different kinds of corruption; institutional mechanisms in place to combat corruption; a legislative framework that outlines the fundamental principles of public service; and the perpetration of theft of state resources (misappropriation of public funds). Regarding the offence of misappropriation of public funds, the scandals that have featured in national and international news point to a specific class of perpetrators: the political elite. Carefully delimited in the earlier part of this paper, we consider a much narrower sect of political elites: those appointed by the President (in the exercise of his constitutional mandate) to ministerial and other senior managerial positions, in whose hands public resources are entrusted, and have misappropriated such resources.

The Endless Fight against Corruption in Cameroon

The establishment of a Special Criminal Court (SCC) in Cameroon in 2011 transmitted a clear signal that there was a need to tackle the issue of theft of state resources. However, and fortunately, the cases investigated and prosecuted by the SCC, so far, reveal the degree of involvement of the political elite in the embezzlement of public funds. Over 95 per cent of the individuals indicted fit into the definition of the political elite also known as "politically exposed individuals."[35]

The success of the SCC in dealing with this specific category of perpetrators validates the view that every anti-corruption law and institution before the SCC was impotent in fulfilling its mandate because of the involvement of the political elite who would have influenced law enforcement. Due to (political and unlawful) interference, numerous cases were neither reported nor investigated. The political character of appointments to leadership in such institutions itself meant that the political elite would consider for appointment only those who would protect them and foster their interests: a self-seeking pursuit of wealth of personal gain at the expense of the state.

Ranked twice by the global anti-corruption watchdog as the most corrupt country in the world,[36] there are various reasons why the numerous laws and institutional mechanisms have not helped in ending corruption in Cameroon. Some of those reasons include the politicisation of law enforcement agents which makes it difficult for them to do their work; the absence of judicial independence as the judiciary is constituted by the executive; and a general climate of corruption wherein every public official seeks personal gain rather than public service.

All those factors militate against legal and institutional mechanisms, ultimately depriving them of the requisite political will to tackle and overcome this conundrum. Without any significant change in those aspects, Cameroon's battle against corruption, especially the theft of resources by the political elite, remains forlorn, and whether the SCC will succeed in infusing the right psyche to the political elite, remains one of the unanswered questions for now.

The Political Elite and Corruption in Cameroon

As mentioned earlier, political elites have been involved in the perpetration of embezzlement of public funds. Unfortunately, due to the political power they possessed and wielded, pertinent details were kept from the public domain. With the establishment of the SCC, the misappropriation of public funds committed by the political elite over a long time has been laid bare.

As of August 2022, over 300 individuals have been indicted and prosecuted by the SCC. Of this number, over 95 per cent constituted the political elite: individuals appointed by the President to cabinet-level positions, directorates of state-owned enterprises, or appointments made by the Prime Minister, Ministers-of-State, or Ministers. All those individuals occupied cabinet-ranking portfolios. Jerome Mendouga, former Ambassador to the United States, was also implicated in the theft of public funds. Numerous directors of state-owned enterprises, appointed by presidential decree, formed part of the clientele of the SCC. The amounts of public funds stolen by those elites are alarmingly high (and outrageous), done in complicity with other individuals.

Combating Corruption in South Africa

At the dawn of its democratic dispensation in the 90s, South Africa stood out as a country with a huge promise to be outstanding: a public service that is transparent and accountable, guided by constitutional ethos. Building from a society scarred and scourged by the decades-long policies of apartheid with shattered lives, devastated communities and broken livelihoods, post-apartheid South Africa, and a nascent democracy as a political choice would ultimately face the challenges of closing the gap between the rich and the poor; ensure economic equality for all; and enhance national and social cohesion.

Such aspirations and expectations of a national government would mean that every available resource should be directed towards those ends. While successive administrations since President Nelson Mandela's era have been devoid of corruption scandals involving the political elite, the former President Jacob Zuma's administration directed the country towards a very different and ugly turn. Developments during the Zuma years and the scandals that dogged his administration (his Cabinet and himself) did not only test the soundness and integrity of the entire South African political and legal systems but further helped in affirming two not-so-nice views.

First, the extent of corruption scandals showed that South Africa is just like any other African country. Roughly translated, this means that in spite of the laws and institutions in place, corruption would find a place in the South African society and ultimately flourish like the Sower's seed that fell on fertile ground. Secondly, the speed at which corruption infiltrated into the ranks of the political elite was unprecedented. In so short a time, specific individuals could be blamed for a perceived state capture, triggering the collapse of the Zuma rule and the establishment of a state capture commission with a mandate to investigate allegations of state capture, headed by the then Deputy Chief Justice Raymond Zondo.[37]

The Zuma years were marked by the adulteration of every political institution; the appointment of his henchmen to state-owned enterprises; associating with the Gupta family in ways that influenced political appointments;[38] and depriving legal and political institutions of the resources, support and will to investigate, prosecute, and convict political elites who were involved in grand corruption.[39]

The Political Elite and Corruption in South Africa

Recent developments in South Africa attest to some disturbing truths: the endemic nature of corruption in South Africa, the involvement of the political elite in corrupt activities, especially misappropriation of public funds; the ineffectiveness and insufficiency of existing legal and institutional mechanisms to combat corruption and the devastating effects it has on service delivery, economic growth, and social development. In other words, South Africa has confirmed that it is just another African country: quite sarcastic but undeniably a continent that is ravaged by corruption scandals, weak institutional mechanisms, and the heavy involvement of the political elite in the theft of state resources. While the corruption scandals have dominated the media in recent years (at least under President Cyril Ramaphosa's administration), a few are worth mentioning. Drawn from the wide pool of the political elite, three individuals have, in recent times, drawn the focus of politicians, special investigating units, and the wider population: Former President Zuma; former Minister of Health, Zweli Mkhize; and the Former Premier of Free State Province, Ace Magashule.

Since its coming into power in 1994, the African National Congress (ANC) has been implicated in, and embroiled in, corruption scandals particularly under the leadership of Zuma that have benefited a few of his associates (obviously at the expense of the poor).[40] During the ANC's 101st birthday celebrations, the former president said:

> Support is fine, and we love it. However, if you just go beyond that and become a member, you will realise everything of yours will go very well. If you are a businessperson business will thrive. Everything you touch will multiply.[41]

Saying such on a public platform meant a few things: the institutionalisation of corruption by the chief executive of the country, which eventually caused corruption to creep and get normalised into the social fabric of South African society, whether formally or informally. Zuma's presidency, as would be seen later, was marked by several corruption scandals. The upgrading of his private residence in Nkandla is one of the few: a topical issue that sparked tensions and violence in Parliament as well as drawing the attention of the Public Protector and the Constitutional Court (ruling on the power of the Public Protector as well as the legal standing of its report). Opportunistic relationships with the Guptas have triggered investigations on whether there was State Capture, resulting in the establishment of a State Capture Commission headed by the then Deputy Chief Justice Raymond Zondo. The Guptas were in business relationships with members of the Zuma family: a relationship that influenced even the composition of the Zuma cabinet and appointments to state-owned enterprises such as Eskom.[42]

Other allegations reveal that President Zuma used his position to enrich himself, his son and the Guptas by giving preferential treatment over their businesses and awarding state contracts to entities linked to the Gupta family.[43] From a public administration perspective, President Zuma compromised fundamental principles of public administration which include accountability and transparency.[44] At the time of writing this chapter, cases of corruption that occurred prior to his presidency have resurfaced. President Zuma's battle with the State Capture Commission had taken a sour turn as he challenged the mandate and independence of the Commission to investigate the financial crimes committed during his presidency. The conviction of the former president for contempt of court not only highlights the incorruptibility of the judiciary but affirms the fact that as a political branch, it is not persuaded by a politician's influence.

Another political elite whose surreptitious activities have been exposed is the former Minister of Health, Zweli Mkhize. As the former minister earned the ire of the public and other political elites, the Special Investigating Unit (SIU) publicly shared the details on the acquisition of personal protective equipment in the wake of the coronavirus (COVID-19) infections across the country: millions of public funds had been misdirected, through unofficial channels, to other individuals.[45] Another scandal that continues to dog the former minister is the payment made by the Department of Health to Digital Vibes for COVID-19 communications work. It is alleged that Mkhize has a vested interest in the company. However, it was found that the contract was authorised outside normal government regulations and procurement procedures.[46] According to a 114-page report by the SIU, a whistleblower alleged that there were irregularities in the award of the tender to Digital Vibes and that the former minister had a vested interest in the award.[47]

It was found that there had been irregular expenditure amounting to "approximately" South African Rands (ZAR) 150 million and an additional "fruitless and wasteful" expenditure amounting to between ZAR 72 million and ZAR 80 million that was incurred by the National Department of Health.[48] Acting in complicity with three other senior officials in the Department of Health, it is alleged that the former Minister did not follow prescribed procedures in getting tenders awarded. The SIU report found incriminating evidence against the Acting Director-General of the Department of Health – he wrote a letter to the National Treasury wherein he made "material intentional misrepresentations" to get approval to deviate from normal procurement procedures.[49] The evidence established that he committed fraud for which he should be indicted. The SIU report found that the former minister lied to the nation that his family and himself did not benefit from the contract that was awarded to Digital Vibes.[50] The scandal resulted in the resignation of the minister; however, so far no criminal charges have been brought against him.

Lastly, the former premier of the Free State, Ace Magashule is another political elite who has been involved in multiple corruption scandals. Magashule has been charged with fraud; corruption and money laundering concerning the 2014 contract the Free State Department of Human Settlements awarded to Blackhead Consulting Joint Venture (JV) to audit and remove asbestos from homes.[51] It is alleged that the amount of money paid to the company is around ZAR 225 million (approximately US$13.1 million). The former premier appeared before the Bloemfontein Magistrates' Court in the summer of 2020 on charges relating to corruption and was released on a ZAR 200 000 (about US$11,600) bail.[52] Following the allegations laid against him, the ANC under President Ramaphosa suspended Ace Magashule from his position as Secretary-General of the ANC in May 2021 until the criminal case is finally disposed of.[53]

The foregoing three scandals, involving the political elite who were at the nucleus of the former cabinet and ANC, are indicative of the culture of corruption that has plagued the ANC as a ruling party and cabinet members. The contents of the State Capture report have recently been made public: a formal disclosure of the involvement of key political elite in the development and deployment of an unprecedented corruption architecture resulting in dismissals from cabinet positions, redeployment of specific individuals to run state-owned enterprises, illicit financial flows from those state-owned entities to specific individuals, and ultimately, the incorporation of corruption into the official business of the state.

Like Cameroon, South Africa's anti-corruption efforts, such as the laws and institutions in place, have not been effective in deterring the political elite from embezzling state resources. Even though many reasons may account for this, the obvious one is the lack of political will – a much-needed element to complement all other efforts. If leaders are to be followed, and they must lead by example, then, by stealing public resources entrusted in their hands, they directly benumb every anti-corruption effort as they set the standard to be followed by all subordinates.

Political Elites and Corruption in Cameroon and South Africa

A look at corruption in both Cameroon and South Africa reveals some commonalities. First, the two countries have a solid legislative framework that prohibits and punishes corruption.[54] Secondly, Cameroon, like South Africa, has institutional mechanisms in place. Those mechanisms are designed to curb the perpetration of corruption at all levels. Thirdly, the political elite in Cameroon and South Africa are actively involved in the perpetration of grand corruption. In Cameroon, individuals who occupied portfolios such as Premier, Ministers, Directors-General, and the diplomatic corps – were all implicated in grand corruption and the details became public only after they were convicted by the SCC. In South Africa, the experience was not different: through the State Capture Inquiry, numerous pertinent details were divulged to the broader South African public – the involvement of the political elite in the theft of state resources, done through syndicates and fraud.[55] Both countries have experienced the worst forms of racketeering that ever struck their countries in recent years.

The question then is this: why those similarities even though those countries are far apart? An answer to that question touches on some key issues: first, the deprivation of the requisite political will to complement the legal framework and institutional mechanisms put in place to combat corruption. Politicians in these countries, like in most other places, do not view, and do politics for the interest of everyone. To them, politics is an opportunity to advance the self, or self-interest.

With such a mindset, the political elite looks for every opportunity to further their interests, even at the detriment of the masses, and would cripple or weaken every institution that stands along their way. The enactment of laws and establishment of institutions to combat corruption need to be complemented by the political will: the firm commitment made by politicians that summons the entire nation to the cause.

Furthermore, they must be credible in anti-corruption movements: this means that they must not only echo words and speeches but lead by examples. The political elite, especially the cabinet, recommends and makes decisions on who to head key agencies in the fight against corruption. To further their goals, the political elite would appoint their stooges to direct those offices, and then deprive them of the political will they need. Such agencies, cognisant of the fact that the political will is absent, become unable to investigate and prosecute prominent politicians who are engaged in corruption.

Conclusion

In the foregoing discussion, we narrowed the definition of the notion of political elite, adopting a vertical appointment approach for this chapter. The vertical appointment approach focuses on politicians appointed by the President to cabinet positions: that being a constitutional duty whose performance is greatly political. For Cameroon, the exercise of that constitutional function extends to appointments to state-owned enterprises. For South Africa, the focus was on three top politicians: a former president and two former cabinet members. From those case studies, some disturbing observations can be made. First, the political elite is deeply involved in the perpetration of grand corruption, especially the theft of state resources. Secondly, by participating in the theft of state resources, the political elite numbs every effort made to combat corruption. Thirdly, they taint political leadership with a legitimacy crisis, making it difficult for their subordinates as well as the broader nation to join in any anti-corruption effort. As they perpetrate corruption within their circles, petty corruption such as bribery and favouritism become rife in the lower ranks of public service, ultimately making public service a sector not governed by any ethical standards but one where you serve who you decide to serve, at a time of your choosing. Lastly, with corruption deeply entrenched in the political class, it is obvious that this enemy amongst us may well be considered a permanent resident as it will not disappear any time soon.

The involvement of the political elite in perpetrating grand corruption is a serious concern for many reasons. First, they are entrusted with state resources which are ring-fenced. Abusing their offices and siphoning those resources for private benefit mean that the public at large is bereft of those resources. Secondly, in a country that is committed to good governance and founded upon the rule of law, those institutions are assaulted when political leadership engage in unethical conduct. Public confidence in political leaders is eroded. The gradual decay of state institutions commences, and ultimately, they lose their credibility in the eyes of the public.

It is quite important to build a cult of responsible, ethical, and responsive politicians who never relent on upholding the core ethics and standards of public administration and management, knowing that once called to serve the public, they are bound to manage and deliver. Like the Cameroonian experience, the establishment of specialised judicial institutions to bring the political elite into its dragnet becomes quite important in that it informs and reminds other political elites that they are not above the law and cases of theft of public property shall be investigated and prosecuted.

Notes

* Professor of Public International Law, School of Postgraduate Studies, Faculty of Law, North-West University.

** Lecturer at North West University, South Africa.

*** Lecturer at the Faculty of Law, North-West University, South Africa.

1 Transparency International "Global Perceptions Index 2021" (pages 2–3) available at: <https://images.transparencycdn.org/images/CPI2021_Report_EN-web.pdf> (accessed on 11 April 2022).

2 Sarah Chayes, "Kleptocracy in America: Corruption is reshaping governments everywhere," *Foreign Affairs* 96, no. 5 (2017): 7.

3 See generally, Abdou Thiao, "The effect of illicit financial flows on government revenues in the West African Economic and Monetary Union countries," *Cogent Social Sciences* 7, no. 1 (2021).

4 Cordelia Onyinyechi Omodero, "Effect of corruption on foreign direct investment inflows in Nigeria," *Studia Universitatis Economics Series* 29, no. 2 (2019).

5 Mohamed Sami Ben Ali and Seifallah Sassi, "The corruption-inflation nexus: evidence from developed and developing countries," *The BE Journal of Macroeconomics* 16, no. 1 (2016).

6 Kwabena Gyimah-Brempong, "Corruption, economic growth, and income inequality in Africa," *Economics of governance* 3, no. 3 (2002).

7 Arolda Elbasani and Senada Šelo Šabić, "Rule of law, corruption and democratic accountability in the course of EU enlargement," *Journal of European Public Policy* 25, no. 9 (2018).

8 Siew Pyng Christine Chong, Chwee Ming Tee, and Seow Voon Cheng, "Political institutions and the control of corruption: a cross-country evidence," *Journal of Financial Crime* 28, no. 1 (2020).

9 Theo Eicher, Cecilia García-Peñalosa, and Tanguy Van Ypersele, "Education, corruption, and the distribution of income," *Journal of Economic Growth* 14, no. 3 (2009).

10 Asaju Kayode, Sunday Onah Adagba, and Silas Felix Anyio, "Corruption and service delivery: the case of Nigerian public service," *Wudpecker Journal of Public Administration* 1, no. 1 (2013).

11 Héctor Flores Marquez et al., "Corruption and extreme wealth. Evidence at country level," *Cogent Social Sciences* 7, no. 1 (2021).

12 Luminiţa Ionescu, "The adverse effects of corruption on growth and development," *Economics, Management, and Financial Markets* 9, no. 4 (2014).

13 Examples include electoral fraud; fraud at examinations; fake identity; bribery; extortion; money laundering; nepotism and favouritism; abuse of discretion; collusion; patronage; and *clientelism*. Anzanilufuno Munyai, *Overcoming the corruption conundrum in Africa: a socio-legal perspective* (Newcastle: Cambridge Scholars Publishing, 2020).

14 Munyai, *Overcoming the corruption conundrum in Africa: a socio-legal perspective*, 54–55.
15 Global Financial Integrity, *Illicit Financial Flows from Developing Countries: 2002–2006*, Global Financial Integrity (Washington, DC, December 2008)
16 Law No. 2011/028 of 14 December 2011 established the Special Criminal Court (SCC) with its mandate stipulated in Section 2.
17 Joshua D Kertzer and Jonathan Renshon, "Experiments and surveys on political elites," *Annual Review of Political Science* 25 (2022).
18 Chapter Nine institutions refer to state institutions established to support constitutional democracy. These include the Public Protector; the Auditor-General; the South African Human Rights Commission; Commission for Gender Equality; Electoral Commission and Commission for the Promotion and Protection of the Rights of Cultural, Religious and Linguistic Communities: Sections 181–194 of the Constitution of South Africa, 1996.
19 Kertzer and Renshon, "Experiments and surveys on political elites," 7.
20 Erik Lin-Greenberg, "Soldiers, Pollsters, and International Crises: Public Opinion and the Military's Advice on the Use of Force," *Foreign Policy Analysis* 17, no. 3 (2021).
21 Mari Teigen and Rune Karlsen, "Influencing elite opinion on gender equality through framing: a survey experiment of elite support for corporate board gender quotas," *Politics & Gender* 16, no. 3 (2020).
22 Enrique Fatas, Tibor Neugebauer, and Pilar Tamborero, "How politicians make decisions: A political choice experiment," *Journal of Economics* 92, no. 2 (2007).
23 Jonathan Renshon, "Losing face and sinking costs: Experimental evidence on the judgment of political and military leaders," *International Organization* 69, no. 3 (2015).
24 Joshua D Kertzer, Jonathan Renshon, and Keren Yarhi-Milo, "How Do Observers Assess Resolve?," *British Journal of Political Science* 51, no. 1 (2019).
25 George Moyser and Margaret Wagstaffe, "Studying elites: theoretical and methodological issues," in *Research methods for elite studies*, ed. George Moyser and Margaret Wagstaffe (Boston: Allen & Unwin, 1987); Robert Putnam, *The Comparative Study of Political Elites* (Englewood Cliffs, NJ: Prentice-Hall, 1976).
26 See generally Kertzer and Renshon, "Experiments and surveys on political elites," 7.
27 Kertzer and Renshon, "Experiments and surveys on political elites," 7.
28 HD Lasswell, "The elite concept," in *The Comparative Study of Elites: An Introduction and Bibliography*, ed. D Lerner HD Lasswell, CE Rothwell (Stanford, CA: Stanford University Press, 1952), 6.
29 Lasswell, "The elite concept," 13.
30 Elizabeth N Saunders, "No substitute for experience: presidents, advisers, and information in group decision making," *International Organization* 71, no. S1 (2017).
31 Kertzer and Renshon, "Experiments and surveys on political elites," 8.
32 Kertzer and Renshon, "Experiments and surveys on political elites," 8.
33 Section 84(2) of the 1996 Constitution of South Africa.
34 Sections 83–85, 91 and 93 of the 1996 Constitution of South Africa.
35 Ministers, Mayors, Director-Generals of state-owned entities; Premiers; Treasury-Inspectors; Tax Inspectors; Secretary-Generals, Chiefs of Service; *etc.*
36 Transparency International, "1998 Corruption Perceptions Index" available at www.transparency.org/en/press/1998-corruption-perceptions-index accessed on 13 April 2022 and Transparency International, '1999 Corruption Perceptions Index" available at <www.transparency.org/en/cpi/1999> accessed on 13 April 2022.
37 RMM Zondo, *Judicial Commission of Inquiry into State Capture Vol. 1: South African Airways and its Associated Companies* (Pretoria, 2022), www.gov.za/sites/default/files/gcis_document/202201/judicial-commission-inquiry-state-capture-reportpart-1.pdf. Accessed on 30 March 2022.
38 BBC, "The Guptas and their links to South Africa's Jacob Zuma," *BBC* (London) 2018, www.bbc.com/news/world-africa-22513410.

39 Zondo, *Judicial Commission of Inquiry into State Capture Vol. 1: South African Airways and its Associated Companies*.
40 Daniel N Mlambo, "Governance and service delivery in the public sector: the case of South Africa under Jacob Zuma (2009–2018)," *African Renaissance* 16, no. 3 (2019): 203.
41 Mandy De Waal, "South Africa's power elite," *Daily Maverick*, 21 January 2013, 2013, www.dailymaverick.co.za/article/2013-01-21-south-africas-power-elite/. Accessed on 30 March 2022.
42 Zondo, *Judicial Commission of Inquiry into State Capture Vol. 1: South African Airways and its Associated Companies*, ii.
43 Zondo, *Judicial Commission of Inquiry into State Capture Vol. 1: South African Airways and its Associated Companies*, iii.
44 Makhura B Rapanyane, "Seizure of State Organs, Corruption and Unaccountability Promotion in South Africa: Case Study of Jacob Zuma Administration," *African Journal of Development Studies* 11, no. 3 (2021): 252.
45 Janine Arcangeli Roze Moodley, "Gauteng Health suspends official linked to PPE scandal," (Pretoria) 2020, www.sanews.gov.za/south-africa/gauteng-health-suspends-offi cial-linked-ppe-scandal.
46 SUI, *Final Report* (Pretoria, 30 June 2021), vii, www.thepresidency.gov.za/download/file/fid/2408.
47 SUI, *Final Report*, vii.
48 SUI, *Final Report*, vii.
49 SUI, *Final Report*, viii.
50 SUI, *Final Report*, 6.
51 EWN, "The charges against Ace Magashule," *Eye Witness News*, 13 November 2020, https://ewn.co.za/2020/11/13/read-the-charges-against-ace-magashule. Accessed on 30 March 2022.
52 EWN, "The charges against Ace Magashule." Accessed on 30 March 2022.
53 P Letshwiti-Jones and Q Hunter, "ANC suspends secretary-general Ace Magashule," *News24* (Johannesburg), 5 May 2021, www.news24.com/news24/southafrica/news/breaking-anc-suspends-secretary-general-ace-magashule-20210505. Accessed on 30 March 2022.
54 See Emmanuel Egbeyong Bechem, "Corruption in Cameroon: Public Perception on the Role and Effectiveness of the Different Anti-Corruption Agencies," *Review Public Administration and Management* 6, no. 1 (2018).
55 Trevor Budhram, "Political corruption and state capture in South Africa," in *Political Corruption in Africa*, ed. Inge Amundsen (Northampton, MA: Edward Elgar Publishing Limited, 2019).

16 The Role of Women as Anti-Corruption Agents

*Chikondi Mandala**

Introduction

The relationship between women and corruption is still evolving. There are three aspects to women and corruption: women as corrupt, women as victims of corruption, and women as anti-corruption agents. According to popular belief, women are less prone to corruption and thus make better anti-corruption agents. However, there is an argument that if given the opportunity, women will engage in corrupt acts on a par with men.[1] Second, women are more likely to be victims of corruption because of their reproductive needs, caregiver jobs, and perceptions of women as the fairer, weaker sex. Women are more vulnerable to solicitation and the use of sex as a form of currency in corruption if they are constantly exposed to government services and officials. The culmination of these factors reduces accessibility to social services such as health and education. Finally, this is related to the argument that women could be effective anti-corruption agents because consistent and continuous exposure to public institutions and officials provides more opportunities for women to expose fraudulent behaviour and practices. As a result of their first-hand knowledge, they are better advocates for the fight against corruption.

This chapter discusses African perceptions of corruption, women, and their complex relationships with corruption – as corrupt, as having natural integrity that dissuades them from being corrupt, and as perfectly situated to fight corruption. The thrust of the argument is that there is nothing that suggests that women are more or less corrupt than men/others, but that there are societal, economic, and other factors that place women in a position to fight corruption. This is compounded by the fact that corruption reduces accessibility to public services, such as education and health, which are accessed by poor people, a demographic that mainly comprises women in Africa.

Corruption Contextualised

A simple definition of corruption is the abuse of entrusted power for personal advantage.[2] The African Union (AU) Convention on Preventing and Combating Corruption offers a thorough list of corruption-related offences in its Article 4.[3] Suggesting, accepting, offering, granting, actions or omissions, diversion, illegal

DOI: 10.4324/9781003326649-19

enrichment, concealment of money generated from the mentioned crimes, and conspiracy to do the listed acts are among the acts that constitute corruption.[4] Corrupt practices include acts such as "demanding or taking money for favours in exchange for services, misuse of public money or granting public jobs to sponsors, friends" and "demanding or accepting money in exchange for favours and/or services, misusing public funds or awarding public employment to sponsors, friends, and families, and companies paying politicians to achieve profitable agreements."[5] As a result, corrupt practices make both the offeror and the offeree liable for prosecution, and they include a wide variety of behaviours.[6]

Women as Corrupt

Perceptions of women as corrupt have been confirmed and denied based on what are perceived to be intrinsic characteristics that women have that make them less corrupt in some instances and more corrupt in other instances. Additionally, societal, economic, and cultural factors suggest that accessibility to corruption for women is more complex than initially perceived. A further complication is where the lines are blurred, and sex is used as a currency for corruption as well as an increased likelihood of women being corrupt in networks where there are more women. The discussion to follow will explore these multi-layered issues and the complexity of women being involved in corrupt practices.

Inherent probity

One of the long-standing arguments for and against women's inclusion in politics has been their possession of inherent probity – the natural, feminine inclination to be morally upright, upstanding, honest, and accountable.[7] This characteristic makes them the perfect candidates for fighting corruption in public institutions and by extension the perfect tool for fighting corruption as a 'broader development goal of good governance.'[8] Taking the situation in Nigeria as an example, Sampson and Decker argue that with increased women's participation in politics, there have also been increasing incidences of women being arrested and prosecuted for grand corruption which was perceived to be a predominantly male act.[9] It seems that women will engage in corrupt practices when given an opportunity. But this would be an overly simplistic conclusion.

Goetz argues that women's inclusion in politics and public office would still leave them excluded from the networks of patronage that their male counterparts have and that the perception of inherent probity excludes them from tapping into the networks of patronage as they are not seen to be good accomplices for corrupt acts.[10] Another claim is that women who work in politics are frequently assigned roles that are stereotypically associated with women (such as Ministers of Gender and/or Treasury Departments of Public Offices) and are there because of family ties.[11] It is not as simple as saying that women will be involved in corrupt acts when they have access, there is a host of factors that ought to come together for women to successfully engage in corruption.

In the instances that women are corrupt, participate in corrupt acts, or are perceived to, their inherent probity subjects them to higher standards and stricter punishments than their male counterparts. The consequences and penalties for women who engage in corruption are more severe than those for men in similar circumstances. Female entrepreneurs were thought to be taking advantage of the Ghanaian economy for their own gain during the country's "high time" (1979, 1982–1992). When they were arrested, they would go through quick trials and have their sentences carried out right away. The punishments frequently included having their goods forfeited and being stripped naked and led through the streets.[12] Due to this perception of women's inherent probity, strict and severe punishments are more likely to be meted out to them, and there is a higher expectation of them to exhibit natural feminine honesty.

Access to networks of patronage

Corrupt acts by women may not be an innate inclination towards corruption when compared to men but are most often a result of institutional structuring of corrupt networks of patronage.[13] Corruption, for both men and women, is supported by an intricate web of class, gender, social differentiation, organisational culture, occupational identity, and interpersonal negotiations of power.[14] The United Nations Office on Drugs and Crime (UNODC) 2020 report on the gendered dimensions of corruption quoted a study that observed that women who joined politics in Brazil often came from civil society organisations as their networks of patronage. The support gained from civil society organisations, therefore, had inherent accountability as their political support came from a group of constituents that may be involved in anti-corruption initiatives.[15]

There was also a reduced need to sustain nepotism, and patrimonialism as their political survival was not dependent on the traditional constituents. This, however, is not merely an altruistic act, as breaking up collusive male-dominated networks could also promote their political progression and ensure their political survival. Female candidates are frequently elected against the backdrop of campaigns that reassure voters that their "interest in politics is as mothers, guardians, and caregivers of the nation."[16] In relation to this, women are often marginalised in institutions and come to power in politics through alternative pathways as opposed to the conventional political networks that might secure a place in politics.[17] These factors combine to create a barrier between women and networks that are or are perceived to be corrupt. Additionally, it might be less likely to pacify the network through favours and services given the unconventional routes to political power.

Sexualised corruption

In conservative societies, interactions between women and men outside their kin may be frowned upon. The nature of corruption is that it is "a 'consensual crime' – both partners consent to the crime (however unwillingly) and neither reports it."[18] It is, therefore, shrouded in secrecy, and those engaging in corruption rarely do so in public. Due to this, there is a sexual danger to women's involvement in patronage networks. According to a study on "illegal" cross-border trade between the Gambia and Senegal, where women are corrupt or offer bribes, there is often a suggestion of a sexual relationship with the male official involved in the transaction.[19] Similarly, in Lima, Peru when the Police Commander commissioned an all-female motorcycle brigade, the explanation was that it would reduce corruption as female police officers

> have an aversion to taking money from male drivers because they feel this act would resemble prostitution . . . engagement in nefarious acts – being seen taking money from men who are not relatives – has drastic implications for women's sexual integrity.[20]

Corruption by women carries with it a lot of shame, and this affects women's involvement in corrupt activities as it is limited by sexual controls.'[21]

It has been hypothesised that women may be more willing to engage in corruption in settings or institutions where there are more women, despite the hypersexualisation of corruption between men and women. According to Goetz's research in microfinance institutions, female professionals were less averse to "extorting unofficial payments for services that ought to be provided as a right" when there were more female clients.[22] The study suggested that opportunities for corrupt acts may be more open for women in female-dominant socially acceptable environments such as the microfinance sector she conducted fieldwork in, or hospitals where nurses and midwives would abuse female patients.[23]

Women as Victims of Corruption

The other caveat to female corruption hinges on female victimisation. Women are particularly vulnerable to corruption because they frequently interact with public officials and officers. They frequently interact with health, education, and registration offices on behalf of their children and other family members in their role as primary caregivers. This also increases their vulnerability to being asked for sex or sexual favours as a form of payment for corruption. Women bear the brunt of both financial and physical exploitation as currency for corruption. The following section will discuss the complexities of women's victimisation during/through corruption.

Women's vulnerability

Women appear to be easy targets for corruption based on the perception of women being the weaker sex.[24] For example, during customs clearance, women are pressurised to bribe clearance agents, who are predominantly male, may pay higher taxes (formal and informal) than their male counterparts, are delayed longer than men by quarantine at border crossings, and might spend more on transportation to get through the border crossing.[25] Additionally, women may be subjected to physical and financial harassment when complying with mandatory processes and procedures which adds to the difficulty of clearing customs.[26]

The triple work burden that consists of productive, reproductive, and social responsibilities[27] involves the functions of caregiver, cleaner, cook, and seamstress, among others, to which can be added, in rural agrarian societies, that of the subsistence food producer. In addition, women have reproductive health needs that are different to men which require them to access health services more often than men. Women have a multifaceted role in the family that exposes them to public services, institutions, and officials more frequently than men. This makes women more likely to encounter corruption in family-oriented public sectors such as social services, health, and education.[28] As a result of the interaction of these factors, women are more likely to be the target of extortion attempts and requests for bribes when seeking out the essential services required for their healthy survival. In order to meet the needs of their families as a result of their complex caregiver roles, women may then be pressured to commit corrupt acts.

Sextortion

Women are more likely to offer their bodies as a form of exchange in corruption, either because a public official has asked them to do so or because they have done so themselves. In Bogota, Colombia, and Johannesburg, South Africa, the Stockholm International Water Institute and the United Nations Development Programme (UNDP) conducted a study on sexual corruption in the water sector in 2017.[29] It was found that women offered sexual favours in exchange for sustained water supply where bills could not be paid, for their water bills to be lowered, and/or to secure water connections. Women were more exposed to dealing with public officials in this realm due to their responsibility for ensuring water supply to their homes. Another layer was that women had less socioeconomic muscle to pay for water connections and bills, so they were more likely to offer sexual favours in exchange. This was particularly common in South Africa. According to the UNODC report, this could be due to legal illiteracy and more extreme poverty in Johannesburg than in Bogota.

There are also instances where sexual favours are solicited by the public official. In 2019, British Broadcasting Corporation (BBC) Africa Eye published the results of an investigation undertaken at the University of Ghana and the University of Lagos in Nigeria where undercover female reporters posed as students and documented academics soliciting sexual favours in exchange for college admissions, and good grades.[30] Another example is from Malawi where, on 18 January 2022, the High Court in Malawi sentenced a 33-year-old police officer to 30-year imprisonment on a rape conviction.[31] The rape victim/survivor was arrested in the middle of the night while waiting for public transportation with two other friends. When she arrived at the police station, the convicted officer recognised her because they attended the same church. When his colleague attempted to make an official record of the arrest at the police station, he was stopped and led the victim/survivor to a different floor of the police station. While there he suggested that the only way she would leave the police station 'was to behave like an adult woman and rescue herself.' He proceeded to rape her twice during that night. He isolated her from her companions while at the police station, raped her in secluded rooms of the police station, and forced her to wash her private parts to conceal evidence of rape. He eventually released her in the middle of the night when there was no public transportation available. The victim spent the night outside the police station with her friends as they waited for public transportation to start operating again.

The examples show that sextortion is a form of corruption that predominantly affects women. While the definition of corruption is broad and encompasses a broad range of acts and/or omissions, sextortion specifically affects women the most.

Recommendations to Empower Women as Anti-corruption Agents

From the analysis above, below are some recommendations to strengthen the role of women in fighting corruption in Africa:

Participation, inclusion, and empowerment

With regard to participation and inclusion, women's participation in public positions improves perceptions of corruption and potentially enhances control of corruption in communities. Women are seen to be less likely to accept bribes, are perceived to be more likely to whistle blow and are seen to be bad accomplices of corruption.[32] Since it is likely that women have encountered corruption and have negative associations with it, when they attain positions of power, they become strong anti-corruption advocates.[33] Both the World Bank's Control of Corruption Index and Transparency International's Corruption Perceptions Index establish that female representation in parliament and positions of power are positively correlated with reduced perceptions of corruption in a nation. In so far as corruption tends to stand in the way of women's political aspirations, they may be more likely than men to fight it. Since women frequently experience discrimination, especially in the political sphere, joining politics may increase their likelihood of fighting corruption, particularly in an effort to advance the interests of women.[34]

In relation to empowerment, women's empowerment allows women to be involved in anti-corruption efforts as they have the confidence and tools to report and resist corruption. The 2012 UNDP study "Seeing beyond the State: Grassroot Women's Perspectives on Corruption and Anti-Corruption" found that organised groupings of women were more empowered to fight corruption by planning and implementing anti-corruption strategies.[35] This buttresses the contention that even at the grassroots level organised and empowered women's groupings can tackle issues relating to corruption and governance.

Systems, institutions, and networks

Systems – disruption of networks of patronage because of exclusion, the more women join the upper echelons the more difficult it could become for corrupt practices to continue. This also depends on their supporter base, as women who come from the non-governmental organisation (NGO) sector have a more accountable supporter base than women who are placed in positions due to familial ties and allegiances. The systems that exist for women's inclusion should, therefore, be democratic and based on merit that will instil fear, promote accountability, and prevent corruption and extortion even in female-dominated institutions.

Institutions – women's responsiveness to women's issues uniquely places women at the precipice of the anti-corruption cause. When women are elected to public office, they tend to focus more on passing legislation and implementing policies in areas benefitting women.[36] By extension, involving women in the anti-corruption cause would be beneficial, especially in the areas where corruption affects women the most, for example, access to public and social services and contributing to the overall fight against corruption.

Networks – women's inclusion in the fight against anti-corruption could potentially disrupt clientelism.[37] Clientelism is 'the practice of providing personal favours – jobs, contracts, welfare support, money, so forth – in exchange for electoral support.'[38] Since women are perceived to be less likely to engage in corruption, they are often shut out of the networks of patronage that engage in and promote corrupt practices. Actively including women in these spaces has the potential to disrupt the patronage networks that allow corruption to thrive. Further, since women are seen to be less risk-averse than men, especially when chances of being caught are high, having more women in public office could reduce instances of corruption.

The socialisation of future generations

The fact that women's involvement in politics is frequently limited to elite women is one of the weaknesses of the claim that women make the best anti-corruption agents. Women who possess the necessary characteristics, such as education, social and financial capital, race and ethnicity, are more likely to be successful in running for political office. This leaves out many women and creates an extremely small pool of women who are capable of organised corruption resistance.

Both male and female leaders place emphasis on women's roles as mothers, guardians, and carers based on women's purity, integrity, and sacrifice, which further qualifies them to not engage in corrupt practices. This is the same argument that was once used to keep women out of the political arena.[39] It is accepted that the idea of women's inherent probity can be a problematic premise from which to begin, their role as mothers, guardians, and carers can be used for the socialisation of future generations – their children, and extended family. Women's triple work burden of productive, reproductive, and social responsibilities affords them more time with their children and extended family.[40] This provides an opportunity for women to instil the virtues inherent to accountability, and anti-corruption into children from an early age.

Socialisation frequently determines one's life's course and instils personal values that are carried well into adulthood. Generations that are familiar with the effects of corruption and generations that are not only equipped but also willing to join the anti-corruption cause can be produced by empowering women at all levels with an understanding of the various forms that corruption takes, the reporting mechanisms, and encouraging kids and extended family to speak up when there is injustice. As Kuwali observes, "Teachings in morality, particularly among the youth, may help to nip corruption in the bud as they promote a culture of ethical conduct."[41]

Notes

* *Doctoral Candidate, University of Kent.*

1 Lisa Kilduff, '*Gender perceptions, risk aversion and intrinsic behaviours: dispelling the purity myth surrounding women and anti-corruption*' www.academia.edu/38188935/Gender_perceptions_risk_aversion_and_intrinsic_behaviours_dispelling_the_purity_myth_surrounding_women_and_anti_corruption (accessed on 19 September 2022).

2 Transparency International, *'What Is Corruption?'* www.transparency.org/en/what-is-corruption (accessed on 13 March 2022).

3 Transparency International, *'What Is Corruption?'* www.transparency.org/en/what-is-corruption (accessed on 13 March 2022).

4 Article 4, African Union, Convention on Preventing and Combating Corruption' August 2006 https://au.int/en/treaties/african-union-convention-preventing-and-combating-corruption (accessed on 13 March 2022).

5 Article 4, African Union, Convention on Preventing and Combating Corruption' August 2006 https://au.int/en/treaties/african-union-convention-preventing-and-combating-corruption (accessed on 13 March 2022).

6 Article 4, African Union, Convention on Preventing and Combating Corruption' August 2006 https://au.int/en/treaties/african-union-convention-preventing-and-combating-corruption (accessed on 13 March 2022).

7 Anne Marie Goetz, *Political Cleaners: How Women Are the New Anti-Corruption Force?* (2007) Development and Change, 38:1, 87–105.

8 Anne Marie Goetz, *Political Cleaners: How Women Are the New Anti-Corruption Force?* (2007) Development and Change, 38:1, 87–105, 88.

9 Isaac Terwase Sampson and Habiba Laraba Decker, "*Gender and Corruption: Understanding the Increasing Role of Nigerian Women in Corrupt Practices*", Gender and Behaviour, (2010) 8:2, 3117–3142.

10 Anne Marie Goetz, *Political Cleaners: How Women Are the New Anti-Corruption Force?* (2007) Development and Change, 38:1, 87–105, 88.

11 Anne Marie Goetz, *Political Cleaners: How Women Are the New Anti-Corruption Force?* (2007) Development and Change, 38:1, 87–105, 88.

12 Isaac Terwase Sampson and Habiba Laraba Decker, "*Gender and Corruption: Understanding the Increasing Role of Nigerian Women in Corrupt Practices*" (2010) Gender and Behaviour, 8:2, 3117–3142.

13 Isaac Terwase Sampson and Habiba Laraba Decker, "*Gender and Corruption: Understanding the Increasing Role of Nigerian Women in Corrupt Practices*" (2010) Gender and Behaviour, 8:2, 3117–3142.

14 Cynthia Howson, "*Women Smuggling and the Men Who Help Them: Gender, Corruption and Illicit Networks in Senegal*" (2012) Journal of Modern African Studies 50:3, 422–445.

15 United Nations Office on Drugs and Crime, The Time is Now: Addressing the Gender Dimensions of Corruption, (2020) accessed at www.unodc.org/documents/corruption/Publications/2020/THE_TIME_IS_NOW_2020_12_08.pdf on 26 April 2022 at 14:04.

16 Anne Marie Goetz, *Political Cleaners: How Women are the New Anti-Corruption Force?* (2007) Development and Change, 38:1, 87–105, 90.

17 Tiffany D Barnes and Emily Beaulieu, *Women Politicians, Institutions, and Perceptions of Corruption* (2019) Journal of Comparative Political Studies 52(1), 134–167.
18 Anne Marie Goetz, *Political Cleaners: How Women are the New Anti-Corruption Force?* (2007) Development and Change, 38:1, 87–105, 93.
19 Cynthia Howson, *Women Smuggling and the Men Who Help Them: Gender, Corruption and Illicit Networks in Senegal* (2012) Journal of Modern African Studies 50:3, 422–445.
20 Anne Marie Goetz, *Political Cleaners: How Women Are the New Anti-Corruption Force?* (2007) Development and Change, 38:1, 87–105, 89.
21 Anne Marie Goetz, *Political Cleaners: How Women are the New Anti-Corruption Force?* (2007) Development and Change, 38:1, 87–105, 101.
22 Anne Marie Goetz, *Political Cleaners: How Women Are the New Anti-Corruption Force?* (2007) Development and Change, 38:1, 87–105, 101.
23 Anne Marie Goetz, *Political Cleaners: How Women Are the New Anti-Corruption Force?* (2007) Development and Change, 38:1, 87–105, 101.
24 Jason Carlo Ong Carranceja, *The Role of Women's Empowerment in Anti-Corruption,* March 2021, Asia Pacific Economic Cooperation Policy Support Unit, Policy Brief Number 9, www.apec.org/publications/2021/04/the-role-of-women-empowerment-in-anti-corruption (accessed on 13 March 2022).
25 The World Bank Group and World Trade Organization, *The Role of Trade in Ending Poverty* (2015) accessed at http://documents.worldbank.org/curated/en/726971467989468997/pdf/97607-REPLACEMENT-The-Role-of-Trade-in-Ending-Poverty.pdf on 8 Oct. 2019 at 3:53 PM.
26 The World Bank Group and World Trade Organization, *The Role of Trade in Ending Poverty* (2015) accessed at http://documents.worldbank.org/curated/en/726971467989468997/pdf/97607-REPLACEMENT-The-Role-of-Trade-in-Ending-Poverty.pdf on 8 Oct. 2019 at 3:53 PM.
27 Food and Agriculture Organization of the United Nations, 'Women's access to rural finance: challenges and opportunities' 2019 www.fao.org/3/ca5167en/CA5167EN.pdf (accessed on 9 October 2019).
28 UNODC.
29 UNDP-SIWI Water Governance Facility, *'Women and corruption in the water sector: Theories and experiences from Johannesburg and Bogota'* (2017) Water Governance Facility Report No. 8 Stockholm: SWI https://siwi.org/wp-content/uploads/2017/09/wgf-report-no-8_final-web-edited.pdf (accessed on 19 September 2022)
30 BBC, "'Sex for grades': Undercover in West African Universities"' BBC Africa, 7 October 2019, www.bbc.co.uk/news/av/world-africa-49907376 (accessed on 14 March 2022).
31 *The Republic v Andrew Chagaga*, in the High Court of Malawi, Criminal Case Number 8 of 2021. (18 January 2022).
32 Jason Carlo Ong Carranceja, *The Role of Women's Empowerment in Anti-Corruption,* March 2021, Asia Pacific Economic Cooperation Policy Support Unit, Policy Brief Number 9, www.apec.org/publications/2021/04/the-role-of-women-empowerment-in-anti-corruption (accessed on 13 March 2022).
33 Jason Carlo Ong Carranceja, *The Role of Women's Empowerment in Anti-Corruption,* March 2021, Asia Pacific Economic Cooperation Policy Support Unit, Policy Brief Number 9, www.apec.org/publications/2021/04/the-role-of-women-empowerment-in-anti-corruption (accessed on 13 March 2022).
34 United Nations Development Programme, *Seeing Beyond the State: Grassroots Women's Perspectives on Corruption and Anti Corruption,* October 2012, www.undp.org/publications/seeing-beyond-state-grassroots-womens-perspectives-corruption-and-anti-corruption (accessed on 13 March 2022).
35 United Nations Development Programme, *Seeing Beyond the State: Grassroots Women's Perspectives on Corruption and Anti Corruption,* October 2012, www.undp.org/publications/seeing-beyond-state-grassroots-womens-perspectives-corruption-and-anti-corruption (accessed on 13 March 2022).

36 Anne Marie Goetz, *Political Cleaners: How Women Are the New Anti-Corruption Force?* (2007) Development and Change 38:1, 87–105, 92.
37 United Nations Development Programme, *Seeing Beyond the State: Grassroots Women's Perspectives on Corruption and Anti Corruption,* October 2012, www.undp.org/publications/seeing-beyond-state-grassroots-womens-perspectives-corruption-and-anti-corruption (accessed on 13 March 2022).
38 Ward Berenschot, *The Political Economy of Clientelism: A Comparative Study of Indonesia's Patronage Democracy* (2018) Journal of Comparative Political Studies 51:12, 1563–1593, 1564.
39 Anne Marie Goetz, *Political Cleaners: How Women Are the New Anti-Corruption Force?* (2007) Development and Change, 38:1, 87–105, 90.
40 Food and Agriculture Organization of the United Nations, '*Women's access to rural finance: challenges and opportunities'* (2019) www.fao.org/3/ca5167en/CA5167EN.pdf (accessed on 9 October 2019).
41 Dan Kuwali, Commend and Condemn: Combating Corruption in Africa, in The Palgrave Handbook of Sustainable Peace and Security in Africa, Dan Kuwali (ed), (2022) Palgrave MacMillan, 581–595, 592.

Part IV

Proactive Strategies to Combat Corruption in Africa

17 Accountable Governance

Fighting Corruption in Africa

*Dan Kuwali**

Introduction

Governance dysfunctions at national and international levels are the major culprits responsible for conflict, instability, and poor socio-economic development in Africa. It is not disputed that corruption has contributed to the continent's stunted growth.[1] Corruption, which has been manifested in ethical shortfalls and accountability deficits in Africa's governance system, has long been a challenge for both the private and public sector performance. Corruption is a systemic issue, which involves society as a whole. Corrupt practices are not exclusively perpetrated by Africans but may also be carried out by foreigners through collaboration with corrupt Africans.[2] Ezeanya-Esiobu has traced the roots of the prevalence of corruption in Africa from the "process of socialization, which commenced with the excessively corrupt colonial government."[3]

According to a survey by Transparency International (TI), an international organization which combats global corruption through concerted anticorruption measures, the police, judiciary, and business executives are seen to have the highest levels of corruption.[4] Corruption is influenced by the education system, public finance management, economic planning, the regulatory system, and the entrenchment of ethical values and culture in a country.[5] Non-African actors are also instrumental in fuelling corruption on the continent through foreign bribery and money laundering.[6]

Among the seven key aspirations listed in Africa Agenda 2063: *The Africa We Want*, one theme stands out as the key to Africa's political and economic transformation.[7] That is "an Africa of good governance, democracy, respect for human rights, justice and the rule of law." According to the former United Nations (UN) Secretary-General, Ghana's Kofi Annan, "good governance is perhaps the single most important factor in eradicating poverty and promoting development."[8] This assertion is in line with Mbaku who argues that corruption in Africa is the direct result of poorly designed institutional patterns and disorganized structures.[9] Momoh maintains that this handicap not only incapacitates states to deal with corruption but also contributes to manipulation and disrespect to the state institutions by the citizens in those states.[10]

DOI: 10.4324/9781003326649-21

Thus, it is safe to assert that accountable governance, including combating corruption, is part of the solutions to most of Africa's problems. The theory is easy to understand. Eradicating poverty and improving human development in Africa must begin with the creation of wealth for inclusive growth, a process that requires a robust entrepreneurial class.[11] To achieve these goals, there must be accountable governance and ethical leadership.

Through a critical analysis of the respect for the rule of law and compliance with anticorruption measures, in both the most and the least corrupt countries in Africa, this chapter addresses how to uphold accountable governance and ethical leadership in order to combat corruption on the continent. The goal is not to provide a catalogue of causes, consequences, and remedies to fighting corruption in Africa but rather to identify more focused strategies to enhance governance and strengthen institutions. Both elements are critical to deter corrupt practices on the continent. The central thesis is that accountable governance and ethical leadership are possible antidotes to corruption in Africa.

The discussion takes the institutional approach to the study of corruption, which derives from the public choice model of human behaviour that divides the society into the public and private spheres.[12] The chapter is organized as follows. The next section outlines the problems of corruption resulting from governance deficits in Africa. The section that follows explains why accountable governance is key to combating corruption. The next section outlines a five-pronged governance approach to combat corruption before providing a conclusion.

The Problem of Corruption and Governance in Africa

Authors such as Gumede and Ezeanya-Esiobu agree that post-independence African countries inherited deeply corrupt institutions, laws, and values from colonial governments.[13] The colonial elite centralized political, economic, and civil power, reserving top jobs in the public and private sectors to fellow colonials.[14] Public institutions such as the judiciary, police, security services, and rule of law selectively served the interests of the elite classes.[15]

Most African countries seem to acknowledge corruption as a normal occurrence and see it as a means to an end.[16] Corruption cases abound on the African continent. There have been reports of grand corruption in President Teodoro Obiang Nguema Mbasogo's regime in Equatorial Guinea; President Jose Eduardo dos Santos's rule in Angola, deposed Sudanese President Omar al – Bashir's leadership; Chad's Idriss Deby Itno; General Sani Abacha's military rule in Nigeria, Charles Taylor's plunder when he became the warlord President of Liberia, Gambia's Yahya Abdul – Aziz Jammeh, who is alleged to have embezzled 100 million during his 22-year rule.[17] While corruption cases of political elites have been well documented, the picture of the nature of the crisis is incomplete if low-level bribes which are ubiquitous on the continent are ignored.[18] Moreso, as discussed earlier, corruption in Africa has internal and external dimensions. Failure to deal with the issue of corruption from both internal and external dimensions is responsible for the increasing level of corruption in Africa.[19]

Corruption is simply defined as "the abuse of entrusted power for private gain."[20] The institutional approach to the study of corruption distinguishes between political (grand) corruption, bureaucratic (administrative) corruption, and economic corruption and differentiates the incentive structures in these three categories.[21] This categorization of corruption is particularly necessary for analysis and design of anti-corruption strategies.[22] Political Corruption is corrupt action by elected politicians and Administrative Corruption by employees of the public sector.[23] Bureaucratic or administrative corruption can be curbed by means of legislation and punishments such as sanctions, but political corruption is far more difficult to combat as those in power would not be in favour of this process.[24]

According to Coetzee, as a systemic problem situation, corruption does not have root causes, but co-producers.[25] However, based on both conceptual and empirical research, different authors have different opinions on the causes of corruption across countries. Forson and others have drawn at least three theories on the causes of corruption, namely: bureaucratic discretionary power; the association of this power with economic rent; and deterrence, which relates to the probability of being apprehended and punished.[26] These causes are broadly categorized under a common theme of costs and benefits, with the first two focusing on the benefits of corruption, while the third relates to the cost of corruption.[27]

While there cannot be a one-size-fits-all explanation for the prevalence of corruption on the continent, poor governance including economic mismanagement, greed, and lack of accountability stands out as common causes of corruption.[28] Across Africa, corruption is fuelled by several factors such as authoritarianism, political and institutional instability, increasing terrorist threats combined with low wage levels of bureaucrats and ineffectiveness of anticorruption measures based on governance and enforcement mechanisms.[29] Protection of human rights, especially access to information and press freedom also affects the fight against corruption.[30] For many, politics in Africa is a realm that attracts courageous crooks and scares away cowardly saints.[31] Political corruption is commonplace on the continent taking the form of state capture as was the case in South Africa, patronage networks, opaque political party financing, vote buying, and unresolved conflicts of interests.[32] In several countries, public officers are scavengers rather than saviours of public resources. In some cases, those mandated to lead the fight against corruption are unable to discharge their function because they wine and dine with the corrupt.

Momoh has classified the factors that impede the fight against corruption at the domestic levels in Africa, into political, economic, socio-cultural, technological, and environmental factors. All these factors centre on weak or poor governance, which is attributed to a lack of leadership skills that makes officials vulnerable to "fertilizing the growth of corruption" on the continent.[33] Unless ethical leadership and accountable governance become prerequisites for holding public office, African nations will continue to be at the mercy of elected officials who assume office to feed their greed and line their pockets. Africa is facing perennial challenges such as intra-state conflict, terrorism, and unconstitutional changes of government, among others. Governance issues, including corruption, are often at the heart of

Table 17.1 List of the Ten Most Corrupt Countries in Africa

No.	*Country*	*Corruption Perceptions Index*
1.	South Sudan	11
2.	Somalia	13
3.	Libya	17
4.	Equatorial Guinea	17
5.	Democratic Republic of the Congo	19
6.	Burundi	19
7.	Chad	20
8.	Sudan	20
9.	Comoros	20
10.	Guinea Bissau	21

these perennial problems. Consequences of corruption in many African states also include retarded economic growth and development.[34]

Transparency International's Corruption Perceptions Index (CPI) ranks countries according to the levels of how their public sector displays corruption. A country's score indicates the perceived level of corruption in its public sector on a scale of 0 to 100, where 0 represents highly corrupt and 100 portrays a corrupt-free society.[35] Corruption has diverse determinants and effects that may be context and country-specific.[36] The degree of corruption, extent of compliance with anticorruption measures, and respect for the rule of law in Africa differ from country to country.[37] Seychelles, Botswana, Cape Verde, Rwanda, Namibia, and Mauritius are among the least corrupt nations in Africa, while South Sudan, Somalia, Libya, Equatorial Guinea and the Democratic Republic of the Congo (DRC) rank amongst the most corrupt countries in Africa.[38]

According to the most recent CPI report, the average index score in Africa is 33, which is the lowest in the world. The report showed that 90 per cent of the 180 countries surveyed had a corruption index score of below 50; 44 of these countries with very low index scores are from Africa.[39] Several African countries dominate the range of the most corrupt nations in the world. At the same time, some European and Asian countries are major benefactors of corruption happening on the African continent. Corrupt practices are deeply intertwined with conflict and state fragility in some African countries, notably the DRC, Libya, Somalia, and South Sudan, among others.[40] Table 17.1 contains a list of the ten most corrupt countries in Africa.

If one compares the Rule of Law Index and the World Justice Project Rule of Law Index, the assertion that "where corruption exists, the rule of law cannot flourish" is rendered true.[41] This implies that the rule of law and corruption are inversely related.[42] It comes as no surprise that countries which have done well in terms of the rule of law index have also done well in dissuading corruption as outlined in the 2021 World Justice Project Rule of Law Index, which ranked 33 countries in Sub-Saharan Africa and eighth in Middle East and North Africa. For example, Rwanda

Table 17.2 List of the Ten Least Corrupt Countries in Africa

No.	*Country*	*Corruption Perceptions Index*
1.	Seychelles	70
2.	Carbo Verde	58
3.	Botswana	55
4.	Mauritius	54
5.	Rwanda	53
6.	Namibia	49
7.	São Tomé and Príncipe	45
8.	Tunisia	44
9.	South Africa	44
10.	Ghana	43

is the highly ranked country in Africa at position one whereas the lowest is the DRC at position 33. Table 17.2 is a list of the ten least corrupt countries in Africa.

Based on a cursory analysis of the corruption index and the rule of law index, there is a negative relationship between the rule of law and corruption, with more respect for the rule of law leading to less corruption. Thus, it can be concluded that both government effectiveness and adherence to the rule of law are critical to combat corruption in Africa.[43]

Why Accountable Governance is Key to Combating Corruption in Africa

Governance relates to processes and stages by which a government carries out its functions.[44] It determines the relationship between the rulers and the ruled in any society.[45] It is also a process of social engagement between the rulers and the ruled.[46] From a governance standpoint, corruption resulting from weak and dysfunctional governance structures continues to prevent many African countries from creating and sustaining the necessary enabling environment for entrepreneurship, and wealth creation. For example, one of the reasons for endemic corruption in South Sudan is the judicial system, which is inefficient and plagued by corruption and a culture of impunity.[47]

From a human rights perspective, corruption, especially bribery, does not affect all people equally; it hits the poorest harder than the wealthiest.[48] While the corrupt political elite amasses wealth, millions of Africans are deprived of their basic needs like food, health, education, housing, access to clean water, and sanitation.[49] Upholding and protection of human rights is critical to combating corruption. An illustration of this point is press freedom, which is a whistleblowing mechanism, especially where the press is to act as a check on those who should represent the public interest. In this case, corruption scandals freely investigated and exposed by mass media act as a deterrent to would-be offenders.[50] However, owing to political patronage, the media has increasingly reneged on its duty as a whistle-blowing institution.[51] The civil society also lacks the means to hold perpetrators to account.[52]

From an economic perspective, corruption creates and increases poverty and exclusion, erodes trust, weakens democracy, and hampers economic development, among other crises.[53] Corruption and bribery circumvent fair tender processes, and the consequences are severe: funding intended for life-enhancing projects (such as schools and hospitals) may be diverted into the hands of corrupt individuals.[54] Where there is corruption, foreign investors are risk averse to put their investment at the mercy of corrupt regimes. Investment has been stunted in Chad where corruption is perpetuated by a weak rule of law and insecurity.[55] In Libya, for instance, bribery and favouritism are common practices in all sectors, and companies may struggle with unfair competition from state-owned businesses, which dominate the local market.[56]

Economic recession occurs when the funds which ought to be used to promote the economy in a given country are illegally externalized or embezzled. A case in point is Somalia's dysfunctional institutions facilitate an environment of lawlessness, and the absence of any form of regulatory framework, which hinders prospects of economic competitiveness.[57] Although Somalia's Provisional Constitution criminalizes corruption, implementation is non-existent.[58]

Accountability is the obligation of government to demonstrate effectiveness in achieving goals and meeting the demands of the public.[59] The absence of accountability, especially when it is lacking on the part of politicians and bureaucrats, creates opportunities for corruption to thrive. This is the case in the DRC where the country is embroiled in a protracted armed conflict and democracy is weak, whistleblowers are usually suppressed.[60] Of late, socio-economic conditions have produced public outrage where Africa has seen a renewed quest for accountable governance expressed itself in the streets, popular culture, the Internet, and social media. These youth-led popular protests and whistleblowing have demonstrated against social injustice, fraudulent elections, corruption, and insecurity, demanding inclusion to participate in governance and a life of dignity as equal citizens.

Before indulging in corrupt practices, officials usually weigh the costs and benefits of being indulging in corrupt practices against those acting with integrity. As noted by Transparency International, where temptation meets permissiveness, corruption takes root on a wide scale.[61] If there is little or no accountability or government control, officials have unfettered discretion or autonomy in making decisions that maximize their self-interest.[62] This assertion is supported by African countries with high CPI such as Botswana, Mauritius, Namibia, and Rwanda, which have a strong antibribery deterrence and enforcement regime, civil service and transparency of financial interests, media freedom, and a high degree of civil society engagement.[63]

Accountable governance is central to the achievement of all the 17 United Nations (UN) Sustainable Development Goals (SDGs).[64] This is particularly clear in Goal 16, which requires States to "promote peaceful and inclusive societies for sustainable development, provide access to justice for all and build effective, accountable, and inclusive institutions at all levels."[65] For example, in the context of the African Continental Free Trade Area (ACFTA), Africa cannot have free trade that creates wealth without governance systems that ensure that all trade within and across the continent is fair.[66]

Countries cannot create jobs that make people self-reliant without governance mechanisms that protect workers from exploitation.[67] States cannot achieve food security without holding cartels that pervert the marketplace accountable to protect farmers.[68] Public office-bearers may ignore their constitutional obligations at their peril where accountability and the rule of law constitute the sharp and mighty sword against impunity. States cannot defeat institutional corruption without independent and impartial oversight mechanisms where public officers are held accountable. Therefore, accountable governance coupled with ethical leadership are the foundations to achieve the Africa We Want.

A Three-Pronged Governance Approach to Combat Corruption

Ezeanya-Esiobu contends that "[t]here is no genetic code that predisposes Africans to corruption."[69] Therefore, to combat corruption, African governments should restore the values of governance and ethical principles.[70] Accountable governance entails respect for the rule of law where the exercise of authority is subject to accountability, just law, open government, and accessible and impartial justice.[71] is built on a foundation of the rule of law particularly accountability and transparency; combating corruption, empowered civil societies including citizen participation in governance, an enabling legal and judicial framework, and an efficient private sector. Accountable governance promotes transparency, respect for the rule of law including equality under the law, fairness in the application of the law, separation of powers, participation in decision-making, legal certainty, avoidance of arbitrariness, and promoting public trust.

Accountable governance is an enabler for socio-economic development in Africa.[72] From an economic perspective, accountable governance is what creates an enabling environment for economic efficiency through equitable rules that promote fair and well-functioning markets, curtail corruption, and ensure the fair delivery of public services. From a social standpoint, accountable governance is what prevents the marginalization of vulnerable social groups by the rich, the powerful, and the well-connected thereby promoting peace. From a development angle, accountable governance is what ensures the equitable distribution of infrastructural developments and provision of welfare programmes. The key challenge then is how to attain accountable governance accompanied by ethical leadership on the continent.

Transparency International has reported that about one in four people pay bribes for public service in Africa.[73] The theory in this chapter is that since corruption is a systemic issue, which involves society, a strong civil society is crucial to report and fight corruption. The argument is that since accountable governance requires transparency, accountability, and participatory citizenship, those serving in public offices or in charge of public funds may desist from corruption if they know that they are accountable to a strong civil society. This may reduce their propensity to indulge in corruption-free, fair, and just political representation.

Accountable governance has the attendant attributes to the improving socio-economic well-being of the population in terms of quality education, affordable health care, job creation, financial security, food security, and an effective criminal justice system that fights corruption and impunity. In the spirit of African solutions to African problems, African states should resolve some of the ethical and governance issues stalling peace and clogging the wheels of growth and development on the continent. This discussion suggests a seven-pronged governance approach to combat corruption in Africa in Africa.

First, countries should entrench mechanisms that promote accountable governance and constitutionalism, reinforce checks and balances, accountability, democracy, and regulate political financing to prevent excessive money and influence in politics. Accountable governance can only be guaranteed by strong public institutions that uphold the rule of law, operate within a human rights framework, and require public duty-bearers to be transparent and accountable.[74] Rather, anti-corruption commissions should have a direct budgetary allocation from the annual budget and report directly to the Legislature.[75] To perform its oversight role, the judiciary should be independent and impartial. Anti-corruption institutions in Africa should be separated from the executive arm of government. Preferably, States should establish independent courts different from the conventional court system to eliminate the delay in the administration of justice that characterized the conventional court system.[76]

Second, a critical imperative to achieve accountable governance is the empowerment of citizens by proving them with political and economic literacy to understand and be involved in democratic governance processes, protection of human rights defenders and whistleblowers and investigative journalism to uncover corrupt practices.[77] States should implement the African Union Convention on Preventing and Combating Corruption, which allows non-state actors such as civil society groups to be critical in anti-corruption issues in the continent. Anticorruption policy decisions should focus on existing educational systems as a conduit for intensifying awareness of the devastating effect of corruption on sustainable national development.[78] Education enhances awareness of the devastating effects of corruption on well-being.[79] To this end, African countries should develop and implement education programmes that help citizens not to only understand and appreciate national constitutions but also recognize the law as a tool that they can use to organize their private lives and resolve their conflicts, at personal and societal levels.[80] This need for legal and constitutional education is particularly urgent among marginalized groups such as the youth and women. They too need to be empowered with the information, whether it be on such topics as security, rights, terrorism, intra-state conflicts, trade laws, unconstitutional changes of government, or laws that regulate our economy, our agriculture, our mining, our media, our elections, and our domestic relationships.

Third, States should professionalize their public services and reduce excessive bureaucracies for basic public services to make it simpler and more transparent in order to reduce the opportunities for corruption.[81] African countries should also embrace merit-based appointments to jobs in public services, regulators, and enforcement agencies to reduce the patronage system, which fosters the environment for corruption.[82]

Fourth, States should regulate political party funding.[83] Finances of political parties have traditionally not been subject to public scrutiny because of the traditional perception that they are private associations, not subject to interference by States in their activities. Since traditional methods of raising money are no longer profitable activities, political parties are tempted to venture into other basis ventures, which are economically more attractive.[84] The other sources of party financing, such as corporate financing and private donations, pose a challenge for the legitimacy of party financing, corruption, and concerns of improper influence of financial means on political decisions.[85] The reason is that certain economic activities may very well profit from favourable political decisions.[86] Complete transparency of the financing of political parties should be ensured with a view to avoiding not only any potentially undesirable influence of money on party politics but also to preserve the trust and confidence of the members in their parties and to avoid its involvement in human rights violations.[87] In this case, both political leaders and business captains should disclose the amount and beneficiaries of their donations to prevent perceptions of corruption and money laundering.

Fifth, ethical leadership is a precursor to accountable governance.[88] Ethical leadership is characterized by a strong social contract between the society and the state that is sufficiently inclusive to permit management of diversity and plurality of views. Ethical leadership is a potent force to propel the body politic to focus on ethical values that serve as a model for the rest of society. Thus, ethical leadership is critical to inculcate a culture of constitutionalism and respect for the rule of law in Africa, where the law is the basis for political decision-making and administrative action. Ethical leadership can also contribute to managing conflicts of interests in public procurement and decision-making.

Sixth, African states should compel external companies to adhere to a set of "integrity" standards when trading in government contracts.[89] As noted earlier, external actors including Asian, American, and European foreign business organizations exarcerbate corruption by colluding in corrupt practices with African partners.[90] In addition to anticorruption measures being made an integral part of governance strategies at the State level, the private sector and civil society must assist governments in fighting the vice.[91]

Seventh, more states should subject themselves to the African Peer Review Mechanism (APRM) to achieve a critical mass of accountable governance on the continent.[92] As a component of the New Partnership for Africa's Development (NEPAD), the APRM is a voluntary mechanism designed to promote structural conflict prevention through good governance.[93] Given the nature of the peace and security on the continent, the APSA cannot work in isolation, it must consistently and coherently coordinate with human rights institutions and organs meant to promote peace, security, and socioeconomic well-being of individuals on the continent.

Accountable governance is key for peace and development in Africa where there is political stability, deepened democracy, equity and justice, and economic prosperity.[94] To achieve this, there must always be a strong social contract between society and the State.[95] On their part, African leaders should redefine their politics to focus not on power but commit to accountability, respect for the rule of law and ethical values that make leadership a people-centred enterprise.

Conclusion

Based on the theoretical and empirical evidence from the literature, the causes of corruption are manifold but can be broadly categorized based on three main perspectives: bureaucratic discretionary power, the association of this power with economic rent, and deterrence, which relate to the probability of being apprehended and punished. These perspectives are further identified under the cost-benefit incentive strands.[96]

One reason corruption is still rampant in Africa is due to a lack of transparency and accountability in several countries. The crux of the chapter is the theory to end corruption; African states should embrace accountable governance by promoting transparency, accountability, and integrity at all levels and across all sectors of society. As people are the centrepiece of governance, states should empower citizens in political and economic literacy to effectively engage in democratic governance processes and check corruption.

To effectively combat corruption in Africa, States must tackle the vice both internally and externally by addressing domestic conditions that facilitate corruption while dissuading foreign perpetrators.[97] To combat corruption and achieve sustainable socio-economic development on the continent, African states should adopt strong institutions to embed accountable governance; establish strong civil society to dissuade corruption and adopt a whistleblower protection legal framework to encourage and support people to safely report corruption; professionalize public services; and reduce bottlenecks to close gaps for corruption; political party funding regulations to curtail corruption including money laundering; embrace ethical leadership to inculcate a culture of honesty and integrity; compel external companies to adhere to integrity standards when trading on the continent; and subject themselves to the African Peer Review Mechanism (APRM) to achieve a critical mass of accountable governance on the continent.

Notes

* Extraordinary Professor of International Law, University of Pretoria.

1 Okwuagbala Uzochukwu, "Corruption in Africa: Overview, Causes, and Solutions," HubPages, 15 April 2020, https://discover.hubpages.com/politics/corruption-in-Africa-Causes-andSolutions (accessed 1 September 2022).

2 Zekeri Momoh, "Corruption and Governance in Africa," Conference: International Multi-Disciplinary Academic Conference on African Transformation and Development organized by Cambridge Publications and Research International, University of Ilorin, Ilorin Kwara state, Volume: vol. 3, no. 10, (March 2015), www.researchgate.net/publication/308792420(accessed 20 July 2022).

3 Chika Ezeanya-Esiobu, "Origins of Corruption In Africa" *The Pan African Review,* 6 October 2019, https//panafricanreview.rw/origins-of-Corruption -in-Africa/(accessed 6 September 2022).

4 Per José Ugaz, Transparency International, "Corruption in Africa: 75 million people pay bribes," www.transparency.org/en/gcb/africa/africa-9th-edition (accessed 3 September 2022).
5 Uzochukwu, "Corruption in Africa: Overview, Causes, and Solutions."
6 Transparency International "Citizens Speak about Corruption in Africa," www.transparency.org/en/news/citizens-speak-out-about-corruption-in-africa (accessed September 2022).
7 African Union, Agenda 2063: The Africa We Want, available at: https://au.int/en/agenda2063.
8 United Nations University, "What Does 'Good Governance' Mean?" available at: https;//unu.edu/publications/articles (accessed 6 September 2022)
9 John Mukum Mbaku, *Bureaucratic and Political Corruption in Africa: The Public Choice Perspective*, Malabar: Kriag (2000).
10 Momoh, "Corruption and Governance in Africa," 6.
11 John Mukum Mbaku, "Good and inclusive governance is imperative for Africa's future," in Deepening Good Governance: Inclusion, Democracy, and Security, Brookings, *Foresight Africa 2020,* https;//brookings.edu/research/html/good-and-inclusive-governance-is-imperative-for- Africa's -future (accessed 5 September 2022).
12 Momoh, "Corruption and Governance in Africa," 4.
13 William Gumede, "Why fighting corruption in Africa fails," Nov 14, 2012, *Pambazuka News,* available at: https://pambazuka.org/why-fighting-corruption-in-Africa-fails. (accessed 6 September 2022). Chika Ezeanya-Esiobu, "Origins of Corruption in Africa."
14 Gumede, "Why fighting corruption in Africa fails."
15 Gumede, "Why fighting corruption in Africa fails."
16 UKEssays. (November 2018). Corruption in Africa – Solutions and Effects, https://www.ukessays.com/essays/politics/politics-of-poor-leadership-and-corruption-in-africa-politics-essay.php?vref=1> (accessed 5 September 2022).
17 Nana Kwaku M. Asamoah, "Corruption in Africa – The Crisis of Our Time?" www.africa.com/ Corruption in Africa – The Crisis of Our Time? - Africa.com/(accessed 5 August 2022).
18 Asamoah, "Corruption in Africa."
19 Momoh, "Corruption and Governance in Africa."
20 Transparency International, "What is Corruption?" www.transparency.org/en/what-is-corruption (4 August 2022).
21 Momoh, "Corruption and Governance in Africa," 4. Ivor Chipkin, "Whither the State? Corruption, Institutions, and State-Building in South Africa," *Politikon, South African Journal of Political Studies*, vol. 40, Issue 2 (July 2013), 211–231, https://doi.org/10.1080/02589346.2013.798457(13 July 2022).
22 Inge Amundsen, ed., *Political corruption in Africa: Extraction and power preservation,* (2019,).
23 Amundsen, *Political corruption in Africa.*
24 Amundsen, *Political corruption in Africa.*
25 Johan J. Coetzee, "Systemic Corruption and Corrective Change Management Strategies: A Study of the Co-Producers of Systemic Corruption and its Negative Impact on Socio-Economic Development," Dissertation presented for the Degree of Doctor of Business Management and Administration at Stellenbosch University, November 2012.
26 Joseph Ato Forson; Theresa Yaaba Baah-Ennumh; Ponlapat Buracom; Guojin Chen; Zhen Peng, "Causes of Corruption: Evidence from sub-Saharan Africa," *South African Journal of Economic and Management Sciences*, vol.19 no. 4 (Pretoria 2016), http://dx.doi.org/10.17159/2222-3436/2016/v19n4a7
27 Forson, "Causes of Corruption."
28 Uzochukwu, "Corruption in Africa."

29 Momoh notes that another impediment to combating corruption in Africa is discretionary anti-corruption laws. Momoh, "Corruption and Governance in Africa," 4. See also Emmanuel Ababa Benson, "20 Most Corrupt Countries in Africa," *Africa Business Insider,* 2 July 2022, africa.business.com (20 June 2022).
30 Forson, "Causes of Corruption."
31 State House, Speech by the President of the Republic of Malawi, His Excellency Dr Lazrus Mccarthy Chakwera at the Opening Ceremony of the African Bar Association Conference Hosted by The Malawi Law Society, Lilongwe, Malawi, statehouse.mw (accessed 4 September 2022).
32 Jorum Duri, "Sub-Saharan Africa: Overview of corruption and anti-corruption," *Transparency International* (20 March 2020), available at: www.u4.no/publications/sub-saharan-africa-overview-of-corruption-and-anti-corruption.pdf (accessed 6 September 2022).
33 Uzochukwu, "Corruption in Africa: Overview, Causes, and Solutions."
34 Chester A. Crocker, "African Governance: Challenges and Their Implications," Hoover Institution, https://hoover.org/researcher/african-governance-challenges- and- their-implications (accessed 6 September 2022).
35 Transparency International, Corruption Perceptions Index (CPI), www.transparency.org/en/cpi (accessed 6 September 2022).
36 *Claire Furphy*, "Corruption in Africa: A Crime against Development," *Polity* (2010), (polity.org.za/corruption-in-africa-a-crime-against-development-2010-11-25).
37 Charles Manga Fombad, "An overview of the crisis of the rule of law in Africa," *African Human Rights Journal* (2018) 18, available at: http://du doi.org/10.17159/1996–2096/2018/vlanla11(accessed 1 September 2022).
38 Talk Africana, "Top 20 Most (Least) Corrupt Countries in Africa, 2022," https://talkafricana.com/top-20-most-and-least-corrupt-countries-in-africa-2020(accessed 5 September 2022).
39 Transparency International, "Corruption Perceptions Index."
40 Duri, "Sub-Saharan Africa."
41 Yury Fedotov, "Where corruption flourishes, development and the rule of law fail" *UNODC Press Release,* 2012, www.unodc.org/unodc/en/press/releases/2012/September/where-corruption-flourishes-development-and-the-rule-of-law-fail-says-unodc-chief.html (accessed 2 September 2022). See also World Justice Project, WJP Rule of Law Index 2021, available at: <https;//worldjusticeproject.org/our-work/research-and data/wjp/rule-of-law-index> (accessed 2 September 2022).
42 Fedotov, "Where corruption flourishes."
43 Michael T. Rock, "Corruption and Democracy," *Economic and Social Affairs*, DESA Working Paper No. 5, ST/ESA/2007/DWP/55,.
44 Momoh, "Corruption and Governance in Africa," 4. Okwudiba Nnoli, *Introduction to Politics* (Enugu, SNAAP Press Ltd, 2003).
45 Momoh, "Corruption and Governance in Africa," 4.
46 Momoh, "Corruption and Governance in Africa," 4.
47 Talk Africana, "Top 20 Most (Least) Corrupt Countries in Africa, 2022"
48 Transparency International "Citizens Speak about Corruption in Africa," www.transparency.org/en/news/citizens-speak-out-about-corruption-in-africa (September 2022).
49 Transparency International, "Corruption in Africa: 75 million people pay bribes," www.transparency.org/en/gcb/africa/africa-9th-edition (3 September 2022).
50 Lindita Camaj, "The Media's Role in Fighting Corruption: Media Effects on Governmental Accountability," *International Journal of Press/Politics,* vol. 18 no. 1 (2013):21–42.
51 Camaj, "The media's role in fighting corruption."
52 Gbenga Lawal, "Corruption and development in Africa: challenges for political and economic change," *Humanity and Social Sciences Journal*, vol. 2, no. 1 (2007): 1–7.
53 Emmanuel Ababa Benson, "20 Most Corrupt Countries in Africa," *Africa Business Insider,* 2 July 2022, africa.business.com (accessed 2 August 2022).

54 Forson et al., "Causes of corruption: Evidence from sub-Saharan Africa."
55 Talk Africana, "Top 20 Most (Least) Corrupt Countries in Africa, 2022."
56 Talk Africana, "Top 20 Most (Least) Corrupt Countries in Africa, 2022."
57 Talk Africana, "Top 20 Most (Least) Corrupt Countries in Africa, 2022."
58 Talk Africana, "Top 20 Most (Least) Corrupt Countries in Africa, 2022."
59 G. Segal and A.B. Summers, *Citizens' budget report: Improving performance and accountability in government*. 2002, eason.org/files/78a6bc2717f984a2b9b783192f5d1bad.pdf (accessed 12 August 2022)
60 Talk Africana, "Top 20 Most (Least) Corrupt Countries in Africa, 2022."
61 www.transparency international.org.
62 María H. Jaen, and Daniel Paravisini, "Wages, Capture, and Penalties in Venezuela," in *Diagnosis Corruption: Fraud in Latin America's Public Hospitals* (Washington, DC: Inter-American Development Bank 2002), 57–94.
63 Talk Africana, "Top 20 Most (Least) Corrupt Countries in Africa, 2022."
64 United Nations, "Sustainable Development Goals," available at: https://sdgs.un.org/goals (accessed 4 September 2022).
65 African Union, "African Continental Free Trade Area (AfCFTA)," available at:<au.int/en/cfta> (accessed 6 September 2022).
66 African Union, "African Continental Free Trade Area (AfCFTA)."
67 Chakwera, "Statement at the African Bar Association Conference."
68 Chakwera, "Statement at the African Bar Association Conference."
69 Chika Ezeanya-Esiobu, "Origins of Corruption in Africa," Sarah Muir and Akhil Gupta, "Rethinking the Anthropology of Corruption," *Current Anthropology*, v. 59 Supplement 18, (April 2018).
70 Ezeanya-Esiobu, "Origins of Corruption In Africa"
71 United Nations Development Programme, available at: <https://undp.org/maldavises-accountable-governance (accessed 6 September 2022).
72 African Union, "The Africa Governance Report: Promoting African Union Shared Values," Report prepared by The African Peer Review Mechanism (APRM) In Collaboration with the African Governance Architecture (AGA) January 2019, available at://https://au.int/36418-doc-eng-_the_africa_governance_report_2019_final-1.pdf (accessed at 2 September 2022).
73 Transparency International "Citizens Speak about Corruption in Africa," www.transparency.org/en/news/citizens-speak-out-about-corruption-in-africa (September 2022).
74 Policies aimed at controlling or reducing corruption in African countries must begin with laying the foundation for a strong institution- economic, political, and social- in all sectors of the economy. UKEssays, "Corruption in Africa."
75 Momoh, "Corruption and Governance in Africa," 8.
76 Momoh, "Corruption and Governance in Africa," 8.
77 Reporting incidents of corruption is one of the best ways to stop corruption. However, whistleblowers are scared to report for fear of retribution and ineffective of reporting mechanisms. Hence protection of whistleblowers from retribution, improving reporting channels, and raising public awareness about how and where to report corruption, assurance about whistleblower protection; and guaranteeing operational and physical freedom of anti-corruption civil society organisations. States should also adopt whistleblower protection legal framework to encourage and support people to safely report corruption, access public information and demand transparent, responsive, and accountable government institutions. Ugaz, "Corruption in Africa."
78 Forson et al., "Causes of corruption: Evidence from sub-Saharan Africa."
79 Forson et al., "Causes of corruption: Evidence from sub-Saharan Africa."
80 Mbaku, "Good and inclusive governance is imperative for Africa's future."
81 William Gumede, "Why fighting corruption in Africa fails."
82 Gumede, "Why fighting corruption in Africa fails."

83 For instance, funding of all political parties should be made public and state funding of political parties should be equal. Momoh, "Corruption and Governance in Africa," 8.
84 Amnesty International, *Injustice Incorporated: Corporate Abuses and Human Right to Remedy*, 7 March 2014, available at: <www.amnesty.org/en/library/info/POL30/001/2014/en. > (accessed 15 July 2017).
85 For example, political parties have developed commercial activities in areas, such as marketing, shopping centres, and house construction through companies owned or shared by the party. Such practices may be susceptible to corruption and have given rise to allegations of money laundering and criminality in some cases. The Council of Europe, *Financing Political Parties and Election Campaigns – Guidelines,* Making democratic institutions work Integrated Project, 19. Momoh, for example, notes that most ruling parties in African states like Nigeria, Botswana, and Cameroun are funded by corrupt politicians who after funding the ruling parties to win elections will not be investigated by the government in power. Momoh, "Corruption and Governance in Africa," 8.
86 Council of Europe, *Financing Political Parties and Election Campaigns – Guidelines*, p. 19.
87 Council of Europe, *Financing Political Parties and Election Campaigns – Guidelines*, p. 9–13.
88 Paul Nantulya, "Wisdom from Africa on Ethical Leadership," 9 *Spotlight,* Africa Center for Strategic Studies, May 2017, <africacenter.org/spotlight/wisdom-from-africa-on-ethical leadership> (accessed 6 September 2022).
89 William Gumede, "Why fighting corruption in Africa fails."
90 Gumede, "Why fighting corruption in Africa fails."
91 *Furphy*, "Corruption in Africa: A Crime against Development.
92 African Union, "African Peer Review Mechanism," https://aprm-au.org (accessed 3 September 2022).
93 New Partnership For Africa's Development (NEPAD), https://aprm-au-org (accessed 5 September 2022).
94 Noah Dallaji, "Good Governance Key to the Africa We Want," *The Eagle Online,* 26 August 2021, https://theeagleonline.com.ng/good-governance-key-to-the-africa-we-want-by-noah-dallaji? (accessed 3 September 2022).
95 Crocker, "African Governance."
96 Forson et al., "Causes of Corruption."
97 Momoh, "Corruption and Governance in Africa," 8.

18 Leadership

Top-Down Approach to Corruption Proofing

*Thokozire Kuwali**

Introduction

African media are flooded with reports of fraud, corruption, embezzlement, and disregard for rules and regulations. Corruption is the misuse of authority for personal gain and is related to fraud. Bribery is a form of corruption, as various authors have pointed out in this volume. According to Transparency International, more than 75 million people in Sub-Saharan Africa have engaged in some form of fraud or corruption through the payment of bribes, either to avoid facing legal repercussions or to gain access to the essential services they so desperately need. Corruption creeps into fraud because these crimes are connected. The media's reporting on corruption has generated a lot of discussion about why fraud cases are increasing in businesses and even at the household level.[1]

Fraud is an intentional act or omission that is mostly designed to deceive others and normally results in the victim suffering a loss while the perpetrator achieves a gain. One finds it simple to engage in such behaviour because they believe everyone else is doing it, so why not them? To make matters worse, fraud cases rarely result in charges being filed against offenders. When such behaviours become the norm in society, it is very unfortunate. Institutions at all levels are vulnerable to fraud and corruption, which has frequently resulted in the demise of some organisations, significant investment losses, high litigation costs, the imprisonment of important individuals, and a decline in confidence in the capital markets. Publicised fraudulent behaviour by key executives has negatively impacted the reputations, brands, and images of many organisations around the globe.[2]

As discussed in this book, corruption can negatively impact a country's investment in general, foreign direct investment and dwindling capital inflows as people will have no confidence to invest. Foreign trade and aid, official growth, inequality, government expenditure, and services can also be affected, leading to an increase amongst masses living below the poverty line and making the achievement of Sustainable Development Goals (SDGs), which countries are thriving to achieve by the year by 2030 a distant reality.[3]

In most cases where corruption occurs, it is partly due to the laxity or tolerance of leaders by not setting the right tone at the top and leading by example to desist from corrupt practices. Various empirical studies outline the following as factors

DOI: 10.4324/9781003326649-22

that influence the occurrence of corruption: the size and structure of governments, the nature of democracy and the political system, the quality and independence of oversight institutions, the extent of economic freedom/openness of the economy, salaries of civil service, press freedom and judiciary, cultural determinants, percentage of women in the labour force and in parliament, colonial heritage, and the endowment of natural resources.[4] Addressing these factors can contribute to combating corruption.

A more pressing question is why corruption appears to be widespread in many African countries. To make matters worse, anti-corruption action in these countries is typically reactive, as evidenced by the launch of investigations and, ultimately, prosecution after losses have occurred, rather than employing preventative or detective measures to avoid loss. Unfortunately, the nature of the crimes is only discovered after the damage has been done, so responses to corruption are viewed as mere publicity stunts or window dressing. While publicity may aid in deterrence, recovering assets and funds stolen adds to the cost of investigation and prosecution, exacerbating the loss of public funds.

Because of the complexity of the environment in which modern African society finds itself, as well as the diversity of needs, it is critical to have effective governance structures and processes in place to enable the achievement of goals and objectives in an efficient manner while minimising loss through corruption and fraud. Transparency and accountability will improve the control environment, lowering the risk of corrupt practices. The Three lines model can assist in bringing the desired corrupt-free environment. A model is a tool that assists institutions in identifying structures and processes that best assist the achievement of objectives and facilitate strong governance and risk management processes. This model can apply to any organisation including government institutions. The model has six principles which if properly adopted can improve the risk management process that in turn reduces the risk of fraud and corruption.[5]

The model site principle number one as governance stipulates that any organisation requires appropriate structures and processes that enable accountability by the governing body to stakeholders and ably provide organisational oversight through integrity, leadership, and transparency. It also provides actions that manage risks to acceptable levels of management to achieve the objectives of the organisation through risk-based decision-making and the application of resources. The last principle talks about assurance and advice by an independent internal audit function that assists in providing clarity and confidence which eventually promotes and facilitates continuous improvement through rigorous inquiry and insightful communication of results.[6]

By framing evaluation results to attract attention for implementation and impact, internal audit functions or external assurance providers play a crucial role in upholding accountability. Auditors should independently assess processes and then communicate results objectively to determine whether controls are in place to thwart elements that serve as a breeding ground for fraud and corrupt behaviour. Corruption and fraud risks can be reduced by properly conducting evaluations and implementing recommendations.

Three Lines Model: Governance Structures to Prevent Corruption

It is safe to assert that accountable governance is part of the solutions to most African problems[7] and corruption inclusive. The three lines model principle number one elevates strong structures of governance that enable accountability by those trusted with providing organisational oversight through integrity, leadership, and transparency. The model further seeks to facilitate risk management to acceptable levels in so doing loopholes for corruption are identified and dealt with before they materialise. African countries have not been spared, with a lot of referred cases where the risk of corruption and fraud materialised, and a lot of money was lost.

For example, in October 2013 Baker Tilly was engaged by the Department for International Development (DFID) to conduct a forensic and system security audit services support to the Government of Malawi (GoM) following the discovery of irregularities by staff at the Accountant General Department in Malawi.[8] These irregularities were discovered during a routine examination of the Budget Exception Report. In-house investigations by the Accountant General in Malawi revealed that significant amounts of government money appeared to have been misappropriated and this incident is widely known and referred to in the Malawi media as the "Cashgate" scandal.[9]

The Malawi Government lost billions of kwachas ($31 million) of the nation's budget through Cashgate, and this is a country where the poverty rate is high rated at 50.7% in 2019/20.[10] The prevalent poverty would have been an urge to cautiously save funds for development and poverty reduction, but some officials did not take this into account and went ahead to defraud the Government.

However, the Cashgate scandal has made financial industry professionals more aware of the need to be proactive and watchful to prevent similar situations from happening again. People became aware of the public sector's porous systems and the need for improved controls because of several factors that came to light. The Integrated Financial Management Information System (IFMIS), an Oracle-based Enterprise Resource Planning (ERP) that was being used as a financial management system to allocate resources and disperse payments in government, was one of the systems that contributed to the looting. This system aims to increase accountability and transparency, but it has proven to be the opposite after the Malawian government discovered widespread looting where controls were circumvented and occasionally overridden, leading to significant losses of public funds.

To proactively prevent abuse, this called for appropriate structures that would strengthen accountability and transparency. The model enables independent assessors and internal auditors, who are the third line of defence, to effectively review and provide independent assurances on how corruption and fraud risks are managed. Internal Auditors are guided by the International Professional Practices Framework (IPPF) where standard 2120. A2 stipulates clearly that Internal Auditors (IA) must evaluate the potential for the occurrence of fraud and how the organisation manages fraud risk. While Standard 2210.A2 requires IA to consider the probability of significant errors, fraud, noncompliance, and other exposures when developing engagement objectives[11] which are normally a feed into corrupt practices. Internal audit has an important role to play in ensuring that management has put in place effective systems to detect and prevent corrupt practices within a system. This is part of its normal role of supporting oversight functions in risk management and does this through the provision of assurance over fraud and corruption controls while playing an advisory role to that chard with executions of action for fulfilment of objectives.

Accountability and Corruption: Abuse of IFMIS in Malawi

The implementation of Integrated Financial Management Systems (IFMIS) is a critical component of financial reforms aimed at increasing efficiency, data security, and comprehensive financial reporting. IFMIS is an integrated computerised financial package that improves the effectiveness and transparency of public resource management by computerising a government's budget management and accounting system.[12] If properly managed, the system (IFMIS) offers a number of advantages, such as improved fiscal management, more efficient resource allocation, improved resource management (value for money), decreased fraud and corruption, improved transparency, increased accountability, and lower transaction costs. However, users of the system exploited the gaps and stole millions of monies from the government coffers at the time of implementation in Malawi in 2014, when security issues were noted. In the system, IFMIS was used to create payments to suppliers, after which checks were issued for payment to suppliers and others.

Before processing checks, the Accountant General's Department manually received all the payment vouchers, minus the supporting documentation from the various Ministries. The system was manipulated to release funds without lawful authority, create and approve unauthorised payments, issue cheques through the Accountant General's Department and transfer funds into supplier accounts without authorisation.[13] It was then discovered that perpetrators exploited these weaknesses through collusion and were able to transfer funds from the government bank accounts to the vendor accounts for goods and services that were never supplied and then delete these transactions from the IFMIS system.

Any effective control system should use a variety of compensating controls that are intended to work in concert to identify control failures, in this case, an IFIMIS failure. To prevent abuse, embedded controls should make it simple to identify unethical and incorrect transactions. By implementing the proper governance control structures recommended by the three-line model, such system abuse can be reduced. These controls should also be complemented by external checks, for example, banks, Financial Intelligence Authority (FIA) and oversight functions such as external audit.[14] With the prevalent abuse that was happening, it is evident that proper structures of governance which allow transparency, responsibility, accountability, participation, and responsiveness (to the needs of the people) were not embodied in the governance structures and systems at that point to curb the malpractice and abuse.[15]

As a result, leaders must devise proper governance structures that increase accountability and responsibility to prevent citizens from rationalising corruption.

Good governance refers to the political and institutional processes and outcomes required to achieve development goals. The true measure of "good" governance is how well it fulfils the promise of human rights: civil, cultural, economic, political, and rights. And one can ask with all the abuse, will institutions of governance effectively guarantee to its citizenry the right to health, adequate housing, sufficient food, quality education, fair justice and personal security?[16] In addition to this, means of curbing these malpractices from reoccurring as the saying goes "prevention is better than cure" must be set by inculcating a deliberate cultural and behaviour setup that would set a tone for non-tolerance of corruption and fraud. This will cascade down from the top (leaders in public, private, and society) down to the people at the grassroots.

Leadership in Combating Fraud and Corruption

Organisations and societies are operating in an increasingly volatile, uncertain, complex, and ambiguous (VUCA) world. In addition, stakeholders' needs are becoming diverse with competing interests. Stakeholders, therefore, entrust oversight to independent bodies such as the Board of Directors, which in turn delegates resources and authority to management or government officials to take appropriate actions that deal with risks that emanate from the VUCA challenges. This fiduciary duty includes risk management and resource allocation which necessitates the need for effective structures and processes to enable the achievement of objectives and the country's agenda while supporting strong governance and risk management. The oversight functions rest with public bodies, oversight institutions (including anti-corruption bodies), human rights institutions, and parliamentary committees, among others are ultimately accountable for governance and results in the form of goal achievements and development.

If the opposite is true for those entrusted with fiduciary and oversight roles, then leadership failure fuels corruption and fraud. A good example can be drawn from South Africa where Institutionalised state corruption was morphed into a phenomenon entitled state capture in South Africa.[17] State capture is the repurposing of the country's institutions towards private individual interests.[18] In the process, public goods and interests are not considered, and instead, the few connected individuals in the private and public sectors reap the benefits not due to them.

Therefore, leaders are key to fighting corruption in their jurisdiction and setting the right tone at the top (TaT) matters most. TaT is commonly defined as leadership and their commitment to being honest and ethical.[19] The tone at the top sets forth a cultural environment and values that detect the way of doing things or the way of working. If leaders choose to live by example and condemn corruption, they will be able to reprimand those who practice it without fear of reproach. The fight against corruption calls for ethical leadership which is a key factor when reducing unethical behaviours that lead to corrupt practices and fraudulent activities. In relation to this, Zambia's President, Hakainde Hichilema, soon after his election on 24 August 2021 told the British Broadcasting Corporation (BBC) that his government discovered "horrifying" amounts of money being stolen. He added that his government would show "zero tolerance" towards corruption and would get to the bottom of what he called the illicit movement of funds "very soon."[20]

With this tone set by Hakainde, a few months into his leadership results started showing in the economy, the Zambia currency started appreciating over major exchange currencies and donor confidence increased which saw Zambia securing an approval of SDR (special drawing rights)[21] 978.2 million (about US$1.3 billion) 38-month Extended Credit Facility arrangement to help restore macroeconomic stability and foster higher, more resilient, and more inclusive growth. The program advances the authorities' home-grown reform plan to restore debt sustainability, create fiscal space for much-needed social spending, and strengthen economic governance.[22] That is what a good tone benefits a country.

Combating Corruption in Africa: Setting the Tone at the Top Approach

In any system, fraud and corruption are difficult to eradicate, but they become even more difficult to eradicate when the leadership is actively involved. One tends to wonder why this group of individuals appears to risk everything, including their reputations and legacies, by engaging in unethical behaviour. A deal whereby a person exchanges something of the utmost moral or spiritual significance, such as one's values or the soul, for some worldly or material benefit, such as knowledge, power, or wealth, is known as a Faustian bargain.[23] Leaders at the helm of organisations or countries' affairs are better placed to set a tone that is later emulated by their followers. People find it easy to commit all sorts of malpractices because they feel everyone is doing it and so, "Why not me"? Everyone can refer to big cases that the so-called "big fish" have committed. To make matters worse, in most instances, the cases against the big fish have not gone far enough to bring the culprits to book.

Corruption and fraud are likely to decline to some extent if the leadership, in whatever capacity, at the national, community, organisational, church, or family level, sets forth the proper cultural environment and values. There won't be anyone to encourage bad behaviour, creating a climate at the top where ethics, risk management, and good governance are prioritised. The next concern is how to establish the proper tone as leaders in any organisation, including the government.

Communicate, Promote, and Display Good Ethics and Values

Leadership should clearly communicate and promote good ethics and values, say it, mention it, and live it. This can go to the extent of engaging in informal conversations that communicate ethics and values. Most importantly, leaders must display their commitment to abiding by the ethics and rules set. For example, Thomas Sankara of Burkina Faso who ruled the country from 1983 to 1987 demonstrated that communicating and promoting good ethical values to citizens yields a strong cultural resilience that in turn stirs development and growth. Within his short reign, Sankara seized power with the goal of eliminating corruption and the dominance of the former French colonial power. He immediately launched one of the most ambitious programs for social and economic change ever attempted on the African continent. To symbolise this new autonomy and rebirth, he renamed the country from Upper Volta to Burkina Faso ("Land of Upright Man").[24] This was on its own a push to promote and deploy good ethical values.

Encourage Reporting of Misconduct

Leadership should establish proper channels for whistleblowers to "safely" report misconduct that occurs anywhere. As argued by Majiga in Chapter 21, governments and organisations need functional whistleblowing programs that will allow reporting on misconduct without any fear of ramifications. In addition, these programmes should necessitate the examination and investigation of whistleblower's reports and bring perpetrators to book. Auditors are key to this aspect so that reports are objectively and independently assessed, and evidence is gathered to reprimand perpetrators through the right jurisdiction, such as courts, police, and other law enforcement agencies. As an extension, as explained by Kabaya in Chapter 20, other professionals like lawyers also have a duty to report illegal activities by their clients without necessarily abusing the lawyer–client privilege.

Punish Misconduct and Reward Ethical Behaviours

Leadership should also ensure that rules and laws are water-tight to punish any form of misconduct, as appropriate. Punishment deters would-be perpetrators from committing fraud or corruption because they know there will be consequences. Moreover, with precedencies around, perpetrators would know exactly what ramifications lie ahead considering that they would be well thought of, being repletion of previous cases. Equally, good behaviours displayed need to be recognised, acknowledged, and rewarded. In punishing misconduct, a case in 2005 where news was all over the media of Malawi's minister of education who was sacked after being implicated in a public fund scandal that he used public funds amounting to MK165,550.00 (US$161) for his wedding. Mr Yusuf Mwawa who was then minister of education became the first minister to be sacked in the new Mutharika administration on corruption charges. During that period, it was unthinkable for ministers to be arrested but a good way to fight corruption through setting straight the right tone on punishing misconduct and rewarding ethical behaviours.

Patriotism and Pursuit to Leave a Positive Legacy in Public Service

Until politicians and public officers start seeing public service as servanthood, which it is meant to be and stop seeing positions as a way of making money, corruption, and fraud will continue to thrive. As discussed by Agbor and others in Chapter 15, political elites should change their perception, and this can only happen if people chosen in public service set the right tone by not only doing but also being seen to be doing what is simply right. Obviously, culture and perceptions are hard to change overnight, but with a strong will and the right tone at the top, the change needed will come by.

So, leaders are key in setting the right tone at the top, in addition, the tone in setting proper structures that can encourage proper risk management as it focuses on achieving objectives and creating value, as well as matters of "defence" and protecting value. Consequently, setting these structures coupled with a continuous and independent evaluation of their adequacy helps to easily uncover and detect incentives that motivate fraud and corruption before actual occurrence. For fraud, a subset of corrupt practices to occur, three elements namely opportunity, pressure (also known as incentive or motivation), and rationalisation (sometimes called justification or attitude) must be present. This is well explained in the fraud triangle theory.[25]

These fraud elements align well with the "perfect place" syndrome of the 10–80–10 rule which highlights a general assumption of capability by the breakdown of the population and the likelihood of fraud occurrences.[26] Essentially, this rule suggests that 10 per cent of the population will never commit fraud in their lifetime while 80 per cent of the population might commit fraud given the right combination of opportunity, pressure, and rationalisation. Lastly, 10 per cent of the population is actively looking at systems and trying to find a way to commit fraud. With this analogy therefore, it is the 80 per cent that needs to be managed, and the independent evaluation of controls set by those entrusted with fiduciary duty can assist in reducing the occurrences of fraud and corrupt acts.

And it has been proved by seeing the many fraud and corruption cases mainly in the Public Service more especially in young democracies and developing countries. To prevent and detect fraud and corruption in the public service, lifestyle audits are a critical and legitimate management tool and form part of risk management. Unfortunately, most cases are difficult to detect, and dishonestly inclined professionals can conceal their fraudulent actions with disturbing alacrity and ease, particularly in work environments with weak controls or limited segregation of duty.[27] The most evident clue to these illicit activities is a sudden and unexplained change in an individual's lifestyle. By adopting lifestyle audits, greater transparency is obtained, and it also serves as a powerful deterrent against unethical behaviour, as it reminds people that their behaviours are subject to scrutiny.

Conclusion

The foregoing chapter has demonstrated that if leaders lead by example and set the right tone at the top, which is a fundamental attribute when it comes to conquering corrupt practices and fraud, a subset of corruption, corruption, and fraud will die down. Those charged with oversight and governance in institutions must instil in their followers a culture of integrity and ethical behaviour. They must create an environment that promotes ethical behaviour and instils accountability, honesty, and transparency.

Additionally, African states should put in place appropriate governance structures, policies, and procedures that enhance control improvement to effectively denounce and combat corruption. Independent and capable auditors must perform valuation and ongoing assessments so that any gaps are promptly closed before criminals have a chance to carry out such crimes. To ascertain the likelihood of fraud and corruption in each sector, fraud and corruption risks must be assessed as part of the planning process for audit reviews. Furthermore, governance and culture reviews must establish a foundation for each review so that key issues related to top-down tone, values, reward, and recognition are evaluated, and gaps are closed to reduce pressure, opportunities, and rationalisation, all of which are incentives and motivation for fraud and corruption.

Lifestyle audits must also be performed to assist in identifying unexplained wealth accumulation, which is a major red flag and a common indicator of potential corruption and fraud. However, it is necessary to ensure that the lifestyle audit is informed by what would be expected of an average earner. In other words, an audit of lifestyle should not be found to unduly regulate sound entrepreneurial spirit by the bureaucrats who have no practice on how actual business is undertaken beyond the theory. It is necessary to explore how far algorithms can be used to establish if one's lifestyle is materially departing from what is expected of their reward for labour. It is time to consider whether science is applied to these things to enhance objectivity.

Audits can also serve as a deterrent to would-be perpetrators by acting as a control. Institutions should implement strong internal control systems to limit the occurrence of risks and detect gaps that can breed corruption and fraud. The detection of such differences can raise red flags, necessitating a thorough investigation of their actions and transactions. In such cases, an examination of the individual's income, assets, and investments can be conducted to determine whether such seemingly extravagant expenditures could have resulted from illegal gains. If the audit shows a mismatch between a person's known income and assets compared to their lifestyle and spending patterns, then there is an increased risk that the person is deriving alternative income from sources that constitute a public conflict of interest or illegal activity, including embezzlement and bribery. As a matter of caution, however, there is a need to walk a fine line between tallying lifestyle with the asset or alternative funding portfolio with the need to not be seen as regulating people's freedoms and choices of what they value at the different stages of their lives.

Lastly, the adoption of the three lines model is a defence and controlling mechanism where prevention and fighting corruption is concerned. The model reinforces organisations by implementing structures and processes that foster accountability and transparency, and this best assists in the achievement of objectives and facilitates strong governance and in turn minimises or eradicates corruption risks.

In the final analysis, the call to action for all parties involved is to exercise caution and reveal wrongdoing at all levels. If these malpractices are to be reduced through corrective measures, proper reporting and implementation follow-up are required. To minimise pressure, opportunities, and rationalisation, leaders should launch organisational governance and culture reviews to assess values, rewards, and recognition and close gaps. The three lines model, which establishes guidelines for governance and sets up appropriate structures and procedures to enable accountability by governing bodies, prompt action by implementers, and assurance and guidance by an independent internal audit function, should be adopted by organisations to instil confidence and foster continuous improvement through rigorous reviews and insightful communication. African countries need to establish proper lifestyle audit frameworks, and their degree of success needs to be looked at by independent assessors who will give assurance on the adequacy and effectiveness of such programmes.

Notes

* Group Chief Internal Auditor, NICO Group PLC.

1 These are petty cases by individuals who may work as messengers, cleaners, and even house helpers.

2 The Institute of Internal Auditors, "Managing the Business Risk of Fraud: A Practical Guide," 27 June 2007. available at: us.aicpa.org (accessed 20 June 2023), 5.

3 United Nations, "Sustainable Development Goals," available at https://sdgs.un.org/ (accessed August 15, 2022).

4 Enste, Dominik Heldman, "Causes and consequences of corruption: An overview of empirical results", IW-Report No. 2, 25 January 2017, available at: Causes and Consequences of Corruption: An Overview of Empirical Results - German Economic Institute (IW) (iwkoeln.de) (accessed 20 June 2023).

5 Institute of Internal Auditor (IIA), "The IIA Three Lines Model: An Update of the Three Lines of Defense," available at:www.theiia.org/globalassets/site/about-us/advocacy/three-lines-model-updated.pdf (2 September 2022).

6 MSFA, "Updated Three Lines Model Promotes Strong Governance and Risk Management," available at: www.mfsa.mt/publication/updated-three-lines-model-promotes-strong-governance-and-risk-management/ (September 30 2022).

7 Dan Kuwali, "Is accountable governance a solution to African problems?", available at: Is Accountable Governance a Solution to African Problems? - The Raoul Wallenberg Institute of Human Rights and Humanitarian Law (accessed 2 September, 2022).

8 Government of Malawi, "Forensic Audit Report," National Audit Office Malawi, 21 February 21, 2014.

9 Baker Tilly, "Report on Fraud and Mismanagement of Malawi Government Finances," National Audit Office, 21 February 2014, available at: vdocuments.mx_the-final-forensic-audit-report-on-cashgate-in-malawi.pdf (accessed 20 June 2023).

10 The World Bank, "Malawi," available at: www.worldbank.org/en/country/malawi/overview#1 (15/08/2022)

11 Institute of Internal Auditors, "IIA's Standards on Corruption and Fraud," available at: ia.org.uk/resources/delivering-internal-audit/position-paper-internal-audit-and-corrupt-practices (accessed 2 September 2022).

12 The Implementation of Integrated Financial Information Management Systems (IFMIS) ttps://www.u4.no/publications/the-implementation-of-integrated-financial-management-systems-ifmis.pdf (April 8, 2009)

13 Baker Tilly, "Report on Fraud and Mismanagement of Malawi Government Finances."

14 Baker Tilly, "Report on Fraud and Mismanagement of Malawi Government Finances."

15 Office of the High Commissioner for Human Rights (OHCHR), "Good Governance," available at: www.ohchr.org/en/good-governance/about-good-governance, 27 September 2022

16 OHCHR, "Good Governance."

17 Sanet Madonsela, "Critical Reflections on State Capture in South Africa," *Insight on Africa,* vol 11, Issue 1 (4 December 2028), available at: https://journals.sagepub.com/,./doi.org/10.1177/0975087818805888 (accessed 20 June 2023).

18 Madonsela, "Critical Reflections on State Capture in South Africa."
19 Corporate Finance Institute, "Tone at the Top," available at: https://corporatefinanceinstitute.com/resources/knowledge/finance/tone-at-the-top/ (accessed 27 September 2022).
20 Hakainde Hichilema, "Corruption at 'Horrifying' Levels," September 2, 2021, *BBC News Africa*, available: at: www.bing.com/videos/search?q=%2bZambian+President+Hichilema%3a+Corruption+at+%27Horrifying%27+Levels%2c++September+2%2c+2021%2c+BBC+News+Africa%2c+Africa&qpvt=%2bZamb (accessed 20 June 2023).
21 International Monetary Fund, "Fact Sheets," available at: www.imf.org/en/About/Factsheets/Sheets/2016/08/01/14/51/Special-Drawing-Right-SDR (accessed 22 May 2023).
22 International Monetary Fund, "IMF Executive Board Approves New Extended Credit Facility (ECF) Arrangement for Zambia," 31 August 2022, available at: IMF Executive Board Approves New Extended Credit Facility (ECF) Arrangement for Zambia (accessed 22 May 2022).
23 Britannica, "Faustian Bargain," available at: www.britannica.com/topic/Faustian-bargain (accessed 27 September 2022).
24 Thomas Sankara, "Facts about Thomas Sankara in Burkina Faso," available at: www.thomassankara.net/facts-about-thomas-sankara-in-burkina-faso/?lang=en (accessed at 29 September 2022).
25 Whistleblowers, "Fraud Triable," available at: www.whistleblowers.org/fraud-triangle/ September 12, 2022
26 Board and Fraud, "Perfect Place Syndrome and the 10–80–10 Rule to Ethics," 6 March 2023, available at: Perfect Place Syndrome and the 10-80-10 Rule to Ethics – BoardAndFraud (accessed 31 May 2023).
27 Republic of South Africa, "Guide to Implement Lifestyle Audits in the Service," Department of Public Service and Administration," March 2021, available at: www.dpsa.gov.za/dpsa2g/documents/iem/2021/Guide%20on%20Lifestyle%20Audits.pdf (October 11, 2022).

19 Prosecuting Corruption

A Case Study of Kenya and Uganda

Godard Busingye, Hadijah Yahyah**, and Rosemary Kanoel****

Defining a Sugar-Coated Bullet: Corruption's Conceptual Fallacies

Corruption can be defined as the misuse of office for personal gain. It includes offering, giving, promising, solicitation, or acceptance of any goods of monetary value or benefit or undue advantage in exchange for any act or omission in the performance of a person's duties.[1] It is an international problem because looted funds are laundered through the global financial system. It is inextricably linked to terrorism and violent extremism because assets stolen through corruption can be used to finance further crimes, including violent extremist and terrorist acts.[2] Corruption responds to standard economic incentive theory. It negatively affects anti-corruption policies.[3] Corruption is a systemic governance issue rooted in the ideology and leadership style of the socio-economic and political elite.[4] Viewed from a negative perspective, corruption is the single largest roadblock to democracy, as well as socio-economic and cultural development for any developing nation on the African continent.[5] Viewed from a positive perspective, however, corruption can act as a springboard upon which poor economies can base to enter into higher income statuses, as was the case for the Western economies during the slave trade, colonial periods, and even today in the neo-colonial era.

Corruption, by its very nature, is a sugar-coated bullet that must explode when the necessary trigger effects are in place. It is a systemic and endemic vice, exogenic to the African cultures but reminiscent of the Western World civilizations. Generically, it is the abuse of entrusted power for private gain.[6] For example, the power unwillingly entrusted to the slave master by the slave, the unwavering trust by the traditional African chiefs and clan leaders to the Western colonial masters, which was betrayed by those wielding superior and witty power. It is now a criminal act under international and national legal regimes, but it is not easy to detect, investigate, prosecute, and secure a conviction in courts of law. It is an act which promotes the existence and glorification of unbalanced and unfair power relations between the poor or weak and the economically, socially, or politically strong individuals. The latter is inherently brutal and aggressive when it comes to the sharing of national resources for the benefit of all citizens.

According to the Transparency International Index, corruption is categorized as grand corruption (committed at a high level of government, enabling leaders to

DOI: 10.4324/9781003326649-23

benefit at the expense of the public good), petty corruption (where low-and mid-level officials abuse their power), and political corruption (where policies and procedures are manipulated by decision makers who want to sustain their power, status and wealth).[7] This categorization does not make sense to whoever is exploited by the corrupt. Corruption must be either condemned as systemic evils that deprive the poor and weak of their riches or commended as a systemic socio-economic and political virtue that is necessary for the economic growth of society, nothing in between will suffice.

The United Nations (UN) Convention against Corruption, adopted by the UN General Assembly resolution 58/4 of 31 October 2003, puts in place various measures to fight corruption. The Convention applies, in accordance with its terms, to the prevention, investigation, and prosecution of corruption and to the freezing, seizure, confiscation, and return of the proceeds of offences established in accordance with the Convention. It imposes a duty on each State Party, in accordance with the fundamental principles of its legal system, to develop and implement or maintain effective, coordinated anti-corruption policies that promote the participation of society and reflect the principles of the rule of law, proper management of public affairs and public property, integrity, transparency and accountability. Each State Party must endeavour to establish and promote effective practices aimed at the prevention of corruption.

The Convention further requires each State Party to endeavour to periodically evaluate relevant legal instruments and administrative measures with a view to determining their adequacy to prevent and fight corruption. There is, however, no identifiable channel through which dictates of this UN Convention can be enforced in municipal jurisdictions. Municipal jurisdictions, depending on their development models, may choose to adhere to its tenets or even ignore them. The European Convention defines corruption as the deliberate action of whosoever promises or gives, directly or through an intermediary, an advantage of any kind whatsoever to an official for himself or for a third party for him to act or refrain from acting in accordance with his duty or in the exercise of his functions in breach of his official duties shall constitute active corruption.[8]

The AU Convention defines "corruption" as an act or practice including related offences prescribed in this Convention.[9] It defines proceeds of corruption to mean assets of any kind corporeal or incorporeal, movable or immovable, tangible or intangible, and any document, or legal instrument evidencing title to or interest in such assets acquired as a result of corruption.[10] Section 1 of the Anti-Corruption Act of 2009 of the Laws of Uganda vaguely defines the term "corruptly" to mean purposely doing an act, which tends to corrupt or influence a person to do an act or omission contrary to established procedures. The Anti-Corruption and Economic Crimes Act, 2003 (Kenya), defines "corruption" to include bribery, fraud, embezzlement, or misappropriation of public funds and abuse of office or breach of trust. It also includes an offence involving dishonesty – (i) in connection with any tax, rate, or impost levied under any Act; or (ii) under any written law relating to the elections of persons to public office.

A scan through the various definitions of the term corruption reveals that logically, all its ingredients amount to defined crimes such as theft, embezzlement, or bribery. For example, the Penal Code Act, Cap. 120 (Laws of Uganda), under section 254 (1) and (3), defines the offence of theft as when: (1). A person fraudulently and without claim of right takes anything capable of being stolen, or fraudulently converts to the use of any person other than the general or special owner thereof anything capable of being stolen. The presumption here is that a person who takes or converts anything capable of being stolen is fraudulent if he or she does so with any of the following intents: (a) an intent permanently to deprive the general or special owner of the thing of it; (b) an intent to use the thing as a pledge or security; (c) an intent to part with it on a condition as to its return which the person taking or converting it may be unable to perform; (d) an intent to deal with it in such a manner that it cannot be returned in the condition in which it was at the time of the taking or conversion; (e) in the case of money, an intent to use it at the will of the person who takes or converts it, although he or she may intend afterwards to repay the amount to the owner. "Special owner" within the meaning of this section includes any person who has any charge or lien upon the thing in question or any right arising from or dependent upon holding possession of the thing in question.

Corruption also includes passive criminal behaviour such as conflict of interest – a situation where individuals are in a position to derive personal benefit from actions or decisions made in their official capacity. Clientelism, which is a system of exchanging resources and favours based on an exploitative relationship between a "patron" and a "client" is another form of corruption.[11] Various other forms of corruption include favouritism, patronage, nepotism, and cronyism (whereby those in official positions exploit their power and authority to provide jobs or favours to family members or friends, even though they may not be qualified or deserving). All these forms of corruption have ingredients of stealing from the public coffers by other means.

For example, the salary earned by a person appointed because of nepotism, or favouritism, or patronage would not have been so earned if the appointment was not corruptly given, that money is thence a stolen public property. The connection between employment and meritocracy is broken by nepotism, favouritism, or patronage, which can lead to governmental abuse.[12] Trading in influence, using one's connections with persons in authority to obtain favours or preferential treatment for a third party (person, institution, or government), usually in return for their loyalty or any undue advantage is also corruption.[13]

Begovic agrees that the term corruption is not succinctly defined and that there are very many definitions of the term, which makes it problematic to address. He is, however, comfortable with a generic definition coined by Vito Tanzi which defines corruption as the intentional non-compliance with the arm's-length principle aimed at deriving some advantage for oneself or for related individuals from this behaviour. According to Begovic, for there to be corruption, there must be some advantage for the individual who commits a violation of the arm's-length principle.[14] Still, such a definition is not helpful to one who wishes either to condemn or to commend corruption. An examination of the acts, omissions, or related offences in these imperfect definitions shows that there is no commitment to criminalize such acts, omissions, or related offences by the powers that may be. What comes out clearly, though, is that corruption is a systemic criminal act embedded in the socio-economic, cultural, legal, and political fabric of the global society.[15] Corruption, by its very nature, remains a sugar-coated bullet, which must at one time explode in the face of the corrupt. It is an anti-social behaviour and a plague that has eaten so deep into the entire fabric of the many societies, it confers undue benefits on few people contrary to legal and moral norms of the society.[16]

Prosecution of Corruption in Selected African States

The UN Convention's robust peer review mechanisms have served as a global framework for international cooperation to strengthen prevention, disrupt money-laundering schemes, and return stolen proceeds from foreign banks and other necessary actions. On 10 September 2018 the UN Secretary General, encouraged all Member States to bring greater resolve to implement this Convention. The African Union (AU) notes that corruption hampers efforts aimed at promoting democratic governance, socio-economic transformation, peace and security, and the enjoyment of human rights in the AU Member States.[17]

AU has, therefore, initiated processes to condemn corruption on the African continent in its policy and legal Instruments. The same spirit of condemning corruption is taken down to the Regional Economic Communities (RECs), such as the East African Community (EAC) and the Southern African Development Community (SADC). Member States on the continent equally condemn corruption in their national legislation. In its Preamble, the Constitutive Act of the African Union expresses the determination of African governments to take up the multifaceted challenges, including corruption, which confront the continent and its peoples in the light of the social, economic, and political changes taking place in the world.[18]

The agenda of the African continent, therefore, is to condemn corruption in all its forms and uproot it from the fabric of its societies.[19] The African continent is now focused towards achieving the goals and priority areas set by its political leadership under Agenda 2063. Agenda 2063 is Africa's blueprint and master plan for transforming Africa into the global powerhouse of the future.[20] Its goals and priority areas, however, cannot be achieved, if corruption is not eliminated from the systems of the continent.

The Agenda 2063 goals and priority areas are having a prosperous Africa based on inclusive growth and sustainable development; an integrated continent politically united and based on the ideals of Pan-Africanism and the vision of African Renaissance; an Africa of good governance, democracy, respect for human rights, justice, and the rule of law; a peaceful and secure Africa; Africa with a strong cultural identity common heritage, values, and ethics; an Africa whose development is people driven, relying on the potential offered by African people, especially its women and youth, and caring for children; and an Africa as a strong, united, resilient, and influential global player and partner. In line with these goals and priority areas for the African continent, African countries are re-examining their stance towards stigmatizing corruption and condemning it through their national legal frameworks. A scan of the AU Member countries' domestic legislation shows that each country has laws and established institutions to fight corruption.

At the RECs level, the Treaty for the Establishment of the East African Community, 1999 under Article 5 (3) (h) emphasizes the need to strengthen and consolidate cooperation in agreed fields that will lead to equitable economic development within the Partner States and which would, in turn, raise the standard of living and improve the quality of life of their populations. Article 6 (d) of the EAC Treaty provides for good governance in the Community. This broadly includes adherence to the principles of democracy, the rule of law, accountability, transparency, social justice, equal opportunities, and gender equality, as well as the recognition, promotion, and protection of human and people's rights in accordance with the provisions of the African Charter on Human and Peoples' Rights. Article 7(1) (f) of the Treaty provides for the equitable distribution of benefits accruing or to be derived from the operations of the Community and measures to address economic imbalances that may arise from such operations.

The Preamble to the Treaty of the Southern African Development Community (SADC), highlights the need to involve the people of the region centrally in the process of development and integration, particularly through the guarantee of democratic rights, observance of human rights and the rule of law. African countries have undertaken to condemn corruption by establishing institutions and enacting appropriate legislation for that purpose. From the foregoing, the achievement of the aspirations of the African continent regarding human rights and security is pegged on how successful the continent will be in tackling corruption and uprooting it from its systems. Short of uprooting it from its systems, the African continental aspirations will only remain flowery and attractive on paper but will not be so realized. Achievements so far made on the continent towards tackling the global pandemic of corruption, however, must be in the limelight, lest the continent remains amenable to unfair judgement by the Western economies.

The South African Constitution, 1996, under section 215 (1) provides that national, provincial, and municipal budgets and budgetary processes must promote transparency, accountability, and the effective financial management of the economy, debt, and the public sector. This constitutional provision is operationalized by the Prevention and Combating of Corrupt Activities Act (PACCA), 2004. The PACCA creates a general offence of corruption that is defined in broad terms, making it rather difficult to successfully prosecute a suspect on its provisions. The PACCA applies to both the public and private sectors. Under the PACCA, a person is guilty of an offence in terms if he or she directly or indirectly accepts or offers to accept a gratification from another person or gives or agrees to give a gratification to any other person for his or her benefit, or that of another. The giving or acceptance must be done in order to induce the other party to act in an improper manner in the performance of that individual's duties.

South Africa, which is probably the continent's highly developed democracy, has not shied away from holding its highly placed politicians accountable for their corrupt deeds. In that spirit, Ex-President Jacob Zuma is facing 16 charges of corruption relating to a multi-billion-dollar arms deal.[21] Ex-President Zuma is accused of taking kickbacks from the US$5 billion purchase of fighter jets, patrol boats, and other arms manufactured by five European firms, including British military equipment maker BAE Systems and French Company Thales. Unfortunately, the South African Courts may never be able to bring to justice those powerful individuals in the Western World who engaged in corrupt deals with ex-President Zuma. The inability to bring to book individuals and Companies based in the Western World is firstly because they are very powerful and hence capable of evading the justice system in South Africa, but secondly, because they are supported by their governments and, therefore, not in the interest of the South African Government to directly antagonize with Western Governments. The South African Government's legal system is equally not robust enough to prosecute foreign nationals and entities operating out of the country's jurisdiction.

Much as Jacob Zuma is being prosecuted after leaving office, South Africans have not waited for incumbent President Cyril Ramaphosa to leave Office and then bring up corruption charges against him since they have gathered glaring evidence against him. South Africa's watchdog is accusing President Cyril Ramaphosa of misleading Parliament and potential money laundering over a campaign donation.[22] Once investigations are completed, President Ramaphosa will be compelled to answer to the charges of corruption in the South African Courts of law. These cases illustrate how committed South Africans are to getting rid of corruption in their country's system in order to rally behind all other African countries in the race towards achieving the set goals and priority areas under Agenda 2063.

Successful prosecution of these cases largely depends on the support the prosecution will get from the Western World, where, in the case of ex-President Jacob Zuma, there was collusion with Western Companies. Prosecuting these cases within the vivid limitations, however, sends a clear signal to other African political leaders that when found corrupt, they will not be spared. The Constitution under Objective XXVI provides that all public offices shall be held in trust for the people; all persons placed in positions of leadership and responsibility shall, in their work, be answerable to the people; and that all lawful measures shall be taken to expose, combat, and eradicate corruption and abuse or misuse of power by those holding political and other public offices.

Article 223 establishes an Inspectorate of Government, whose functions are to promote and foster strict adherence to the rule of law and principles of natural justice in administration; eliminate and foster the elimination of corruption and abuse of authority and of public office; promote fair, efficient, and good governance in public offices; subject to the provisions of the Constitution to supervise the enforcement of the Leadership Code of Conduct; investigate any act, omission, advice, decision, or recommendation by a public officer or any other authority to which this article applies, taken, made, given, or done in exercise of administrative functions; and stimulate public awareness about the values of constitutionalism in general and the activities of its office, in particular, through any media and other means it considers appropriate. These constitutional provisions are operationalized by the 2002 Inspectorate of Government Act, which sets up the institutional structure of the Inspectorate and provides for the procedures through which the leadership Code can be enforced.

Under Article 233, the Constitution empowers Parliament to, by law establish a Leadership Code of Conduct for persons holding such offices as may be specified by Parliament. The Leadership Code of Conduct so established requires specified officers to declare their incomes, assets and liabilities from time to time and how they acquired or incurred them, as the case may be; and prohibits conduct likely to compromise the honesty, impartiality and integrity of specified officers; or likely to lead to corruption in public affairs; or which is detrimental to the public good or welfare or good governance. The 2002 Leadership Code Act provides for a minimum standard of behaviour and conduct for leaders; requires leaders to declare their incomes, assets, and liabilities; and puts in place an effective enforcement mechanism to ensure that the constitutional normative demands are realized.

Other key organs of government that are at the helm of fighting corruption in Uganda include the Auditor General, established under the 2008 National Audit Act, Parliament, which provides an oversight role to government and private entities in Uganda, the Judiciary, which manages cases brought to it by the various organs of government and private individuals, the Central Bank, which implements the Anti-Money Laundering Act.[23] According to section 4 of the Bank of Uganda Act, one of the functions of the Bank of Uganda is to supervise, regulate, control, and discipline all financial institutions and pension funds institutions.[24]

All these initiatives are capped by mechanisms under the Whistleblowers Protection Act, which enables a whistleblower to make a disclosure of information where that person reasonably believes that the information tends to show that a corrupt, criminal, or other unlawful act has been committed, is being committed, or is likely to be committed.[25] Or, that a public officer or employee has failed, refused, or neglected to comply with any legal obligation to which that officer or employee is subject. It also applies where a whistleblower believes that a miscarriage of justice has occurred, is occurring, or is likely to occur or that any matter referred to herein has been, is being, or is likely to be deliberately concealed.

In the case of Uganda, a number of high-ranking civic leaders have been charged and convicted for corruption and corruption-related offences. In the case of *Uganda v. Lwamafa Jimmy and 2 others*[26] The Principal State Attorney, prosecuting the case asked the court to send out a clear message that corruption is a risky business. The Principal State Attorney invited the court to follow the sentencing patterns in cases such as *Uganda v. John Kashaka and others, Anti-Corruption Court of Uganda*[27] and the case of *Uganda v. Teddy Ssezi Cheeye*, where the Anti-Corruption Court imposed ten-year imprisonment against each convict yet the sums involved were much less than in this case.[28]

In the *Lwamafa Case*, a sentence of ten-year imprisonment was given as the highest custodial punishment, while the three convicts were ordered to jointly compensate the Government of Uganda to the tune of 50 billion shillings. In arriving at the order for compensation, the court took note of the fact that corruption is a systemic vice and that the convicts could not have managed to commit this crime without the assistance of others deployed at various points in the criminal chain.

The case clearly demonstrates that condemning corruption by any other means, without devising means of uprooting it from the operating systems of governments does not answer in affirmative whether or not corruption should be condemned or commended.

In the case of Kenya, several high-profile cases have in the recent past been investigated and prosecuted. Onyango, however, observes that there are over 15 mega corruption scandals in Kenya, which have never been resolved.[29] Regarding the 15 mega corruption scandals in Kenya, Onyango pointed out that (a) almost all the suspects named in the multi-billion graft scandals were never jailed; (b) some of the corruption cases, involving Senior State Officials, are several years old, implying that there was no will to bring them up for prosecution; (c) the courts cite lack of or insufficient evidence as the reason why suspects were let off the hook. Kenya, however, does not condone corruption but must be suffering the same fate as is suffered by other African states, such as South Africa in the drive to eliminate corruption in its systems. In recent years, high-profile Kenyans, including the former Sports Cabinet Secretary, and a retired Police Boss who was an official in the same Ministry, and former Kenya Medical Research Institute (KEMRI) Director, a former nominated Senator, three employees of the Ministry of Education and former Kasarani Lawmaker, were convicted of corruption and economic crimes such as abuse of public office, theft, and mismanagement of public funds.[30]

It is important to note that the successful prosecution of corruption cases largely depends on the will of the people to get rid of the vice. This is usually expressed in the laws of a country. The Constitution of Kenya, 2010 under Chapter 6 sets out the requirements of leadership and integrity expected of all public and state officers. In this regard, section 72 (2), of the Constitution, which is under Chapter 6, provides for the guiding principles of leadership and integrity. They include selection on the basis of personal integrity, competence and suitability, or election in free and fair elections; objectivity and impartiality in decision making, and in ensuring that decisions are not influenced by nepotism, favouritism, other improper motives or corrupt practices; selfless service based solely on the public interest, demonstrated by honesty in the execution of public duties; and the declaration of any personal interest that may conflict with public duties; accountability to the public for decisions and actions; and discipline and commitment in service to the people. The letter and spirit of the Constitution are cascaded down for implementation through Acts of Parliament.

The 2003 Anti-Corruption and Economic Crimes Act establishes the Kenya Anti-Corruption Commission (KACC), as a public body. The KACC became fully operational in August 2005 and replaced previous agencies and units working on corruption-related issues. The KACC is responsible for investigating and preventing corruption and economic crimes and educating the public on the dangers of corruption. The KACC does not have any prosecution powers but forwards cases to the Attorney General for further management. The KACC receives regular funding and has a full-time staff, which, according to the 2008 Global Integrity report, is among the best-paid public officials in Kenya.

The 2011 Ethics and Anti-Corruption Commission Act under section 11 provides for additional functions to the Commission, in addition to those under the Constitution. The Commission is clothed with powers to develop and promote standards and best practices in integrity and anti-corruption, in relation to State officers. It also has the responsibility to develop a code of ethics and work with other State and public offices in the development and promotion of standards and best practices in integrity and anti-corruption. It receives complaints on the breach of the code of ethics by public officers, investigates, and recommends to the Director of Public Prosecutions the prosecution of any acts of corruption or violation of codes of ethics or other matter prescribed under this Act or any other law enacted pursuant to Chapter 6 of the Constitution. It recommends appropriate action to be taken against State officers or public officers alleged to have engaged in unethical conduct and oversees the enforcement of codes of ethics prescribed for public officers.

The Commission further advises on its own initiative, any person on any matter within its functions and raises public awareness on ethical issues. It educates the public on the dangers of corruption, enlists, and fosters public support in combating corruption but with due regard to the requirements of the Anti-Corruption and Economic Crimes Act.[31] Subject to Article 31 of the Constitution, it monitors the practices and procedures of public bodies to detect corrupt practices and to secure the revision of methods of work or procedures that may be conducive to corrupt practices. It has the authority to institute and conduct proceedings in court for purposes of the recovery or protection of public property or for the freezing or confiscation of proceeds of corruption or related to corruption, or the payment of compensation, or other punitive and disciplinary measures.

Kenya's Leadership and Integrity Act establishes procedures and mechanisms for the effective administration of Chapter 6 of the Constitution.[32] Section 3 provides that the primary purpose of this Act is to ensure that State officers respect the values, principles, and requirements of the Constitution. Section 6 prescribes a general Leadership and Integrity Code for State officers. The 2016 Bribery Act provides for the prevention, investigation, and punishment of bribery in Kenya.[33] The Act applies to the public, public officers, and private entities in Kenya. An overview of these specific anticorruption laws shows how Kenya is on the right track to condemn corruption and having uprooted from its public and private systems.

Key Findings

Corrupt is a global vice that is associated with negative effects regarding human rights, democracy and good governance, economics, and social and cultural arenas. It is a function of power relations, whereby the rich and the elite bourgeoisie middle class, both in the Western World and on the African continent partner to deprive the poor of the God-given human rights to property and even life. The Western economies, however, historically corruptly took a lion's share of African riches and continue to do so in the neo-colonial era. The core of corruption is the transfer of wealth from the powerless to the powerful. In its totality, corruption leads to injustices against the poor but also to disrespect of government and loss of trust in government systems.

Citizens who watch government insiders get rich by stealing resources or demanding bribes are ripe for recruitment for terrorists.[34] When the weight of this burden becomes too much for the people to endure, they inevitably react. The resulting instability and outflows of desperate people demonstrate that corruption is not just an internal matter. It is a regional and global concern for all of us.

Failure to have a succinct definition, coupled with conceptual fallacies about the phenomenon of corruption paints it as negative and devilish without critically analysing its positive aspects. This problem is accentuated by the long-time de-popularization and demonization of corruption by those who hitherto benefited from it, but who do not wish to be asked to account for how they moved into the socio-economic class they were propelled into by the very acts they now seek to criminalize. In its current conceptualization, corruption is a vice that is already stigmatized and that no one can praise publicly. It should, however, not be branded negatively without considering its historical positive contribution to the socio-economic and political development agenda of the present-day developed Western democracies.[35]

Condemning or commending corruption without taking into account its historical benefits to the development agenda of individual States cannot yield any positive outcomes. Any effort to fight corruption will be fought by the corrupt elite who work for international corporations and individual capitalist business communities. The developed economies that outrightly condemn corruption today do not wish the less developed economies to get near to them in terms of socio-economic and political development. Moreover, condemnation of corruption is now championed by agencies of the developed economies such as the World Bank and the IMF, which are highly capitalized by States that benefited from corrupt tendencies that include slave trade in the colonized territories on the African continent.

Due to the stigmatization of corruption, States that condoned corruption and which have prospered due to its benefits are constrained to praise or even condemn it openly. The latent silence of such States creates a problematic situation, especially at the international level, where developing economies, especially on the African continent are condemned as corrupt, while the condemners are not wholly clean. Well-functioning legal and judicial systems, if supported by the political elite can fight the devilish corrupt tendencies in society. It suffices to note, however, that development paths cannot be uniform for all economies of the world. During the Industrial Revolution, for example many Western economies, including the United States saw a rise in corporations. Corporations became more powerful than States and, through corruption, influenced States' development agendas, thereby creating affluent political classes.[36]

Commending or condemning corruption in Africa and any approaches to combating it cannot be well articulated without linking the vice to the continent's slave trade and colonial history. To an African, slave trade and colonialism destabilized the culture of unity, cultural identity and the slow, but sure path of socio-economic and political development. The African development strategy was drastically replaced by an already corrupted and inhuman Western ideology of self-aggrandizement, looting, and plundering of the continental human and natural resources. Lopes and Hirsch argue that 'going back to the post-independence era, the colonial legacy continued to weigh against Africa's economic development.'[37] The structure and nature of economies still reflect inherited enclaves, preventing departure from resource dependence and attempts to change the economic trajectory.[38]

Being continuously linked to the colonial systems, the African post-colonial economic rubric, which is characterized by corruption, becomes systematically interdependent with its colonial roots. Commending or condemning approaches to combat corruption in Africa, can, therefore, only be succinctly done using the lenses of systems analysis approach.[39] Simply put, a systems thinking approach is thinking about systems and how they operate to release or further constrain an economic model from or into its chains. A systems thinking approach helps to better understand the deep roots of these complex behaviours in order to better predict them and, ultimately, adjust their outcomes.[40] Entrenched corrupt practices within the public sector (official systemic corruption) hamper the clear definition and enforcement of laws.[41] This makes it difficult to unpack corruption and deal with it from an informed point of view.

Conclusion

The definition of corruption falls short of informing anyone wishing to condemn or commend corruption to know exactly what it is. For example, does any act or omission which is done contrary to established procedures amount to corruption? Condemning or commending corruption in the current globalized world is a risky venture. Some of the giants behind the gimmicks of condemning corruption are corrupt themselves or are beneficiaries of the corrupt past of their ancestors, on whose behalf they do not wish to apologize. That makes them protective of the corrupt regimes and may harm anyone who attempts to cross into their comfort zones. Moreover, they do not wish those who are not yet corrupt to get into the arenas of corruption so that they too, amass ill-begotten wealth and compete with those already established in the highly revered economic class.

Corruption is a serious impediment to the rule of law and sustainable development. It obstructs economic growth and development, erodes public confidence, legitimacy, and transparency and hinders making fair and effective laws, as well as their administration, enforcement, and adjudication. Modern means of communication can facilitate corruption to unimaginable levels. European slave trade reparations could be used in Africa and the New World to indemnify the descendants of the formerly enslaved. That, however, will not cleanse the already tainted image of those who engaged in the slave trade and obtained benefits, which, after all, cannot be disclosed, even when reparations are offered. In the final analysis, it remains a debatable issue whether, much as it is devilish, corruption can be condemned, severely punished and hence stigmatized, or commended publicly.

Scholars, politicians, and legislators should unpack the ingredients of the crime of corruption and categorize outright it as theft so that it can be stigmatized and condemned by everyone in the globalized world order. A systems-based approach should be used to clean the dirty enclaves of society that commend corruption, with a view to enabling the African continent to achieve its goals and priority areas set out under Agenda 2063.

Governments should enhance anti-corruption efforts by ensuring independent judiciaries, a vibrant civil society, freedom of the media and effective whistle-blower protections. The international community should complement those efforts by working more effectively against money laundering, tax evasion, and the illicit financial flows that have deprived countries of much-needed resources, and that feed further corruption.

A corruption-free environment is a prerequisite to the socioeconomic and political development of society. Those who benefited from corruption, before stigmatizing it should, therefore, come out and declare the known proceeds of their predecessors' corrupt actions and be ready to account to those who were deprived of their rights, especially during the slave trade and colonial eras. The ultimate is to accept past wrongdoing to promote accountability and equitable sharing of the resources hard-earned by everyone on the globe.

Notes

* Chief of Legal Services in the Uganda Peoples' Defence Forces/Ministry of Defence and Veteran Affairs.

** Doctoral Candidate at the University of Nairobi.

*** Advocate of Courts of Judicature of Uganda, a Lecturer School of Law at Kampala International University.

1 Cissy Kagaba Cissy, "Realizing Public Accountability in Uganda's Public Service Delivery System – A Myth or Reality?" The Third Annual Anti-Corruption Week, A Paper presented at the Anti-Corruption Coalition Uganda at Uganda Christian University, Mukono Monday 29th October 2018.

2 António Guterres, "Remarks to the Security Council on Corruption in Conflict," *United Nations*, September 10, 2018, www.un.org/sg/en/content/sg/speeches/2018.

3 Benjamin A. Olken Rohini Pande, "Corruption in Developing Countries," *NBER Working Paper* No. w17398, 19 Jul 2022, www.nber.org/papers/w17398.

4 Seth Kaplan, "Is Corruption Always Bad?"

5 Vindho Saundarajan, "Corruption–A Social, Moral and Economic Bane," December 8, 2016, www.linkedin.com/pulse/corruption-social-moral-economic-bane-vinodh-soundarajan/.

6 Transparency International, "What is Corruption," www.transparency.org/en/what-is-corruption (accessed 22 June 2022).

7 Transparency International, "What is Corruption."

8 Convention drawn up on the basis of Article K.3 (2) (c) of the Treaty on European Union on the fight against corruption involving officials of the European Communities or officials of Member States of the European Union, Official Journal C 195, 25/06/1997 P. 0002–0011.

9 African Union (AU), "Convention on Prevention and Combating Corruption," Addis Ababa, 2003 ("AUCPCC), Article 1.

10 AUCPCC, 2003, Article 1.

11 James. A. Robinson, "The Political Economy of Clientelism", *Scandinavian Journal of Economics* 115 no. 2 (2013): 260–291, DOI: 10.1111/j.1467–9442.2013.12010.x.

12 Nii Ntreh. "This is why African governments cannot give up on nepotism", *Face 2 Face Africa*, July 22, 2021, https://face2faceafrica.com/article/this-is-why-african-governments-cannot-give-up-on-nepotism.

13 "European Parliament", Corruption in the European Union: Prevalence of corruption, and anti-corruption efforts in selected EU Member States, September 18, 2017, www.europarl.europa.eu/thinktank/en/document/EPRS_STU(2017)608687.

14 Boris Begovic, Corruption: Concepts, types, causes and consequences, *ResearchGate*, (January 2005), www.researchgate.net/publication/265364211.
15 David O Iyanda, Corruption: Definitions, Theories and Concepts, *Arabian Journal of Business and Management Review (OMAN Chapter)* 2, no.4, (November 2012), www.arabianjbmr.com/pdfs/OM_VOL_2_(4)/4.pdf.
16 David O Iyanda, "Corruption: Definitions, Theories and Concepts".
17 African Union Convention on Preventing and Combating Corruption, Adopted by the 2nd Ordinary Session of the Assembly of the Union Maputo, Mozambique 11th July 2003.
18 Adopted at Lome, Togo on 11 July 2000.
19 Dan Kuwali, "Commend and Condemn: Combating Corruption in Africa", in *The Palgrave Handbook of Sustainable Peace and Security in Africa* (Palgrave Macmillan, 25 May 2022), 581–595.
20 African Union, 2013.
21 BBC News, "South Africa ex-President Jacob Zuma Charged with Corruption", 16 March 2018, www.bbc.com/news/world-africa-43658953.
22 B.B.C. News, "South Africa's President Cyril Ramaphosa accused in corruption row", 19 July, 2019, www.bbc.com/news/world-africa-49052112.
23 Act number 12 of 2013 of the Laws of Uganda.
24 Chapter 51 of the Laws of Uganda.
25 No. 6 of 2010 (Laws of Uganda).
26 Anti-Corruption Division, at Kololo, Criminal Session Case 9 of 2015.
27 HCT-00-AC-SC 0047–2012.
28 High Court of Uganda, Criminal Case No; 1254 of 2008.
29 Jacob Onyango, 15 mega corruption scandals in Kenya which have never been resolved, May 22, 2018, www.tuko.co.ke/274539-15-mega-corruption-scandals-kenya-resolved.html.
30 Joseph Wangui. "Working towards a Corrupt Free Zone, Kenya: Recent High-Profile Convictions Boost War on Corruption", *Daily Nation,* October 31, 2021, https://allafrica.com/stories/202110140214.html.
31 No. 3 of 2003 of the Laws of Kenya.
32 Chapter 182 of the Laws of Kenya.
33 No. 47 of 2016 of the Laws of Kenya.
34 Haley, "Remarks at a UN Security Council Briefing on Corruption and Conflict".
35 Chika Ezeanya, "Corruption and Nation Building in Sub-Saharan Africa: A Historical Analysis, in Challenges to Democratic Governance in Developing Countries", (*Springer Link*, November 26, 2013) 181–194, https://link.springer.com/chapter/10.1007/978-3-319-03143-9_12.
36 Christopher Klein, "How the Gilded Age's Top 1 Percent Thrived on Corruption, Vast corporate wealth and a fee-based governance structure fuelled widespread corruption during America's Gilded Age", January 27, 2020, www.history.com/news/gilded-age-corruption-corporate-wealth.
37 Carlos Lopes and Alan Hirsch, "African narratives vs. African development strategy", *OECD*, September 28, 2020, https://oecd-development-matters.org/2020/09/28/.
38 Lopes and Hirsch, "African narratives vs. African development strategy."
39 Ross Arnold D and Wade Jon P, "A Definition of Systems Thinking: A Systems Approach, Science Direct", *Procedia Computer Science*, November 25, 2015, www.sciencedirect.com/science/article/pii/S1877050915002860.
40 Ross Arnold D and Wade Jon P, "A Definition of Systems Thinking: A Systems Approach, Science Direct".
41 Edgardo Buscaglia and Maria Dakolias, "An Analysis of the Causes of Corruption in the Judiciary, Legal and Judicial Reform Unit", The World Bank, August 1999, https://documents1.worldbank.org/curated/en/322431468744322656/pdf/multi-page.pdf.

20 Arresting Money Laundering in Zimbabwe

*Sandra Fungai Kabaya**

Introduction

Money laundering is a peculiar modern evil that has persisted over time. Other related crimes like corruption, terrorism, tax evasion, fraud, and smuggling were all prevalent in ancient times and remain so today.[1] The overarching goal of this chapter is to identify gaps in the anti-money laundering Framework and direct attention towards combating money laundering. The first section of this chapter is a conceptual analysis of money laundering, and it sets the tone for the rest of the chapter. The second section analyses the history of anti-money laundering in Zimbabwe as well as the Zimbabwean legal and institutional framework. The third section assesses the international legal framework and control mechanisms for combating money laundering, as well as Zimbabwe's position in this regard. The fourth section discusses various gaps in anti-money laundering implementation and concludes with anti-money laundering recommendations.

Money laundering is a broad and complex crime.[2] It is inextricably linked to a slew of social ills and predicate crimes, including drug trafficking, fraud, terrorism, smuggling, tax evasion, and corruption.[3] Evidence suggests that combating money laundering is a multifaceted exertion that necessitates sound legislation, competent law enforcement agencies, and coordination among states.[4] To effectively prevent money laundering, anti-money laundering regimes must not only detect and chastise perpetrators but also confiscate all proceeds of crime.[5] To be effective, anti-money laundering regimes must be flexible to both local anti-money laundering imperatives and international collaboration.[6] As a result, most countries are constantly bolstering their anti-money laundering regimes.

Money laundering is the concealment of the original illicit source of funds by directing funds engendered from illicit activities through legitimate institutions.[7] It is exactly what it is: dirty (Illegal) money is washed in water (through various transactions), resulting in clean (legal) money. Any person who profits and/or obtains any benefit from a criminal endeavour such as corruption may be committing an act of money laundering.[8] The goal of money laundering is to incorporate proceeds of crime universally denoted as dirty money into legitimate financial systems.[9] It is vital to note that money laundering cannot exist in isolation; typically,

DOI: 10.4324/9781003326649-24

it is at the tail-end of predicate crimes.[10] Organised crime syndicates use money laundering to clean their ill-gotten profits.[11]

In several instances, organised crime employs money laundering to integrate stolen funds into the global financial system.[12] For instance, proceeds from the sale of illicit drugs can be directed into legitimate financial systems, by enticing bank officials to open bank accounts.[13] A further example is when senior government officials receive bribes and mishandle important levels of power to favour contracts and businesses operated by coordinated crime syndicates.[14] Often, public officials are bribed to ignore criminal syndicates' pursuits, to the detriment of many. As a result, bribery, and abuse of office aid money laundering.[15] This has corrosive consequences on societies as it undermines the rule of law.[16]

Decoding Money Laundering in Zimbabwe

The laundering process is in three distinct phases: placement, layering, and/or integration.[17] The first phase of money laundering is placement, in which the money launderer grants illegally acquired profits into the formal financial system.[18] This can be achieved by splitting substantial sums of money into smaller, less visible sums before depositing them in financial institutions.[19] This is done to thwart any suspicions that may perhaps arise if such money was deposited in hefty amounts by the money launderer.[20]

Layering denotes the process by which the money launderer splits, blurs, and transfers the laundered funds away from the illicit source.[21] Layering frequently entails investing in cash-oriented institutions such as the sale of real estate or even the transfer of funds to offshore accounts.[22] All this can be accomplished by transferring funds to jurisdictions that do not comply with anti-money laundering legislation. Finally, integration denotes the process by which a money launderer reintroduces previously laundered funds into the economy, typically through financial institutions, so that the funds are the result of his or her legitimate business activities.[23]

The difference between layering and integration is that in the former, the movement and use of money are solely for the purpose of garbling the origins. The latter entails passage and usage for a legitimate economic purpose.[24] Once the launderer has completed all phases, the implication of money laundering becomes inescapable, making criminals profit effortlessly from ill-gotten gains.

Money Laundering has expanded exponentially in Africa over the past decade. Yearly, money laundering engenders approximately US$10,000,000 in proceeds.[25] United Nations reckons that 2–5% of global GDP is laundered yearly.[26] This is expected to range between US$800,000,000 and US$2,000,000,000,000.[27] According to the Economic and Financial Crimes Commission (EFCC), African states lose US$50,000,000,000 yearly due to money laundering.[28] The total of money estimated to be lost by African states as of money laundering can settle their debts.[29] The covert nature of money laundering has made it problematic to precisely predict the total amount of money that is part of money laundering. Money laundering is a menace to the integrity and operation of any country's financial sector.[30]

Clearly from above, money laundering is a global phenomenon and Zimbabwe is no exception.[31] Zimbabwe was hitherto categorised as a perilous state due to tactical inadequacies in its anti-money laundering framework.[32] In Zimbabwe, wire fund transfers permit funds to transfer between corporate entities and financial institutions in Zimbabwe in the flicker of an eye, making unravelling complicated at each stage.[33] It is problematic to approximate the amount of illicit money that enters the Zimbabwean financial system yearly. However, some institutions have endeavoured to approximate the extent of money laundering over the years. According to the 2021 Corruption Perceptions Index (CPI) indicator, Zimbabwe is one of the world's most corrupt states, with a score of 23 out of 100 on the corrupt state list, a drop from the 2020 score of 24 out of 100.[34]

Zimbabwe's money laundering problem occurred because of and is intertwined with the state's socioeconomic challenges.[35] Zimbabwe's economy experienced recession, cash deficiencies, hyperinflation, record echelons of unemployment, and food shortages between 2000 and 2010.[36] Zimbabwe was transformed from Africa's breadbasket to the region's basket case.[37] As a result of the dwindling economy and lack of job prospects, the economy suddenly turned out to be informal. Many Zimbabweans relied on informal currency arbitrage, cross-border trading, and foreign exchange trading to survive.[38] Illegal foreign currency and illegal markets also sprang up all over Zimbabwe.[39] Corruption, drug trafficking, tax evasion, smuggling, and fraud quickly became part of the day-to-day Zimbabwean economy.[40]

Criminals have used Zimbabwe's unstable cash supply to legitimise illicit proceeds. Dirty dollars are being obtained illegitimately and sold on the illegal market to stranded Zimbabweans for daily utilisation[41] There is also illegal transfer/export of foreign currency and/or assets from Zimbabwe, as well as offshore retention of foreign currency and/or assets due to Zimbabwe, without the necessary regulatory authorisations.[42] Dirty money in the hands of Zimbabwean cartels is simply being concealed under the mattress.[43]

Due to the negative effect of money laundering, Zimbabwe has developed tools to fight it, including recommendations to the designated business entities, as well as other reporting parties.[44] Zimbabwe's anti-money laundering efforts are into two distinct phases: pre-2013 and post-2013.[45] Prior to 2013, the legal framework was disjointed. Of the statutes, only the Serious Offences Act gave the police investigative, confiscation and forfeiture powers in money laundering cases.[46] Prior to 2013, specific elements of money laundering, such as concealment and disguise of proceeds of crime, were not captured[47] There was also no framework outlining the powers that authorise competent authorities' investigation and prosecution capabilities.

Upon identifying the inadequacies of the erstwhile legal framework, the Zimbabwean government moved to a unified anti-money laundering legal framework.[48] In 2013, the Money Laundering and Proceeds of Crime Act (MLPCA)[49] was enacted and in 2018, legislation and amendments to support the MLPCA were introduced, further aligning Zimbabwe with international instruments.[50]

The Legal Regime to Arrest Money Laundering in Zimbabwe

The Money Laundering and Proceeds of Crime Act of 2013 (MLPCA) is Zimbabwe's primary anti-money laundering legislation.[51] In terms of anti-money laundering in Zimbabwe, the MLPCA serves two crucial functions. For starters, it criminalises money laundering. Second, it authorises the establishment of an independent and functional Financial Intelligence Unit (FIU).[52] In turn, the FIU establishes regulatory authority over designated institutions. The MLPCA's goals[53] include averting the abuse of Zimbabwe's legitimate financial systems, facilitating the identification of proceeds of unlawful acts, including terrorism and other serious crimes, as well as the tracing, freezing, and eventual confiscation of such proceeds.[54]

Other pertinent anti-money laundering legislation includes the Bank Use Promotion and Suppression Act,[55] the Trafficking in Persons Act,[56] which criminalises human trafficking, the Criminal Matters (Mutual Legal Assistance) Act,[57] and the Criminal Law (Codification and Reform) Act,[58] which permits the country's legal framework to deal with proceeds of crime derived from piracy-related activities.

Designated Anti-Money Laundering Institutions in Zimbabwe

The FIU and law enforcement agencies such as the Anti-Corruption Commission, the Zimbabwe Republic Police, the National Prosecuting Authority, the Zimbabwe Revenue Authority, and the Department of Immigration are among Zimbabwe's designated anti-money laundering competent authorities.[59] These oversee the monitoring and regulation of anti-money laundering. Each of the roles of these institutions will be briefly discussed in turn.

The Financial Intelligence Unit

The main drive of the FIU is to scrutinise suspicious transaction reports and all financial data and then disseminate the outcome.[60] In collaboration with competent supervisory bodies, the FIU regulates DNFBPs for anti-money laundering compliance.[61] Furthermore, it monitors and ensures that all stakeholders are following the MLPCA.[62] The FIU also helps to coordinate measures for seizure, detention, and forfeiture of currency, bearer negotiable instruments, and precious metals.[63]

The Zimbabwe Anti-Corruption Commission (ZACC)

Corruption must be taken seriously because of the inherent relationship between it and money laundering. The mission of ZACC is to investigate and expose cases of corruption in both the public and private sectors. The Criminal Law (Codification and Reform) Act[64] empowers the conducting of criminal investigations involving corruption.[65] The existence of the Zimbabwe Anti-Corruption Commission is consistent with international perspectives, which call for state parties to form an authoritative body to combat corruption.[66] Even though the government demonstrated its political will by establishing a national anti-corruption body, there are numerous challenges. The Commission is solely funded by the Consolidated Revenue Fund, and it has faced budgetary constraints since its inception, which has hampered most efforts to combat corruption more effectively.[67]

ZACC's capacity has been described as substandard.[68] Insufficient capacity has an impact on the organisation's effectiveness. Not only is this institution understaffed, but it is questionable whether those in the ranks are up to date on best practices in investigation and general enforcement.[69] The Zimbabwe Anti-Corruption Commission (ZACC) has been described as a "toothless bulldog."[70] Even though anti-corruption laws are in place, they are selectively enforced to protect some ruling elite "sacred cows."[71] Although the Zimbabwe Anti-Corruption Commission has highlighted its effectiveness through numerous arrests of corrupt public officials,[72] there has been a dearth of convictions for money laundering and terrorist financing.[73] Clearly, ZACC requires capacity-building to improve and strengthen its national capacity to investigate corruption.

The President's Office has also established a Special Anti-Corruption Unit that will work alongside the ZACC and the Zimbabwe Republic Police to combat corruption.[74] The Special Anti-Corruption Unit was formed to support the President of Zimbabwe's anti-corruption agenda. Its role is to improve the effectiveness of the government's anti-corruption efforts and to prosecute corruption cases designated to it by other law enforcement agencies. However, according to Transparency International Zimbabwe (TIZ), the Special Anti-Corruption Unit is an illegal entity that unnecessarily duplicates the prosecuting authority's roles.[75] It is simply duplicating the roles of the National Prosecuting Authority, which has the mandate to prosecute all cases on behalf of the state.[76]

The National Task Force

The National Task Force is chaired by the FIU's Director-General, and its membership includes all key Ministries and institutions tasked with combating money laundering. The responsibilities of the National Task Force on anti-money laundering and Counter-Terrorism Financing set up under the MPLCA include developing comprehensive and adequate risk mitigating measures and guidelines for implementing the national anti-money laundering policy.[77]

The Anti-Money Laundering Advisory Committee

This is a committee mandated to advise the Minister of Finance and Economic Development on Anti-Money Laundering policy. The committee constitutes of the FIU's Director-General, heads of competent authorities, and qualified experts in financial analysis, law, accounting, forensic auditing, law enforcement, and any other field deemed relevant by the Advisory Committee.[78]

The Law Society of Zimbabwe

The Law Society of Zimbabwe is an independent organisation tasked with representing, regulating, and controlling the legal profession. In keeping with its core values, the Law Society of Zimbabwe is committed to maintaining transparency and equity through impartial and fair performance of its duties.[79] Lawyers hold a unique position in the anti-money laundering regime because they deal directly with the law and have the ability to "make or break" the regime by either advising money launderers to continue with their illicit dealings or choosing to bring them to justice by openly declaring any illicit dealings.[80]

Indeed, lawyers are gatekeepers who hold the keys to secure financial systems.[81] Lawyers frequently know the source of their client's wealth and funds, and if they are complicit, they risk allowing financial system abuse to prevail. This is consistent with what Mdala argues in Chapter 14 that corrupt officials would opt to use lawyers in their transactions to disassociate themselves from the unexplained wealth that can trigger inquiries. This may be done, for example, by instructing lawyers to incorporate a company or a trust and transfer the corrupt proceeds to the legal entity.

The Law Society of Zimbabwe has signed a Memorandum of Understanding with the FIU in support of the global fight against anti-money laundering.[82] Furthermore, the Memorandum of Understanding is intended to assist them in effectively performing their role as a competent supervisory authority and in complying with DNFBP provisions in the MLPCA.[83]

Through the enactment of the MLPCA, Zimbabwe's legal and institutional framework prioritised the criminalisation of money laundering.[84] This is consistent with international instruments that require state parties to transpose anti-money laundering legislation into domestic law and establish designated institutions to enforce compliance as well as monitor and regulate anti-money laundering requirements.[85]

International Anti-Money Laundering Initiatives

The Vienna Convention, the Palermo Convention, and the United Nations Convention Against Corruption are the three main conventions (UNCAC) for anti-money laundering.[86] Each of these conventions will be discussed in turn.

The United Nations Convention Against Illicit Traffic in Narcotic Drugs and Psychotic Substances of 1988 (Vienna Convention)

The Vienna Convention was the drive behind the global fight against illicit trafficking and money laundering.[87] The Vienna Convention[88] places an obligation on state parties to include legislation criminalising all offences related to illicit trafficking in their domestic laws. It criminalises the conversion or transfer of property with the knowledge that such property is derived from the illicit drug trade.[89] Similarly, it makes it a crime to conceal or disguise the true nature and source of property derived from the illicit drug trade. In general, the Vienna Convention makes it for state-specific legislation to deprive criminals of the profits made from money laundering and its precursor crime(s). Further, the Vienna Convention requires member states to enact forfeiture legislation that permits for the identification and freezing of property or proceeds from drug trafficking and related offences. The Convention established a solid legal framework to undermine those who obstruct the provision of information by using laws for customer confidentiality and bank secrecy to facilitate an asset forfeiture legal framework.[90] State parties must assist each other in the confiscation and seizure of property beyond their jurisdiction by cooperating.

The United Nations Convention Against Transnational Organised Crime

The Convention's goal is to endorse collaboration and effectively prevent and combat transnational organised crime.[91] The Palermo Convention goes beyond simply criminalising predicate offences like corruption; it also criminalises individuals' participation in organised crime.[92] International cooperation is also encouraged.[93]

United Nations Convention Against Corruption (UNCAC)

The UNCAC was established because states recognised the link between corruption and various other types of crime, including money laundering.[94] The overarching goal of UNCAC is to promote, facilitate, and support international cooperation and technical assistance in the prevention and fight against corruption, including asset recovery among state parties.[95] In this regard, the UNCAC requires state parties to develop regulatory and supervisory measures for monitoring financial and non-financial institutions.[96]

To achieve effectiveness in combating corruption including money laundering, state parties must develop and promote global cooperation among the judicial, law enforcement, and financial regulatory authorities.[97] According to UNCAC, states parties must establish legal frameworks that facilitate the confiscation of proceeds of crime derived through corruption including money laundering.[98]

The Financial Action Task Force (FATF)

The FATF is an intergovernmental organisation founded in 1989 as a response to criminals laundering drug money and funding terrorism.[99] Its mandate is to specialise in the expansion of global anti-money laundering standards. To that end, the FATF seeks to harmonise national legislation and regulatory reforms in anti-money laundering strategies by developing guidelines for anti-money laundering frameworks.[100] Although the FATF's recommendations are not legally binding, member countries are obligated to comply.[101] It is also important to note that failure to cooperate and comply with the recommendations frequently results in penalties.

The FATF has issued recommendations emphasising money laundering prevention, detection, and deterrence. These recommendations detail customer due diligence procedures based on the Know Your Client (KYC) principle, which aids in identifying and collecting relevant information from customers. Well-maintained customer data is the backbone of an effective anti-money laundering regime. Furthermore, the FATF endorses the filing of Suspicious Transaction Reports (STRs), which keeps the DNFBPs alert to money laundering activity and aids the coordination of anti-money laundering efforts. Anti-money laundering is perilous to the obliteration of transnational crime because it allows for asset recovery between states.

Customer due diligence can be used as an anti-money laundering tool by collecting, identifying, and verifying customer information in any business transaction. Customer due diligence can also be a deterrent measure for money launderers seeking to introduce criminally obtained proceeds into the financial system.[102] As a result, whenever there is a suspicion of money laundering or a doubt about previously verified information, customer due diligence must be valued.[103]

It is the best practice for DNFBs to store information collected during customer due diligence on file for at least five years.[104] Customer databases that are well-maintained can aid law enforcement agencies to trace identified proceeds of crime.[105] This is critical in the fight against money laundering and increases the effectiveness of anti-money laundering efforts. Accurate records also have the potential to be useful as evidence and to provide competent authorities with information in money laundering investigations and prosecutions.

For the anti-money laundering regime to be effective, a supervisory and regulatory system for all Designated Non-Financial Businesses and Professions (DNFBPs) must be in place.[106] Appropriate legislation should empower supervisory authorities to conduct their operational procedures and domestic laws must specifically criminalise money laundering.[107] Legislation should also impose severe enough penalties to deter potential money launderers. Furthermore, anti-money laundering legislation should include asset forfeiture laws that allow competent authorities to seize ill-gotten gains from criminals and return them to victims.[108] To protect its financial system and work in the global community against money laundering, a country like Zimbabwe must prioritise meeting global compliance in anti-money laundering.

The African Union Convention on Preventing and Combating Corruption

The AU Convention on Preventing and Combating Corruption aims to address the root causes of corruption that inhibit transparency and accountability by public officials.[109] It also criminalises the acquisition, possession, and association of property derived from human trafficking. Similarly, Article 6 of the AU Convention emphasises the importance of member states enacting legislation to make the laundering of corrupt proceeds and all related criminal offences.[110]

As far as alignment and compliance with the international perspective are concerned, Zimbabwe has a sound legal and institutional framework in place. The MLPCA can be celebrated as it addresses deficiencies by providing a clear definition of money laundering, which in turn facilitates the criminalisation of money laundering constituent elements such as concealment, conversion, disguise, and acquisition and use of proceeds of crime, among others.[111] However, as much as the law can be celebrated, there are several gaps that must be addressed, as will be discussed later.

Gaps in Anti-Money Laundering Implementation

Lack of enforcement of anti-money laundering regulations by competent authorities is a major impediment to combating money laundering in Zimbabwe.[112] The lack of enforcement appears to offer limited deterrence, which researchers argue is a factor in the significant increase in money laundering activities in Zimbabwe.[113]

Gaps in the implementation of effective AML measures have been identified, particularly in government institutions. Government institutions' compliance and implementation were found to be underperforming, owing primarily to budget constraints, political reasons, competition, duplication of institutions, and lack of training. The lack of resources and trained personnel in the Financial Intelligence Unit (FIU) has also hampered the effective fight against anti-money laundering.[114]

For the regime's success, adequate operational, financial, and human resources must be made available. Zimbabwe requires sufficient and consistent political will that reflects a commitment to a national agenda, as well as government unity of purpose. Anti-money laundering policies and measures are easily undermined by a lack of political will.

When analysing the institutional framework, it is obligatory to assess how the institutions conduct their mandate. Zimbabwe's anti-money laundering institutional frameworks do not appear to be capable of combating the spread of financial crime.[115] Although the chapter has highlighted how they have been numerous arrests of corrupt public officials, there has been a dearth of convictions for money laundering and terrorist financing.[116] The fight against money laundering in Zimbabwe has almost become futile, and the institutional framework has nearly shot itself in the foot. The state must therefore compel accountability and transparency in all its institutions.

Close examination also reveals that the MLPCA was both rushed and lacked due process, with the draft bill lacking thorough debate before the Senate,[117] thereby violating the constitution.[118] This has affected how the law is perceived and operationalised on paper, demonstrating a lack of seriousness on the part of the legislators as the MLPCA appears to have been more of a FATF compliance exercise than a genuine anti-money laundering measure.[119] The MLPCA also does not address virtual currency trading, which is a novel phenomenon that many countries are still grappling with.

Conclusion

This chapter evaluated Zimbabwe's anti-money laundering regime. Overall, there is an indication that Zimbabwe is rolling towards instituting an anti-money laundering regime that addresses money laundering while also being consistent with international best practices. Without proper legislation, it is undoubtedly difficult to combat money laundering. It should be noted that, while Zimbabwe signed and ratified international conventions, the implementation of the provisions is taking time. The failure of Zimbabwe and developing countries to implement international conventions renders them ineffective and is a major vulnerability that must be managed. To arrest money laundering, Zimbabwe and other African countries should strive to align their anti-money laundering regimes with international law and abandon adoption without enforcement.[120]

Unquestionably, Zimbabwe is vulnerable to money laundering activities, necessitating the enhancement of money laundering prevention mechanisms in the country. After reviewing the state of anti-money laundering in Zimbabwe, the chapter makes the following recommendations to arrest money laundering:

Provision of Adequate Financial Resources

Institutions must be provided with adequate financial resources to function. The outcomes of successful prosecutions, convictions, and asset forfeitures can be used to assess the effectiveness of competent authorities.[121] To strengthen the anti-money laundering regime, political leaders are also encouraged to set a good example by not instigating financial system manipulation and all perpetrators of money laundering must be brought to book.

Coordination of Competent Authorities

Coordination of competent authorities is required for effective anti-money laundering implementation. Domestic cooperation is critical, but international cooperation is also necessary. The FIU should consider joining the international community to improve its effectiveness and connections with other FIUs. This would keep Zimbabwe up to date on the latest money laundering trends and help to align international standards and best practices.

Effective Regulatory System

Zimbabwe must align its law with international anti-money laundering best practices. Key institutions must also update their systems to speed up the collection and movement of financial data, allowing for more timely investigations into financial crimes. Key institutions must strictly adhere to the required measures for the anti-money laundering strategy to become efficient and effective. The lack of strong institutions is also noted by Agbor, Tsatsipe, and du Pukoy in Chapter 15. Those who formulate and develop anti-money laundering policies must also ensure that institutions' policies are consistent.[122]

Training for Competent Authorities

To keep up with dynamic money laundering typologies and foster continuous skill improvement, training for competent authorities should be conducted on a regular basis. Competent anti-money laundering supervisory authorities in Zimbabwe must develop and implement ongoing anti-money laundering training programs. Adequate training will equip personnel with the ability to investigate money laundering cases, gather evidence, and supervise asset recovery.

Anti-Money Laundering Helpline

The FIU must set up a free and private anti-money laundering hotline. Once this helpline is operational, designated entities gain a better understanding of the anti-money laundering guidelines on the application of proceeds of crime and anti-money laundering, as well as the scenarios discussed in this Chapter.

Appointment of Compliance Officers

In Zimbabwe, compliance officers are only appointed on paper, exemplifying adoption without enforcement. One of the reasons for increased money laundering in Zimbabwe is a lack of enforcement.[123] All designated entities must hire compliance personnel to monitor compliance with money laundering regulations. Failure to do so must be met with calibrated and primed punishments.

Notes

* Associate Legal Counsel, BeraMasamba Law Firm, Zimbabwe.

1 Masimba Tafirenyika, "Illicit Financial Flows from Africa: Track It, Stop It Get It," available at: www.un.org/africarenewal/magazine/december-2013/illicit-financial-flows-africa-track-it-stop-it-get-it (Accessed 27 August 2022).

2 Alexander K (2001) "The International Anti-Money Laundering Regime: The Role of the Financial Task Force," *Journal of Money Laundering Control*:231–248.

3 Rusanov G and Pudovochkin Y (2018) "Money Laundering Predicate Offenses: Models of Criminological and Legal Relationships" *Journal of Money Laundering Control*: 22–32.

4 Alexander, ibid., 231.

5 Bridges M J (1997) "Taking the Profit out of Crime" *Journal of Money Laundering Control*:26–39.

6 Financial Action Task Force (2019) "Methodology: For Assessing Technical Compliance with the FATF Recommendations and the Effectiveness of AML/CFT Systems" www.fatfgafi.org/media/fatf/documents/methodology/FATF%20Methodology%2022%20Feb%202013.pdf (Accessed 23 August 2022).

7 Friedrich Schneider, 2021 Economic and Financial Crime: Corruption, Shadow Economy, and Money Laundering, Book Review by Monica Violeta Achim and Sorin Nicolae Borlea. (Springer Nature: Cham, Switzerland, 2021). ISBN 97 20–21.

8 Mens M "Beyond Placement, Layering and Integration -The Perception of Trade-Based Money Laundering Risk in UK Financial Services "*Journal of Money Laundering Control* (2019) 614–625

9 Organisation of Economic Cooperation and Development (2002) "Glossary of Statistical Terms", available at https://stats.oecd.org/glossary/detail.asp?ID=5081 (Accessed 20 August 2022).

10 C Goredema, "Money Laundering in Southern Africa: Incidence, Magnitude and Prospects for its Control" Institute for Security Studies (2004), 92.

11 See www.fatf-gafi.org/faq/moneylaundering (Accessed 24 August 2022)

12 UNDOC www.unodc.org/e4j/en/organized-crime/module-4/key-issues/money-laundering.htMoney Laundering (Accessed 27 July 2022).

13 Senate Hearing: Combating Money Laundering and Other forms of Illicit Finance: Administration Perspectives on Reforming and Strengthening Bank Secrecy Act Enforcement January 17 2017 www.govinfo.gov/content/pkg/CHRG-115shrg29913/htMoneyLaundering/CHRG115shrg29913.htm (Accessed 20 August 2022).

14 Transparency International (2016) "What is Grand Corruption and How can we stop it?", available at www.transparency.org/news (visited 20 August 2022).
15 Helping Countries Combat Corruption: The role of the world bank: http://www1.worldbank.org/publicsector/anticorrupt/corruptn/cor02.htm (nd) *Accessed 20 July 2022
16 Annan K (2004) United Nations Office of Drugs and Crime "UNCAC: Foreword" United Nations: New York, available at: www.unodc.org/documents/brussels/UN Convention_Against_Corruption.pdf (Accessed 20 July 2022).
17 Cox D Handbook of Anti-Money Laundering 2 January 2012 John Wiley & Sons, 6.
18 Lokanan ME and Nasimi N "The Effectiveness of Anti-Money Laundering Policies and Procedures within the Banking Sector in Bahrain" 2020 *JMONEY LAUNDERINGC* 769–781.
19 What are the three stages of Money Laundering October 5, 2020 https://alessa.com/blog/3-stages-of-money-laundering Accessed 3 July 2022.
20 FATF 2020 www.fatf-gafi.org/faq/moneylaundering. (Accessed 20 July 2022)
21 Stages of Money Laundering Explained 21 February 2021 www.stpaulschambers.com/stages-of-money-laundering-explained/ (Accessed 21 August 2022).
22 Layering in Money Laundering Everything you need to know March 12 2021 www.tookitaki.com/compliance_hub/layering-in-money-laundering/ (Accessed 1 August 2022)
23 Teichmann, F. Recent trends in money laundering. *Crime Law Soc Change* 73, 237–247 (2020). https://doi.org/10.1007/s10611-019-09859-0 (Accessed 20 August 2022).
24 Parkman T (2012) "Mastering anti-money laundering and counter-terrorist financing: A compliance Guide for Practitioners" Great Britain: Pearson Education, 5.
25 The Second Money Laundering and Terrorist Financing National Risk Assessment Key Findings (2019), 18.
26 United Nations Money Laundering www.unodc.org/unodc/en/money-laundering/overview.htMoney Laundering (Accessed 20 August 2022).
27 11 of the biggest FinCrime and money laundering facts www.napier.ai/post/financial-crime-statistics-2022 (Accessed 20 August 2022).
28 Masimba Tafirenyika Africa loses 50 Billion every year. www.un.org/africarenewal/magazine/december-2013/africa-loses-50-billion-every-year (Accessed 22 August 2022).
29 Masimba Tafirenyika Africa loses 50 Billion every year. www.un.org/africarenewal/magazine/december-2013/africa-loses-50-billion-every-year (Accessed 22 August 2022).
30 Gjoni M, Gjoni AK and Kora HB "Money Laundering Effects, 2015" in *Proceedings of the International Conference on Management, Business and Economics* (November 2015) 13–20–19.
31 Van Duyne Critical Handbook of Money Laundering1; Gubbay 1998 MONEY LAUNDERINGC277–278; Goredema Money Laundering in East and Southern Africa.
32 Eastern and Southern Africa Anti-Money Laundering Group August 2007 www.esaa Money Launderingg.org/reports/Zimbabwe_detailed_report.pdf (Accessed 20 August 2022).
33 Reserve Bank of Zimbabwe Guidelines for retail payment and systems www.rbz.co.zw/documents/nps/payment-systems-guidelines-august-2017.pdf (Accessed 15 August 2022).
34 Transparency International 2021 Corruption Perceptions Index: Press Release www.tizim.org/2022/02/01/2021-corruption-perceptions-index-press-release/ (Accessed 3 September 2022.
35 Zimbabwe The Social and Economic Challenges are huge 21 July 2016 www.boell.de/en/2016/07/21/zimbabwe-socio-economic-challenges-are-huge (Accessed 10 August 2022).
36 Reserve Bank of Zimbabwe, Masiyandima N, Ngundu T, Kupeta K, Moyo P, S, Ngwenya S Optimal Inflation for Zimbabwe. www.rbz.co.zw/documents/working_papers/optimal-inflation-for-zimbabwe-research-paper--2.pdf (Accessed 20 July 2022)

37 Rosie Dimano Zimbabwe from breadbasket to basketcase 24 June 2010 www.thestar.com/news/world/2010/07/24/zimbabwe_from_breadbasket_to_basket_case.htMoney Laundering (Accessed 20 August 2022).
38 Mazarura Onisimo L, Exploring the dynamics of informal foreign currency trading: the case of Harare's black market traders. https://researchspace.ukzn.ac.za/xMoney Launderingui/handle/10413/912 (Accessed 20 July 2022)
39 Farai Shawn Matiashe Winning the battle but losing the war. Zimbabwe is cracking down on illegal money changers but that is not stopping its runaway inflation Wednesday, 20 October 2021 10:07 www.theafricareport.com/137137/zimbabwe-is-cracking-down-on-illegal-money-changers-but-that-is-not-stopping-its-runaway-inflation/ (Accessed 25 August 2022).
40 Shambare M An appraisal of the Anti-Money Laundering Regime in Zimbabwe https://etd.uwc.ac.za/handle/11394/8986 (Accessed 20 August 2022).
41 The Guardian Dirty dollars: how tattered US notes became the latest street hustle in Zimbabwe www.theguardian.com/global-development/2021/nov/17/dirty-dollars-how-tattered-us-notes-became-the-latest-street-hustle-in-zimbabwe (accessed 8 July 2022).
42 Prosper Simbarashe Maguchu Challenges of Money Laundering for sovereign states that use the US dollar Public International Law. www.emerald.com/insight/content/doi/10.1108/JMoneyLaundering-06-2021-0056/full/htMoney Laundering (Accessed 17 July 2022).
43 Prosper Simbarashe Maguchu Challenges of Money Laundering for sovereign states that use the US dollar Public International Law. www.emerald.com/insight/content/doi/10.1108/JMoneyLaunderingC-06-2021-0056/full/htMoney Laundering (Accessed 17 July 2022).
44 Chitimira H M Ncube Towards Ingenious Technology and the Robust Enforcement of Financial Markets Laws to Curb Money Laundering in Zimbabwe www.scielo.org.za/scielo.php?script=sci_arttext&pid=S1727-37812021000100034 (Accessed 10 July 2022).
45 Shambare Jane An Appraisal of the Anti-Money Laundering Regime in Zimbabwe University of Western Cape https://etd.uwc.ac.za/bitstream/handle/11394/8986/shambare_m_law_2021.pdf?sequence=3&isAllowed=y (Accessed 10 August 2022).
46 Eastern and Southern African Anti-Money Laundering Group (2007) "Mutual Evaluation/Detailed Assessment Report: Anti-Money laundering and Combating the Financing of Terrorism" Republic of Zimbabwe, https://esaaMoney Launderingg.org/reports/Zimbabwe_detailed_report.pdf (Accessed 28 June 2022).
47 Goredema C (2001) "Beyond Declarations of Intent" African Security Studies 10 (3) 80.
48 Shambare M An appraisal of the Anti-Money Laundering Regime in Zimbabwe https://etd.uwc.ac.za/handle/11394/8986 (Accessed 20 August 2022).
49 Money Laundering and Proceeds of Crime Act (Amendment Act No. 12) of 2018.
50 Maguchu P (2018) "Revisiting Money-Laundering Legislation in Zimbabwe and the Role of International Organisations' African Security Review 1–13 at 4. http://etd.uwc.ac.za (Accessed 3 July 2022)
51 Money Laundering and Proceeds of Crime Act (Amendment No.1) [Chapter 9:24] of 2019.
52 Jane Shambare Research Paper Submitted in Partial Fulfilment of the Requirements for the MPHIL Degree 2021 https://etd.uwc.ac.za/bitstream/handle/11394/8986/shambare_m_law_2021.pdf?sequence=3&isAllowed=y (Accessed 24 August 2022).
53 Money Laundering and Proceeds of Crime Act (Amendment No. 1) [Chapter 9:24] of 2019.
54 Financial Intelligence Unit Republic of Zimbabwe (2019) "A Money Laundering/CFT Framework", available at www.fiu.co.zw/aMoney Launderingcft-framework/ (Accessed 7 July 2022).
55 Bank Use Promotion and Suppression Act [Chapter 24:24] of 2004.

56 Trafficking in Persons Act [Chapter 9: 25] of 2014.
57 Criminal Matters (Mutual Legal Assistance) Act [Chapter 9: 06] of 1990.
58 Criminal Law (Codification and Reform) Act, Chapter 9:23.
59 Eastern and Southern African Anti-Money Laundering Group (2007) "Mutual Evaluation/Detailed Assessment Report: Anti- Money laundering and Combating the Financing of Terrorism" Republic of Zimbabwe https://esaaMoneyLaunderingg.org/reports/Zimbabwe_detailed_report.pdf (Accessed 28 June 2022).
60 Financial Intelligence Unit Reserve Bank of Zimbabwe www.fiu.co.zw/home/functions/ (Accessed 20 July 2022).
61 Reserve Bank of Zimbabwe Guidance to Financial Institutions and Designated Non-Financial Businesses and Professions on the Risk Based Approach to Implementation of Anti Money Laundering and Combating Financing of Terrorism Obligations www.fiu.co.zw/wp-content/uploads/2021/06/AMONEY LAUNDERINGCFT-Guidance-for-Financial-Institutions-2021.pdf Accessed 20 August 2022.
62 FIU Republic of Zimbabwe (2019) "AMONEY LAUNDERING/CFT Framework" www.fiu.co.zw/aMoney Launderingcft-framework/ (visited 29 July 2022).
63 MONEY LAUNDERINGPCA (2019) sec 12 A.
64 Criminal Law (Codification and Reform) Act, s. 174.
65 Criminal Law (Codification and Reform) Act, s. 174
66 Article 6 (1) UNCAC (2003). http://etd.uwc.ac.za/.
67 Charity Matumbi (nd) Combating Corruption through effective criminal justice practices international cooperation and engagement of the civil society: The Zimbabwean Perspective, available at www.unafei.or.jp/publications/pdf/RS_No107/No107_32_IP_Zimbabwe.pdf (Accessed 3 September 2022).
68 The Zimbabwean 17 May 2012; www.thezimbabwean.co.uk/news/zimbabwe/58309/news-roundup.html (Accessed 22 September 2022).
69 Transparency International Zimbabwe (2013) Enforcement of Anti-Corruption Laws Zimbabwe UNCAC Civil Society Review, available at https://uncaccoalition.org/files/cso-review-reports/year2-zimbabwe-report.pdf (Accessed 2 September 2022).
70 Allen Choruma (nd) Corruption Stalls Zimbabwean Economic Agenda, available at http://iffoadatabase.trustafrica.org/iff/Corruption%20stalls%20Zimbabwe%E2%80%99s%20economic%20agenda%20_%20The%20Financial%20Gazette.pdf (Accessed 2 September 2022).
71 Allen Choruma (nd) Corruption Stalls Zimbabwean Economic Agenda, available at http://iffoadatabase.trustafrica.org/iff/Corruption%20stalls%20Zimbabwe%E2%80%99s%20economic%20agenda%20_%20The%20Financial%20Gazette.pdf (Accessed 2 September 2022).
72 Taruvinga M (15 May 2020) "NetOne boss, board members arrested by ZACC" New Zimbabwe News www.newzimbabwe.com/netone-boss-board-members-arrested-by-zacc (visited 25 May 2022).
73 Eastern and Southern African Anti-Money Laundering Group (2007) "Mutual Evaluation/Detailed Assessment Report: Anti- Money laundering and Combating the Financing of Terrorism" Republic of Zimbabwe, available at: https://esaamlg.org/reports/Zimbabwe_detailed_report.pdf (Accessed 28 June 2022).
74 The Sunday Mail Special Anti-Corruption Unit begins work on 8 July 2018 www.sundaymail.co.zw/special-anti-corruption-unit-begins-work (Accessed 10 August 2022).
75 Zimbabwe " Mnangagwa's Special Anti-Corruption Unit Illegal", 2 November 2020, available at https://allafrica.com/stories/202011021020.html (Accessed 2 September 2022).
76 Zim Morning Post (October 30, 2020) TIZ slams special anti-corruption unit, available at www.zimmorningpost.com/tiz-slams-special-anti-corruption-unit/ (Accessed 2 September 2022
77 The Republic of Zimbabwe National Anti-Money Laundering and Combating Financing of Terrorism Strategic Plan 2020–2025 Contributing to Zimbabwe's economic growth by achieving high-level effectiveness in combating AML/CFT www.fiu.co.zw/

wp-content/uploads/2017/07/Zimbabwe-AMONEYLAUNDERING.CFT-Strategic-Plan-for-2015-2020.pdf (Accessed 20 August 2022).

78 MLPCA (2019), s. 12 C.

79 Law Society of Zimbabwe (2019) "About Us" http://lawsociety.org.zw/AboutUs (Accessed 17 July 2022).

80 Trautman L J (2017) "Following the money: Lesson learnt from Panama papers" Penn State Law Review 121(3): 808–873 at 830.

81 Transparency International (2015) "Incentivizing Integrity in Banks" Working Paper 2: 1–9 at 5.

82 Shambare M An appraisal of the Anti-Money Laundering Regime in Zimbabwe https://etd.uwc.ac.za/handle/11394/8986 (Accessed 20 August 2022).

83 Shambare M An appraisal of the Anti-Money Laundering Regime in Zimbabwe https://etd.uwc.ac.za/handle/11394/8986 (Accessed 20 August 2022).

84 Zimbabwe Risk and Compliance Report May 2017 http://knowyourcountry.info/files/zimbabweaMoney Launderingreportaug 14_2.pdf (Accessed 20 August 2022).

85 Navin Beekarry The International Anti-Money Laundering and Combating the Financing of Terrorism Regulatory Strategy: A Critical Analysis of Compliance Determinants in International Law www.law.gwu.edu/sites/g/files/zaxdzs2351/f/downloads/BeekarryInternationalLaw.pdf (Accessed 15 August 2022).

86 International Monetary Fund Anti Money Combating the Financing of Terrorism (AMONEY LAUNDERING/CFT) www.imf.org/external/np/leg/aMoneyLaundering cft/eng/aMoney Laundering4.htm (Accessed 25 August 2022).

87 Simpson M (2010) "International Initiatives" in Smith & Srivastava (eds) International Guide to Money Laundering Law and Practice Bloomsbury Publishing, USA at 193.

88 Article 3 Vienna Convention (1988).

89 Mugarura N (2012) "The Global Anti-Money Laundering Regulatory Landscape in Less Developed Countries" Surrey: Ashgate at 65.

90 Article 5 (3) Vienna Convention (1988).

91 Article 1 Palermo Convention (2000).

92 Article 5 Palermo Convention (2000).

93 Article 16–30 Palermo Convention (2000).

94 Preamble UNCAC (2003).

95 Article 1 UNCAC (2003).

96 Article 14 (1) (a) UNCAC (2003)

97 Article 14 (4) (5) (f) UNCAC (2003).

98 Article 31 (1) UNCAC (2003).

99 Muller W H Kalin C H & Goldsworth J G (2007) "Anti-Money Laundering: International Law and Practice" West Sussex: John Wiley & Sons Ltd.at 6.

100 Mugarura, N. (2011). The institutional framework against money laundering and its underlying predicate crimes. *Journal of Financial Regulation and Compliance*, 19(2), 174–194.

101 United Nations Charter Chapter VII binds member states to Anti-Money Laundering conventions that complement FATF Recommendations.

102 Stessens G (2008) "Money Laundering: A New International Law Model" Cambridge: Cambridge University Press at 146. FATF Recommendation 10. at 146.

103 The Elements of an Effective Anti-Money Laundering CFT Framework www.unodc.org/documents/southeastasiaandpacific/2009/02/TOCAMONEYLAUNDERINGO/08-CHAPTER_III.pdf Accessed 20 August 2022.

104 Anti-Money Laundering Global Anti-Money Laundering Regulatory Issuance (B) No 1 Series of 2018 Anti Money Laundering/Counter Terrorism Financing Guidelines.

105 Stessens G (2008) "Money Laundering: A New International Law Model" Cambridge: Cambridge University Press at 146.

106 The Elements of an Effective AML CFT Framework www.unodc.org/documents/southeastasiaandpacific/2009/02/TOCAMONEY LAUNDERINGO/08-CHAPTER_III.pdf (Accessed 20 August 2022)

107 The Elements of an Effective AMONEY LAUNDERING CFT Framework www.unodc.org/documents/southeastasiaandpacific/2009/02/GO/08-CHAPTER_III.pdf (Accessed 20 August 2022)
108 Asset Recovery Inter-Agency Network South Southern Africa Taking the Proceeds from Crime the Story of Arinsa. www.unodc.org/documents/southernafrica/The_story_of_ARINSA.pdf (Accessed 20 August 2022)
109 Preamble AU Convention (2003).
110 Article 6 AU Convention (2003)
111 S vs Chikukwa HH 813/16.
112 Dzomira S (2014) "Electronic Fraud (cyber fraud) Risk in the Banking Industry, Zimbabwe" Risk, Governance & Control: Financial Markets and Institutions 4(1): 19. http://etd.uwc.ac.za (Accessed 7 July 2022)
113 Fundira B "Money Laundering in Zimbabwe, 2004 to 2006" at 70 in Goredema C (ed) *Confronting the Proceeds of Crime in Southern Africa: An Introspection* (ISS Pretoria 2007) 47–72.
114 Simwayi M & Haseed M (2011) "The Role of Financial Intelligence Units in Combating Money Laundering: A comparative analysis of Zambia, Zimbabwe and Malawi" Journal of Money Laundering Control 15(1): 122.
115 Zimbabwe Broadcasting Cooperation (25 September 2019) "SECZ move to curb money laundering", www.zbc.co.zw/secz-moves-to-curb-money-laundering/ (Accessed July 2022).
116 Eastern and Southern African Anti-Money Laundering Group (2007) "Mutual Evaluation/Detailed Assessment Report: Anti- Money laundering and Combating the Financing of Terrorism" Republic of Zimbabwe, available at: https://esaamlg.org/reports/Zimbabwe_detailed_report.pdf (Accessed 28 June 2022).
117 Maguchu (2018) http://etd.uwc.ac.za (Accessed 7 July 2022)
118 Shambare M An appraisal of the Anti-Money Laundering Regime in Zimbabwe. Available at: https://etd.uwc.ac.za/handle/11394/8986 (Accessed 20 August 2022).
119 Maguchu (2018) at 7. http://etd.uwc.ac.za (Accessed 7 July 2022)
120 Nance M T (2018) "The regime that FATF built: An introduction to the Financial Action Task Force" Crime Law Society Change 69: 109–129 at 123. http://etd.uwc.ac.za (Accessed 23 August 2022).
121 S v Tapfuma HH 565–19
122 Reserve Bank of Zimbabwe Monetary Policy statements from 2018 to 2020 www.rbz.co.zw/index.php/monetary-policy (Accessed 7 July 2022).
123 Chitimira H M Ncube Towards Ingenious Technology and the Robust Enforcement of Financial Markets Laws to Curb Money Laundering in Zimbabwe www.scielo.org.za/scielo.php?script=sci_arttext&pid=S1727-37812021000100034(Accessed 10 July 2022)

21 Whistleblowers

The Role of Citizens in Fighting Corruption

*Prince Bright Majiga**

Introduction

Corruption has been proven to undermine confidence in public institutions, weaken management of government budgets, and limit the development of small- and medium-sized enterprises.[1] There is little doubt that successfully fighting corruption can lead to better fiscal performance. Corruption is a notoriously secretive activity, and it is usually only those engaged in corrupt deals or those who work with them who are aware of it. Mostly, insiders are among the few people who can report cases of corruption (past or ongoing) and identify the risk of future wrongdoing. As a matter of fact, detection of corruption is a pre-condition to initiate related investigations and prosecution. By bringing corrupt practices to bear, whistleblowers play a critical part in turning what is generally agreed to be a vicious cycle into one that is virtuous in nature.

Why Whistleblowing Is Instrumental to Combating Corruption

Research has shown that whistleblowing is one of the most effective ways to detect fraud and wrongdoings in any country and facilitate measures to minimise or prevent further losses. Data show that occurrences of fraud in companies often come to light thanks to whistleblowers who have detected internal problems more frequently than any other actor, including regulators, auditors, and the media.[2] It has also been argued that whistleblowing promotes accountability by allowing an individual to disclose information on misconduct while at the same time protecting the individual from possible reprisals.[3]

Yet the importance of whistleblowing in the detection and prevention of wrongdoing is still generally undervalued. This has led to fewer efforts by Civil Society Organisations (CSOs) and other stakeholders to propagate its use. All the same, whistleblowing remains an inexpensive risk management tool with benefits for emerging democracies with less established oversight mechanisms. Whistleblowing is also a tool which can be employed to sound the alarm at early stages, potentially even before any damage has been done.

Studies on the use of whistleblowing to combat corruption and fraud have focused on developed countries and not on African and other developing countries.[4]

DOI: 10.4324/9781003326649-25

The research focused specifically on the continental level of whistleblower activity and potential protection is underdeveloped, and studies in this field are scanty.[5] Not only is the dearth of literature problematic, but the infrequent use of whistleblowing due to fear of reprisals, lack of feeding, or general ignorance as an attempt to enhance governance is worrisome.

The Nature of Whistleblowing

There are no generally agreed definitions of whistleblowing. The term whistleblowing could be seen as an act of dissent or defined more precisely as a disclosure of significant malicious or corrupt conduct by concerned citizens with an intention to bring into light an issue of public interest.[6] Whistleblowing is also seen as the disclosure of wrongdoing(s) that needs to be dealt with to protect the public interest.[7] Other authorities have described whistleblowing as the discovery by an individual, usually an employee in a public institution or private institution made to the public of illegality, corruption, mismanagement, or other wrongdoings.[8]

What is important is to note that two perspectives seem to persist in the conversation around whistleblowing. The first views whistleblowing as an act of justice, serving or intending to right a wrong, such as the case of former WorldCom's Cynthia Cooper.[9] It has also been suggested that the perceived transparency gained from whistleblowing and the contention that whistleblowing is in the public interest provide practical and moral legitimacy.[10]

To that end, whistleblowers are not passive participants, and they are active participants in quest of both economic and social justice. Intending to right a wrong, the potential whistleblower may set out to correct malpractice or malfeasance. This belief would motivate a potential whistleblower to do what s/he believes is right. On the contrary, reasonably and interestingly, the second view considers whistleblowing as a breach, an unprofessional act, or a form of betrayal.[11] In this regard, whistleblowers are a target of retaliation and tend to face considerable backlash from friends and foes. These two perspectives are valid to various extents and apply to various scenarios on the African continent. They can be separated in their epistemological nature but may not be divorced in their application as regards the act itself.

Whistleblowing has also been discussed from the perspective of civil disobedience as two forms of dissent.[12] Considering the weak and at times failed efforts in combating corruption in Africa, whistleblowing is an attractive practice of resort, especially by those who feel duty-bound to expose corruption but are not sure of whether the perpetrators will be prosecuted. For whistleblowing to occur three elements are required. These are as follows: first, there must be a wrongdoer who commits the alleged wrongdoing; second, an individual who observes the wrongdoing, defines it as such, and reports it; and third, there must be a recipient (an individual or platform) of the alleged wrongdoing report.[13]

Over time, whistleblowing as a phenomenon has been a debatable and delicate issue because it involves revealing or exposing unethical secrets that a given individual, organisation, government institution, and company is involved in and found wanting. There are debates on whether lawyers and other practitioners should report illegal transactions by their clients while not violating the concept of privileged information.

Ordinarily, whistleblowing is a dominant anti-corruption instrument with the objective of supporting accountability by disclosing information about misconduct concerning fraud and corruption and also safeguarding the whistleblower against retaliation and sanctions of all kinds. This is supported by the argument that effective whistleblowing requires basically an initial report, which is an achievement and solid perseverance in reporting.[14] This extends to the provision of financial rewards and protection for whistleblowers. However, this does not take into consideration that the selfish quest for fame and vengeance can also influence individuals to engage in whistleblowing.

Whistleblowing has been instrumental in the fight against corruption and other unlawful conduct in both the private and public arena as it promotes a culture of openness and transparency. It is fundamentally linked to ensuring transparency and political accountability in relation to the use and management of public and private resources and property. Thus, the role of civil society organisations and the youth in activism cannot be overemphasised. It has promoted responsible and accountable use of public resources and property.[15]

Whistleblowing as a Norm, Not an Exception

The benefits of whistleblowing are many, and yet it appears that the phenomenon itself has not been normalised in many African states. The fact that whistleblowing is the exception and not the norm has severely hampered efforts to combat corruption in Africa. The reality that whistleblowing is still on the peripherals means that those who partake in it or advocate for it remain in danger of being ostracised.

Corruption has greatly undermined citizens' trust and confidence in social and political institutions in Africa. To that end, the need for transparency is non-negotiable. Accountable government cannot be achieved without transparency, and governments that allow corruption to take root and flourish undermine their own legitimacy. While transparency holds the key to this societal malaise, transparency depends on the critical element of access to information. The law in most democratic countries on the continent provides for the right of a citizen to access information created and maintained by their government and governmental institutions.[16] Thus, many developing and developed countries have adopted the Right to Information laws ostensibly to expose and prevent corruption, enhance citizens' participation in public affairs, and protect human rights.[17]

Unfortunately, the passage of the right to access to information (RTI) laws in Africa has shown little impact on democratic governance in Africa. More importantly, most RTI laws in Africa, when interrogated, appear to have a lot of bottlenecks that still make public information difficult to access. Whistleblowing is thus likely to remain an exception rather than a norm.

The Employment of Technology in Whistleblowing

Having considered some advantages of whistleblowing, it is important to look into how it can be harnessed. It is important that whistleblowing be employed in an appropriate manner considering the issues associated with moral and lawful ways of whistleblowing, coupled with the government's unwillingness to enact or operationalise RTI laws on the continent and the general and yet unjustified apprehension towards whistleblowing. To that end, the employment of whistleblowing needs to be done in consideration of ethics, morality, and laws and by taking advantage of potential benefits that information communication and technology (ICTs) such as social media and e-governance offer. This section focuses on the employment of ICTs in whistleblowing.

General Use of Technology Combat Corruption

There have been attempts to introduce ICT-enabled opportunities to express voice and the degree to which public service providers respond to expressions of citizens' voices.[18] ICT interventions are broadly categorised into two types of interventions. The first type involves transactional reforms that aim to control and automate government processes, restrict the discretion of officials, and enhance the detection of corruption. The second type involves transparency reforms that focus on opening up the state and enhancing the flow of information between government and citizens, thus increasing the visibility of that state and its agents' actions.[19]

As a result of the seemingly endless potential of ICTs to fight corruption, new technologies have been used to: facilitate the reporting of corruption; provide access to official information; monitor the efficiency and integrity of social services and of a country's political life; and to make financial information more transparent. There are also examples of technology being used to support campaigning efforts, and over the last decade, governments have launched an increasing number of e-government initiatives to enhance the efficiency and transparency of public administration and improve interaction with citizens.[20]

However, it has been noted that new ICTs tend to favour those already in power and elites.[21] Literature suggests that social media has a lot of potential to be used for governance purposes, but that this is not utilised in most contexts. Many governments are using e-government strategies and disseminating information through online channels but not soliciting citizen feedback. Where there are two-way channels, it is very unclear whether citizen feedback is acted upon.[22] Lack of feedback mechanisms is akin to making noise in a crowded ballroom and means that the effectiveness of this particular medium is difficult to assess and, if possible, improve.

Social Media/Online Activism

Similar to offline civic participation, types of online civic participation can be situated in the informal–formal differentiation or along a spectrum ranging from expressive to collective participation. Online activism has been categorised and being defined as a politically motivated movement relying on the Internet based on the direction of initiatives.[23] That is, whether one sends out information or receives it, calls for action or is called upon, or initiates an action or reacts to one. The three areas that online activism focuses on are firstly, awareness/advocacy; secondly, organisation/mobilisation; thirdly, action/reaction.

Awareness and Advocacy

Online civic participation could be either technology-enhanced or technology-based. Technology-enhanced civic participation refers to civic activities on the Internet and social media that enhance traditional participation such as by serving as an additional communication channel or by coordinating action more efficiently for mobilisation purposes.[24] This category also includes electronic versions of traditional forms of offline participation for which there is a clear offline counterpart such as online voting, online petition signing, and e-mailing a government official as opposed to sending a letter) and donating money online as opposed to cash transactions. On the other hand, technology-based civic participation refers to civic activities on the Internet and social media that are only possible online.[25]

The Internet, as the latest form of alternative media, offers activists a fast, easy, malleable and cheap way to create and spread their message without interference from the gatekeepers of mainstream media.[26] Globalisation, or the transnational spread of economic, technological, and cultural forces, is intrinsically connected to the rise of the Internet and new communication technologies.[27] Just as globalisation deterritorialises space and extends boundaries beyond geographic and political lines, technology allows activists to communicate with and mobilise disparate populations simultaneously, unencumbered by geographic or temporal restraints.[28]

Organisation and Mobilisation

Social media have a great potential for enabling the quick mobilisation of many participants for a particular cause, as demonstrated by the role it played in social movements such as *Ushahidi* in Kenya and Nigeria.[29] This is made possible by the key benefits social media brings in terms of collaboration, participation, empowerment, and time. As a collaborative and participatory media, it allows users to connect and form communities to socialise, share information, or achieve a common goal or interest. Equipped with the ability to publish or disseminate information in real time at low cost, this opens new avenues and doors for alternatives to traditional media, as can be seen through popular social media applications and platforms such as Wikileaks[30] and ipaidabribe, which is an Indian corruption reporting platform created in 2009.[31] The success of platforms such as IPaidABribe.com programmes has demonstrated the enormous potential of such methods. However, its replication and success on the African continent remains to be seen.

Action and Reaction

The idea behind these applications and platforms is straightforward, involving three main mechanisms through which these tools are expected to assist in the fight against corruption. First, providing easy access to an instantaneous anonymous and straightforward reporting tool empowers citizens to complain safely, loudly, and visibly when corrupt officials and public service providers abuse their positions of entrusted power to extort bribes from citizens.[32] Through public shaming, these applications seek to deter corruption. Second, crowd-reporting helps break the silence around the daily occurrence of corruption. That is, most citizens end up realising that other citizens are also facing similar or related corruption challenges. The realisation that corruption is systemic and not limited to individual experience is important in influencing a call to action. This greatly reduces the general error of attribution which is the tendency to see problems not in their systemic nature but rather from an individual or self-centred fashion. Third, corruption-reporting apps can also help promote collective action.[33]

In sum, social media and ICTs can also be used for social mobilisation and citizen empowerment, with some evidence of internet and Facebook penetration having a sizable and negative impact on corruption.[34] Facebook is the most visited website among all of Africa's Internet users, who make up 10 per cent of the continent's population. However, this implies that social media usage is restricted to elites.[35] Limited internet access means these channels are currently out of reach of the poorest and most marginalised. This has a bearing on the sensitisation and mobilisation of large portions of the population.

In short, by removing the cover of secrecy, empowering victims of corruption to speak up and showing that a sizeable sector of the population does not approve of or tolerate these practices, reporting apps make it harder for corrupt public officials and service providers to solicit or receive bribes.[36] All the same, this does not imply that social media-enabled platforms are destined for success. It must always be borne in mind that technology is just but a tool, a means and its employment does not offer any guarantee of success.

Use of E-Government

E-governance is gaining popularity as a tool for improved public service delivery and reduced corruption in developing countries. Case studies and statistical analyses indicate that ICTs can help address corruption by automating and streamlining government processes, restricting the discretion of officials and the need for citizen interaction with gatekeepers for key services, improving monitoring of public officials and by enhancing the effectiveness of internal and managerial control over corrupt behaviours. Thus, e-government may possibly eliminate many opportunities for corruption.[37]

ICT-based methods of communication, and especially new forms of social media, offer parliaments the opportunity to communicate with citizens and engage them in the political process more effectively. This is important in the context of declining levels of trust in parliaments where new media is often identified as a tool to address poor engagement with politics. However, the use of ICT poses significant challenges to parliaments, many of which do not readily adopt new technology. As a result, most parliaments have acquired some of the forms and elements of ICT and the new social media.[38] The use of social media by parliaments is more tentative. This may reflect the lack of internet penetration in low-income countries, where radio is more likely to reach citizens.

Despite these high expectations and massive investments in e-government, evidence of impact is mixed and limited and there is a high rate of failure of e-government projects, due to contextual factors as well as the type of the ICT interventions. It thus follows that e-government is not a silver bullet for addressing corruption. In fact, despite massive investment in information technology in recent years in many countries, various estimates indicate that many e-government projects fail. About 30 per cent of these projects are total failures, with the project abandoned before completion and fewer than 20 per cent considered as successes.[39]

Although whistleblowing is not a panacea for corruption and corporate malfeasance, it has proven highly effective as a last line of defence against behaviour that is both economically harmful and politically destabilising.[40] To that end, several contextual factors are important to consider for effectively addressing corruption through e-governance, including technology access and literacy, with the need to provide training to enable broad participation in e-government services, technology penetration, technology capabilities, and access to government agencies, as well as social and technology readiness of citizens. Beyond the technology itself, legal frameworks, organisational processes, leadership, and campaign strategies may all be necessary complements of digital tools in order to secure effective change.

Finally, it must be noted that technology does not replace a solid, evidence-based anti-corruption strategy. If anything, technology simply expands the reach of previously tested tactics by adding new tools to the mix. The introduction of e-governance and ICT may also not be equally effective on all types of corruption. Such approaches can be effective in addressing petty corruption involving street-level bureaucrats but less so in dealing with grand corruption involving higher-level officials.[41] It is important that groups or organisations and individuals, who design initiatives, should always bear in mind alternative methods to promote and enhance social accountability.

Corruption Fights Back!

The secretive nature of corruption, the complicity of powerful elites and deep-seated cultural perceptions about corruption have led to a situation whereby measures taken to fight against the problem are not only treated with contempt or disregarded but also actively and systemically resisted. Fighting corruption in many parts of the world, especially developing countries, is still risky. Institutions are weak while those who engage in corruption are often powerful political and economic elites able to buy or command inaction. Consequently, whistleblowing encounters challenges.

An investigation into whistleblowing listed four major institutional obstacles to effective whistleblowing: first, whistleblowing regulatory institutions are by design understaffed and do not have the required resources to adequately process reported cases. Secondly, regulators responsible for processing whistleblowing cases also by design lack significant experience. Thirdly, regulators are usually under deliberate pressure from their appointing authorities and end up ignoring whistleblowing cases that are connected to those in echelons of power; and fourthly, whistleblowers face significant risks enough to deter them from engaging in the act.[42]

Risks to Whistleblowers

The most common risks whistleblower face in the Middle East and North Africa (MENA) appear to be threats to income, life and personal safety.[43] In Morocco, for example, physical assaults on whistleblowers have been reported, while several journalists have reportedly been killed for exposing corruption in the region.[44] In Egypt and Tunisia, the risk of physical assault is also considered to be acute.[45]

Examples abound. On 17 January 2015, a Kenyan blogger Abraham Mutai was arrested and detained for close to 24 hours before being released. The arrest was closely followed by the temporary suspension of Muta's blogs and Twitter account. Mr Mutai had published information on his online platforms, with a plethora of credible documentary evidence, of alleged corruption and fraud in a public agency and some county governments. In April 2022, a Malawian investigative journalist named Gregory Gondwe was reportedly arrested for his role in exposing corruption through his *Platform for Investigative Journalism* website.[46] The arrest of Gondwe came after Malawi's Attorney General announced that he would act against those who leaked a document meant for the country's Anti-Corruption Bureau. Whistleblowers still live in fear in South Africa, despite that country's relatively advanced whistleblower protection laws, with most individuals still facing serious threats and persecution, some of them losing their jobs in some way, many suffering personal threats and violence, and more. In fact, two central figures in a major corruption scandal are to this day.[47]

This is inconsistent with the oft-stated commitment to the fight against corruption and crime generally. It is worth noting that for almost every investigation or prosecution that is carried out, there is inevitably a whistleblower involved. However, what is glaringly clear is that in most African states, blowing the whistle carries a high personal risk – particularly when there is little legal protection against dismissal, humiliation, or even physical abuse.

Whistleblowing is one of the most effective ways of detecting fraud and wrongdoing and facilitating measures to minimise or prevent further losses. One would therefore expect the relevant authorities to act on the information provided by whistleblowers by conducting further investigations on the alleged corruption incidents rather than oppress whistleblowers. Individuals who come forward to disclose wrongdoing should be embraced and protected, not harassed and ostracised. It is as surprising as it is disturbing that a whistleblower rather than being embraced by the official system should be harassed and vilified for playing a most critical role in calling attention to wrongdoing.

Lack of Whistleblower Protection Legislation

Whistleblower protection legislation is only the first piece of the puzzle, but even in that regard, the situation on the ground is disturbing. In fact, only eight of 54 African countries have passed these laws, and even those are weak. In practice, there is a need for comprehensive protection for whistleblowers and measures to enhance anonymity through secure means of reporting and how to link up with the media so as to relay the information to the public.[48]

Above and beyond what is available on the ground, and aside from politicians' rhetoric, there is little political will to offer whistleblowers more protection. This contrasts with what most political parties state in their manifestos when they are seeking power. It thus comes as no surprise that there is little distinction between "informants," "disgruntled workers," "trouble makers," "enemies of the state," and "whistle blowers." All the same, lack of awareness or political support for whistleblowing measures should not deter civil society from promoting whistleblowing where possible. Nevertheless, whistleblowers are often perceived as disloyal rather than as champions of the public interest. In many countries, they are viewed as untrustworthy and sometimes even as spies or traitors.[49] This makes them possible targets by elites whose feathers are ruffled following damaging disclosures.

As can be seen earlier, the muzzling of whistleblowers is an active, hard power measure that corrupt authorities use to silence critics. On the other hand, deliberate neglect or delays to enact laws that encourage and promote whistleblowers are passive measures but all the same powerful and systemic ways that those who engage or benefit from corruption use to weaken the fight against corruption. While a distinction may be made in terms of the nature of these measures, they usually co-exist and are applied at the earliest or timely convenience by powerful elites.

Whither Whistleblowing?

While whistleblowing is not a panacea for ending corruption, its role in the fight cannot be overemphasised, and its criticality cannot be downplayed. Despite the perils that the act poses to its partakers and the sometimes-lackadaisical attitude by states to promote whistleblowing, available documentation and results from practice show that whistleblowing is too important to be ignored. This section discusses some measures that can be adopted to enhance whistleblowing. These measures are in the form of possible changes in laws, policy and practice by various stakeholders including governments, Civil Society Organisations (CSOs) and the citizenry. In presenting these recommendations, it must be noted that they are not blanket in nature and that their customisation to particular contexts in different states would be more practical.

Protection Regime for Whistleblowers

It is important that public employees and those outside the traditional employee–employer relationship such as consultants, temporary workers, and trainees should be protected from reprisal for honestly reporting concerns. More importantly, those who attempt to report or corroborate reports must be protected as well. This extends to all individuals that are closely related to whistleblowers such as family members. Whistleblowers should be protected against any damages suffered because of their disclosure. At the societal level, whistleblowers should be professionally recognised for their acts in preventing harm to society. This extends to financial rewards, with due diligence applied in taking different legal and national contexts into account.

Post-reporting Follow-Up

Another promising strategy can be to move away from a simple reporting mechanism to an accountability and citizen–government conversation tool that ensures clear processes of communication and post-reporting follow-up at the local and regional levels. While this is equally relevant at the national level, it has been noted that it has the potential to be a significant deterrent at the local level due to generating a lack of good-faith resolution.[50] In fact, local authorities could even help national-level protection if they give clear reasons justifying why a report may not be investigated, hence providing room for resolving any possible misconduct.

Make Data Available and More Relevant

There is always a need to treat data received through corruption-reporting platforms. These platforms do not necessarily depict an objective picture of corruption in that particular community. This is attributed to that most online applications are mostly used by specific sectors of the population and may not be within reach of people who are greatly subjected to the effects of corruption. Reaching a significant number of users can be difficult.[51] It is difficult to ascertain whether there is an increase in a number of users or simply being used by citizens who are already engaged in civic issues given the anonymous nature of reports.[52] This presents a trade-off: when participants are anonymous, an initiative cannot systematically follow up with them to learn about the impact of participation while, at the same time, being able to report anonymously is a key feature for many of these platforms.

Civic Education/Sensitisation

As noted earlier, whistleblowers may be perceived as traitors or betrayers to criminal enterprises. This may lead to their ostracisation and further discourage would-be whistleblowers. To change this perception, whistleblowing needs to be promoted as an effective tool for stopping corruption and serving the public interest. Governments should lend their support to public information campaigns as well as initiatives to promote whistleblowing that are carried out by professional groups, Ombudspersons, industry, media, trade unions, and other civil society organisations. Whistleblowers should be not only protected by public authorities but also honoured and actively supported.

Conclusion

This chapter examined the conceptual issues that surround the issue of whistle-blowing. In doing so, it has tackled the moral, ethical and legal intricacies associated with whistleblowing. Despite the advantages that whistleblowing offers, it still remains an exception rather than a norm in most African countries, with CSOs employing it sparingly. This has significantly affected the fight against corruption.

The chapter also identified several impediments to the employment of whistle-blowing. These challenges are mostly systemic. They relate to deliberate under-staffing of corruption fighting bodies, lack of experience amongst those tasked to investigate incidents of whistleblowing and little protection for whistleblowers. These arm-twisting manoeuvres by the political elite have made whistleblowing not only unattractive but also dangerous. Despite advances in technologies, low internet penetration among other flawed planning considerations make feedback, or at least perception of feedback, have meant that various stakeholders have not done much to harness the potential benefits of using ICTs in combating corruption.

The sceptre of corruption cannot be merely wished away. Similarly, whistleblowing, for all its potential benefits cannot be left to its own devices. There is a need for urgency by states, CSOs and the general citizenry to harness the power of whistle-blowing in attempts to fight corruption. While admitting that whistleblowing is not a panacea in preventing corruption on the continent, it is a step in the right direction.

Notes

* Captain, Malawi Defence Force and Researcher, National Defence College, Malawi.

1 Transparency International. The Impact of Corruption on Growth and Inequality, 15 March 2015, available at: www.transparency.org/files/content/corruptionqas/Impact_of_corruption_on_growth_and_inequality_2014.pdf.

2 KPMG, Profile of a Fraudster, Survey 2007, p. 26 (Zurich, Switzerland: KPMG, 2007) www.kpmg.co.uk/pubs/ProfileofaFraudsterSurvey(web).pdf. (Accessed 6 October 2022).

3 Samuel Kimeu, Adili, Whistleblowers Kenya needs them for the war against corruption to succeed Issue No 150

4 Adriana S. Cordis and Elizabeth M. Lambert, "Whistleblower laws and corporate fraud: Evidence from the United States," *Accounting Forum*, 41:4 (2017): 289–299, DOI: 10.1016/j.accfor.2017.10.003.

5 AS Rahaman, "Critical accounting research in Africa: whence and whither", Critical Perspectives on Accounting, 21:5(2010):420–427.

6 James Dungan, Adam Waytz and Liane Young, "The Psychology of Whistleblowing," *Current Opinion in Psychology*. (2015) 6.10.1016/j.copsyc.2015.07.005.

7 FO Oyebade, "Whistle-Blowing as a Panacea for Fighting corruption in Nigeria." Paper Presented at a Public Lecture Organized by Ibadan and District Society of the Institute of Chartered Accountants of Nigeria (ICAN), 2016.

8 Ogunkeye, "Whistle-Blowing as a Panacea for Fighting Corruption in Nigeria."

9 Dungan, Waytz, and Young, "The Psychology of Whistleblowing."

10 W Maroun and JF Solomon, "Whistle-blowing by External Auditors: Seeking legitimacy for the South African Audit Profession? *Accounting Forum*, 38 (2014):111–121.
11 P Alleyne, M Hudaib, and R Pike, "Towards a conceptual model of whistle-blowing intentions among external auditors", The British Accounting Review, Vol. 45 No. 1, (2013):10–23.
12 FA Elliston, "Civil disobedience and whistleblowing: a comparative appraisal of two forms of dissent", Journal of Business Ethics, Vol. 1 No. 1 (1982):23–28.
13 MP Miceli, and JP Near, "Individual and situational correlates of whistleblowing", *Personnel Psychology*, Vol. 41 No. 2 (1988): 267–281.
14 Taylor, E.Z. and Curtis, M.B. (2010), "An examination of the layers of workplace influences in ethical judgments: whistleblowing likelihood and perseverance in public accounting", Journal of Business Ethics, Vol. 93 No. 1, pp. 21–37.
15 See UNDP (2013) Enhancing Youth Political Participation Throughout the Electoral Cycle [online]. Available at www.undp.org/content/dam/undp/library/Democratic%20Governance/Electoral%20Systems%20and%20Processes/ENG_UN-Youth_Guide-LR.pdf (Accessed on 03 October 2022).
16 See, for example, section 37 of the Constitution of the Republic of Malawi, Malawi Government, The Constitution of the Republic of Malawi, Lilongwe, 2018. See also Access to Information Act 2016 (No. 13 of 2017), available at: https://malawilii.org/akn/mw/act/2017/13/eng%402017-02-16, Act No. of the Laws of Malawi.
17 Calland, Richard and Bentley, Kristina A., The Impact and Effectiveness of Transparency and Accountability Initiatives: Freedom of Information (July 2013). Development Policy Review, Vol. 31, pp. s69-s87, 2013, Available at SSRN: https://ssrn.com/abstract=2305479 or http://dx.doi.org/10.1111/dpr.12020
18 Peixoto, T and Fox, J When Does ICT-Enabled Citizen Voice Lead to Government Responsiveness? 2016 World Development Report Background Paper Digital Dividends
19 Davies, T., & Fumega, S. (2014). Mixed incentives: Adopting ICT innovations for transparency, accountability, and anti-corruption.
20 Wickberg, S. (2013). Technological innovations to identify and reduce corruption. Anti-Corruption Resource Centre. Available at: www.u4.no/publications/technological-innovations-to-identify-and-reduce-corruption (Accessed on 6 September 2022).
21 Peixoto, T and Fox, J When Does ICT-Enabled Citizen Voice Lead to Government Responsiveness? 2016 World Development Report Background Paper Digital Dividends
22 Browne, E. (2015). Social media and governance (GSDRC Helpdesk Research Report 1191). Birmingham, UK: GSDRC, University of Birmingham.
23 Vegh, S. (2003) Classifying Forms of Online Activism: The Case of Cyber protests against the World Bank. In Ayers, D. and Mccaughey, M. (Eds) CyberActivism: Online Activism in Theory and Practice. New York & London: Routledge.
24 Christensen, H. (2011) Political activities on the internet: Slactivism or political participation by other mean? First Monday. 16:2. [online] http://firstmonday.org/htbin/cgiwrap/bin/ojs/inde x.php/fm/article/view/3336/2767(accessed on 6 September 2022).
25 Christensen, H. (2011) Political activities on the internet: Slactivism or political participation by other mean? First Monday. 16:2. [online] http://firstmonday.org/htbin/cgiwrap/bin/ojs/inde x.php/fm/article/view/3336/2767(accessed on 6 September 2022).
26 Postmes, T., & Brunsting, S. (2002). Collective action in the age of the Internet: Mass communication and online mobilization. Social Science Computer Review, 20, 290–301.
27 Thussu, D. K. (2006). International communication: Continuity and change. London: Arnold.
28 Monica Chadha & Summer Harlow, The Writing Is on the Wall, or Is It? Exploring Indian Activists' Beliefs About Online Social Media's Potential for Social Change. International Journal of Communication 9(2015), 672–693
29 Ushahidi means "testimony" in Swahili. See www.ushahidi.com/; Juliana Rotich, Ushahidi: Empowering Citizens through Crowdsourcing and Digital Data Collection », Field

Actions Science Reports Special Issue 16 available at: http://journals.openedition.org/factsreports/4316 (accessed on 13 October 2022).

30 See www.wikileaks.org.

31 Bertot, J. C., Jaeger, P. T. and Grimes, J. M., 2010, Using ICTs to create a culture of transparency: E-government and social media as openness and anti-corruption tools for societies. Government Information Quarterly, 27(3), p. 264–271 https://doi.org/10.1016/j.giq.2010.03.001.

32 Zinnbauer, Dieter, The Vexing Issue of the Revolving Door (April 30, 2015). Edmond J. Safra Working Papers, No. 61, Available at SSRN: https://ssrn.com/abstract=2600633 or http://dx.doi.org/10.2139/ssrn.2600633

33 Zinnbauer, "The Vexing Issue of the Revolving Door."

34 Jha, Ch and Sarangi, S. (2014). Social Media, Internet and Corruption. SSRN Electronic Journal. http://ssrn.com/abstract=2391904.10.2139/ssrn.2391904.

35 Hollands, G. (2012). Putting participation at the heart of development//putting development at the heart of participation, A Civil Society Perspective on Local Governance in South Africa, Good Governance Learning Network. 38–49. http://ggln.org.za/ggln-state-of-localgovernance-publication-2012.pdf#page=40

36 Kukutschka, RMB Technology against corruption: the potential of online corruption reporting apps and other platforms u4 Expert Answer 28 November 2016 Number: 20

37 Shrivastava, U. & Bhattacherjee, A. (2014). ICT development and corruption: An empirical study. 20th Americas Conference on Information Systems, AMCIS 2014; Elbahnasawy, N.G E-Government, Internet Adoption, and Corruption: An Empirical Investigation, World Development, Volume 57, 2014, https://doi.org/10.1016/j.worlddev.2013.12.005.

38 Griffith, J., & Leston-Bandeira, C (2012) How Are Parliaments Using New Media to Engage with Citizens?, The Journal of Legislative Studies, 18:3–4, 496–513, DOI: 10.1080/13572334.2012.706058

39 Peixoto, T and Fox, J When Does ICT-Enabled Citizen Voice Lead Voice Lead to Government Responsiveness? 2016 World Development Report Background Paper Digital Dividends

40 Dambisa Moyo, "The Wisdom of Whistleblowers," available at: www.project-syndicate.org/onpoint/whistleblower-solution-to-corruption-corporate-malfeasance-by-dambisa-moyo-2021-11 Nov 19, 2021(Accessed on 6 September 2022).

41 Transparency International, www.transparency.org/files/content/corruptionqas/Literature_review_The_use_of_ICTs_in_the_fight_against_corruption_2016.pdf

42 RP Nielsen, Whistle-Blowing Methods for Navigating Within and Helping Reform Regulatory Institutions. Journal of Business Ethics, 112(3)(2013): 385–395. https://doi.org/10.1007/s10551-012-1247-0

43 Transparency International Expert Survey on Whistleblowing in the MENA Region 2014.

44 Transparency International Whistleblowing Overview for Morocco.

45 Transparency International Whistleblowing Overview for Egypt, Lebanon and Tunisia.

46 According to the document that Gondwe used in his story, published on 30 March 2022, it appeared that the government made payments to the corruption suspect, Zuneth Sattar. Available at: www.voanews.com/a/malawi-police-arrest-journalist-seize-his-it-equipment/6517873.html (Accessed on 6 September 2022).

47 Wendy Trott, "PPLAAF: Protecting and Empowering Whistleblowers in Africa," 25 January 2021 https://luminategroup.com/posts/news/protecting-and-empowering-whistleblowers-in-africa

48 Trott, "PPLAAF: Protecting and Empowering Whistleblowers in Africa."

49 Transparency International, "Alternative to Silence – Whistleblower Protection in 10 European Countries," (Berlin, Germany: TI, 2009). www.transparency.org/publications/publications/alternative_to_silence_whistleblower

50 Tiago Peixoto, Jonathan Fox When Does ICT-Enabled Citizen Voice Lead to Government Responsiveness? 2016 World Development Report Background Paper (January 2016).
51 Kukutschka, RMB, Technology against corruption: the potential of online corruption reporting apps and other platforms u4 Expert Answer 28 November 2016 Number: 20
52 Transparency International We seek to put a stop to the impunity of the corrupt 11 November 2012. Available at: www.transparency.org/en/news/we-seek-to-put-a-stop-to-the-impunity-of-the-corrupt (accessed on 6 October 2022)

22 Corruption Proofing

A Whole of Society Approach

*Dan Kuwali**

Introduction

Corruption cannot be reduced to a single definition due to its complexities and varying perceptions of crime. However, a common understanding is that corruption entails abusing public resources for private gain.[1] The World Bank expanded its definition and replaced "public office" with "trusted office."[2] The implication is that private "office" is included in the expanded definition, which means that corruption is not just a problem occurring in public institutions, but also a problem in the private sector, often acting in conjunction with the public sector. From a public choice theory, corruption can be viewed as actions by unscrupulous individuals or groups to subvert existing rules and generate extralegal income and wealth for themselves.[3] Corruption includes bribery, extortion, abuse of discretion, abuse of office, and conflict of interest, elite and state capture, among others. Corruption should be distinguished from fraud, which can loosely be seen as wrongful or criminal deception intended to result in financial or personal gain.

This discussion focuses on political or grand corruption, which is an elephant in the room that can make other forms of administrative and petty corruption even more challenging to combat. The prevalence of grand corruption in Africa and its highly devastating effects on human development explains why most countries on the continent have ratified the African Union (AU) Convention on Preventing and Combating Corruption (AUCPCC).[4] Apart from Eritrea, North Korea, and Syria, all members of the United Nations (UN) have ratified the UN Convention against Corruption (UNCAC) thereby manifesting their intention to combat this global vice.[5] The UNCAC requires States to enact laws criminalising varying forms of corruption. Both the AUPCC and the UNCAC oblige their respective State parties to prevent, detect, investigate, and punish acts of corruption and related offences.[6] Notwithstanding the nearly universal condemnation of corruption, the untethered power and influence of elite kleptomaniacs render anticorruption laws to be honoured more in breach than in compliance.[7]

For this reason, the purpose of this discussion is to curtail the likelihood of political elites abusing public resources for their private gain with no legal or political consequences by recommending effective strategies to deter grand corruption. The discussion develops a people-centric approach to corruption-proofing by deterring

DOI: 10.4324/9781003326649-26

and preventing grand corruption through naming and shaming depriving the perpetrators and beneficiaries of the proceeds of crime and repurposing the loot to the people. The approach is people-centric because, contrary to the mundane belief that corruption is a victimless crime, it is the ordinary people who bear the brunt of this vice. This people-centric anticorruption approach involves diagonal accountability where non-state actors (the media and civil society) utilise their principal–agent power to raise red flags where there is a suspicion or risk of corruption to question their governments and demand accountability.[8]

The discussion is divided into five parts excluding the conclusion. Apart from this introduction, the second part diagnoses why it is complex to combat grand corruption at both domestic and international levels. The third part discusses the political economy of corruption in Africa complete with facts and figures. The fourth exposes the challenges encountered in fighting grand corruption and demonstrates how to overcome them. The fifth recommends measures addressing loopholes in combating grand corruption with an emphasis on Africa. The goal is to inform actionable legal and policy approaches to combat grand corruption.

The central thesis of this discussion is that diagonal accountability in which external actors outside the formal political institutions such as the media and civil society are keys to holding the government accountable for grand corruption. This reasoning is anchored by Article 12 of the AUCPCC which enjoins African states to create an enabling environment to allow the media and the civil society to hold governments to the highest levels of transparency and accountability in the management of public affairs. Similarly, Article 13 of the UNCAC obliges States to promote active participation of individuals and groups outside the public sector, particularly civil society, non-governmental organisations (NGOs), and community-based organisations in the antigraft fight. The diagonal accountability advanced in this discussion resonates with Article 3(3) of the AUCPCC, which requires transparency and accountability in public affairs.

The reason is that vertical accountability, which is the ability of a country's population to hold its government accountable, involves a relationship between unequal entities (the government and its citizens) and may not be timely to halt grand corruption. The involvement of the public in elections is the most obvious instance of vertical accountability. However, the population can also lawfully protest, strike, publicise, and engage in conscientious objection. Equally, horizontal accountability, which is the extent to which state institutions hold the executive branch of government accountable involves the relationship between equals (different branches of government) who may equally be entangled in state capture. Although non-state actors can execute diagonal accountability, they do not have the power to prosecute and punish perpetrators of corruption. Therefore, the point is that a combination of vertical, horizontal, and diagonal accountability (whole-of-society approach) can arrest the intractable problems of grand corruption by deterring not only the perpetrators of corruption but also the enablers of these practices and the beneficiaries.

Dealing with grand corruption cannot take the same approach as there are different environments involving big and small kleptocrats in developed and developing countries. Therefore, the discussion adopts systems thinking to understand the complex structural causes of grand corruption to address those challenges more holistically. In grand corruption, systems thinking helps to understand situations where, for example, the affluent and influential elites practice nepotism by recruiting their relatives or providing businesses to their associates and thus concentrate wealth further lead to more land, higher quality education, better health care, and access to more influential people. While certain dynamics help the privileged get more privileged, others work directly or indirectly against the disadvantaged, especially minorities and the poor.[9] A systems approach aims to transform the culture of corruption by changing the environment that contributes to corruption such as eliminating factors that promote corruption, developing moral and transformational leaders and role models through commend and condemn campaigns, and by developing innovative, transparent, and accountable institutions from the grassroots to the topmost leadership.

Grand Corruption: Diagnosis, Measurement, and the Challenges of Detection

The World Bank distinguishes between "isolated" and "systemic" corruption.[10] Political or grand corruption, which is typically orchestrated by political elites or elected politicians, such as state capture that took place in South Africa, is typically divided into two categories: administrative corruption, which is typically committed by employees in the public sector (public officials), along with their private enablers and beneficiaries.[11] Administrative or bureaucratic corruption is sometimes called petty corruption such as the type usually practised by some errant traffic police officers on the roads of Kenya, Malawi, Nigeria, and such other countries.[12] Political or grand corruption is further seen through the lenses of extractive political corruption and power-preserving political corruption. The former is when a politician uses corrupt means to extract wealth to the benefit of themselves, their families, friends, and business associates (e.g. embezzlement, bribery, and fraud), whereas the latter takes place when the corruptly gained resources are utilised to strengthen the position of the politician and political party in question. This is one of the ways in which political party funding is achieved.[13]

Understanding the different kinds of corruption is important to develop actionable and effective responses. For example, power-preserving corruption cannot be measured using the Corruption Perceptions Index (CPI) developed by Transparency International (TI) as it may not be detected by such a methodology. The fact that developed countries show lower levels of perceived corruption than developing countries may mask the involvement of beneficiary countries who provide a safe haven to the illicit financial flows from Africa.[14] The variables of measuring corruption using CPI do not cover grand corruption and compliance with public procurement legislation, among other such factors. As its name suggests, CPI does not reflect the experience of corruption but rather perception, which alludes to the public as grand corruption is covert and complex. Grand corruption is difficult to detect because of the illicit practices of powerful kleptocrats who can beat the system with impunity by operating under the anticorruption radar.

While administrative corruption can be curbed by law enforcement means such as legislation, prosecution, and punishments, political corruption is difficult to detect and complex to combat since its powerful perpetrators can indulge in state capture and undermine the anticorruption efforts. Most strategies to fight corruption hinge on criminal prosecution although it has generally proved ineffective as the cases in most African countries, particularly Nigeria and South Africa have shown.[15] In any event, prosecution usually happens after public resources have already been purloined making asset seizure and recovery largely an academic exercise.

Grand corruption is defined as "the abuse of high-level power that benefits the few at the expense of the many and causes serious and widespread harm to individuals and society."[16] Examples of grand corruption include state capture, embezzlement, trading in influence, and bribe payments. Grand corruption can be a one-off transaction or systematic pattern often with significant and harmful repercussions to societies, including damage to the rule of law, economic development, and social harmony.

Although the fight against grand corruption is elusive, politically exposed persons (PEP) who are motivated by greed and power are the most susceptible to committing this form of corruption, hence making it easy for non-state actors to detect the red flags. The red flags or risk indicators for grand corruption include unexplained wealth, bid fixing or non-competitive contract steering, and registration of successful suppliers in tax havens, suggesting concealment of vested interests. Red flags can also be seen where PEP-connected bank accounts are registered in tax havens, receive a greater percentage of wire transfers from tax havens, have frequent traffic of account activity, and have substantially higher account balances, among other risk factors.[17] Granted, PEP-connected accounts are not evidence of grand corruption *per se* but PEPs have a high propensity to grand corruption such that suspicious transactions may point to illegality. Other red flags are prevalent and evident in defence spending and other high-stakes procurement of medical supplies, power-generating equipment, agricultural inputs, construction projects, and other such high-value procurement which usually use the single-sourcing method of procurement.

Overcoming Obstacles in Combating Corruption

Corruption-proofing is creating a vigilant environment with measures to deter and prevent corruption. Corruption proofing requires a systems approach to design strategies to overcome obstacles posed by powerful individuals and political elites to address specific types of corruption. While Africa is regarded as the most corrupt continent, anticorruption strategies tend to leave out the foreign beneficiaries who facilitate the illicit financial flows from Africa. Addressing these challenges requires an understanding of perpetrators and beneficiaries of grand corruption and how these schemes operate in practice at both the domestic and international levels.

Article 2(4) of the AUCPCC enjoins African states to promote socio-economic development by removing obstacles to the enjoyment of economic, social, and cultural rights and civil and political rights. Below are some of the obvious obstacles to overcoming grand corruption.

State and Elite Capture

State capture weakens institutions by creating an environment where corruption may be regarded as a norm. For example, grand corruption can neutralise the legislative branch of government to be unable to provide meaningful parliamentary scrutiny of corrupt practices of other branches of government (i.e. horizontal scrutiny). Elite capture may erode the independence of the judiciary and politicise judicial processes. State capture may undermine audit institutions and anticorruption agencies in the executive branch to only target the small fish and leave political elites to go scot-free. Grand corruption may influence the executive to oppress media freedom, shut down civil society groups or force them to look the other way in the face of rampant corruption. In some situations, Oligarchs may even put the media and vocal activists in their pockets.

Powerful Politically Exposed Persons Undermine Anticorruption Efforts

Grand corruption is invariably committed by politically exposed persons (PEPs) making it particularly challenging and uniquely difficult to arrest the "big fish" without external interference thereby only targeting perpetrators of petty corruption. Article 52 of the UNCAC defines PEPs as individuals who are, or have been, entrusted with prominent public functions and their family members and close associates. PEPs do not only political elites but also their family members, and business associates. In most cases, PEPs can commit grand corruption with impunity because they control the instruments of state power including law enforcement machinery.[18] In Ghana, for example, 22 circuit court judges and magistrates were either suspended or investigated for alleged involvement in corrupt practices in 2015.[19] In South Africa, former President Jacob Zuma is facing graft charges in the procurement of military materiel.[20]

Obscurity in Funding of Political Parties and Campaigns

Article 10 of the AUCPCC requires that States adopt legislation and other measures to proscribe the usage of corruptly obtained funds to finance political parties and to include principles of transparency in political party funding.

Lack of Conflict-of-Interest Registers

Most public procurement legislation requires procuring entities to document conflicts of interest by those involved in administering tenders. The absence of conflict-of-interest registers facilitates manipulating public procurement processes for personal gain.[21] Some officials engage in bid-fixing or collusive patterns by abusing shell companies where they hold a vested interest.

Political Party Funding

Political party and campaign fundraising activities may be susceptible to corruption where certain economic activities may very well profit from favourable political decisions. The growing importance of other sources of party financing, such as state funding, corporate financing, and private donations, poses a challenge to the legitimacy of party financing. To the extent that costly electoral campaigns largely determine the outcome of the elections, it is clearly undesirable that parties depend on or represent the interests of closely allied financial contributors.[22]

"Miracle Money": Weak Oversight of Religious Contributions

Religious institutions generally have fewer oversight mechanisms than any other major institution. The apparent lack of financial oversight in many religious institutions has resulted in high incidences of misuse of donations, and schemes involving the abuse of charities to facilitate tax evasion, embezzlement, corruption, money laundering, and other luxurious expenses. Montague has noted that religious institutions are prone to financial abuse because of reasons such as many religious institutions lack basic forms of oversight and accountability, thereby revealing too much trust in the honesty of religious people. Unlike other nonprofit organisations, religious leaders can exert ostensible religious authority over their members. The propensity of religious organisations to be more susceptible to grand corruption calls for public scrutiny and oversight mechanisms.

Impunity and Weak Tone of Anticorruption Campaign

An effective anticorruption strategy and legislation should send a clear message to potential perpetrators that a State or the international community is determined to prevent and deter corruption.[23] The weak tone and tenor of national anti-corruption legislation such as the Nigerian Corrupt Practices and Other Related Offences Act does not scare potential perpetrators. The same is the case with the Corrupt Practices Act of Malawi, which *prima facie* seems to only list a catalogue of corrupt practices. If one is to judge a book by its cover, the name of the legislation should set the raison d' être of the statute. The gold standard in nomenclature is the Convention on Preventing and Combating Corruption, which clearly declares the continental body's abhorrence against corruption. In addition, impunity or the absence of risk of punishment, particularly imprisonment due to non-criminal sanctions such as civil recovery orders (CROs) of assets may have the undesired effect of contributing to the pervasiveness and persistence of grand corruption in some cases.[24]

Mindset and Culture of Corruption

A culture of corruption thrives where there is nonexistence or docility of national systems to promote ethics and integrity and where the law is not supported by mechanisms that promote integrity and ethical values to eradicate moral decadence. In cases where the leadership sets the tone of abhorring corruption from the top, there is usually public support for antigraft measures including an enabling environment for law enforcement agencies. Expressing political will by a country's leadership may help garner public support for antigraft campaigns including motivating law enforcement agencies for a well-coordinated and successful anti-corruption campaign.

Lack of Coordination and Networking by Law Enforcement Agencies

A silos approach to anticorruption contributes to a lack of vigilance in sectoral anti-corruption initiatives where fighting corruption is seen as the responsibility of the anti-corruption authorities alone, and not the citizenry, which demotivates law enforcement and anticorruption agencies. The absence of a multiagency approach to combat grand corruption may not provide for a system of checks and balances including the sharing of information between and amongst agencies thereby weakening the antigraft strategy. Such loopholes may also allow corrupt elites to infiltrate the system and compromise other agencies. Fighting corruption requires coordination of law enforcement agencies together with the media, civil society organisations, and the public who act as whistleblowers for effective cooperation between those agencies, including information sharing such as access to records for taxation, asset ownership, and criminal history, among others.

Lack of International Cooperation

Corruption is not a domestic matter, but a transnational phenomenon that affects all societies and economies worldwide, making international cooperation to combat the vice essential.[25] Grand corruption is facilitated and exacerbated by the globalisation of the world economy, allowing political elites to hide their loot offshore or outside their home countries. The fact that grand corruption is usually a cross-border crime calls for a supranational approach to combat the vice. Although Article 19 of the AUCPCC and Article 43 of the UNCAC create a multilateral legal framework for cooperation in fighting corruption, their enforcement depends on national implementation and bilateral relations through mutual legal assistance cooperation frameworks.[26] Even where the necessary political will exists, the lack of capacity and financial resources, inadequate domestic legal implementation, and operational hurdles especially in developing States inhibit international antigraft campaigns.[27]

Whistleblower Ambivalence

Where there are no laws to protect whistleblowers, those who notice corruption have no interest in reporting it for fear of recrimination and reprisals. The same is the case where there is impunity as blowing the whistle on the offenders would not lead to action being taken. In such cases, potential whistleblowers would rather turn a blind eye than risk their lives for what they perceive to be futile endeavours. The situation is the same where there are no laws to protect whistleblowers, witnesses, experts and victims.[28]

Covert Means of Grand Corruption

Grand corruption by nature is a secretive activity that does not happen in the presence of bystanders. The way grand corruption is perpetrated is discreetly covert and more complex for ordinary citizens to notice unless it is of scandalous proportions detected by the media. As a result, it is difficult to observe and report grand corruption.

Towards a Whole-of-Society Approach to Deterring Grand Corruption in Africa

Article 5(4) of the AUPCC dictates that African states adopt legislative and other measures to create, maintain, and strengthen internal accounting, auditing, and follow-up systems, particularly, in the public income, customs, and tax receipts, expenditures and procedures for hiring, procurement and management of public goods and services. Thus, combating grand corruption cannot be achieved using linear solutions but should be addressed systematically. In this case, systems thinking helps understand the complex structural causes of grand corruption to address those challenges more holistically. In doing so, the complex challenges in combating grand corruption cited earlier are viewed through the lenses of system archetypes of two collective action problems.

First is the tragedy of commons where everyone is keen on plundering public funds, a phenomenon which can be addressed by deterrent strategies. Second, is the success to the successful, which is the archetype that plays out where disadvantages grow against the marginalised and advantages accrue to the privileged. Success to the successful represents two reinforcing structures that may be in a delicate balance as soon as one gains a small advantage, the resource allocation favours the more successful and the result is then rapidly skewed in the direction of the more successful. In other words, opportunity breeds success, success breeds opportunity and the opposite is true.[29] The tendency exists in most societies in Africa as is also manifested by the political elites who are prone to grand corruption.

While there cannot be a one-size-fits-all approach to combating corruption, the purpose of corruption prevention should be to minimise, as much as possible, its crippling effect on the economy, human rights, national security, and social welfare.[18] A systems approach helps to deter and prevent grand corruption by changing the environment that contributes to corruption through, among others, diagonal accountability to develop innovative, transparent, and accountable institutions. Corruption prevention requires a robust system to detect and eliminate the causes and conditions of corruption through the development and implementation of appropriate measures for seizing the proceeds of corruption, deterrence, and preventing corruption from occurring in the first place. Below is a ten-point whole-of-society strategy on corruption-proofing (deterrence and prevention of grand corruption) and reversing its effects in Africa:

Transparency in Public Procurement (Competitive Bidding) Processes

Anticompetitive behaviour in public procurement is a recipe for grand corruption. Anticompetitive practices occur, for example, where one bidder or supplier is offered contracts very frequently and dominantly to the exclusion of others.[30] While the dominance of awards of tenders by one supplier does not necessarily indicate corruption by itself, the frequency alone may indicate the risk of a probability of corruption. Transparency in public procurement processes and efficient and effective service delivery by removing bureaucratic bottlenecks may prevent kickbacks for cutting corners by public officials and bidders. Deciding bids on merit and not corruption is good for business as it ensures value for the quality of goods and services. The United Kingdom Chapter of Transparency International has developed guidelines for defence spending whose use may curtail corruption in the defence and security sector. The Kimberly Process initiative in the extractive industry has gained traction to curb corruption and irresponsible practices in the diamond sector.

Promotion of Public Finance Management Practices

Corruption encompasses abuse and misuse of public resources. Diversion of public resources for private gain can be curbed by following public finance management practices. By demanding financial accountability, the public can promote financial probity and professionalism in handling public resources. Vertical and diagonal accountability can promote public involvement in public finance management.[20] Kenya and Tanzania have good examples of legislative and institutional frameworks where the public is involved to promote integrity and transparency at the national level.[31]

Institutionalise Supranational Law Enforcement Efforts

The high mobility of corruptly obtained assets and the data ecosystem resulting from the interconnectedness of financial systems present an opportunity to confront grand corruption. Supranational anticorruption law enforcement is especially critical in combating grand corruption since political elites who perpetrate it usually are limited to having influence only at a local level.[32] Hence political elites may be powerless to influence supranational efforts against grand corruption. The current campaign to establish an International Anticorruption Court may be a step in the right direction.[33] However, what may be more effective is the exercise of universal jurisdiction to create an interconnected web of enforcement so that political kleptomaniacs should have nowhere to hide their illegally obtained wealth.

In the meantime, African civil society groups may ably demand accountability of their governments for grand corruption using the African Court of Human Rights and Justice mechanisms. According to Article 30(f) of the African Court of Justice and Human Rights Statute, individuals and non-governmental organisations accredited to the AU or to its organs can only submit cases against States if the State concerned has made a declaration accepting the competence of the African Court to do so under Article 8 of the "Single Protocol."[34] A supranational approach to combat corruption may also not be affected by the intermitted political will to combat corruption due to changes in government at national levels.

Deter Illicit Financial Flows and Money Laundering

Money laundering is rampant in some philanthropic endeavours, sports betting, art purchases, real estate, trusts, and such other innocent activities that may be abused by kleptocrats. Measures to control trace and seize illicit financial flows (IFFs) of different types can deter or prevent grand corruption by making it more difficult to conceal or benefit from the proceeds of corruption. The follow-the-money methods employed by money laundering, corruption, and tax evasion investigators have contributed to depriving beneficiaries of the grand corruption of their proceeds of crime. Embracing smart technology to encourage arms-length relationships between officials and the public as well as promote footprints in financial transactions has assisted to curb IFFs. The vast network of stakeholders from law enforcement and private-sector firms interested in combating IFFs presents a formidable shield to deter grand corruption by closing safe havens.

Due Diligence

Some PEPs have formed shell companies to mask their conflict of interest and hide from being directly seen as benefiting from their corrupt practices. Lifting or penetrating the veil of incorporation is a procedure used in corporate law to determine the actual owners of a commercial entity. Diagonal accountability by civil society organisations and the media has been instrumental in introducing Beneficial Ownership Registers (BORs) in several countries to curb IFFs. BORs require companies to penetrate their veil of incorporation and reveal the actual owners making it more difficult for corrupt entrepreneurs to avoid local and international oversight. Despite legal questions about breaching the right to privacy, BORs provide a useful database to trace IFFs and the involvement of PEPs and corrupt entrepreneurs in grand corruption.[35]

Institutionalising Integrity Checks for Politically Exposed Persons

PEPs are, by virtue of their access to power, at risk of corruption, and hence monitoring and regulating aspects of their finances can be a useful way of identifying risks. Integrity checks (and lifestyle audits) including the mandatory declaration of assets for public officers to assess the legality of their assets is a potent tool to reduce the probability of grand corruption by PEPs. Institutionalising the obligation to undertake due diligence before entering business relationships with PEPs may be an effective strategy to deter corruption if it can be systematised globally.[36]

Confiscation and Seizure of the Proceeds and Instrumentalities of Corruption

Article 16 of the AUCPCC and Article 31 of the UNCAC make provisions for unexplained wealth orders for asset seizure, confiscation, and forfeiture. Article 20 of the UNCAC requires the criminalisation of illicit enrichment, which is defined as a significant increase in the assets of a public official that they cannot reasonably explain about their lawful income. Asset seizure, confiscation, and forfeiture through Unexplained Wealth Orders (UWOs) is a widely used legal mechanism to deter criminal activity by nullifying its financial benefits although its effectiveness has been modest.[37]

Amplifying Diagonal Accountability

As outlined in Article 3(3) of the AUCPCC, accountability – the constraints on public officials' use of power – is the cornerstone of good governance and the key to combating grand corruption. Beyond the extent to which governments are accountable to citizens (vertical accountability) and other state institutions (horizontal accountability), the media and civil society provide diagonal accountability. Diagonal accountability entails that non-state actors have the power to hold the government accountable. As required by Article 12 of the AUPCC, given their perceived independence and detachment from grand corruption, the media and civil society should amplify diagonal accountability by demanding transparency, accountability, and access to information from governments.

In this way, diagonal accountability can promote public participation in public finance management to increase the responsiveness of public bodies and provide support to watchdog institutions to fight corruption. To achieve this, the media and whistleblowers should systematically report on corruption and inculcate a culture of integrity and honesty to promote ethical conduct, especially among the youth. The Panama Papers, Pandara Papers, and the International Consortium of Investigative Journalists (ICIJ) have been keys to reporting corrupt practices.[38] For diagonal accountability to work, States should provide laws and other measures to protect whistleblowers as required by Article 33 of the UNCAC.

Commend and Condemn Campaign

While punishing corruption is a vital component of any effective anti-corruption effort, civil society should adopt the commend and condemn policy to increase the benefits of honesty and the costs of being corrupt.[39] This shows the need to formulate a policy where good character and professionalism are commended and rewarded by providing relevant incentives while bad character and corruption are condemned and punished. A sensible combination of reward and punishment should be the driving force for reforms to fight corruption. It is also necessary to incentivise civil servants adequately. There is an inverse relationship between the level of public sector wages and the incidence of corruption. Whether civil servants are appropriately compensated or grossly underpaid will affect motivation and incentives. If the public sector wages are too low, employees may find themselves under pressure to supplement their income in "unofficial" ways.

Multiagency Anticorruption Approach

Corruption affects human rights, human development, peace, and security. Therefore, in addition to independence from political interference, inter-agency cooperation and networking are keys in the fight against grand graft. Non-state actors should motivate anticorruption and other oversight institutions to end impunity and deter potential perpetrators by providing information for an effective antigraft campaign including corporate criminal liability, public interest litigation, civil litigation, and asset recovery. Investigating complex grand corruption requires specialised skills to break sophisticated codes in the face of powerful and well-resourced defendants.[40] To close this financial and capacity gap, anticorruption civil society organisations and the media should also share their research and development expertise to assist anticorruption bodies in analysing data to identify risks and intervene to timely deter and prevent corruption before public resources vanish.[41] Such expertise should also extend to continuous monitoring and evaluation of the anti-corruption strategies to ensure they can be easily adapted to situations on the ground as tactics for grand corruption are dynamic.

Conclusion

Corruption is a progressive problem in Africa manifested in state capture and misappropriation of significant public resources. African states have the moral and legal obligation to protect their populations against corruption including the adoption of appropriate legislative and adequate preventive measures.[42] While administrative or petty corruption can be arrested by law enforcement, political corruption is far more difficult to combat as the affluent and influential perpetrators tend to undermine antigraft efforts. Neither can a one-size-fits-all approach be used to combat corruption. Nor can different situations be dealt with the same approach. A systems approach is necessary to deter, detect, and invest in corrupt practices to prevent grand corruption. The systems and people-centric strategy suggested in this discussion implies extinguishing corruption by diminishing its benefits and creating an environment that abhors vice.

A combination of vertical, horizontal, and diagonal accountability (whole-of-society approach) can arrest the intractable problems of grand corruption by deterring not only the perpetrators of corruption but also the enablers of these practices as well as the beneficiaries thereby closing safe-havens for elite kleptocrats to conceal their corruptly gained wealth. The whole-of-society approach advanced in this discussion entails that the fight against corruption is the responsibility of everyone through active participation in the implementation of anti-corruption legislation and strategies by demanding justice. Fighting grand corruption primarily through criminal prosecution has proven ineffective in the face of affluent and influential perpetrators. Although law enforcement is a vital component of any effective anti-corruption effort, it may be short-term and ineffective to combat grand corruption hence the need for proactive prevention strategies to reward integrity and punish perpetrators of the vice.

Corruption involves unlawful enrichment through unlawful means that deprive the public of their social benefits. The motive of perpetrators of grand corruption is the accumulation of wealth and power at the expense of integrity-based structures that benefit the public. Therefore, the normative and policy strategies to deter grand corruption should aim at commending integrity and condemning illegality, naming and shaming kleptocrats as well as malign corporate interests, and disincentivising corruption by depriving perpetrators of the power, influence, and proceeds of crime while incentivising repurposing of wrongfully diverted assets to the public and the country's economy.

This discussion has argued that the media and civil society organisations have a critical role to play through diagonal accountability to name and shame elite kleptomaniacs, commend merit and legality as well as condemn mediocrity and illegality. In line with Article 12 of the AUCPCC, diagonal accountability can also help to disincentivise corruption by seizing proceeds of crime and redirecting them for public use to incentivise antigraft action. To be sure, corruption-proofing measures should include the provision of transparency in public procurement processes, promotion of public finance management practices, institutionalise supranational law enforcement measures, deterrence of IFFs, the establishment of BoRs, institutionalising integrity checks for PEPs, provision of UWOs, amplifying diagonal accountability, adopting commend and condemn campaigns, and strengthening anticorruption and oversight institutions. This transformation may help to spur economic development on the continent, which is the poorest and least peaceful continent in the world.

Notes

* Extraordinary Professor of International Law, University of Pretoria.

1 World Bank, *Helping Countries Combat Corruption: The Role of the World Bank. Poverty Reduction and Economic Management*, New York, September 1997, 9–10.

2 World Bank, *Helping Countries Combat Corruption*, 434.

3 John Mukum Mbaku, *Corruption in Africa: Causes, Consequences and Cleanups* (Lexington Books, 2010), 4.

4 African Union, AU Convention on Preventing and Combating Corruption, available at:<https://au.in/sites/default/files/treaties/36382-treats-0028-african-union-convention-on-preventing-and-combating-corruption-e.pdf>(accessed 20 February 2023).

5 As of 18 May 2023, UNCAC has 189 States Parties.

6 See for example Article 18 of the AUPCC and Article 1(a) of the UNCAC.

7 Sabine E. Nölke, "Toward A More Effective Implementation of Anti-Corruption Measures: Suggestions for the Strengthening of Existing Frameworks and Institution," Discussion Paper, Canadian Task Force Against Global Corruption March 2023, 5.

8 Anna Lührmannm Kyle L. Marcuardt, and Valeriya Merchkova, "Constraining Government: New Indices of Vertical, Horizontal, and Diagonal Accountability", *American Political Science Review,* vol 114, no. 3: (2020): 811–820.
9 David Peter Stroh, *Systems Thinking for Social Change* (White River Junctions, VT: Chelsea Green Publishing, 2015), 60–61.
10 World Bank, *Helping Countries Combat Corruption,* 9–10.
11 Neil Arun, "State capture: Zuma, the Guptas, and the sale of South Africa," *BBC News*, 15 July 2019, available at: https??www.bbc.com/news/world-africa-48980964 (Accessed 22 May 2023).
12 Inge Amundsen (ed.), *Political corruption in Africa: Extraction and Power Preservation,* (Cheltenham: Edward Elgar Publishing, 2019).
13 Dan Kuwali, " 'Bloody Bucks: Preventing War Profiteering,' in Juan-Pablo Bohosi and Jerney Letnar Černič (eds), *Making Sovereign Financing and Human Rights Work* (Oxford: Hart Publishing, 2014), 271–288.
14 Pornanong Budsaratragoon and Boonlert Jitmaneeroj, "A critique on the Corruption Perceptions Index: An interdisciplinary approach," Socio-Economic Planning Sciences, vol 70 (June 2020), available at: https://doi.org/10.1016/j.seps.2019.100768 (Accessed 22 May 2023).
15 Human Rights Watch, "Nigeria: Corruption Fuelling Police Abuses," 17 August 2010, available at: www.hrw.org/news/2010/08/17/nigeria-corruption-fueling-police-abuses (accessed 11 May 2023).
16 Transparency International, "Grand Corruption," available at: www.transparency international/en/our-priorities/grand-corruption (accessed 1 March 2023).
17 Nölke, "Toward A More Effective Implementation of Anti-Corruption Measures," 5.
18 Mark L. Wolf, Richard Goldstone, and Robert I. Rotberg, *The Progressing Proposal for an International Anti-Corruption Court* (Cambridge, Mass.: American Academy of Arts and Sciences, 2022), 1.
19 Nana Boakye-Yiadom and Godwin A. Allotey, "Chief Justice cracks whip: 22 'corrupt' judges suspended," https://*citifmonline*. (Accessed 24 May 2023).
20 John Eligon, "Jacob Zuma, Former South African President, Is Arrested," *The New York Times*, 7 July 2021.
21 See sections 14, 15, and 29 of the Public Procurement and Disposal of Assets, Act, available at: <Public-Procurement-Regulations-2020.pdf (ppda.mw)> (accessed 2 May 2023).
22 Biezen, *Financing Political Parties and Election*, 19–23.
23 See also Kofi A. Annan, "Foreword," in United Nations Office on Drugs and Crime, *United Nations Convention against Corruption,* (New York: United Nations, 2004), iii.
24 Wolf, Goldstone, and Rotberg, *The Progressing Proposal for An International Anti-Corruption Court,* 5.
25 United Nations Office on Drugs and Crime, *United Nations Convention against Corruption,* (New York: United Nations, 2004), preambular para. 4.
26 Nölke, "Toward A More Effective Implementation of Anti-Corruption Measures," 13–14.
27 Nölke, "Toward A More Effective Implementation of Anti-Corruption Measures," 13–14. See also Article 18 of the AUCPCC and Article 46 of the UNCAC.
28 See Articles 32 and 33 of the UNCAC.
29 Stroh, *Systems Thinking,* 60–61.
30 Mihály Fazekas and Gábor Kocsis, "Uncovering High-Level Corruption: Cross-National Objective Corruption Risk Indicators Using Public Procurement Data," *British Journal of Political Science,* vol 50, issue 1(January 2020):155–164.
31 Tanzania and Kenya have entrenched guiding principles for ethical conduct, leadership, and integrity.
32 Nölke, "Toward A More Effective Implementation of Anti-Corruption Measures," 15.

33 Wolf, Goldstone, and Rotberg, *The Progressing Proposal for an International Anti-Corruption Court,* 5.
34 *See* Article 8 of the Protocol on the Statute of the African Court of Justice and Human Rights [the 'Single Protocol'], *available at*: <www.africa-union.org/root/au/Documents/Treaties/treaties.htm> (12 December 2023). See also Article 30 (f) of the African Court of Justice and Human Rights.
35 See Transparency International, "EU Court of Justice Delivers Blow to Beneficial Owner Transparency," available at: www.transprancy,org/en/eu-court-of-justice-delivers-blow (accessed 17 May 2023).
36 See also Ruta Mrazauskaite and Matthew C. Stephenson, "A Proposal for a Global Database of Politically Exposed Persons, " *Stanford Journal of International Law*. vol 56, issue 153 (2020)
37 Peter Sproat, "Unexplained Wealth Orders: An Explanation, Assessment and Set of Predictions," *The Journal of Criminal Law,* vol 82, issue 3 (June 2018), https://doi.org/10.1177/00220183187732
38 International Consortium of Investigative Journalists, see www.icij.org (Accessed 22 May 203).
39 Dan Kuwali, "Commend and Condemn: Combating Corruption in Africa" in Dan Kuwali (Editor), *The Palgrave Handbook of Sustainable Peace and Security,* Springer/Palgrave, 2022, 581–595.
40 See Austin F. Cullen Commissioner, "Commission of Inquiry into Money Laundering in British Columbia Interim Report," November 2020 "The Cullen Commission Report"), available at:<https://cullencommission/ca/files/reports/cullencommission-interimReport.pdf>(accessed 12 May 2023).
41 Luís de Sousa, Anti-corruption Agencies: Between Empowerment and Irrelevance," *Crime, Law, and Social Change*, vol. 53 no. (2010):5–22.
42 African Union, AUPCC, preambular para. 9 and Art 2(3).

Conclusion

*Dan Kuwali**

In Chapter 4, Happy Kayuni draws perspectives from political science to investigate the concept of corruption in the context of its political and cultural significance in Africa using political and anthropological lenses. Kayuni specifically seeks to respond to the question-how corruption is understood or interpreted in everyday African life, where the vice has contributed to dwindling peace, stability, development, and public service delivery as noted by Jonathan Makuwira in Chapter 7. Considering the thin line between a gift and graft in Africa, in Chapter 2, Dan Kuwali attempted to find a common definition of corruption having explored the different layers of omission, commission, and perpetrators of the crime. Understanding the different categories of corruption and different measurement methodologies enables the diagnosis of the problem and devising effective strategies for combating the vice.

Since the motive for corruption is greed to accumulate wealth and access to power, in Chapter 3, Avitus A. Agbor draws lessons from Cameroon's Special Criminal Court (SCC) to navigate the nexus between greed and corruption. Agbor argues that the insatiable desire for more wealth and money may explain why some individuals, even when affluent, are still willing and able to concoct and hatch fraudulent schemes to steal public funds. Greed by the elite is further explained by Johan J. Coetzee in Chapter 8 that political elites have centralised power and facilitated bid rigging, contract splitting and 'sale of contract papers'. The larger the capital-intensive projects, the bigger the bribes, Coetzee notes and recommends a combination of a state- and citizen-centric approach that is multifaceted and country-specific. Hence, as argued by Kuwali in Chapter 22, the central thesis of this book is that efforts to combat corruption in Africa should focus on disincentivising the vice by depriving the perpetrators of the proceeds of crime and incentivising whistleblowing to scare potential perpetrators.

However, Chikondi Chidzanja and Charles Kajoloweka in Chapter 11 rightly note that corruption is partly influenced by external actors whether positively or negatively. The West's approach to only condemn instances of corruption in Africa and not commend cases where the vice has been curbed obscures best practices to combat the vice on the continent. Such a tendency also shields beneficiaries of stolen assets from the continent that are invested in developed states and benefits

DOI: 10.4324/9781003326649-27

those economies, thereby reducing the political will to fight the vice effectively and holistically. Nonetheless, the responsibility to ensure the prevention and eradication of corruption is in the hands of all states and individuals. In Chapter 17, Kuwali argued that governance deficits are the major contributors to corruption in Africa, which was inherited from the colonial elites. In most cases, external actors collude with African partners and are major benefactors of corruption happening on the African continent. Therefore, to effectively combat corruption in Africa, Kuwali suggests that states must tackle it both internally and externally by addressing domestic conditions that allow corruption to strive while dissuading foreign perpetrators.

In Chapter 9, Kezzie Mkandawire and Maureen Mwalabu prescribe practical strategies for mitigating corruption in public service delivery based on an assessment of the political context, capacity, cost, and other socio-economic factors. George Chikondi Lwanda explained in Chapter 10 the persistent patterns of palm-oiling in the natural resources sector, especially in Africa's oil and gas licensing process. Lwanda laments that a culture of concealing the identity of licence winners exacerbates the risks. Avitus A. Agbor and Rorisang Matlala advise that the fight against corruption must not be limited to public officials but should also be extended to the private sector where uncountable surreptitious illegal activities take place, resulting in loss to the state, leaving monies in the hands of the perpetrators and giving those involved a considerable market edge over their competitors. This is why in Chapter 13, Gilbert Mittawa and William Kwabiah recommended strategies to combat corruption in sports.

Having noted the strengths and weakness of existing legal frameworks to find a solution to the systemic problem of corruption in Africa exposed by Hajer Gueldich in Chapter 6, Avitus A. Agbor and Rorisang Matlala in Chapter 12, advocate for a legal system to embrace and implement a non-conviction-based confiscation system, empowering the judiciary and law enforcement personnel to shift the burden to asset owners to prove the lawful origins of their property. In this case, Unexplained Wealth Orders (UWOs) could be one of the tools of law enforcement where owners of property cannot justify their acquisition or ownership. Salome Chapeyama Mdala in Chapter 14 narrates how anti-money laundering (AML) measures limit the channels through which criminals can legitimise their illicit funds. If corrupt individuals fail to utilise their gains, it would demotivate them and would-be practitioners to engage in corruption. Consequently, in Chapter 20, Sandra Fungai Kabaya advised on how lawyers and other fiduciary duty bearers can contribute to anti-money laundering initiatives, using an example of Zimbabwe but with potential replication elsewhere.

Hence, combating corruption to avoid impunity and protect public resources requires the implementation of effective corruption-proofing (prevention, detection, and deterrence) strategies for deterrence and prevention by changing the environment that contributes to corruption through, among others, diagonal accountability to develop innovative, transparent, and accountable institutions. Common to this discussion are recommendations that for Africa to deter corruption and achieve sustainable socio-economic development, African states should among others: adopt strong institutions to embed accountable governance, professionalise public services, and reduce bottlenecks to close gaps for corruption; political party funding regulations to curtail corruption, including money laundering, embrace ethical leadership to inculcate a culture of honesty and integrity and compel external companies to adhere to integrity standards when trading on the continent.

In Chapter 21, Prince Bright Majiga proposes that citizen-centred whistleblowing should be innovative enough to detect and report sophisticated grand corruption schemes. Further, in Chapter 22, Kuwali suggests taking advantage of the perceived independence and detachment from grand corruption of the media, civil society, and community-based organisations to deter corruption through diagonal accountability, spurring a whole-of-society approach and supranational law enforcement to close safe havens for elite kleptocrats to conceal their corruptly gained wealth. The role of women as anti-corruption agents should not be overlooked and is spotlighted in Chapter 16 by Chikondi Mandala. Mandala contends that women's roles in the fight against corruption can be strengthened by promoting gender parity and equity. A holistic inclusion would allow for women's full participation in decision-making in politics or the economy where they have access to the networks, circles, and structures that build corruption and thus can participate in dismantling the same.

Agbor and his colleagues Refilwe Tsatsimpe and Chevaure du Pokoy in Chapter 15 argue that without a change in the ideological mindset that influences and shapes the political elite, efforts to end corruption will be limited to rhetoric uttered on political podiums and not be more than an empty thunderbolt. This point resonates with Coetzee's recommendation that political support is paramount to transforming procurement processes. This underscores the systems approach taken by Frantuono who argues that transformation of the corrupt sub-optimal system requires the application of high-power leverage points to existing subsystems. Overall, Thokozire Kuwali in Chapter 18, contends that leadership is crucial in combating corruption, especially by setting the right tone from the top to deter fraud and corrupt practices in Africa. Leadership in any environment is key to setting the reverberating tone by condemning corruption and eradicating elements that trigger corrupt practices such as pressure, opportunity, and rationalisation.

As Kabaya recommends in Chapter 20, there is a need for a global fight, starting at local levels to dismantle money-laundering syndicates through aggressive law enforcement. But as Godard Busingye, Hadijah Yahyah, and Rosemary Kanoel advise in Chapter 19, practices that are interpreted as corrupt in one jurisdiction might not be considered so in other jurisdictions. This is in concurrence with what Kuwali in Chapter 22 noted that combating grand corruption primarily through criminal prosecution has proven ineffective as this crime is perpetrated covertly by affluent and influential motivated by greed and power who can undermine anti-graft efforts. Godard Busingye, Hadijah Yahyah, and Rosemary Kanoel in Chapter 19 recommend that prosecution should be complemented by establishing citizen oversight bodies for compliance, complaint, and redress mechanisms. Bearing in mind the complex nature of the vice and the multiplicity of actors involved, Kuwali calls for a whole-of-society approach to combating corruption which he outlines in Chapter 22. This is in line with the systems thinking approach to combating corruption outlined by Michael J Frantuono in Chapter 5. Indeed, the gap between actual and acceptable levels of corruption and of well-being that currently exist in many African countries requires a fundamental change to close it.

Note

* Extraordinary Professor of International Law, University of Pretoria.

Index

Note: Page numbers in *italic* indicate a figure, and page numbers in **bold** indicate a table on the corresponding page.

Milton Keynes UK
Ingram Content Group UK Ltd.
UKHW051905230624
444477UK00005B/81